Beginning Cryptography with Java™

Beginning Cryptography with Java™

David Hook

Wiley Publishing, Inc.

Beginning Cryptography with Java™

Published by
Wiley Publishing, Inc.
10475 Crosspoint Boulevard
Indianapolis, IN 46256
www.wiley.com

Copyright © 2005 by Wiley Publishing

Published by Wiley Publishing, Inc., Indianapolis, Indiana

Published simultaneously in Canada

ISBN-13: 978-0-7645-9633-9

ISBN-10: 0-7645-9633-0

Manufactured in the United States of America

10 9 8 7 6 5 4 3 2 1

1MA/SV/QX/QV/IN

For general information on our other products and services or to obtain technical support, please contact our Customer Care Department within the U.S. at (800) 762-2974, outside the U.S. at (317) 572-3993 or fax (317) 572-4002.

Wiley also publishes its books in a variety of electronic formats. Some content that appears in print may not be available in electronic books.

Library of Congress Cataloging-in-Publication Data
Hook, David, 1962–
  Beginning cryptography with Java / David Hook.
      p. cm.
  Includes bibliographical references and index.
  ISBN-13: 978-0-7645-9633-9 (paper/website)
  ISBN-10: 0-7645-9633-0 (paper/website)
1. Computer security. 2. Cryptography. 3. Public key infrastructure (Computer security) 4. Java (Computer program language) I. Title.
  QA76.9.A25H645 2005
  005.8--dc22
                                                                    2005011272

About the Author

David Hook

David Hook has been writing software in a variety of domains and languages for the last 20 years. He has worked with Java since 1995, originally doing medical imaging before moving into cryptography and security a year or so later. In April 2000, he co-founded the open source Bouncy Castle cryptography project and has played an active role in it ever since. He currently works as a freelance consultant, mainly in Java, doing the odd bit of lecturing and writing on the side. When he is not using his spare time to work on Bouncy Castle, he spends it pursuing his other interest in computer graphics. He lives in Melbourne, Australia, with his most patient wife Janine and a cat named Hamlet, who really seems to think he's a little cryptographer in a fur coat. David can be reached at dgh@bund.com.au.

Credits

Acquisitions Editor
Carol Long

Development Editor
Kezia Endsley

Production Editor
Angela Smith

Copy Editor
Joanne Slike

Editorial Manager
Mary Beth Wakefield

Vice President & Executive Group Publisher
Richard Swadley

Vice President and Publisher
Joseph B. Wikert

Project Coordinator
Erin Smith

Graphics and Production Specialists
April Farling
Denny Hager
Jennifer Heleine
Julie Trippetti

Quality Control Technician
Carl Pierce
Brian H. Walls

Proofreading and Indexing
TECHBOOKS Production Services

To FB and HC.

Acknowledgments

First of all, I'd like to thank Peter Grant for reviewing the chapters and exercises during the development of this book, Jon Eaves who also provided additional feedback, and Bernard Leach, who, with Peter and Jon, helped bring the Bouncy Castle project to life.

I would also like to thank Simon McMahon for additional feedback and comments, Jan Leuhe and Sharon Liu for answering my questions on early JCE history for this book, not to mention many of the other questions I've had over the years. Thanks must also go to all the people making up the Bouncy Castle user community — where the project has been successful; it is as much due to your feedback, comments, contributions, and patience, as to any other efforts.

To the Wrox crew, especially Carol Long and Carol Griffith for helping me get started and keeping me on track, and to my development editor Kezia Endsley, who never commented on the fact, that as a first time author, I clearly had no idea what I was doing. If this book provides you with all you expected, it is as much due to Kezia's patient editing and direction as it is with any knowledge I have of the subject.

Finally, I would like to thank the members of my family. To my parents, Geoff and Pauline, brothers, Brendan, Martin, and Warwick, and my sister, Sarah, you have all been a constant source of inspiration and support. To my parents-in-law, Ron and Maureen, who quietly went about helping my wife Janine repaint our house while I was hiding in the office typing furiously, and to my wife Janine who found time to support me through the book as well, what can I possibly say? Thank you.

Contents

Contents

Contents

Contents

Contents

Contents

Contents

Contents

Contents

Contents

Contents

Introduction

This book is about using cryptography with Java.

Depending on who you are, you may think of cryptography as a great menace or as a very useful tool. The truth is that in some ways it is neither, in other ways it is both. It's neither because, if you choose, you could easily reduce it to an interesting mathematical game, with no application. It's both because it most definitely gets applied, not always well, and not always for purposes that everyone agrees with. Whichever side of the fence you are on, the one thing everyone agrees with is that the politics surrounding cryptography and access to the technology that allows you to use it have been intense.

Java, on the other hand, is simply a programming language. It arrived on the popular scene in 1995 and has become very popular as a language for writing applications involving the Internet, electronic commerce, or a combination of the two. Other than the odd, often "religious," issue between programmers or companies, the language itself has carried none of the political problems that have accompanied cryptography. However, a language by itself won't allow you to develop secure Internet applications, so it quickly became apparent that it would be necessary to introduce into Java APIs that allowed people to make use of cryptography. When this happened the politics arrived and, for some, using Java suddenly got intense as well. Finally, the politics subsided and we arrived where we are now, with a rich set of APIs that allow developers to use cryptography effectively in application development — providing they know how.

This brings me to why this book was written. People will still wax lyrically about key sizes and PKI (Public Key Infrastructure), but what does it all mean, and what does it mean when you are using Java? The Java APIs afford you a great deal of flexibility, and although this will allow you to implement an application using cryptography at a fundamental level, it will also allow you to tie yourself into some terrible knots. You can avoid this if you understand a few principals about the way the APIs are put together. Furthermore, by understanding the relationships between the high-level APIs and the more fundamental ones, debugging becomes easier and you can recognize when it is not necessary to build things from scratch, as, in some cases, the hard work has already been done. In short, with the right understanding, you can save yourself a lot of work. This book has been written with the aim of providing that understanding.

Who This Book Is For

This book is written for people who are Java developers and are trying to make use of cryptography in their applications and for people who simply want to understand what's going on when cryptography is being used in Java applications. It does assume you are familiar with the Java language, but it does not assume you have any familiarity with any of the APIs it discusses, such as the JCA, JCE, the Bouncy Castle APIs, and JavaMail.

If you are already very familiar with the JCE and the JCA, you might want to skim the first four chapters quickly and start reading thoroughly from Chapter 5 onward; otherwise, I would recommend you start at the beginning. If you do skim the first four chapters, you should pay attention to the development of the utilities class that is added at the start of most chapters. The reason is that the utilities class used in Chapter 5 and onward builds on the work done in the first four chapters.

What This Book Covers

This book has been written to provide you with a basic understanding of how cryptography is done in Java, what some of the issues are in using cryptography in Java, and the higher-level APIs that can save you from both having to reinvent the wheel and also save you from rediscovering mistakes that others have already made.

Of course, discussion is generally not as useful as experience, and the book has been written with numerous examples, each of which should allow you to investigate a specific issue and learn about specific parts of the various Java APIs available to you for implementing cryptography and PKI. In it, you will see how to make use of the APIs available to allow you to

- ❑ Do symmetric encryption, asymmetric encryption, and integrity checking.
- ❑ Create, validate, and revoke certificates.
- ❑ Create and process secured messages and mail.
- ❑ Create and use secured channels using SSL.

Naturally, implementing anything in any language always leaves the door open to shooting oneself in the foot, and cryptography is definitely no exception. With this in mind, where possible, examples and their associated explanations have been written to help you avoid some of the common pitfalls, and as this is a beginning book, further reading has also been suggested to allow you to take the concepts further if you need to.

The book has been written to allow you to take full advantage of recent updates in the security APIs with J2SE 5.0; however, you will also find that almost all the examples can be used, with minor modifications, with older JDKs. Barring some specific uses of J2SE 5.0, the minimum version of Java you need to be using to use every API described in the book is JDK 1.3. If you are using an earlier JDK, you can still use this book, but you will find that you will not be able to use all of the examples, such as those dealing with secure mail and SSL.

How This Book Is Structured

This book has been structured with a deliberate ordering in mind. The main thing you will notice is that a utilities class is developed over the course of most chapters and that later chapters make use of functionality that was introduced in earlier ones. Likewise, the examples in each chapter have been introduced in a specific order and build on previous ones, so if you want to get the most out of each chapter, it is best to start at the beginning and work through to the end.

The book has 10 chapters. The first five chapters cover the basic principles of Java APIs and the technology involved to deal with the higher-level APIs and concepts covered in the last five chapters. As with the rest of the book, the first five chapters are example-oriented and cover the following topics:

- ❑ Chapter 1 discusses the basic architecture of JCE and JCA, provides some historical background, and shows you how to properly set up a provider, as well as how to determine if your provider has not been properly set up.

❑   Chapter 2 introduces the basic concepts behind symmetric, or secret, key encryption, including how it is done in Java, how keys are generated, and how to use password-based encryption. It includes discussions about what algorithms there are, what the various modes and padding mechanisms available with symmetric algorithms are for, and what they mean.

❑   Chapter 3 introduces message digests and message authentication codes, shows why they are used, demonstrates how they are used in Java, and discusses some of the issues you may encounter when using them.

❑   Chapter 4 introduces asymmetric, or public key, encryption and digital signatures. It covers the popular algorithms, how they are used, and which Java API is required to generate and reconstruct keys, as well as how to make use of the algorithms themselves.

❑   Chapter 5 provides a general introduction into ASN.1 — the language in which most secure protocols and messaging formats are described. It shows you how to read an ASN.1 module, interpret some of the common syntactic constructs, and then use the API provided by the Bouncy Castle ASN.1 packages to create your own Java implementations of ASN.1 structures.

After Chapter 5, the book moves on to high-level topics, building on the work covered in the first five chapters. Each of the following chapters is written to give you practice with the topics being discussed:

❑   Chapter 6 shows you how to make your own X.509 digital certificates, handle certificate extensions, create and process certification requests, and build your own certificate paths, or chains.

❑   Chapter 7 shows you how to create your own certificate revocation lists (CRLs) and make use of the Online Certificate Status Protocol (OCSP). It discusses what trust anchors are and teaches you how to use the Java certificate path validation API with both CRLs and OCSP. It also shows you how to use the certificate path builder API to recover certificate paths from collections of certificates and CRLs.

❑   Chapter 8 shows you how to make use of the Java KeyStore API for managing keys and certificates. The personal credential standard PKCS #12 is also discussed, as are a number of the interoperability issues that surrounds its use and how to deal with them.

❑   Chapter 9 shows you how to make use of CMS, a messaging protocol for creating signed and encrypted messages. It builds on this further to show you how to use S/MIME, the secure MIME standard that allows you to create signed and encrypted e-mail. Validations and processing of these messages when you receive them is covered as well.

❑   Chapter 10 shows you how to make use of SSL and TLS, socket-level protocols that allow you to create secure channels between two end points for transferring data. The typical situations with the use of SSL and TLS, where the client is authenticated or the client is unauthenticated, are covered, as are the methods for specifying which servers to trust and how to identify whom you have connected to.

❑   The appendixes include supplementary material, including the answers to the exercises at the end of each chapter, algorithms provided by the Bouncy Castle provider, using Bouncy Castle with elliptic curve interfaces, and a bibliography to reference for additional information.

What You Need to Use This Book

To get the most out of this book, you need access to J2SE 5.0, the Bouncy Castle provider, and the JavaMail API. That being said, the Bouncy Castle provider supports earlier versions of Java, back to JDK 1.1. Consequently, most of the examples in the book will work with earlier versions of Java as well. When they don't, I have included pointers as to how to get them to work with earlier versions of Java.

I'm assuming you're already aware that both the JDK and JavaMail APIs are freely available from `http://java.sun.com`. As for the open source Bouncy Castle provider, you can find it at `http://www.bouncycastle.org`. This book also discusses a number of standards that are available online at no charge, so if you want to do further reading it is easy to do so. You can find these standards listed in Appendix D, "Bibliography and Further Reading," and if you want to cover the content of a particular chapter in depth, you might find it useful to download the relevant standard so you can consult it as you go.

Conventions

To help you get the most from the text and keep track of what's happening, we've used a number of conventions throughout the book.

Examples that you can download and try out for yourself generally appear in a box like this:

Try It Out

Try It Out is an exercise you should work through, following the text in the book.

1. They usually consist of a set of steps.
2. Each step has a number.
3. Follow the steps through with your copy of the database.

How It Works

After each *Try It Out*, the code you've typed will be explained in detail.

> **Boxes like this one hold important, not-to-be forgotten information that is directly relevant to the surrounding text.**

As for styles in the text:

- ❑ We *highlight* new terms and important words when we introduce them.
- ❑ We show keyboard strokes like this: Ctrl+A.
- ❑ We show filenames, URLs, and code within the text like so: `persistence.properties`.

❑ We present code in two different ways:

```
In code examples we highlight new and important code with a gray
background.
```

```
The gray highlighting is not used for code that's less important
in the present context, or has been shown before.
```

Source Code

As you work through the examples in this book, you may choose either to type in all the code manually or to use the source code files that accompany the book. All of the source code used in this book is available for download at www.wrox.com. Once at the site, simply locate the book's title (either by using the Search box or by using one of the title lists) and click the Download Code link on the book's detail page to obtain all the source code for the book.

Because many books have similar titles, you may find it easiest to search by ISBN; for this book the ISBN is 0-764-59633-0.

Once you download the code, just decompress it with your favorite compression tool. Alternately, you can go to the main Wrox code download page at www.wrox.com/dynamic/books/download.aspx to see the code available for this book and all other Wrox books.

Errata

We make every effort to ensure that there are no errors in the text or in the code. However, no one is perfect, and mistakes do occur. If you find an error in one of our books, like a spelling mistake or faulty piece of code, we would be very grateful for your feedback. By sending in errata you may save another reader hours of frustration, and at the same time, you will be helping us provide even higher-quality information.

To find the errata page for this book, go to www.wrox.com and locate the title using the Search box or one of the title lists. Then, on the book details page, click the Book Errata link. On this page you can view all errata that has been submitted for this book and posted by Wrox editors. A complete book list including links to each book's errata is also available at www.wrox.com/misc-pages/booklist.shtml.

If you don't spot "your" error on the Book Errata page, go to www.wrox.com/contact/techsupport.shtml and complete the form there to send us the error you have found. We'll check the information and, if appropriate, post a message to the book's errata page and fix the problem in subsequent editions of the book.

p2p.wrox.com

For author and peer discussion, join the P2P forums at p2p.wrox.com. The forums are a Web-based system for you to post messages relating to Wrox books and related technologies and interact with other readers and technology users. The forums offer a subscription feature to e-mail you topics of interest of your choosing when new posts are made to the forums. Wrox authors, editors, other industry experts, and your fellow readers are present on these forums.

At http://p2p.wrox.com you will find a number of different forums that will help you not only as you read this book, but also as you develop your own applications. To join the forums, just follow these steps:

1. Go to p2p.wrox.com and click the Register link.

2. Read the terms of use and click Agree.

3. Complete the required information to join as well as any optional information you wish to provide and click Submit.

4. You will receive an e-mail with information describing how to verify your account and complete the joining process.

You can read messages in the forums without joining P2P, but in order to post your own messages, you must join.

Once you join, you can post new messages and respond to messages other users post. You can read messages at any time on the Web. If you would like to have new messages from a particular forum e-mailed to you, click the Subscribe to this Forum icon by the forum name in the forum listing.

For more information about how to use the Wrox P2P, be sure to read the P2P FAQs for answers to questions about how the forum software works as well as many common questions specific to P2P and Wrox books. To read the FAQs, click the FAQ link on any P2P page.

The JCA and the JCE

The basic functionality for using cryptographic techniques in Java is provided by the Java Cryptography Architecture (JCA) and its sibling, the Java Cryptography Extension (JCE).

In this chapter, you will look at how the architecture works, as well as why the architecture is the way it is. You will look at the policy files associated with the JCA and JCE, how signing of cryptographic services providers works, and how the JCA and JCE decide which provider to use if an algorithm you have requested is implemented by more than one. Finally, you will see how to install a provider either statically in the Java runtime or dynamically when an application starts up.

In this chapter, you will learn

- ❑ How the JCA and JCE are architected
- ❑ What patterns apply to their use as an API
- ❑ What a cryptographic services provider is
- ❑ How to add a services provider to your Java runtime, either dynamically or by static configuration changes
- ❑ How to confirm a provider has been installed and what its capabilities are
- ❑ What the common issues are if there are problems

Basic Architecture

The first thing you will notice about the JCA and the JCE is that there is little reference to actual algorithm implementation in the classes and interfaces that make them up. Instead, the JCA and, subsequently, the JCE is architected to provide an abstraction layer for application developers, and the objects that provide the implementations of the algorithms you wish to use are created using factory classes.

This architecture is what is referred to as *provider-based architecture*; in this case, it means that the JCE and JCA provide a set of classes and interfaces that an application developer writes to, together with factories that enable the creation of the objects that conform to the interfaces and classes. The objects that ultimately give the functionality that the application developer is using are provided by an underlying implementation through a *factory pattern* and are not directly visible to the developer. In the JCA and JCE, the collections of classes that provide these implementation objects are, not surprisingly, called *providers*, and the JCA and JCE have some simple mechanisms for allowing people to add providers and to choose specific providers.

A quick look at Figure 1-1 shows how the various parts work together. Application code is written that calls the appropriate JCE/JCA API classes; these in turn invoke the classes in a provider that provides implementations for the JCE/JCA service provider interface (SPI) classes. The classes then invoke the internal code in the provider to provide the actual functionality requested.

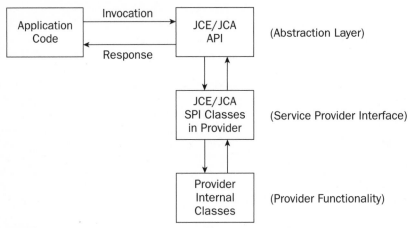

Figure 1-1

This might seem like a roundabout way of doing things at first, but it does make sense after a bit of thought as to why. It helps you see why it is important to understand two major items in the history of the APIs.

The first is that at the time the JCE and JCA were originally developed, export controls on encryption technology, at least in the United States, were a lot stricter than they are now. This is the main reason why the original JCA concerned itself only with authentication, which is generally exempt as long as the underlying algorithms cannot be used for encryption. It is also the reason that the JCE ended up as an extension, rather than as was originally intended, part of the regular security APIs. Export control extends not only to underlying implementations but also to what is referred to as "crypto in the hole" or, more clearly, frameworks that can be used for encryption if some magic component — in this case a cipher implementation — is added later. In this case, as the JCE was a framework for doing encryption, it was covered by "crypto in the hole." Hence, it was deemed to be covered by cryptography export laws, to the point where the original specification was actually presented as a white paper at a conference in May 1997, academic presentation being the only legal means of publishing it.

The next issue was that algorithms like RSA were still under patent, so it was not possible to include implementations of them directly; however, the API had to be able to allow people to write code that dealt with things like RSA signatures and ciphers as well as the padding and hashing mechanisms that accompany them. In the light of this, having the facility for pluggable providers accessed via a factory pattern not only makes sense but is a necessity.

A consequence of the use of the factory pattern is that it makes it very simple for people to plug and play with providers, which can be very useful. For example, you may be planning to deploy an application using a hardware cryptography device, be it external or a bus adapter. In this case the device will have a thin JCA/JCE provider built on top of a JNI interface. On the other hand, you will probably find it a lot easier and cheaper to allow your developers to use a software-only provider when developing the application. Another consequence is that, at least from an application developer's point of view, it does make the API easier to learn: All ciphers look the same, all cryptographic hashes look the same, and the only change that needs to be made is the string passed to the factory to select the implementation. Further, new implementations of algorithms can be added without increasing the apparent complexity of the API. As an example of the kind of "complexity creep" I am talking about here, it is worth considering that in the Bouncy Castle Lightweight API there are 23 engine classes in the `org.bouncycastle.crypto.engines` package, all of which are encapsulated by the single `Cipher` class in the JCE.

Now you are probably wondering what changed that allowed the JCE to go from being something that was not available in other than clean room implementations outside of the United States to something that is now being included with the JDK. Well, cryptography export controls relaxed a bit and at the same time changes were made to the JCE being shipped by Sun. This allowed the JCE to meet the relaxed controls. Sun introduced the use of policy files, which allowed the use of algorithms and key sizes to be restricted and also introduced the idea of signed providers. The changes were signed off by the National Security Agency (NSA) and the U.S. Department of Commerce, and here we are today: JCE 1.2.2, which is for JDK 1.2 and JDK 1.3, ships with unrestricted policy files and works with any signed provider, and every JDK that has shipped since JDK 1.4 ships with the JCE included and restricted policy files that allow access to certain key sizes. The JDK 1.4 and later versions of the JCE will work with any correctly signed provider and have unrestricted policy files available for them. Considering that there are a number of commercial and open source providers that are now signed, when you consider where we were five years ago, this is quite a good result!

> **Note** I have said that the JDK since 1.4 ships with restricted policy files. The reason for this has nothing to do with U.S. cryptography export laws; it is because the JDK ships only with the key sizes that all countries it can be imported into find acceptable. If you need to run the JCE without restrictions, you need to download the unrestricted policy files separately, if it is legal in the country where you are.

This brings us to the two lessons that can be learned from this history. As mentioned, export controls in the United States have relaxed, but it does not mean they do not exist, nor does it mean that if you are not in the United States, your local government does not have laws in with regard to the development of encryption technology. If you want to play in this space, possibly developing products that may be exported overseas, or in some cases even used within your nation's borders, make sure you understand what the legal situation is first. Encryption technology, including software and hardware, is still widely regarded as munitions, and consequently the penalties for ignoring the law on the export and use of encryption technology are very similar to those handed out for arms smuggling. In addition, some algorithms, such as the symmetric cipher IDEA, are still patented in some countries. If you use an algorithm in a country where it is still patented, you are obliged to pay royalties regardless of whether you paid for the software.

So, enough about history, the next things I need to cover in dealing with the JCA and the JCE are the issues of provider signing and the workings of the JCE policy files.

Provider Signing

Provider signing is enforced using root certificates that are embedded in the Java runtime. If you want to write a provider for use with the Java runtime, you need to create a private key and get an associated certificate created, which is signed by a certificate chain that starts with one of the root certificates embedded in the Java runtime.

I will not go into any real detail on provider signing here, as it is only relevant if you need to create your own provider jars. In brief, getting a signing certificate to validate a provider requires getting a certificate from Sun; you can find the details on how to do this in the document entitled "How to Implement a Provider for the Java Cryptography Extension," which is distributed with the document set for the JDK. (This is normally in a file called `docs/guide/security/HowToImplAProvider.html` under the Java documentation tree.) Apart from this fact, the other item you need to be aware of is that if you need to take advantage of the way policy files are used by the Java runtime, you can do so by creating your own application jar and incorporating a policy file. You might want to use an existing code base and create a special provider as part of the application you ship. In any case, the details can be found in the document "Java Cryptography Extension (JCE) Reference Guide" (normally found in `docs/guide/security/jce /JCERefGuide.html` under the Java documentation tree). This can be important if you need to develop a product that must conform to either corporate or government restrictions and enforce algorithm restrictions, limited key sizes, mechanisms such as key escrow, or some combination of all three.

Jurisdiction Policy Files

The normal JDK download ships with a set of policy files that places certain restrictions on the key sizes that can be used. Key sizes are limited in general to 128 bits (except for the symmetric cipher Triple-DES) and RSA key generation is limited to 2,048 bits. The easiest way to deal with this restriction if it need not apply to you is to download the unrestricted policy files.

Installing the Unrestricted Policy Files

> **The following information applies only if you are dealing with JDK 1.4 or later; if you are using JDK 1.2 or JDK 1.3 and using the JCE 1.2.2, the unrestricted policy files come preinstalled in the JCE 1.2.2 distribution.**

You can find the unrestricted policy files on the same page as the JCE/JDK downloads are found. Normally it will be a discrete link at the bottom of the download page entitled something like

"Unlimited Strength Jurisdiction Policy Files." The download is a ZIP file, and providing it is legal for you to do so; you should download the ZIP file and install the two JAR files it contains according to the instructions in the README file contained in the ZIP file.

If you are installing these on a Linux, or some other Unix variant, you need to make sure you install the policy files in the Java runtime you are using, and you will probably need root access or the assistance of a root user to do so, unless you have installed a personal runtime of your own.

If you are installing on Windows, you also need to be extra careful about installing the policy files, as the default install for the JDK installs a runtime for the JDK and a separate JRE, which will normally appear under C:\Program Files\Java.

Try It Out   Testing that the Policy Files Are Installed

Once you have installed the policy files, it is a good idea to make sure they really are installed where you think they are. Try typing and running the following test program. It will not only tell you if the policy files are installed but give you an introduction to the use of the Cipher class and the simple creation of SecretKey objects. There is also an electronic version available for download on the book's Web site.

```
package chapter1;

import javax.crypto.*;
import javax.crypto.spec.*;

public class SimplePolicyTest
{
    public static void main(String[]  args) throws Exception
    {
        byte[]     data = { 0x00, 0x01, 0x02, 0x03, 0x04, 0x05, 0x06, 0x07 };

        // create a 64 bit secret key from raw bytes
        SecretKey  key64 = new SecretKeySpec(
                    new byte[] { 0x00, 0x01, 0x02, 0x03, 0x04, 0x05, 0x06, 0x07 },
                    "Blowfish");

        // create a cipher and attempt to encrypt the data block with our key
        Cipher     c = Cipher.getInstance("Blowfish/ECB/NoPadding");

        c.init(Cipher.ENCRYPT_MODE, key64);
        c.doFinal(data);
        System.out.println("64 bit test: passed");

        // create a 192 bit secret key from raw bytes
        SecretKey  key192 = new SecretKeySpec(
                        new byte[] { 0x00, 0x01, 0x02, 0x03, 0x04, 0x05, 0x06, 0x07,
                                     0x08, 0x09, 0x0a, 0x0b, 0x0c, 0x0d, 0x0e, 0x0f,
                                     0x10, 0x11, 0x12, 0x13, 0x14, 0x15, 0x16, 0x17 },
                    "Blowfish");

        // now try encrypting with the larger key
        c.init(Cipher.ENCRYPT_MODE, key192);
        c.doFinal(data);
```

```
                System.out.println("192 bit test: passed");


                System.out.println("Tests completed");
        }
    }
```

If the files are installed, your class path is correct, and you have compiled the test program, it should be a matter of executing

```
java chapter1.SimplePolicyTest
```

If all is well you will see

```
64 bit test: passed
192 bit test: passed
Tests completed
```

On the other hand if it does not work the most likely thing you will see is

```
64 bit test: passed
Exception in thread "main" java.lang.SecurityException:
        Unsupported keysize or algorithm parameters
        at javax.crypto.Cipher.init(...)
        at chapter1.SimplePolicyTest.main(SimplePolicyTest.java:38)
```

If the preceding happens, it means the policy files are not installed correctly. Check the README file that came with the unrestricted policy file distribution and make sure it has been followed.

> **Blowfish has been chosen as the cipher to use above because it allows for large keys and is present in all versions of the provider that comes by default with the Sun JCE, as well as the clean-room JCE implementations that are available. I will deal with what algorithms are useful to use in production code later.**

How It Works

Whenever an attempt is made to utilize any of the functionality in a JCE provider, the runtime code supporting the API checks the policy restrictions associated with that piece of functionality. In this example, one of two things can happen:

- ❏ It will work, in which case the Java runtime has determined from the JCE policy files that the key size you requested to use with the Cipher class is permissible.

- ❏ It will fail, in which case the Java runtime will have determined from the JCE policy files that the key size you requested to use is not permissible.

You probably noticed that the exception also included the term *algorithm parameters* in its message. This will make sense as you go further. You will see that key size is not the only way of expressing the arguments that are used to initialize objects, like Cipher, that provide the functionality available to you in the JCE.

Troubleshooting Other Issues

You may also run into some other problems while compiling or running the test. The most likely ones are presented here:

❑   **Test does not compile, error message is** `package javax.crypto does not exist.` If this happens, the JCE is not installed. Make sure there is a JAR file containing the `javax.crypto` package tree in either the `jre/lib/ext` (`jre\lib\ext`) directory or the `jre/lib` (`jre\lib`) directory under your install of Java. If you see this and you are running JDK 1.4 or later, there is a problem with your Java installation, and you should reinstall it. If you are running JDK 1.2 or JDK 1.3 and you do not have the JCE, you can download it from `http://java.sun.com`—the release you will be looking for in this case is the JCE 1.2.2.

❑   **Test compiles; however, the runtime exception `java.security.NoSuchAlgorithm Exception: Algorithm Blowfish not available` occurs.** In this case the problem is with the provider. Check that the `java.security` files in your installation have not been tampered with and the SunJCE provider is present. Once again, if this happens and you are running Java 1.4 or later, there is a problem with your installation. If you are running JDK 1.2 or JDK 1.3, check that the install instructions for the JCE have been followed properly.

If you see any other problems, the most likely causes are as follows:

❑   **If you are running JDK 1.4 or later.** These come with the JCE preinstalled. There will be a problem with your installation and it would probably be simpler to reinstall it.

❑   **If you are running JDK 1.2 or JDK 1.3.** For these the JCE would have had to have been installed by hand. Check that the installation instructions have been followed correctly.

How Do You Know the Policy Files Really Behave as Sun Says They Do?

When you look at the history behind the JCE, it is easy to see why some people would be inclined to feel it is all a conspiracy by Sun, the U.S. government, the UN, the Illuminati, the Greys, or some other "organization" and that anything running under the JCE should not be trusted, as you cannot see the code that deals with key strength and various other control mechanisms that the policy files allow you to turn on or off. If this is a concern for you, remember, just as you would test a hardware cryptography adapter by comparing its outputs for given inputs against the outputs produced by an alternative implementation for the same set of outputs, you can also treat the JCE and the underlying provider as a black box and perform the same tests. As it happens the Bouncy Castle provider was first developed as a lightweight library for MIDP, so if you are feeling really enthused, you can start by verifying that the Bouncy Castle provider and the JCE is producing the same output as its lightweight equivalent. It is true that in matters like these you should not take what people tell you at face value, but always remember you can test and investigate the truth of other people's claims yourself.

Installing the Bouncy Castle Provider

There are two ways to install a provider for the JCE and JCA. You can do it dynamically at runtime, or you can configure the JRE to preload the provider for you so that it is "naturally" available in the environment. Which one is best for you will vary according to circumstance, but in general, you will experience fewer issues if you install providers by configuring the Java runtime.

> Note that while this book is largely written for use with the Bouncy Castle provider, the installation instructions that follow should work for any appropriately signed JCE/JCA provider.

Installing by Configuring the Java Runtime

This is by far the simplest and most convenient mechanism for dealing with a provider. On the downside, it also involves changing the configuration of the Java runtime.

There are two steps involved in installing by configuring the Java runtime. First you need to install the JAR file containing the provider, and then you need to enable the provider so the Java runtime can find it.

Install the JAR File Containing the Provider

Under your Java installation you should find the directory `jre/lib/ext`, or if you are using Windows, `jre\lib\ext`. The purpose of this directory is to provide a home for standard extensions to the runtime, which are not normally distributed with the default setup. This is where the provider JAR should go.

In the case of the Bouncy Castle provider you can find the JAR file you need on the page `http://www.bouncycastle.org/latest_releases.html`. The naming convention used for provider JARs in Bouncy Castle is `bcprov-JdkVersion-Version.jar`. So for example, if you were after the JDK 1.4 provider JAR and the release you were looking for was version 1.29, the name of the JAR file you want to download would be `bcprov-jdk14-129.jar`.

Download the JAR file and copy it to the `jre/lib/ext` directory of your Java install. Remember, if you are using Windows, you will probably have two installations, one for the full JDK and one that just contains the JRE, which will normally be under your `Program Files` directory tree. If you have an install of the JRE, you will need to make sure the provider is present under its `lib/ext` directory.

Enable the Provider by Adding It to the java.security File

If you have already been through the installation of the unrestricted policy files, you will probably have noticed that in addition to `jre/lib/ext` under every Java install, there is also a `jre/lib/security`. One of the files contained in `jre/lib/security` specifies, amongst other things, what providers are enabled for the JCE and JCA, as well as their *precedence*. We will look at what precedence means in the next section but for now it is enough to say if you open the file for editing and scroll down a bit, you will see a group of lines like the following:

```
#
# List of providers and their preference orders (see above):
#
security.provider.1=sun.security.provider.Sun
security.provider.2=com.sun.net.ssl.internal.ssl.Provider
security.provider.3=com.sun.rsajca.Provider
security.provider.4=com.sun.crypto.provider.SunJCE
```

The list may have more, or fewer, providers largely depending on which version of Java you have installed. Add the following line to the end of the list:

```
security.provider.N=org.bouncycastle.jce.provider.BouncyCastleProvider
```

N needs to be the next number in the sequence. So, for the previous example list, you would add the line:

```
security.provider.5=org.bouncycastle.jce.provider.BouncyCastleProvider
```

Save the file after making the change, again being making sure you have changed the `java.security` files in all the installs of Java you are using (remember, you may have two installs under Windows, in which case the second one will be under `lib/security` of your JRE install), and you are finished.

> **It might be tempting to put the Bouncy Castle provider first and move all the other ones down one. Do not do this; some Java system software rely on the Sun providers being the first ones in the list, and things will stop working if they aren't.**

Try It Out   Verifying Bouncy Castle Provider Installation

If you have added the Bouncy Castle provider to the `java.security` file and correctly installed the provider JAR file in `jre/lib/ext`, compiling and running the following program, `SimpleProviderTest`, will indicate everything is correct by printing

```
BC provider is installed
```

If the program prints the message `BC provider not installed` instead, first check that the provider has been added to the `java.security` file in `jre/lib/security`, and then check that the provider JAR has been installed in the `jre/lib/ext` directory. You also need to be sure that only one version of the provider has been installed — for example, if you are dealing with JDK 1.4, having both `bcprov-jdk14-128.jar` and `bcprov-jdk14-129.jar` in `jre/lib/ext` at the same time will cause confusion and the provider will not work as expected.

```java
package chapter1;

import java.security.Security;

/**
 * Basic class to confirm the Bouncy Castle provider is
 * installed.
 */
public class SimpleProviderTest
{
    public static void main(String[] args)
    {
        String providerName = "BC";

        if (Security.getProvider(providerName) == null)
        {
            System.out.println(providerName + " provider not installed");
        }
        else
        {
            System.out.println(providerName + " is installed.");
        }
    }
}
```

How It Works

If you look back to the changes made to the `java.security` configuration file, you will see that the following line was added:

```
security.provider.5=org.bouncycastle.jce.provider.BouncyCastleProvider
```

The `Provider` class has a `getName()` method on it that returns a simple name for the provider. It is this simple name that the JCE/JCA classes in the Java runtime are trying to match when a request to create an object is made using the `getInstance()` factory pattern that includes a provider name. In the case of the `BouncyCastleProvider` class, its simple name is just `BC`.

You can also use this simple name to get a copy of the provider via the static `Security.getProvider()` method. Because it is provider implemented by the `BouncyCastleProvider` class that you are interested in, you just pass its simple name (`BC`) to `Security.getProvider()` to retrieve it. Of course, if there is no match for the simple name `BC` and a `null` is returned, it means the provider has not been installed correctly.

As a useful aside, the `Security` class also allows you to retrieve an array of all the providers available using the static `Security.getProviders()` method.

Installing During Execution

A provider can also be added during the execution of your program. This is done via the class `java.security.Security` using the `addProvider()` method. In the case where you wanted to add the Bouncy Castle provider at runtime, you could add the following imports:

```
import java.security.Security;
import org.bouncycastle.jce.provider.BouncyCastleProvider;
```

Then insert the line:

```
Security.addProvider(new BouncyCastleProvider());
```

This line must be added before the provider is referred to in your program. For example, if you were modifying the previous test program, you would obviously need to use the `Security.addProvider()` method before attempting to use `Security.getProvider()`.

> **The examples in the book and on the book Web site assume you have installed the Bouncy Castle provider by configuring the JRE. If you have not, you will need to modify the examples according to the previous instructions for them to work correctly.**

How Provider Precedence Works

You saw earlier that the `java.security` configuration file had precedence numbers associated with each provider installed. Now you will look at how precedence is used. When you instantiate a JCA/JCE object that is created using the `getInstance()` factory pattern, you can either specify the provider you wish to use or leave it up to the Java runtime to choose the provider for you. So, if you wish to specify you want to use the Bouncy Castle provider to create the object, you mightsay, in the case of a `Cipher` object:

```
Cipher.getInstance("Blowfish/ECB/NoPadding", "BC");
```

Or if you do not care which provider is used to create the object you want, you might say

```
Cipher.getInstance("Blowfish/ECB/NoPadding");
```

In this case the Java runtime will select the first provider it can find that can satisfy the request, according to the list of providers in the `java.security` file and the provider's precedence as given there. Providers with a lower preference number take precedence over those with a higher one.

Try It Out   **Precedence Demonstration**

To demonstrate how precedence rules apply, try running the following program:

```
package chapter1;

import javax.crypto.Cipher;

/**
 * Basic demonstration of precedence in action.
 */
public class PrecedenceTest
{
    public static void main(String[] args) throws Exception
    {
        Cipher          cipher = Cipher.getInstance("Blowfish/ECB/NoPadding");

        System.out.println(cipher.getProvider());

        cipher = Cipher.getInstance("Blowfish/ECB/NoPadding", "BC");

        System.out.println(cipher.getProvider());
    }
}
```

The output will probably look something like:

```
SunJCE version 1.42
BC version 1.29
```

How It Works

Although the version numbers may be slightly different, the principle is the same: If you do not specify a particular provider, the provider with the lowest preference order will be used. The SunJCE provider has a higher precedence than the BC provider, so if you do not specify a provider for the Blowfish cipher, you will always get the SunJCEs version.

In general, if you are deploying an application, it is well worth your while to specify the provider in addition to the full algorithm name for the JCA/JCE objects you want to use. Relying on precedence rules can get you into trouble if there are incompatibilities that you are not aware of between providers that you might be mixing or incompatibilities between your code and other providers.

Examining the Capabilities of a Provider

Providers make their capabilities available to the JCA and JCE using a property table that is publicly available, so it is a fairly simple process to write a program that will tell you what a given provider provides support for.

Listing Provider Capabilities

The following program dumps out the base algorithm names and the factory classes so they can be used with the BC provider. As you can see, it just iterates through the entries in the property table the provider contains.

```java
package chapter1;

import java.security.Provider;
import java.security.Security;
import java.util.Iterator;

/**
 * List the available capabilities for ciphers, key agreement, macs, message
 * digests, signatures and other objects in the BC provider.
 */
public class ListBCCapabilities
{
    public static void main(
        String[]    args)
    {
        Provider        provider = Security.getProvider("BC");

        Iterator  it = provider.keySet().iterator();

        while (it.hasNext())
        {
            String      entry = (String)it.next();

            // this indicates the entry actually refers to another entry

            if (entry.startsWith("Alg.Alias."))
            {
                entry = entry.substring("Alg.Alias.".length());
            }

            String  factoryClass = entry.substring(0, entry.indexOf('.'));
            String  name = entry.substring(factoryClass.length() + 1);

            System.out.println(factoryClass + ": " + name);
        }
    }
}
```

How It Works

As you saw before, `Security.getProvider()` allows you to retrieve a provider based on its simple name. In the case of a `Provider` implementation, it is the key set for the provider's property table that contains the types associated with each entry, and that determines whether that entry is simply an alias for another one. The result is that you can get a fairly clear idea of what a provider supports from the strings contained in its property table's key set.

When you run the program, you will probably notice there is quite a bit of output. I will not go into detail about exactly what the output means here, other than to say it will be covered in later chapters. Basically, however, if you see

```
Cipher: AES
```

the line means that a `Cipher.getInstance()` call like

```
Cipher.getInstance("AES/ECB/NoPadding", "BC");
```

or some variant, should produce an object, likewise for MessageDigest, Mac, SecretKeyFactory, and so on.

You can find out more information about the provider capabilities tables, such as how the aliasing works in the "How to Implement a Provider for the Java Cryptography Extension" document referred to earlier in the chapter.

Summary

This chapter has been aimed at making sure you are properly set up to understand and practice what is discussed in the rest of the book.

You have had a brief look at how the JCE and JCA APIs evolved the way they have, and a discussion about how to utilize the policy mechanisms that they provide. As mentioned earlier, for the most part configuring policy for JCE and JCA providers will primarily be a matter of just downloading and installing the unrestricted policy files. It is important to remember that you can make use of your own policy files if you need to as well. The details on how to do this ship with the JCE documentation that Sun provides.

In addition to this, in this chapter you learned

- ❑ How to confirm the policy files for the JCE, and that the JCA are configured as you thought they were
- ❑ How to install a provider into your Java runtime and verify this fact
- ❑ How to examine a provider to see what algorithms it contains
- ❑ How the `getInstance()` factory pattern works and how precedence works

In the next chapter, I will begin to expand beyond basic setup to the practicalities of using the JCE, starting with making use of the JCE for doing symmetric key encryption.

Exercises

1.   Some colleagues come to you with a problem they are having using a JCE provider they have downloaded. They have installed the provider correctly in the `jre/lib/ext` area and added it to the configuration file in `java.security` but are getting a `java.lang.SecurityException` with the message `Unsupported keysize or algorithm parameters`. What have they forgotten?

2.   You are running in a Windows environment. You have downloaded and installed everything into your JDK that is required to support the provider you want to use, but you still find that some Java applications you are using fail to find the provider, even though you are sure you have installed it. Why might this be happening?

3.   You are attempting to use an algorithm that is available in a provider you have installed, but you are finding that when you create an object to use it via the `getInstance()` method, the object does not have all the capabilities that the documentation that comes with the provider indicates. Why might this be the case?

Symmetric Key Cryptography

Symmetric key ciphers are one of the workhorses of cryptography. They are used to secure bulk data, provide a foundation for message authentication codes, and provide support for password-based encryption as well. As symmetric key cryptography gains its security from keeping a shared key secret, it is also often referred to as *secret key* cryptography, a term that you will see is used in the JCE.

This chapter introduces the concept of symmetric key cryptography and how it is used in the JCE. I will cover creation of keys for symmetric key ciphers, creating Cipher objects to be used for encryption, how modes and padding mechanisms are specified in Java, what other parameter objects can be used to initialize ciphers and what they mean, how password-based encryption is used, methods for doing key wrapping, and how to do cipher-based I/O.

By the end of this chapter you should

- ❑ Be well equipped to make use of a variety of symmetric key ciphers
- ❑ Understand the various cipher modes and paddings and what they are for
- ❑ Be able to construct or randomly generate symmetric keys
- ❑ Understand key wrapping
- ❑ Be able to utilize the I/O classes provided in the JCE

Finally, you should also have a few ideas about where to look when you are trying to debug applications using symmetric key ciphers and what might go wrong with them.

A First Example

To get anywhere in this area, you have to first be able to create a key, and then you have to be able to create a cipher so that you can actually do something with it. If you recall the policy file test in the last chapter, you will remember it used two classes, `javax.crypto.Cipher` and `javax .crypto.spec.SecretKeySpec`. These two classes provide you with enough of a starting point to write a simple example program.

A Basic Utility Class

In the policy test program, you were mainly interested in whether you could create a cipher with a given key size and use it. This time you will carry out a simple encryption/decryption process so you can see how ciphers get used from end to end. Before you can do this, you need to define some basic infrastructure that allows you to look at the output of your programs easily. Encrypted data, as you can imagine, is only human-readable by chance, so for the purposes of investigation, it is best to print the bytes you are interested in using hex, which, being base-16, nicely maps to two digits a byte.

Here is a simple utility class for doing hex printing of a byte array:

```
package chapter2;

/**
 * General utilities for the second chapter examples.
 */
public class Utils
{
    private static String   digits = "0123456789abcdef";

    /**
     * Return length many bytes of the passed in byte array as a hex string.
     *
     * @param data the bytes to be converted.
     * @param length the number of bytes in the data block to be converted.
     * @return a hex representation of length bytes of data.
     */
    public static String toHex(byte[] data, int length)
    {
        StringBuffer    buf = new StringBuffer();

        for (int i = 0; i != length; i++)
        {
            int    v = data[i] & 0xff;

            buf.append(digits.charAt(v >> 4));
            buf.append(digits.charAt(v & 0xf));
        }

        return buf.toString();
    }

    /**
     * Return the passed in byte array as a hex string.
     *
     * @param data the bytes to be converted.
     * @return a hex representation of data.
     */
    public static String toHex(byte[] data)
    {
        return toHex(data, data.length);
    }
}
```

Copy and compile the utility class. Now you have done that, look at the example that follows.

Try It Out   **Using AES**

Because this example is fairly simple, I'll explain the API I am using after it. However, you should note that the example is using an algorithm called AES. Prior to November 2001, the stock standard algorithm for doing symmetric key encryption was the Data Encryption Standard (DES) and a variant on it, namely, Triple-DES or DES-EDE. Now, following the announcement of the Advanced Encryption Standard (AES), your general preference should be to use AES. You will look at some other algorithms a bit later; however, a lot of work went into the development and selection of AES. It makes sense to take advantage of it, so AES is what you'll use in this example.

```
package chapter2;

import javax.crypto.Cipher;
import javax.crypto.spec.SecretKeySpec;


/**
 * Basic symmetric encryption example
 */
public class SimpleSymmetricExample
{
    public static void main(String[] args) throws Exception
    {
        byte[]          input = new byte[] {
                        0x00, 0x11, 0x22, 0x33, 0x44, 0x55, 0x66, 0x77,
                        (byte)0x88, (byte)0x99, (byte)0xaa, (byte)0xbb,
                        (byte)0xcc, (byte)0xdd, (byte)0xee, (byte)0xff };
        byte[]          keyBytes = new byte[] {
                        0x00, 0x01, 0x02, 0x03, 0x04, 0x05, 0x06, 0x07,
                        0x08, 0x09, 0x0a, 0x0b, 0x0c, 0x0d, 0x0e, 0x0f,
                        0x10, 0x11, 0x12, 0x13, 0x14, 0x15, 0x16, 0x17 };

        SecretKeySpec key = new SecretKeySpec(keyBytes, "AES");

        Cipher          cipher = Cipher.getInstance("AES/ECB/NoPadding", "BC");

        System.out.println("input text : " + Utils.toHex(input));

        // encryption pass

        byte[] cipherText = new byte[input.length];

        cipher.init(Cipher.ENCRYPT_MODE, key);

        int ctLength = cipher.update(input, 0, input.length, cipherText, 0);

        ctLength += cipher.doFinal(cipherText, ctLength);

        System.out.println("cipher text: " + Utils.toHex(cipherText)
                                        + " bytes: " + ctLength);
```

```
        // decryption pass

        byte[] plainText = new byte[ctLength];

        cipher.init(Cipher.DECRYPT_MODE, key);

        int ptLength = cipher.update(cipherText, 0, ctLength, plainText, 0);

        ptLength += cipher.doFinal(plainText, ptLength);

        System.out.println("plain text : " + Utils.toHex(plainText)
                                            + " bytes: " + ptLength);
    }
}
```

Readers who also spend their time browsing through the NIST FIPS publications may recognize this as one of the standard vector tests for AES in FIPS-197. As an aside, if you are planning to get seriously involved in this area, you would do well to have some familiarity with the relevant NIST FIPS publications. The most relevant ones have been listed in Appendix D, and amongst other things, they are a big help if you need to confirm for yourself the validity of an implementation of an algorithm they describe.

If all is going well, and your class path is appropriately set up, when you run the program using

```
java chapter2.SimpleSymmetricExample
```

you will see

```
input text : 0112233445566778899aabbccddeeff
cipher text: dda97ca4864cdfe06eaf70a0ecd7191 bytes: 16
plain text : 0112233445566778899aabbccddeeff bytes: 16
```

You may also get the exception:

```
Exception in thread "main" java.security.NoSuchProviderException:
                                        Provider 'BC' not found
```

which means the provider is not properly installed.

Or you may get the exception:

```
Exception in thread "main" java.lang.SecurityException:
                        Unsupported keysize or algorithm parameters
```

which instead means it can find the provider, but the unrestricted policy files are not installed.

If you see either of these exceptions, or have any other problems, look through Chapter 1 again and make sure the Bouncy Castle provider has been correctly installed and the Java environment is correctly configured.

On the other hand, if everything is working, it is probably time you looked at how the program works.

How It Works

As you can see, the example demonstrates that carrying out a symmetric key encryption operation is a matter of providing a key to use and a suitable object for doing the processing on the input data, be it plaintext to be encrypted or ciphertext to be decrypted. In Java the easiest way to construct a symmetric key by hand is to use the `SecretKeySpec` class.

The SecretKeySpec Class

The `javax.crypto.spec.SecretKeySpec` class provides a simple mechanism for converting byte data into a secret key suitable for passing to a `Cipher` object's `init()` method. As you'll see a bit later, it is not the only way of creating a secret key, but it is certainly one that is used a lot. Looking at the previous Try It Out ("Using AES"), you can see that constructing a secret key can be as simple as passing a byte array and the name of the algorithm the key is to be used with. For more details on the class, see the JavaDoc that comes with the JCE.

> One thing the `SecretKeySpec` will not do is stop you from passing a weak key to a `Cipher` object. Weak keys are keys that, for a given algorithm, do not provide strong cryptography and should be avoided. Not all algorithms have weak keys, but if you are using one that does, such as DES, you should take care to ensure that the bytes produced for creating the `SecretKeySpec` are not weak keys.

The Cipher Class

A look at the previous example program quickly reveals that the creation and use of a `javax.crypto.Cipher` object follows a simple pattern. You create one using `Cipher.getInstance()`, initialize it with the mode you want using `Cipher.init()`, feed the input data in while collecting output at the same time using `Cipher.update()`, and then finish off the process with `Cipher.doFinal()`.

Cipher.getInstance()

A `Cipher` object, rather than being created using a constructor directly, is created using the static factory method `Cipher.getInstance()`. In the case of the example, it was done by passing two arguments, one giving the kind of cipher you want to create, the other giving the provider you want to use to create it — given by the name `"BC"`.

In the case of the cipher name `"AES/ECB/NoPadding"`, the name is composed of three parts. The first part is the name of algorithm — AES. The second part is the mode in which the algorithm should be used, ECB, or Electronic Code Book mode. Finally, the string `"NoPadding"` tells the provider you do not wish to use padding with this algorithm. Just ignore the mode and padding, as you will be reading about them soon. What is most important now is that when the *full name* of the `Cipher` object you want to be created is given, it always follows the *AlgorithmName/Mode/TypeOfPadding* pattern. You can also just give the algorithm name and provider, as in:

```
Cipher.getInstance("AES", "BC");
```

However if you do, it is purely up to the provider you are using as to which mode and padding will be used in the `Cipher` object that has been returned. It is advised against doing this in the interests of allowing your code to be portable between providers. Specify exactly what you need and you should be spared unnecessary surprises.

Cipher.init()

Having created a `Cipher` object using `Cipher.getInstance()` at a minimum, you then have to initialize it with the type of operation it is to be used for and with the key that is to be used. `Cipher` objects have four possible modes, all specified using static constants on the `Cipher` class. Two of the modes are connected with key wrapping, which you'll look at later, and the other two are `Cipher.ENCRYPT_MODE` and `Cipher.DECRYPT_MODE`, which were used previously. The `Cipher.init()` method can take other parameters as well, which you'll look at later. For the moment it is enough to understand that if you do not call the `init` method, any attempt to use the `Cipher` object will normally result in an `IllegalStateException`.

Cipher.update()

Once the `Cipher` object is set up for encryption or decryption, you can feed data into it and accept data from it. There are several convenience update methods on the `Cipher` class that you can read about in the JavaDoc, but the one used in the example is the most fundamental. Consider the line:

```
int ctLength = cipher.update(input, 0, input.length, cipherText, 0);
```

Cipher objects usually acquire a chunk of data, process it by copying the result into the output array (the argument `cipherText`), and then copy the next chunk and continue, filling the output array as they go. Thus, you cannot be sure how much data will be written each time you do an update; the number of output bytes may be O (zero), or it may be between 0 and the length of the input. The starting offset that the processed blocks are written to is the last argument to the method, in this case 0. Regardless of how many bytes get output during an update, you will only know how many bytes have been written to the output array if you keep track of the return value.

Cipher.doFinal()

Now consider the line:

```
ctLength += cipher.doFinal(cipherText, ctLength);
```

`Cipher.doFinal()` is very similar to `Cipher.update()` in that it may also put out 0 or more bytes, depending on the kind of `Cipher` object you specified with `Cipher.getInstance()`. Likewise, it also has a return value to tell you how many bytes it actually wrote to the output array (again the `cipherText` array). Note that the second argument is the offset at which writing of the output will start and is a value that has been preserved from the last `Cipher.update()`.

> **Failing to keep track of the return values from the `int` returning methods of `update()` and `doFinal()` is one of the most common error programmers make using the `Cipher` class. It is never okay to ignore the return values if you want to write flexible code.**

Symmetric Block Cipher Padding

While the value of the test vector used in the last example was not due to random chance, neither was the length of it. Most of the popular ciphers are block ciphers, and their block size is normally more than 1 byte long; DES and Blowfish, for example, have a block size of 8 bytes. AES, the latest addition to the family, has a block size of 16 bytes. The effect of this is that the input data to a cipher that is being used in a blocking mode must be aligned to the block size of that cipher. Truth is, for most of us, the data we wish to encrypt is not always going to be a multiple of the block size of the encryption mechanism we want to use. So while we can find out what the block size is using the `Cipher.getBlockSize()` method and then try to take it into account, the easiest way to deal with this issue is to use padding mechanisms.

PKCS #5/PKCS #7 Padding

PKCS #5 padding was originally developed for block ciphers with a block size of 8 bytes. Later, with the writing of PKCS #7, the authors of the standard specified a broader interpretation of the padding mechanism, which allowed for the padding mechanism to be used for block sizes up to 255 bytes. The PKCS in PKCS #5 and PKCS #7 comes from Public-Key Cryptography Standards that were developed by RSA Security. They are also worth a read, and a list of the most relevant appears in Appendix D.

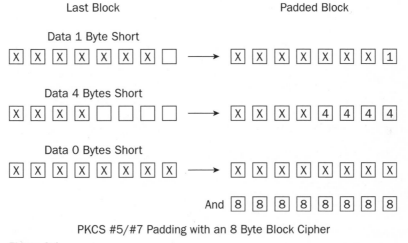

PKCS #5/#7 Padding with an 8 Byte Block Cipher

Figure 2-1

You can see from Figure 2-1 that the padding mechanism is quite simple; if you need to pad a block of data where the last input block is 3 bytes shorter than the block size of the cipher you are using; you add 3 bytes of value 3 to the data before encrypting it. Then when the data is decrypted, you check the last byte of the last decrypted block of data and remove that many bytes from it. The only shortcoming of this approach is that you must always add the padding, so if the block size of your cipher is 8 bytes and your data is a multiple of 8 bytes in length, you have to add a pad block with 8 bytes with the value 8 to your data before you encrypt it, and as before, remove the extra 8 bytes at the other end when the data is decrypted. The advantage of this approach is that the mechanism is unambiguous.

Try It Out   Adding Padding

Fortunately, as a by-product of the use of the factory pattern, the JCE allows you to introduce padding in a manner that makes its effect on the application developer almost invisible. Looking back at the example program again, imagine that you wanted to encrypt and decrypt a hex string which is not block aligned, say, 50 percent longer than the test vector. Here is what the example looks like with PKCS #7 padding introduced and the important changes highlighted:

```java
package chapter2;

import javax.crypto.Cipher;
import javax.crypto.spec.SecretKeySpec;


/**
 * Basic symmetric encryption example with padding
 */
public class SimpleSymmetricPaddingExample
{
    public static void main(String[] args) throws Exception
    {
        byte[]        input = new byte[] {
                        0x00, 0x01, 0x02, 0x03, 0x04, 0x05, 0x06, 0x07,
                        0x08, 0x09, 0x0a, 0x0b, 0x0c, 0x0d, 0x0e, 0x0f,
                        0x10, 0x11, 0x12, 0x13, 0x14, 0x15, 0x16, 0x17 };
        byte[]        keyBytes = new byte[] {
                        0x00, 0x01, 0x02, 0x03, 0x04, 0x05, 0x06, 0x07,
                        0x08, 0x09, 0x0a, 0x0b, 0x0c, 0x0d, 0x0e, 0x0f,
                        0x10, 0x11, 0x12, 0x13, 0x14, 0x15, 0x16, 0x17 };

        SecretKeySpec key = new SecretKeySpec(keyBytes, "AES");

        Cipher        cipher = Cipher.getInstance("AES/ECB/PKCS7Padding", "BC");

        System.out.println("input : " + Utils.toHex(input));

        // encryption pass

        cipher.init(Cipher.ENCRYPT_MODE, key);

        byte[] cipherText = new byte[cipher.getOutputSize(input.length)];

        int ctLength = cipher.update(input, 0, input.length, cipherText, 0);

        ctLength += cipher.doFinal(cipherText, ctLength);

        System.out.println("cipher: " + Utils.toHex(cipherText)
                                        + " bytes: " + ctLength);

        // decryption pass

        cipher.init(Cipher.DECRYPT_MODE, key);
```

```
            byte[] plainText = new byte[cipher.getOutputSize(ctLength)];

        int ptLength = cipher.update(cipherText, 0, ctLength, plainText, 0);

        ptLength += cipher.doFinal(plainText, ptLength);

        System.out.println("plain : " + Utils.toHex(plainText)
                                        + " bytes: " + ptLength);
    }
}
```

Run the program and you will see the following output:

```
input : 000102030405060708090a0b0c0d0e0f1011121314151617
cipher: 0060bffe46834bb8da5cf9a61ff220aefa46bbd3578579c0fd331874c7234233 bytes: 32
plain : 000102030405060708090a0b0c0d0e0f10111213141516170000000000000000 bytes: 24
```

Looking through the example, you can see there are not many changes. Looking at the output, you are probably wondering why there are 32 bytes in the plainText array when outLength is 24. Why are there an extra 8 zero bytes on the end? I will get to that in a minute; first, take a look at the how it works.

How It Works

The key to getting this example to function the way it does is in the string passed in the padding section of the cipher name. Rather than specifying, as you did in the previous Try It Out ("Using AES") :

```
Cipher          cipher = Cipher.getInstance("AES/ECB/NoPadding", "BC");
```

you replace the padding term in the cipher name, in the above "NoPadding", with the name of the padding you wish to use "PKCS7Padding". This results in the following:

```
Cipher          cipher = Cipher.getInstance("AES/ECB/PKCS7Padding", "BC");
```

The padding has another effect on the code as well. The first thing you will notice is that Cipher.init() method is now called before the output arrays are created, and the output array is created by calling Cipher.getOutputSize() and passing in the length of the input as an argument. In the case of decryption, this gives you these two lines:

```
cipher.init(Cipher.DECRYPT_MODE, key);

byte[] plainText = new byte[cipher.getOutputSize(cipherText.length)];
```

The Cipher.init() needs to be first as, if you recall the earlier discussion, a cipher must be initialized before it makes sense to use any of its other methods. In this case, the method you want to use is Cipher.getOutputSize(). Note that the JavaDoc for this method specifies that the length returned by Cipher.getOutputSize() may be greater than the actual length returned by Cipher.update() or Cipher.doFinal(), and it often is—especially when decrypting. This is another reason why you need to pay attention to the return values from Cipher.update() and Cipher.doFinal(). People occasionally make the mistake of thinking this means that there is something broken about the Cipher class. If you are wondering about this, remember when a padded message is being decrypted, the Cipher class has no way of knowing how much padding there is *until it decrypts the block with the padding*. You could say it is a fact of life—the best you can do with just the length of the input is guess. Consequently that is all the API offers.

In later examples, you'll use the two-parameter version of `Utils.toHex()` so that only the generated bytes in the output arrays are printed. For the most part, however, you can assume extra bytes will be getting allocated as a result of `Cipher.getOutputSize()`. It is just that they will be ignored, as they should be, by keeping track of the length of the data using the return values from `Cipher.update()` and `Cipher.doFinal()`.

> **Always remember that the estimated size of the output array returned by** `Cipher.getOutputSize()` **will almost always be larger than the number of bytes produced by the cipher. If you do not take this into account, you will end up with spurious zeros at the end of your data.**

Other Padding Mechanisms

A number of other padding modes are available. The following ones are available in the Bouncy Castle provider. If you are using another provider, you might find some or all of the following in addition to NoPadding and PKCS5Padding and/or PKCS7Padding:

- ❑ **ISO10126-2Padding.** A padding mechanism defined in ISO10126-2. The last byte of the padding is the number of pad bytes; the remaining bytes of the padding are made up of random data.

- ❑ **ISO7816-4Padding.** A padding mechanism defined in ISO7816-4. The first byte of the padding is the value 0x80; the remaining bytes of the padding are made up of zeros.

- ❑ **X9.23Padding.** A padding mechanism defined in X9.23. The last byte of the padding is the number of pad bytes; outside of the last byte, the pad bytes are then either made up of zeros or random data.

- ❑ **TBCPadding.** For Trailing Bit Complement padding. If the data ends in a zero bit, the padding will be full of ones; if the data ends in a one bit, the padding will be full of zeros.

- ❑ **ZeroBytePadding.** Do not use this one unless you have to deal with a legacy application. It is really only suitable for use with printable ASCII data. In this case the padding is performed by padding out with one or more bytes of zero value. Obviously, if your data might end with bytes of zero value, this padding mechanism will not work very well.

In addition to padding mechanisms that affect the processing of the last block of the data stream, there are cipher modes that affect the processing of each block in the data stream as well. The next section looks at the cipher modes.

Symmetric Block Cipher Modes

Quite a number of modes have been proposed for symmetric block ciphers. This chapter restricts itself to the most well known, but you can find further details on cipher modes by referring to *Applied Cryptography — Second Edition* and *Practical Cryptography*, both of which are listed in Appendix D.

The first one, known as ECB mode, is the mode closest to the actual cipher. The other modes—CBC mode, CTS mode, CTR mode, OFB mode, and CFB mode—are all really constructed on top of ECB mode and attempt to work around problems that can result from using ECB mode directly or because the cipher requires a block of bits at a time to do its job, rather than being able to stream the data.

Let's start with ECB mode.

ECB Mode

ECB, or *Electronic Code Book*, mode describes the use of a symmetric cipher in its rawest form. The problem with ECB mode is that if there are patterns in your data, there will be patterns in your encrypted data as well. A *pattern*, in this case, is any block of bytes that contains the same values as another block of bytes. This is more common than you might imagine, especially if you are processing data that is structured.

Try It Out   **Ciphertext Patterns in ECB Mode**

Try running the following example. The example uses DES not so much as a recommendation, but more because having an 8-byte block size (rather than the 16-byte one AES has) makes it much easier to see the patterns.

```
package chapter2;

import javax.crypto.Cipher;
import javax.crypto.spec.SecretKeySpec;


/**
 * Basic symmetric encryption example with padding and ECB using DES
 */
public class SimpleECBExample
{
    public static void main(String[] args) throws Exception
    {
        byte[]          input = new byte[] {
                    0x00, 0x01, 0x02, 0x03, 0x04, 0x05, 0x06, 0x07,
                    0x08, 0x09, 0x0a, 0x0b, 0x0c, 0x0d, 0x0e, 0x0f,
                    0x00, 0x01, 0x02, 0x03, 0x04, 0x05, 0x06, 0x07 };
        byte[]          keyBytes = new byte[] {
                    0x01, 0x23, 0x45, 0x67,
                    (byte)0x89, (byte)0xab, (byte)0xcd, (byte)0xef };

        SecretKeySpec key = new SecretKeySpec(keyBytes, "DES");

        Cipher          cipher = Cipher.getInstance("DES/ECB/PKCS7Padding", "BC");

        System.out.println("input : " + Utils.toHex(input));

        // encryption pass

        cipher.init(Cipher.ENCRYPT_MODE, key);

        byte[] cipherText = new byte[cipher.getOutputSize(input.length)];
```

```
          int ctLength = cipher.update(input, 0, input.length, cipherText, 0);

          ctLength += cipher.doFinal(cipherText, ctLength);

          System.out.println("cipher: " + Utils.toHex(cipherText, ctLength)
                                             + " bytes: " + ctLength);

          // decryption pass

          cipher.init(Cipher.DECRYPT_MODE, key);

          byte[] plainText = new byte[cipher.getOutputSize(ctLength)];

          int ptLength = cipher.update(cipherText, 0, ctLength, plainText, 0);

          ptLength += cipher.doFinal(plainText, ptLength);

          System.out.println("plain : " + Utils.toHex(plainText, ptLength)
                                             + " bytes: " + ptLength);
       }
    }
```

When you run this example, you should see the output:

```
input : 000102030405060708090a0b0c0d0e0f0001020304050607
cipher: 3260266c2cf202e28325790654a444d93260266c2cf202e2086f9a1d74c94d4e bytes: 32
plain : 000102030405060708090a0b0c0d0e0f0001020304050607 bytes: 24
```

How It Works

The words "Code Book" really sum up ECB mode. Given a particular block of bytes on input, the cipher performs a set of deterministic calculations, looking up a virtual code book as it were, and returns a particular block of bytes as output. So given the same block of input bytes, you will always get the same block of output bytes. This is how a cipher works in its rawest form.

Notice how the hex string 3260266c2cf202e2 repeats in the ciphertext as the string 001020304050607 does in the input. If you imagine you know nothing about the input data and are looking at the encrypted data and hoping to work out what the input data might contain, that pattern will tell you the input data is repeating. If you already know something about the input data and would like to know more, the pattern might tell you a lot. If the person who is generating the encrypted data is also using the same key repeatedly, a beautiful world might be about to unfold for you if you are the attacker. As for the person doing the encryption, you can see there is a problem.

CBC Mode

CBC, or *Cipher Block Chaining*, mode reduces the likelihood of patterns appearing in the ciphertext by XORing the block of data to be encrypted with the last block of ciphertext produced and then applying the raw cipher to produce the next block of ciphertext.

Try It Out   Using CBC Mode

Try the following example:

```
package chapter2;

import javax.crypto.Cipher;
import javax.crypto.spec.IvParameterSpec;
import javax.crypto.spec.SecretKeySpec;

/**
 * Basic symmetric encryption example with padding and CBC using DES
 */
public class SimpleCBCExample
{
    public static void main(String[] args) throws Exception
    {
        byte[]          input = new byte[] {
                            0x00, 0x01, 0x02, 0x03, 0x04, 0x05, 0x06, 0x07,
                            0x08, 0x09, 0x0a, 0x0b, 0x0c, 0x0d, 0x0e, 0x0f,
                            0x00, 0x01, 0x02, 0x03, 0x04, 0x05, 0x06, 0x07 };
        byte[]          keyBytes = new byte[] {
                            0x01, 0x23, 0x45, 0x67,
                            (byte)0x89, (byte)0xab, (byte)0xcd, (byte)0xef };
        byte[]          ivBytes = new byte[] {
                            0x07, 0x06, 0x05, 0x04, 0x03, 0x02, 0x01, 0x00 };

        SecretKeySpec   key = new SecretKeySpec(keyBytes, "DES");
        IvParameterSpec ivSpec = new IvParameterSpec(ivBytes);
        Cipher          cipher = Cipher.getInstance("DES/CBC/PKCS7Padding", "BC");

        System.out.println("input : " + Utils.toHex(input));

        // encryption pass

        cipher.init(Cipher.ENCRYPT_MODE, key, ivSpec);

        byte[] cipherText = new byte[cipher.getOutputSize(input.length)];

        int ctLength = cipher.update(input, 0, input.length, cipherText, 0);

        ctLength += cipher.doFinal(cipherText, ctLength);

        System.out.println("cipher: " + Utils.toHex(cipherText, ctLength)
                                        + " bytes: " + ctLength);

        // decryption pass

        cipher.init(Cipher.DECRYPT_MODE, key, ivSpec);

        byte[] plainText = new byte[cipher.getOutputSize(ctLength)];

        int ptLength = cipher.update(cipherText, 0, ctLength, plainText, 0);
```

```
        ptLength += cipher.doFinal(plainText, ptLength);

        System.out.println("plain : " + Utils.toHex(plainText, ptLength)
                                    + " bytes: " + ptLength);
    }
}
```

You should see the following output:

```
input : 000102030405060708090a0b0c0d0e0f0001020304050607
cipher: 8a87d41c5d3caead0c21f1b3f12a6cd75424fa086e029e404c89d4c1b9457818 bytes: 32
plain : 000102030405060708090a0b0c0d0e0f0001020304050607 bytes: 24
```

Notice that this time every block of the encrypted output is different, even though you can see that the first and third blocks of the input data are the same. The other item of interest about the ciphertext in this example is that the first block is also different from the first block in the ECB example, despite the fact that they use the same key.

How It Works

You can see from the highlighted changes that we are now passing "CBC" rather than "ECB" to the static `Cipher.getInstance()` method. This explains how I have moved from ECB to CBC mode, but how does that explain the change in the output?

Remember, I said earlier that CBC mode works by XORing the last block of ciphertext produced with the current block of input and then applying the raw cipher. This explains how the first and the third blocks of the ciphertext are now different, as the third block of the ciphertext is now the result of encrypting the XOR of the third block of input with the second block of ciphertext. The question is, what do you do about the first block? At that stage nothing has been encrypted yet.

This is where the `javax.crypto.spec.IvParameterSpec` object comes in. It is used to carry the initialization vector, or IV, and as the name indicates, the `IvParameterSpec` is required, in addition to the key, to initialize the `Cipher` object. It is the initialization vector that provides the initial block of "cipher text" that is XORed with the first block of input.

> **Forgetting to set the IV or setting it to the wrong value is a very common programmer error. The indicator for this error is that the first block of the message will decrypt to garbage, but the rest of the message will appear to decrypt correctly.**

Inline IVs

As you can see, the JCE assumes that the IV will be passed as an out-of-band parameter. Although this is often the case, there is another way of dealing with IVs apart from introducing the IV as an out-of-band parameter to the encryption. In some cases people also write the IV out at the start of the stream and then rely on the receiver to read past it before attempting to reconstruct the message. It's okay to do this, as the IV does not need to be kept secret, but if you are using the JCE, you still need to provide an IV to `Cipher.init()` if you are using a cipher and mode that expects one. Fortunately, this is easy to do as well; in this case you can simply use an IV, which is a block of zeros.

Using an Inline IV

Look at the following example:

```java
package chapter2;

import javax.crypto.Cipher;
import javax.crypto.spec.IvParameterSpec;
import javax.crypto.spec.SecretKeySpec;

/**
 * Symmetric encryption example with padding and CBC using DES
 * with the initialization vector inline.
 */
public class InlineIvCBCExample
{
    public static void main(String[] args) throws Exception
    {
        byte[]          input = new byte[] {
                            0x00, 0x01, 0x02, 0x03, 0x04, 0x05, 0x06, 0x07,
                            0x08, 0x09, 0x0a, 0x0b, 0x0c, 0x0d, 0x0e, 0x0f,
                            0x00, 0x01, 0x02, 0x03, 0x04, 0x05, 0x06, 0x07 };
        byte[]          keyBytes = new byte[] {
                            0x01, 0x23, 0x45, 0x67,
                            (byte)0x89, (byte)0xab, (byte)0xcd, (byte)0xef };
        byte[]          ivBytes = new byte[] {
                            0x07, 0x06, 0x05, 0x04, 0x03, 0x02, 0x01, 0x00 };

        SecretKeySpec   key = new SecretKeySpec(keyBytes, "DES");
        IvParameterSpec ivSpec = new IvParameterSpec(new byte[8]);
        Cipher          cipher = Cipher.getInstance("DES/CBC/PKCS7Padding", "BC");

        System.out.println("input : " + Utils.toHex(input));

        // encryption pass

        cipher.init(Cipher.ENCRYPT_MODE, key, ivSpec);

        byte[] cipherText = new byte[
                        cipher.getOutputSize(ivBytes.length + input.length)];

        int ctLength = cipher.update(ivBytes, 0, ivBytes.length, cipherText, 0);

        ctLength += cipher.update(input, 0, input.length, cipherText, ctLength);

        ctLength += cipher.doFinal(cipherText, ctLength);

        System.out.println("cipher: " + Utils.toHex(cipherText, ctLength)
                                            + " bytes: " + ctLength);

        // decryption pass

        cipher.init(Cipher.DECRYPT_MODE, key, ivSpec);
```

```
        byte[] buf = new byte[cipher.getOutputSize(ctLength)];

        int bufLength = cipher.update(cipherText, 0, ctLength, buf, 0);

        bufLength += cipher.doFinal(buf, bufLength);

        // remove the iv from the start of the message

        byte[] plainText = new byte[bufLength - ivBytes.length];

        System.arraycopy(buf, ivBytes.length, plainText, 0, plainText.length);

        System.out.println("plain : " + Utils.toHex(plainText, plainText.length)
                          .            + " bytes: " + plainText.length);
    }
}
```

Run this example and you should see the following output:

```
input : 00010203040506070809a0b0c0d0e0f0001020304050607
cipher: 159fc9af021f30024211a5d7bf88fd0b9e2a82facabb493f39c5a9febe6a659e85039332be5
6f6a4 bytes: 40
plain : 00010203040506070809a0b0c0d0e0f0001020304050607 bytes: 24
```

How It Works

You can see by examining the highlighted pieces of code that there are only two real changes, apart from the use of an IvParameterSpec with an array of zero value. First, you now call update twice when you encrypt the message, once to feed in the IV and a second time to feed in the message. Second, you trim the IV block off the start of the plaintext so that you only display the bytes making up the message.

This does save you the trouble of passing the IV out of band with the encrypted message; on the other hand, it makes the encrypted message a block longer, thus increasing the overhead required to send the message. It also complicates the code required to process it.

Creating an IV

The examples in this chapter use a fixed IV. Although this is very useful for demonstrating what is going on, as it makes the output of the examples predictable, producing predictable ciphertext is not something you want in a real-life application. In real life the messages your applications are encrypting are often very similar, and in any case, you often cannot control what will be encrypted generating IVs, dealing with the worst-case scenario appears to be the best approach. A sensible IV should be as random as you can make it and preferably unique to a given message. This gives you two ways of generating an IV: generate a random IV from a random source or generate a pseudorandom IV using some piece of data unique to the message you want to encrypt, such as the message number.

As you can see, there are a few things to think about. If you are interested in a more thorough but still approachable discussion of IV generation, read the discussion on initialization vectors in Chapter 5 of *Practical Cryptography*. (See Appendix D.)

Random IVs

How you generate an IV depends a lot on what the environment is like. If you are thinking about using a random IV, the major consideration is really whether the overhead that is added when you use one is acceptable. If your messages are short and you are sending a lot of them, this can rapidly build up. That being said, if you decide to use a random IV, your best bet is to use a `SecureRandom` object, see that it is seeded appropriately, and generate the bytes you need. You will look at creating a `SecureRandom` object in the next section. For now, it enough to say that generating a random IV will often involve no more than the following:

```
byte[]              ivBytes = new byte[cipherBlockSize];
        random.nextBytes(ivBytes);
IvParameterSpec  ivSpec = new IvParameterSpec(ivBytes);
```

where *cipherBlockSize* is the block size of the particular cipher you are using and *random* is a `SecureRandom` object.

Alternatively, you can let the `Cipher` object generate an IV for you. This will only happen on encryption — obviously, to decrypt a message, you need to be told the IV. In any case, you could replace the encryption initialization step in the CBC example with

```
        cipher.init(Cipher.ENCRYPT_MODE, key);
        IvParameterSpec ivSpec = new IvParameterSpec(cipher.getIV());
```

and take advantage of the `Cipher` object's ability to generate a random IV. Of course, in real life, you would probably just retrieve the raw bytes using `Cipher.getIV()` and pass them along with the message to the receiver, who would then create an `IvParameterSpec`.

Creating a SecureRandom Object

An object based on the `java.security.SecureRandom` class can be as simple or as complicated to create as you want. Initially, they were created solely using constructors and a Sun provider implementation based on using a SHA-1 hash. In earlier versions of the JDK, the default initialization of the class caused major performance issues. These days there is support for the creation of `SecureRandom` objects through the factory pattern, meaning that the JCA provider implementers can provide their own, and the default `SecureRandom` implementation will take advantage of hardware support for random number generation as well.

The upshot is that for the most part, `new SecureRandom()` will probably do the right thing by you.

If you are using an older version of the JDK and the default seeding mechanism is destroying performance by causing a substantial delay when the first `SecureRandom` is created, you can prevent the default initialization from taking place by using the `SecureRandom` constructor that takes a byte array. Just make sure you add enough *seed material,* in the shape of random timings from mouse events, network events, or input from the keyboard or any other source available to you, to the `SecureRandom` object you have created to make sure you are getting a good-quality random seed. Things like just the process identifier and system time are not enough. You need to have enough sources of entropy to make sure the initial state of your `SecureRandom` is not easily guessable. Covering all the possible ways to collect seed material is a discussion that is not really appropriate to this book; however, if you are interested in looking into this further, you might want to look at RFC 1750 and also Chapter 10 of *Practical Cryptography* (see Appendix D for more information about this book).

Pseudorandom IVs

Most systems incorporate some idea of message numbering, if for no other reason than to avoid replay attacks. In any case, I mention message numbers because they are generally unique to the message across the system, but the general idea is to find something that travels along with the message that occurs only once. Another name for such a value is a *nonce*, which is short for *number used once*.

Having found a suitable nonce value, you can generate an IV for your message by using the nonce as a seed to some other function that will generate the bytes you need for the IV. As you are after a block size for the cipher worth of bytes and you would like it to be unique, just encrypting the nonce with the cipher will work nicely. In this case you only need to use ECB mode; however, you can avoid creation of an extra `Cipher` object by using the CBC cipher with a zero IV — which is exactly the same.

Try It Out   Using an IV Based on a Nonce

Try the following example:

```
package chapter2;

import javax.crypto.Cipher;
import javax.crypto.spec.IvParameterSpec;
import javax.crypto.spec.SecretKeySpec;

/**
 * CBC using DES with an IV based on a nonce. In this
 * case a hypothetical message number.
 */
public class NonceIvCBCExample
{
    public static void main(String[] args) throws Exception
    {
        byte[]          input = new byte[] {
                    0x00, 0x01, 0x02, 0x03, 0x04, 0x05, 0x06, 0x07,
                    0x08, 0x09, 0x0a, 0x0b, 0x0c, 0x0d, 0x0e, 0x0f,
                    0x00, 0x01, 0x02, 0x03, 0x04, 0x05, 0x06, 0x07 };
        byte[]          keyBytes = new byte[] {
                    0x01, 0x23, 0x45, 0x67,
                    (byte)0x89, (byte)0xab, (byte)0xcd, (byte)0xef };
        byte[]          msgNumber = new byte[] {
                    0x00, 0x00, 0x00, 0x00, 0x00, 0x00, 0x00, 0x00 };

        IvParameterSpec zeroIv = new IvParameterSpec(new byte[8]);

        SecretKeySpec   key = new SecretKeySpec(keyBytes, "DES");

        Cipher          cipher = Cipher.getInstance("DES/CBC/PKCS7Padding", "BC");

        System.out.println("input : " + Utils.toHex(input));

        // encryption pass
```

```
        // generate IV

        cipher.init(Cipher.ENCRYPT_MODE, key, zeroIv);

        IvParameterSpec encryptionIv = new IvParameterSpec(
                                        cipher.doFinal(msgNumber), 0, 8);

        // encrypt message

        cipher.init(Cipher.ENCRYPT_MODE, key, encryptionIv);

        byte[] cipherText = new byte[cipher.getOutputSize(input.length)];

        int ctLength = cipher.update(input, 0, input.length, cipherText, 0);

        ctLength += cipher.doFinal(cipherText, ctLength);

        System.out.println("cipher: " + Utils.toHex(cipherText, ctLength)
                                        + " bytes: " + ctLength);

        // decryption pass

        // generate IV

        cipher.init(Cipher.ENCRYPT_MODE, key, zeroIv);

        IvParameterSpec decryptionIv = new IvParameterSpec(
                                        cipher.doFinal(msgNumber), 0, 8);

        // decrypt message

        cipher.init(Cipher.DECRYPT_MODE, key, decryptionIv);

        byte[] plainText = new byte[cipher.getOutputSize(ctLength)];

        int ptLength = cipher.update(cipherText, 0, ctLength, plainText, 0);

        ptLength += cipher.doFinal(plainText, ptLength);

        System.out.println("plain : " + Utils.toHex(plainText, ptLength)
                                        + " bytes: " + ptLength);
    }
}
```

Run this example and you will now see the following output:

```
input : 000102030405060708090a0b0c0d0e0f0001020304050607
cipher: eb913126049ccdea00f2d86fda94a02fd72e0914fd361400d909f45f73058fc3 bytes: 32
plain : 000102030405060708090a0b0c0d0e0f0001020304050607 bytes: 24
```

As you can see, the ciphertext in the output has now changed substantially as a consequence of the change in IV.

How It Works

Looking at the code, there is only really one major change from the original CBC example: the creation of and handling of the IV. Note that in both cases when the IV is calculated from the message number, the `Cipher` object is initialized for encryption. The reason is that you are not so much encrypting the message number (stored in the array `msgNumber`) as using the cipher's encryption mode to calculate an IV from the message number.

This example also introduces one of the convenience methods on `Cipher`, a `Cipher.doFinal()`, which does the full processing on the input array and produces the resulting ciphertext, complete with padding. The presence of the padding is the reason why you specify that you only want the first 8 bytes of the ciphertext used in the creation of the `IvParameterSpec` object; otherwise, the IV will be two blocks, rather than the required one.

A Look at Cipher Parameter Objects

You have seen already how an IV can be passed into `Cipher.init()` using an `IvParameterSpec` object. You may have noticed that `Cipher.init()` can also take `AlgorithmParameters` objects. Likewise, just as there is a `Cipher.getIV()`, there is also a `Cipher.getParameters()` method.

> `Cipher.getIV()` **and** `Cipher.getParameters()` **should only be called after** `Cipher.init()` **has been called on the cipher of interest.**

At this point it would be worth looking briefly at what the difference is between parameter objects that end in the word `Spec` and those that do not. As a rule, in the JCE, objects ending in the word `Spec` are just value objects. Although these are useful in their own right, there are also situations where you need to be able to retrieve the parameters of a `Cipher`, or some other processing class, not as a value object but as an object that will produce an encoded version suitable for transmission to someone else, or for preservation in a platform-independent manner.

The AlgorithmParameters Class

The `AlgorithmParameters` objects serve this purpose and contain not just the values for the parameters but also expose methods such as `AlgorithmParameters.getEncoded()`, which allow the parameters to be exported in a platform-independent manner. The most common encoding method that `AlgorithmParameters` objects use is one of the binary encodings associated with ASN.1, which is discussed in Chapter 5. The `AlgorithmParameters` class also has a method on it, `AlgorithmParameters.getParameterSpec()`, which enables you to recover the value object associated with the parameters contained in the `AlgorithmParameters` object.

Consequently, calling `Cipher.getParameters()` will, amongst other things, return the IV, but in an object that can be used to generate an encoded IV, suitable for export.

CTS Mode: A Special Case of CBC

You could make use of CTS, or Cipher Text Stealing, mode in the previous example by replacing the `Cipher.getInstance()` call with

```
Cipher              cipher = Cipher.getInstance("DES/CTS/NoPadding", "BC");
```

CTS is defined in RFC 2040 and combines the use of CBC mode with some additional XOR operations on the final encrypted block of the data being processed to produce encrypted data that is the same length as the input data. In some ways, it is almost a padding mechanism more than a mode, and as it is based around CBC mode, it still requires the data to be processed in discrete blocks. If you want to be able to escape from having to process the data in blocks altogether, you need to use one of the streaming block modes, which are covered next.

Streaming Symmetric Block Cipher Modes

Both ECB and CBC mode use the underlying cipher in its most basic way, as an engine that takes in a block of data and outputs a block of data. Of course, the result of doing this was that in situations where you did not have data that was a multiple of the block size in length, you needed to use padding. Although this is an improvement on the situation, it would be useful to be able to use a regular block cipher in a manner that allows you to produce encrypted messages that are the same length as the initial unencrypted messages without having to resort to the kind of shenanigans that take place in CTS. Streaming block cipher modes allow you to use a block cipher in this way.

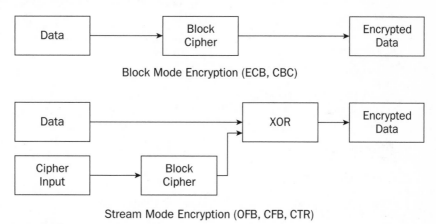

Block Mode Encryption (ECB, CBC)

Stream Mode Encryption (OFB, CFB, CTR)

Figure 2-2

Look at Figure 2-2 and you will see how the streaming is possible. Unlike ECB and CBC modes, the three following modes work by producing a stream of bits that is then XORed with the plaintext. One major thing you need to be careful of: Reusing an IV and a key together is fatal to the security of the encryption. As mentioned previously, you should not do this with CBC mode either, but your exposure, if you do so, will normally be limited. In the case of the stream modes, your exposure from reusing the initialization vector will be total. The reasons for this vary slightly depending on which mode you are using, but the principle remains the same.

CTR Mode

Also known as SIC (*Segmented Integer Counter*) mode. CTR, or *Counter* mode, has been around for quite a while but has finally been standardized by NIST in SP 800-38a and in RFC 3686.

Try It Out   CTR Mode

Consider the following example:

```java
package chapter2;

import javax.crypto.Cipher;
import javax.crypto.spec.IvParameterSpec;
import javax.crypto.spec.SecretKeySpec;

/**
 * Basic symmetric encryption example with CTR using DES
 */
public class SimpleCTRExample
{
    public static void main(String[] args) throws Exception
    {
        byte[]          input = new byte[] {
                            0x00, 0x01, 0x02, 0x03, 0x04, 0x05, 0x06, 0x07,
                            0x08, 0x09, 0x0a, 0x0b, 0x0c, 0x0d, 0x0e, 0x0f,
                            0x00, 0x01, 0x02, 0x03, 0x04, 0x05, 0x06 };
        byte[]          keyBytes = new byte[] {
                            0x01, 0x23, 0x45, 0x67,
                            (byte)0x89, (byte)0xab, (byte)0xcd, (byte)0xef };
        byte[]          ivBytes = new byte[] {
                            0x00, 0x01, 0x02, 0x03, 0x00, 0x00, 0x00, 0x01 };

        SecretKeySpec   key = new SecretKeySpec(keyBytes, "DES");
        IvParameterSpec ivSpec = new IvParameterSpec(ivBytes);
        Cipher          cipher = Cipher.getInstance("DES/CTR/NoPadding", "BC");

        System.out.println("input : " + Utils.toHex(input));

        // encryption pass

        cipher.init(Cipher.ENCRYPT_MODE, key, ivSpec);

        byte[] cipherText = new byte[cipher.getOutputSize(input.length)];

        int ctLength = cipher.update(input, 0, input.length, cipherText, 0);

        ctLength += cipher.doFinal(cipherText, ctLength);

        System.out.println("cipher: " + Utils.toHex(cipherText, ctLength)
                                        + " bytes: " + ctLength);

        // decryption pass

        cipher.init(Cipher.DECRYPT_MODE, key, ivSpec);

        byte[] plainText = new byte[cipher.getOutputSize(ctLength)];

        int ptLength = cipher.update(cipherText, 0, ctLength, plainText, 0);
```

```
        ptLength += cipher.doFinal(plainText, ptLength);

        System.out.println("plain : " + Utils.toHex(plainText, ptLength)
                                        + " bytes: " + ptLength);
    }
}
```

Running the example, you should see the following output:

```
input : 000102030405060708090a0b0c0d0e0f00010203040506
cipher: 61a1f886ff9bc709dd37cd9ce33adc6ff9ab110e46f387 bytes: 23
plain : 000102030405060708090a0b0c0d0e0f00010203040506 bytes: 23
```

As you can see, the `Cipher` object has produced ciphertext that is the same length as the input data.

How It Works

From a coding point of view, because of the benefit of the factory pattern, the only major change from the CBC example is that you have called `Cipher.getInstance()` with `CTR` rather than `CBC` specified in the mode position, and as you are using a streaming mode, `NoPadding` rather than `PKCS7Padding` giving a specification string of `"DES/CTR/NoPadding"`. You do not need to specify any padding because the mode allows you to work with any length of data.

Note also that the IV ends in 3 zero bytes and a one byte. In this case, it is a way of telling yourself that you should limit your processing to data that is no more than 2^{35} bytes (2^{32} times the block size). After that, the counter will go back to zero and begin cycling at the next block. You can see that encrypting two messages with the same IV and the same key will result in encrypting both messages with the same stream of bits. How many messages you can encrypt with a single key depends on how you treat the first four bytes of the IV. In a situation like this, you might divide the four bytes in half and use the first two for the message number and the second two for random data. This would allow you to process 2^{16} messages before recycling keys.

If you follow these rules, CTR mode works very well. There are three nice things about CTR mode: It is a stream mode, so is very easy to work with as you do not have to worry about padding; it allows for random access to the encrypted data, as you just need to know the counter value for a particular block; and finally, the areas where you can get into trouble using CTR mode are obvious from the design for construction of the IV. Given a particular method of constructing an IV, it is easy to see how large a message you can encrypt and how many messages you can process before you have to change keys. You can be certain of this, as you know that the cipher will be producing a different block for each increment of the counter until the counter begins to cycle. You will not have any surprises—in cryptography, this is a good thing.

OFB Mode

You can make use of OFB, or *Output Feedback*, mode in the previous example by replacing the `Cipher.getInstance()` to create the CTR cipher with the following:

```
Cipher          cipher = Cipher.getInstance("DES/OFB/NoPadding", "BC");
```

Like CTR mode, OFB mode works by using the raw block cipher to produce a stream of pseudorandom bits, which are then XORed with the input message to produce the encrypted message. The actual input message is never used. With OFB mode, rather than considering part of the IV to be a counter, you just load the IV into a state array, encrypt the state array, and save the result back to the state array, using the bits you generated to XOR with the next block of input and generate the ciphertext.

You might also see the following:

```
Cipher          cipher = Cipher.getInstance("DES/OFB8/NoPadding", "BC");
```

If this is the case, the OFB mode is set so that the cipher behaves like it has a block size of 8 bits. Virtual block sizes of 16, 24, 32, and so on are also possible. Do not do this unless you do so for reasons of compatibility. Security analysis of OFB mode has shown that it should be used only with an apparent block size that is the same as the block size of the underlying cipher.

The next biggest problem with OFB mode is that if the repetition of encrypting the state initialized by the IV leads to another state value that has occurred before, the value of the state will simply become a repetition of what occurred previously. You have to process a lot of data, and be unlucky, for this to be a problem. As a general rule in cryptography, it is better to avoid anything that involves the word *luck* where possible. Current wisdom is to use CTR instead of OFB, as it gives you more control over the key stream.

CFB Mode

CFB, or *Cipher Feedback*, is one you will encounter a lot. Its most widespread application is probably in the OpenPGP message format, described in RFC 2440, where it used as the mode of choice.

You can make use of CFB mode in the previous example by replacing the `Cipher.getInstance()` to create the CTR cipher with the following:

```
Cipher          cipher = Cipher.getInstance("DES/CFB/NoPadding", "BC");
```

Like OFB mode and CTR mode, CFB mode produces a stream of pseudorandom bits that are then used to encrypt the input. Unlike the others, CFB mode uses the plaintext as part of the process of generating the stream of bits. In this case, CFB starts with the IV, encrypts it using the raw cipher and saves it in a state array. As you encrypt a block of data, you XOR it with the state array to get the ciphertext and store the resulting ciphertext back in our state array.

Like OFB you can also use CFB mode in the following manner:

```
Cipher          cipher = Cipher.getInstance("DES/CFB8/NoPadding", "BC");
```

This actually changes the way the plaintext gets fed into the state array. Using the 8-bit mode described previously, after each encryption step, the bytes in the state array will be shifted left 8 bits, and the byte of ciphertext that was produced will be added to the end (something very similar happens in OFB mode as well, but since you should avoid using OFB mode unless you have to, you probably do not need to worry about it). Obviously one downside here is that the smaller the block size dictated by the mode, the more encryption operations there are. In the case of AES where you have a 16-byte block, using CFB in a 16-bit mode will mean you will have eight times as many encryption operations. The downside of using CFB in full block mode is you then risk running into the same problem as OFB with the bit stream starting to repeat. CFB mode does have some interesting properties in respect to dealing with synchronization errors, so for some applications it is probably a contender. It depends on what you are trying to do.

Symmetric Stream Ciphers

For the purposes here, stream ciphers are basically just ciphers that, by design, behave like block ciphers using the streaming modes. Once again, the idea is for the cipher to create a stream of bits that are then XORed with the plaintext to produce the ciphertext. From the point of view of using stream ciphers in the JCE, you will not notice much difference, other than in the creation of the `Cipher` objects. Stream ciphers do not have modes or require padding — they will always produce output the same length as the input. The result is that only the name of the algorithm is required.

Try It Out　　**Using the ARC4 Stream Cipher**

Here is a simple example using a 128-bit key, for what is probably the most widely used stream cipher on the net — ARC4, apparently based on RSA Security's RC4 cipher. Note that `Cipher.getInstance()` is just passed the name of the algorithm.

```
package chapter2;

import javax.crypto.Cipher;
import javax.crypto.spec.SecretKeySpec;


/**
 * Basic stream cipher example
 */
public class SimpleStreamExample
{
    public static void main(
        String[]    args)
        throws Exception
    {
        byte[]      input = new byte[] {
                    0x00, 0x11, 0x22, 0x33, 0x44, 0x55, 0x66, 0x77,
                    (byte)0x88, (byte)0x99, (byte)0xaa, (byte)0xbb,
                    (byte)0xcc, (byte)0xdd, (byte)0xee, (byte)0xff };
        byte[]      keyBytes = new byte[] {
                    0x00, 0x01, 0x02, 0x03, 0x04, 0x05, 0x06, 0x07,
                    0x08, 0x09, 0x0a, 0x0b, 0x0c, 0x0d, 0x0e, 0x0f };

        SecretKeySpec key = new SecretKeySpec(keyBytes, "ARC4");

        Cipher      cipher = Cipher.getInstance("ARC4", "BC");


        System.out.println("input text : " + Utils.toHex(input));

        // encryption pass

        byte[] cipherText = new byte[input.length];

        cipher.init(Cipher.ENCRYPT_MODE, key);

        int ctLength = cipher.update(input, 0, input.length, cipherText, 0);
```

```
        ctLength += cipher.doFinal(cipherText, ctLength);

        System.out.println("cipher text: " + Utils.toHex(cipherText)
                                        + " bytes: " + ctLength);

        // decryption pass

        byte[] plainText = new byte[ctLength];

        cipher.init(Cipher.DECRYPT_MODE, key);

        int ptLength = cipher.update(cipherText, 0, ctLength, plainText, 0);

        ptLength += cipher.doFinal(plainText, ptLength);

        System.out.println("plain text : " + Utils.toHex(plainText)
                                        + " bytes: " + ptLength);
    }
}
```

Running this example should produce the following output:

```
input text  : 00112233445566778899aabbccddeeff
cipher text: e98d62ca03b77fbb8e423d7dc200c4b0 bytes: 16
plain text  : 00112233445566778899aabbccddeeff bytes: 16
```

As you can see, the ciphertext is the same length as the input text.

How It Works

This example is pretty well the same as any other symmetric cipher example. The only real difference is that you have not specified a mode or a padding, as, in this case, none is required.

One further note on stream ciphers and the JCE: Block size is not really relevant; consequently, the JCE allows a stream cipher to present itself in a manner that allows `Cipher.getBlockSize()` to return 0. If you are trying to write a general-purpose application that will work with any symmetric cipher in the JCE, make sure you do not assume that the return value of `Cipher.getBlockSize()` will always be nonzero.

Generating Random Keys

Up until now, you have been relying on the `SecretKeySpec` class as the object used to create keys for passing into `Cipher.init()`. Looking at the generation of random initialization vectors, you could imagine that one way for generating keys would simply be to generate an array of random bytes and then pass that to a `SecretKeySpec`. Another way, which is preferred, is to use `javax.crypto.KeyGenerator` class.

Try It Out	Random Symmetric Key Generation

Look at the following example, which is built around AES in CTR mode, rather than DES as you saw in the previous Try It Out ("CTR Mode"), and try running it a few times.

```
package chapter2;

import java.security.Key;

import javax.crypto.Cipher;
import javax.crypto.KeyGenerator;
import javax.crypto.spec.IvParameterSpec;
import javax.crypto.spec.SecretKeySpec;

/**
 * Basic example using the KeyGenerator class and
 * showing how to create a SecretKeySpec from an encoded key.
 */
public class KeyGeneratorExample
{
    public static void main(String[] args) throws Exception
    {
        byte[]          input = new byte[] {
                            0x00, 0x01, 0x02, 0x03, 0x04, 0x05, 0x06, 0x07,
                            0x08, 0x09, 0x0a, 0x0b, 0x0c, 0x0d, 0x0e, 0x0f,
                            0x00, 0x01, 0x02, 0x03, 0x04, 0x05, 0x06, 0x07 };
        byte[]          ivBytes = new byte[] {
                            0x00, 0x00, 0x00, 0x01, 0x04, 0x05, 0x06, 0x07,
                            0x00, 0x00, 0x00, 0x00, 0x00, 0x00, 0x00, 0x01 };

        Cipher          cipher = Cipher.getInstance("AES/CTR/NoPadding", "BC");
        KeyGenerator    generator = KeyGenerator.getInstance("AES", "BC");

        generator.init(192);

        Key encryptionKey = generator.generateKey();

        System.out.println("key   : " + Utils.toHex(encryptionKey.getEncoded()));

        System.out.println("input : " + Utils.toHex(input));

        // encryption pass

        cipher.init(Cipher.ENCRYPT_MODE, encryptionKey,
                                    new IvParameterSpec(ivBytes));

        byte[] cipherText = new byte[cipher.getOutputSize(input.length)];

        int ctLength = cipher.update(input, 0, input.length, cipherText, 0);

        ctLength += cipher.doFinal(cipherText, ctLength);

        // create our decryption key using information
        // extracted from the encryption key

        Key     decryptionKey = new SecretKeySpec(
                    encryptionKey.getEncoded(), encryptionKey.getAlgorithm());

        cipher.init(Cipher.DECRYPT_MODE, decryptionKey,
                                    new IvParameterSpec(ivBytes));

        byte[] plainText = new byte[cipher.getOutputSize(ctLength)];
```

```
                int ptLength = cipher.update(cipherText, 0, ctLength, plainText, 0);

                ptLength += cipher.doFinal(plainText, ptLength);

                System.out.println("plain : " + Utils.toHex(plainText, ptLength)
                                                        + " bytes: " + ptLength);
        }
    }
```

You should find that while the key keeps changing, the input and the decrypted plaintext stay the same, indicating that the generated key has been successfully converted to a SecretKeySpec.

How It Works

Looking at the example, there are a few things you will notice. The IV is now 16 bytes as opposed to 8 bytes, reflecting the larger block size AES has over DES. Next, you have created a javax.crypto .KeyGenerator class, initialized it, and used it to create a java.security.Key object. The Key object is then used to initialize the Cipher object and encrypt the data, producing the ciphertext. Finally, you can see that before decryption, a SecretKeySpec is created by using Key.getEncoded() and Key .getAlgorithmName(), and you then initialize the Cipher object with the SecretKeySpec as you would normally do and decrypt the ciphertext.

The Key Interface

The javax.security.Key interface is the base interface implemented by all objects that can be used as cryptographic keys, including SecretKeySpec. It has three methods, all of which you will look at here, although you have only needed two of them so far.

Key.getAlgorithm()

This returns the name of the algorithm that the key is for. In the case of the example, this would simply be the string "AES", which is exactly what is required for the second parameter of SecretKeySpec.

Key.getEncoded()

In the case of a symmetric key, this just returns the bytes making up the key material. As you will see in Chapter 4, it gets a little more complicated with asymmetric keys. In the case of the previous example, though, you can see that the result of Key.getEncoded() can be passed to SecretKeySpec in the same way a byte array can.

Key.getFormat()

This returns the format of the byte array returned by Key.getEncoded(). As you get further into the JCE, you'll see that this can return a variety of values, but for keys used for symmetric algorithms, the name of the format returned is normally the string "RAW", indicating that Key.getEncoded() returns the bytes making up the key material without any additional packaging.

The KeyGenerator Class

The javax.crypto.KeyGenerator class is used to generate keys for use with symmetric encryption algorithms.

KeyGenerator.getInstance()

`KeyGenerator`, like `Cipher`, uses a factory pattern for creating instance objects. Unlike the `Cipher` class, there is no mode or padding to specify, so no additional syntax to know. Just the name of the algorithm and the provider is sufficient, as in:

```
KeyGenerator    generator = KeyGenerator.getInstance("AES", "BC");
```

As with any other `getInstance()` method, you can leave the provider name off and the Java runtime will return the first `KeyGenerator` for the passed-in algorithm name that it finds. Remember, you may inadvertently mix incompatible providers if you do this.

KeyGenerator.init()

At a minimum, `KeyGenerator` objects should be given at least the key size to be generated; otherwise, it is largely up to the internals of the generator what size key you get back. You can also pass the `init()` method of a `KeyGenerator` a source of randomness in the shape of a `java.security.SecureRandom` object you have created and seeded yourself. If you do not pass in a source of randomness, the `KeyGenerator` will generate one internally.

There is also an `init()` method that takes an `AlgorithmParameterSpec` object. Whether you wind up using that depends on what algorithm you are using. To date I have found, in the case of symmetric key generation, using `init()` with a key size and a source of randomness has been enough.

KeyGenerator.generateKey()

Returns a key generated according the parameters passed in by `KeyGenerator.init()`. If you look at the JavaDoc for this method you will see that it really returns a `javax.crypto.SecretKey` object. `SecretKey` is an empty interface that extends `Key` to provide type safety for symmetric key objects.

Password-Based Encryption

So far, you have looked at specifying keys by hand and generating them by using random numbers. Another method for generating keys is to take some human-friendly data like a password, process it using some function, or set of functions, and produce something suitable for use with a symmetric cipher. Encryption carried out in this fashion is known as *password-based encryption,* or PBE.

The most widespread PBE mechanisms are published in PKCS #5 and PKCS #12. There is also a PBE scheme that can be used with S/MIME, which is published in RFC 3211. In the latter case, the key generated from the password is used to generate another key.

This brings up an important point. Outside of dealing with the implementation issues, any PBE scheme must make sure that when people choose passwords, they make sense, from a security point of view, with what is being protected. Passwords are very convenient for people to use. Having said that, left to our own devices, we do have a tendency to take advantage of as much of the convenience as we can. If you are using AES and generating 256-bit keys using a PBE scheme, while at the same time allowing your users to use the password "a," you would not be entirely honest if you claim you are taking full advantage of 256-bit AES.

> PBE key generation mechanisms do employ methods to prevent trivial attacks, but a determined user can easily thwart them by choosing inappropriate passwords. If you use PBE, make sure you have a policy on passwords that's appropriate to the security your application requires and that the policy is enforced.

Basic PBE

PBE mechanisms are based on cryptographic hashing mechanisms. In essence, a password and a *salt*, which is just random data, is fed in some fashion into a mixing function based around a secure hash and the function is applied the number of times dictated by an *iteration count*. Once the mixing is complete, the resulting byte stream coming out of the PBE mechanism is used to create the key for the cipher to be used and possibly an initialization vector as well.

Most mixing functions are built on top of message digests, which I will cover in more detail in Chapter 3, but you can also find out more about the internals of them by looking at the documents for the standards referred to previously. If you look at Figure 2-3, you will realize that the salt and the iteration count must somehow be stored with the encrypted data so that the original data can be recovered later. Briefly the details about the roles the various inputs play are as follows.

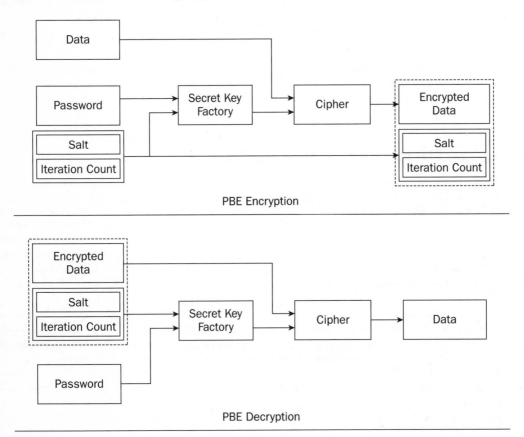

Figure 2-3

The Password

As you have already probably realized, this is the bit that must not only be kept secret, but be at least as hard to guess as the security of your application requires. How much bandwidth you get out of a password in Java depends on the PBE scheme you are using. Most, like PKCS #5, only consider characters in the ASCII range — that is, you will only get the bottom 8 bits of each Java character being mixed into the function. If you are using PKCS #12-based mechanisms, you will be able to utilize the full 16 bits of each Java character.

The Salt

As you can see from Figure 2-3, the salt is a public value — as in you should assume an attacker can find it. The reason for the salt is that by adding a string of random bytes to the password, the same password can be used as a source for a large number of different keys. This is useful because it forces attackers to perform the key generation calculation every time they wish to try a password, for every piece of encrypted data they wish to attack.

If you can, make the salt at least as large as the block size of the function used to process the password. Usually the block size of the function is the same as that of the underlying message digest used by it.

The Iteration Count

As you can see from Figure 2-3, the iteration count is also a public value. The sole purpose of the iteration count is to increase the computation time required to convert a password to a key. For example, imagine someone is trying to launch an attack on data that has been encrypted using PBE by using a dictionary of common words, phrases, and names — more commonly referred to as a *dictionary attack*. If the PBE mechanism has been used with an iteration count of 1,000 rather than 1, it will require 1,000 times more processing to calculate a key from a password.

Make the iteration count as large as you can comfortably. Users usually will cope if an authentication process takes a second or two, and you will be making life a lot harder for someone trying a dictionary attack.

PBE in the JCE

So how does this work in the JCE? There are actually two mechanisms for dealing with PBE in Java, one of which should work across any compliant provider and is based on the `PBEParameterSpec` class. The other mechanism, which is preferred, was introduced in JDK 1.4 and gives the provider more flexibility as to how the key gets generated. You will see the advantage of this a bit later, but which mechanism you choose to use will also depend on whether supporting earlier versions of the JCE is important to you. If you are using the JCE 1.2.2, or a clean room version of the same, the older method is the one you should use.

The following examples have been written for Triple-DES, also referred to as DESede. DESede, a contraction of DES-Encrypt-Decrypt-Encrypt, is derived from the fact that Triple-DES is a three-step single DES process involving first encrypting the input block using single DES with one key, then decrypting the input block using single DES with another key, then encrypting the block again with either the first key used (Two-Key Triple-DES) or a completely different key (Three-Key Triple-DES). At this writing, standards for PBE mechanisms for AES have not yet being established, so I recommend using either Two- or Three-Key Triple-DES.

The other point of interest is the naming convention used for PBE in the JCE. PBE mechanisms are named using the rule PBEwith<*function*>And<*cipher*> where *function* is the algorithm used to support the mechanism that generates the key and *cipher* is the underlying cipher used for the encryption. In the following example, the function used is based on SHA-1 — a message digest, or cryptographic hash. You will look at message digests in Chapter 3, but for now it is enough to know that SHA-1 provides a useful mechanism for mixing bits together in a manner that is not predictable but still deterministic.

Take a look at the original method for using PBE first.

Try It Out   **PBE Using PBEParameterSpec**

Consider the following example; it uses a regular cipher to encrypt the input data and then uses a PBE cipher to decrypt it. In this case, the password is used to create a `javax.crypto.spec.PBEKeySpec`, which is converted to key material by a `javax.crypto.SecretKeyFactory`. The salt and the iteration count are then passed in with the processed key using a `javax.crypto.spec.PBEParameterSpec`.

```
package chapter2;

import java.security.Key;

import javax.crypto.Cipher;
import javax.crypto.SecretKeyFactory;
import javax.crypto.spec.IvParameterSpec;
import javax.crypto.spec.PBEKeySpec;
import javax.crypto.spec.PBEParameterSpec;
import javax.crypto.spec.SecretKeySpec;

/**
 * Example of using PBE with a PBEParameterSpec
 */
public class PBEWithParamsExample
{
    public static void main(String[] args) throws Exception
    {
        byte[]          input = new byte[] {
                    0x00, 0x01, 0x02, 0x03, 0x04, 0x05, 0x06, 0x07,
                    0x08, 0x09, 0x0a, 0x0b, 0x0c, 0x0d, 0x0e, 0x0f,
                    0x00, 0x01, 0x02, 0x03, 0x04, 0x05, 0x06, 0x07 };
        byte[]          keyBytes = new byte[] {
                    0x73, 0x2f, 0x2d, 0x33, (byte)0xc8, 0x01, 0x73,
                    0x2b, 0x72, 0x06, 0x75, 0x6c, (byte)0xbd, 0x44,
                    (byte)0xf9, (byte)0xc1, (byte)0xc1, 0x03, (byte)0xdd,
                    (byte)0xd9, 0x7c, 0x7c, (byte)0xbe, (byte)0x8e };
        byte[]          ivBytes = new byte[] {
                    (byte)0xb0, 0x7b, (byte)0xf5, 0x22, (byte)0xc8,
                    (byte)0xd6, 0x08, (byte)0xb8 };

        // encrypt the data using precalculated keys

        Cipher cEnc = Cipher.getInstance("DESede/CBC/PKCS7Padding", "BC");

        cEnc.init(Cipher.ENCRYPT_MODE,
            new SecretKeySpec(keyBytes, "DESede"),
```

```
                        new IvParameterSpec(ivBytes));

            byte[] out = cEnc.doFinal(input);

            // decrypt the data using PBE

            char[]          password = "password".toCharArray();
            byte[]          salt = new byte[] {
                                0x7d, 0x60, 0x43, 0x5f,
                                0x02, (byte)0xe9, (byte)0xe0, (byte)0xae };
            int             iterationCount = 2048;
            PBEKeySpec      pbeSpec = new PBEKeySpec(password);
            SecretKeyFactory keyFact =
                    SecretKeyFactory.getInstance("PBEWithSHAAnd3KeyTripleDES", "BC");

            Cipher cDec = Cipher.getInstance("PBEWithSHAAnd3KeyTripleDES","BC");
            Key    sKey = keyFact.generateSecret(pbeSpec);

            cDec.init(Cipher.DECRYPT_MODE,
                                sKey, new PBEParameterSpec(salt, iterationCount));

            System.out.println("cipher : " + Utils.toHex(out));
            System.out.println("gen key: " + Utils.toHex(sKey.getEncoded()));
            System.out.println("gen iv : " + Utils.toHex(cDec.getIV()));
            System.out.println("plain  : " + Utils.toHex(cDec.doFinal(out)));
        }
    }
```

If you run this example, you will see the following output:

```
cipher : a7b955896f750665ba71eb50ac3071d9832a8b02760c600bf619a75a0697c87c
gen key: 00700061007300730077006f007200640000
gen iv : b07bf522c8d608b8
plain  : 000102030405060708090a0b0c0d0e0f0001020304050607
```

The line labeled gen iv gives you the real IV used, and as you would expect, it is the same as the one used in the DESede encryption step. However, if you look at the generated key, labeled gen key, it is the password broken down into bytes at 2 bytes per character with 2 zero bytes added to the end. As mentioned earlier, this is the method used by PKCS #12 to convert a password into bytes so that it can be fed into the key generation function.

How It Works

When the preprocessed key is passed to the Cipher.init() method, the extra information in the PBEParameterSpec object is used and the password is mixed into a password generation function and used to create the actual key used for encryption. As you will see in the next section, the actual key generated bears no apparent resemblance to the password that was used to create it.

This need for the PBEParameterSpec can be unfortunate because it means, in the event you need to pass it on to an outside application, you have no way of working out what the actual key used by the PBE is. The newer method of using PBEKeySpec addresses this drawback, but first it would be worth having a look at the classes introduced by the example in more detail.

The PBEParameterSpec Class

The `javax.crypto.spec.PBEParameterSpec` class is available as a carrier for the salt and the iteration count so that they can be passed to the `Cipher.init()` method. As indicated next, you will see it used in any code that was written for versions of the JCE prior to JDK 1.4, or more recent versions where the provider has not yet caught up with the changes in the `PBEKeySpec`.

The PBEKeySpec Class

Originally `javax.crypto.spec.PBEKeySpec` was just a holder for the password. Since JDK 1.4, it is also able to carry the salt and the iteration count if required for the key generation mechanism. Depending on what provider you are using, the newer version of `PBEKeySpec` obsoletes the `PBEParameterSpec` class.

The SecretKeyFactory Class

Having created a `PBEKeySpec` that contains the password, and possibly the other key generation parameters as well, you need some way of getting the provider you are using to convert the specification into a `Key` object suitable for use with one of the provider's ciphers. The `javax.crypto.SecretKeyFactory` class is provided for this purpose.

Like the other JCE classes, the `SecretKeyFactory` is created using a factory pattern based on the `getInstance()` method, which behaves in exactly the same way as other JCA/JCE `getInstance()` methods. It is a fairly straightforward class with methods on it to make it possible to translate secret keys from one provider to another, generate key specifications from `SecretKey` objects, and take key specifications and convert them into keys. You will look at the first two capabilities later, but in the case of PBE, it is this last capability you are interested in. As you will see in the examples, the `SecretKeyFactory` allows you to reduce the conversion of the `PBEKeySpec` into a `SecretKey` object suitable for passing to `Cipher.init()` to a single method call — `SecretKeyFactory.generateSecret()`.

Try It Out   PBE Based Solely on PBEKeySpec

Having seen the original method for handling PBE, you now look at a more up-to-date one. As you can see here, the changes required in the example are both very minor, but there is a major difference in what is returned from the `SecretKeyFactory.generateSecret()` method. Look at the following:

```
package chapter2;

import java.security.Key;

import javax.crypto.Cipher;
import javax.crypto.SecretKeyFactory;
import javax.crypto.spec.IvParameterSpec;
import javax.crypto.spec.PBEKeySpec;
import javax.crypto.spec.SecretKeySpec;

/**
 * Example of using PBE without using a PBEParameterSpec
 */
public class PBEWithoutParamsExample
{
    public static void main(String[] args) throws Exception
    {
```

```
byte[]              input = new byte[] {
                        0x00, 0x01, 0x02, 0x03, 0x04, 0x05, 0x06, 0x07,
                        0x08, 0x09, 0x0a, 0x0b, 0x0c, 0x0d, 0x0e, 0x0f,
                        0x00, 0x01, 0x02, 0x03, 0x04, 0x05, 0x06, 0x07 };
byte[]              keyBytes = new byte[] {
                        0x73, 0x2f, 0x2d, 0x33, (byte)0xc8, 0x01, 0x73,
                        0x2b, 0x72, 0x06, 0x75, 0x6c, (byte)0xbd, 0x44,
                        (byte)0xf9, (byte)0xc1, (byte)0xc1, 0x03, (byte)0xdd,
                        (byte)0xd9, 0x7c, 0x7c, (byte)0xbe, (byte)0x8e };
byte[]              ivBytes = new byte[] {
                        (byte)0xb0, 0x7b, (byte)0xf5, 0x22, (byte)0xc8,
                        (byte)0xd6, 0x08, (byte)0xb8 };

// encrypt the data using precalculated keys

Cipher cEnc = Cipher.getInstance("DESede/CBC/PKCS7Padding", "BC");

cEnc.init(Cipher.ENCRYPT_MODE,
    new SecretKeySpec(keyBytes, "DESede"),
    new IvParameterSpec(ivBytes));

byte[] out = cEnc.doFinal(input);

// decrypt the data using PBE

char[]              password = "password".toCharArray();
byte[]              salt = new byte[] {
                       0x7d, 0x60, 0x43, 0x5f,
                       0x02, (byte)0xe9, (byte)0xe0, (byte)0xae };
int                 iterationCount = 2048;
PBEKeySpec          pbeSpec = new PBEKeySpec(
                                   password, salt, iterationCount);
SecretKeyFactory    keyFact =
          SecretKeyFactory.getInstance("PBEWithSHAAnd3KeyTripleDES", "BC");

Cipher cDec = Cipher.getInstance("PBEWithSHAAnd3KeyTripleDES", "BC");
Key     sKey = keyFact.generateSecret(pbeSpec);

cDec.init(Cipher.DECRYPT_MODE, sKey);

System.out.println("cipher : " + Utils.toHex(out));
System.out.println("gen key: " + Utils.toHex(sKey.getEncoded()));
System.out.println("gen iv : " + Utils.toHex(cDec.getIV()));
System.out.println("plain  : " + Utils.toHex(cDec.doFinal(out)));
    }
  }
```

If you run the example, you should see the following output:

```
cipher : a7b955896f750665ba71eb50ac3071d9832a8b02760c600bf619a75a0697c87c
gen key: 732f2d33c801732b7206756cbd44f9c1c103ddd97c7cbe8e
gen iv : b07bf522c8d608b8
plain  : 000102030405060708090a0b0c0d0e0f0001020304050607
```

Note that this time gen key is now the actual DESede key.

How It Works

This is possible because the `SecretKeyFactory` now has all the information required to create a proper key, rather than being able to do only some basic preprocessing and leaving the final pass to the `Cipher` object to perform using the information in the `PBEParameterSpec`. Being able to do this is an option the Bouncy Castle provider takes full advantage of, as this can be useful when you are carrying out encryption using a variety of applications. While all of the applications may support encryption—say, in the form of Three-Key Triple-DES—they may not all support PBE. In such a situation you may need to know what key was actually produced by the PBE key generation process as well as what IV was used at the start of the encryption process. As you can see here, with the newer method it becomes possible to get both the real encoded key and, after calling `Cipher.init()`, the required IV as well—an enormous improvement.

Key Wrapping

As you have probably already noticed from the JavaDoc for the `Cipher` class, in addition to `Cipher.ENCRYPT_MODE` and `Cipher.DECRYPT_MODE`, the `Cipher` class also has two other modes, `Cipher.WRAP_MODE` and `Cipher.UNWRAP_MODE`.

The wrap modes are provided for the purpose of allowing providers to provide facilities for "key wrapping," or the encryption of the encoded form of the keys. There are two reasons for doing this. The first is simple convenience—you do not have to extract the key's data; to wrap it, you just call `Cipher.wrap()` and the key is extracted for you and returned as an encrypted byte array. The second reason is that some providers will store the actual key material on hardware devices where it is safe from prying eyes; the wrapping mechanism provides a means of getting the key material out of the device without exposing the raw material unencrypted. The alternative would be to force the provider to return the key material using `Key.getEncoded()`, not really acceptable if you have gone to the expense of investing in hardware adapters to protect your keys.

The `Cipher.unwrap()` method is provided to reconstruct the key from the encrypted key material. It is slightly more complicated than the `Cipher.wrap()` method in that it expects the algorithm name and the type of the key. The key types make up the other constants provided in the `Cipher` class. They are: `Cipher.PUBLIC_KEY`, `Cipher.PRIVATE_KEY`, and `Cipher.SECRET_KEY`. The algorithm name should be a string that is meaningful to the provider you are creating the key for.

Try It Out   Symmetric Key Wrapping

You will see an example of the use of `Cipher.PUBLIC_KEY` and `Cipher.PRIVATE_KEY` in Chapter 4. In the meanwhile, the following example shows basic key wrapping as applied to symmetric keys:

```
package chapter2;

import java.security.Key;

import javax.crypto.Cipher;
import javax.crypto.KeyGenerator;

public class SimpleWrapExample
{
```

```
      public static void main(String[] args) throws Exception
   {
      // create a key to wrap
      KeyGenerator generator = KeyGenerator.getInstance("AES", "BC");
      generator.init(128);

      Key    keyToBeWrapped = generator.generateKey();

      System.out.println("input    : " +
                                  Utils.toHex(keyToBeWrapped.getEncoded()));

      // create a wrapper and do the wrapping

      Cipher cipher = Cipher.getInstance("AESWrap", "BC");

      KeyGenerator keyGen = KeyGenerator.getInstance("AES", "BC");
      keyGen.init(256);

      Key wrapKey = keyGen.generateKey();

      cipher.init(Cipher.WRAP_MODE, wrapKey);

      byte[] wrappedKey = cipher.wrap(keyToBeWrapped);

      System.out.println("wrapped  : " + Utils.toHex(wrappedKey));

      // unwrap the wrapped key

      cipher.init(Cipher.UNWRAP_MODE, wrapKey);

      Key key = cipher.unwrap(wrappedKey, "AES", Cipher.SECRET_KEY);

      System.out.println("unwrapped: " + Utils.toHex(key.getEncoded()));
   }
}
```

Run this and you should see that after the key to be wrapped is printed, an encrypted wrapped key will be printed that is longer than the original key, and then, on the last line, you will see that after unwrapping the original key has been recovered.

How It Works

The easiest way to see how this process works is to consider how you would do it using encryption and decryption. For example, you could replace

```
      Cipher cipher = Cipher.getInstance("AESWrap", "BC");
```

with

```
      Cipher cipher = Cipher.getInstance("AES/ECB/NoPadding", "BC");
```

You could then replace the call to `cipher.init()` and the `cipher.wrap()` methods with

```
cipher.init(Cipher.ENCRYPT_MODE, wrapKey);

byte[] wrappedKey = cipher.doFinal(keyToBeWrapped.getEncoded());
```

and rather than use `cipher.unwrap()` to the recover the key, replace it and the second `cipher.init()` with

```
cipher.init(Cipher.DECRYPT_MODE, wrapKey);

Key key = new SecretKeySpec(cipher.doFinal(wrappedKey), "AES");
```

and you would achieve almost the same effect.

In essence, the wrapping mechanism calls `Key.getEncoded()` on the symmetric key under the covers and encrypts what `getEncoded()` returns. When the key is unwrapped, the key is reassembled using the extra information passed into the `unwrap()` method and the encrypted bytes. The `SecretKeySpec` class provides you with a general way of assembling a symmetric key, although the provider may use some other mechanism internally if it suits it.

Using the `NoPadding` works, in this case, as the key being wrapped is a multiple of the block size. You will notice if you compare the output from `SimpleWrapExample` with the output from the version modified to use `"AES/ECB/NoPadding"` that the wrapped key in `SimpleWrapExample` appears to have some padding added to it—the wrapped text is longer than the input text. The reason is that the purpose-built key-wrapping mechanism includes an integrity check that is used to ensure that the key probably decrypted properly. A symmetric key is just a string of random bytes and one string of random bytes looks very much like another; so, in general, if you have a purpose built wrapping mechanism available to you, it is better to use it than try to roll your own.

> **Use purpose-built key-wrapping mechanisms where you can for wrapping keys.**

The last thing to note in the example, modified or otherwise, is that the key doing the wrapping is a larger bit size than the key being wrapped. If it were the other way around, it would be easier to guess the wrapping key than guess the key being wrapped. Put another way, if you were to wrap a 256-bit AES key using a 40-bit ARC4 key, you only have 40 bits of security, not 256, protecting the data encrypted with the AES key.

> **Keys used for wrapping should always be at least as secure, if not more so, than the key being protected.**

Doing Cipher-Based I/O

The JCE contains two classes for doing I/O involving ciphers: `javax.crypto.CipherInputStream` and `javax.crypto.CipherOutputStream`. These classes are not only useful but very easy to use as well. You can use them anywhere you would use an `InputStream` or an `OutputStream`.

The stream classes are a case where the usual factory pattern seen elsewhere in the JCE is not used. Instances of both `CipherInputStream` and `CipherOutputStream` are created using constructors that take an `InputStream`, or `OutputStream`, to wrap, and a `Cipher` object to do the processing.

Try It Out   **Using Cipher-Based I/O**

Look at the following example, which uses `CipherInputStream` and `CipherOutputStream`.

```java
package chapter2;

import java.io.ByteArrayInputStream;
import java.io.ByteArrayOutputStream;

import javax.crypto.Cipher;
import javax.crypto.CipherInputStream;
import javax.crypto.CipherOutputStream;
import javax.crypto.spec.IvParameterSpec;
import javax.crypto.spec.SecretKeySpec;

/**
 * Basic IO example with CTR using AES
 */
public class SimpleIOExample
{
    public static void main(
        String[]    args)
        throws Exception
    {
        byte[]          input = new byte[] {
                            0x00, 0x01, 0x02, 0x03, 0x04, 0x05, 0x06, 0x07,
                            0x08, 0x09, 0x0a, 0x0b, 0x0c, 0x0d, 0x0e, 0x0f,
                            0x00, 0x01, 0x02, 0x03, 0x04, 0x05, 0x06 };
        byte[]          keyBytes = new byte[] {
                            0x00, 0x01, 0x02, 0x03, 0x04, 0x05, 0x06, 0x07,
                            0x08, 0x09, 0x0a, 0x0b, 0x0c, 0x0d, 0x0e, 0x0f,
                            0x10, 0x11, 0x12, 0x13, 0x14, 0x15, 0x16, 0x17 };
        byte[]          ivBytes = new byte[] {
                            0x00, 0x01, 0x02, 0x03, 0x00, 0x01, 0x02, 0x03,
                            0x00, 0x00, 0x00, 0x00, 0x00, 0x00, 0x00, 0x01 };

        SecretKeySpec   key = new SecretKeySpec(keyBytes, "AES");
        IvParameterSpec ivSpec = new IvParameterSpec(ivBytes);
        Cipher          cipher = Cipher.getInstance("AES/CTR/NoPadding", "BC");


        System.out.println("input : " + Utils.toHex(input));

        // encryption pass

        cipher.init(Cipher.ENCRYPT_MODE, key, ivSpec);

        ByteArrayInputStream    bIn = new ByteArrayInputStream(input);
        CipherInputStream       cIn = new CipherInputStream(bIn, cipher);
        ByteArrayOutputStream   bOut = new ByteArrayOutputStream();
```

```
int     ch;
while ((ch = cIn.read()) >= 0)
{
    bOut.write(ch);
}

byte[] cipherText = bOut.toByteArray();

System.out.println("cipher: " + Utils.toHex(cipherText));

// decryption pass

cipher.init(Cipher.DECRYPT_MODE, key, ivSpec);

bOut = new ByteArrayOutputStream();

CipherOutputStream      cOut = new CipherOutputStream(bOut, cipher);

cOut.write(cipherText);

cOut.close();

System.out.println("plain : " + Utils.toHex(bOut.toByteArray()));
    }
}
```

Running the example produces the following:

```
input : 000102030405060708090a0b0c0d0e0f00010203040506
cipher: bbfe17383cc002047c11be5dfc524e4ead5f2a887d197b
plain : 000102030405060708090a0b0c0d0e0f00010203040506
```

How It Works

The example demonstrates the flexibility of the stream model by reading from a stream of plaintext that is encrypted as it is read, and then writing a stream of ciphertext through a suitably configured output stream that will decrypt the ciphertext as it passes it through. CipherInputStream and CipherOutputStream simply wrap the streams passed to their constructors and then filter anything read, or written, to them through the Cipher object passed to their constructor as appropriate.

There is really only one important point to remember with cipher streams. If close on the stream is not called, Cipher.doFinal() will not be called on the underlying cipher either. For example if the line

```
cOut.close();
```

is removed from the example, the output would probably look more like the following:

```
input : 000102030405060708090a0b0c0d0e0f00010203040506
cipher: bbfe17383cc002047c11be5dfc524e4ead5f2a887d197b
plain : 000102030405060708090a0b0c0d0e0f
```

The reason for the missing data in the final output is that, because `Cipher.doFinal()` is not called, the `Cipher` object `cipher` never flushes the bytes it is holding on to as it tries to assemble a block.

> **Forgetting to call** `CipherOutputStream.close()` **or** `Cipher.doFinal()` **is a very common error. If you find your messages truncated with a block or so of data missing from the end, make sure** `close()` **or** `doFinal()` **have been called.**

Summary

You have looked at JCE support for symmetric key encryption and the mechanism by which `Cipher` objects are created so that they will function in particular modes and use specified padding mechanisms if required.

Over the course of the chapter you learned the following:

❑　Some modes such as CBC mode and CTR mode also require an initialization vector (IV) to be set.

❑　IVs can be generated by a `Cipher` object automatically or passed in using an `IvParameterSpec` or a suitable `AlgorithmParameters` object. Where the IV is generated automatically by the `Cipher` object, it can be recovered using `Cipher.getIV()` or `Cipher.getAlgorithmParameters()`.

❑　A symmetric key can be created from raw bytes, using the `SecretKeySpec` class, or generated randomly using the `KeyGenerator` class.

❑　Keys can also be created from passwords using password-based encryption (PBE).

❑　Key-wrapping mechanisms can be used for the safe transport of symmetric keys by encrypting them using other symmetric keys.

❑　How to integrate `Cipher` objects with Java I/O streams by using the `CipherInputStream` class and the `CipherOutputStream` class.

One problem that symmetric key encryption does not address is making sure that the ciphertext has not been tampered with. Providing encryption and decryption mechanisms only solve part of the problem. You will start looking at mechanisms for dealing with this in the next chapter.

Exercises

1.　A colleague has written a program for decrypting a padded byte stream that was created by encrypting with a block cipher. For some reason the program the colleague has written is appending one or more zero bytes to the data created by decrypting the stream. What is the most likely reason for the extra bytes? How would you fix the program?

2.　You have written a program that is decrypting a block cipher encrypted stream created using CBC mode. For the most part, the data appears to be encrypting correctly, but the first block of the decrypted data is always wrong. What is the most likely cause of this?

3. If you have a `Cipher` object initialized in encryption mode that uses an IV, what are the two ways you can retrieve the IV's value?

4. If you have a `Cipher` object that is using PBE, how would you retrieve the parameters passed to the key generation function, other than the password?

5. What is the most likely problem if data written through a `CipherOutputStream` appears to be truncated?

Message Digests, MACs, and HMACs

It is one thing to encrypt a message for transmission to another party; it is something different again to make sure it arrived unchanged.

This chapter looks at methods for authenticating messages and verifying that they have not been tampered with. You can do this by creating message digests and message authentication codes (MACs) using the `MessageDigest` class and the `Mac` class, respectively. You will also see that you can use message digests, also known as *cryptographic hashes*, as the basis for MAC creation by using Hash MACs (HMACs).

Finally, you will look at how digests can be used as the sources of pseudorandom data. You will also look at linking message digests with Java I/O streams and learn how to get a final value from the digest or take a snapshot of it.

By the end of this chapter you should

- ❏ Understand why message digests and MACs are used, as well as how to create them
- ❏ Understand what makes message digests and MACs different and where they can be applied
- ❏ Understand how digests are used as the basis of other functions for PBE and masking
- ❏ Be able to use the stream support available for message digests in Java

Finally, you should also have some understanding of the security issues associated with these two methods.

Getting Started

This chapter uses message digests and MACs in conjunction with encrypted messages. To simplify the examples, you need to take advantage of the following utility class, which has some helper methods in it that incorporate some of the facilities you read about in the last chapter. Type it in or download it from the book's Web site. Once you have it compiled, read on.

```java
package chapter3;

import java.security.NoSuchAlgorithmException;
import java.security.NoSuchProviderException;
import java.security.SecureRandom;

import javax.crypto.KeyGenerator;
import javax.crypto.SecretKey;
import javax.crypto.spec.IvParameterSpec;

/**
 * General utilities for the third chapter examples.
 */
public class Utils
    extends chapter2.Utils
{
    /**
     * Create a key for use with AES.
     *
     * @param bitLength
     * @param random
     * @return
     * @throws NoSuchAlgorithmException
     * @throws NoSuchProviderException
     */
    public static SecretKey createKeyForAES(int bitLength, SecureRandom random)
        throws NoSuchAlgorithmException, NoSuchProviderException
    {
        KeyGenerator generator = KeyGenerator.getInstance("AES", "BC");

        generator.init(256, random);

        return generator.generateKey();
    }

    /**
     * Create an IV suitable for using with AES in CTR mode.
     * <p>
     * The IV will be composed of 4 bytes of message number,
     * 4 bytes of random data, and a counter of 8 bytes.
     *
     * @param messageNumber the number of the message.
     * @param random a source of randomness
     * @return an initialised IvParameterSpec
     */
    public static IvParameterSpec createCtrIvForAES(int messageNumber,
                                                    SecureRandom random)
    {
        byte[]          ivBytes = new byte[16];

        // initially randomize
```

```
        random.nextBytes(ivBytes);

        // set the message number bytes

        ivBytes[0] = (byte)(messageNumber >> 24);
        ivBytes[1] = (byte)(messageNumber >> 16);
        ivBytes[2] = (byte)(messageNumber >> 8);
        ivBytes[3] = (byte)(messageNumber >> 0);

        // set the counter bytes to 1

        for (int i = 0; i != 7; i++)
        {
            ivBytes[8 + i] = 0;
        }

        ivBytes[15] = 1;

        return new IvParameterSpec(ivBytes);
    }

    /**
     * Convert a byte array of 8 bit characters into a String.
     *
     * @param bytes the array containing the characters
     * @param length the number of bytes to process
     * @return a String representation of bytes
     */
    public static String toString(byte[] bytes, int length)
    {
        char[]   chars = new char[length];

        for (int i = 0; i != chars.length; i++)
        {
            chars[i] = (char)(bytes[i] & 0xff);
        }

        return new String(chars);
    }

    /**
     * Convert a byte array of 8 bit characters into a String.
     *
     * @param bytes the array containing the characters
     * @param length the number of bytes to process
     * @return a String representation of bytes
     */
    public static String toString(byte[] bytes)
    {
        return toString(bytes, bytes.length);
    }
```

```
/**
 * Convert the passed in String to a byte array by
 * taking the bottom 8 bits of each character it contains.
 *
 * @param string the string to be converted
 * @return a byte array representation
 */
public static byte[] toByteArray(String string)
{
    byte[]  bytes = new byte[string.length()];
    char[]  chars = string.toCharArray();

    for (int i = 0; i != chars.length; i++)
    {
        bytes[i] = (byte)chars[i];
    }

    return bytes;
}
}
```

One point about the helper class that's worth discussing: There are two functions in the helper class that might seem unnecessary, the toByteArray() and toString() methods. It is true that the String object in Java has a method called getBytes() and a constructor that takes a byte array that seems to do the same thing. If you look at the JavaDoc for String, you should notice that it mentions that string-to-byte conversion and byte-to-string conversion is affected by the default charset your JVM is using. Most JVMs ship using a default charset that causes String.getBytes() and the String byte constructor to behave like the methods detailed in the utility class. Not all do, though, and while you could have specified the charset explicitly, say, using String.getBytes("UTF8"), not all JVMs support all the charset names either. So, at least for these purposes, the most robust way of dealing with string-to-byte array conversion and back is to do it the long way.

> **It is important to remember about the properties of charsets. Programmers often make the mistake of assuming that String.getBytes() will return 2 bytes a character and the String byte array constructors will create a String that has one character for each 2 bytes in the byte array. This is rarely, if ever, what happens, so attempting to pass encrypted messages around by simply creating String objects and converting back to byte arrays using String.getBytes() will normally result in corrupted data.**

The Problem of Tampering

So you are happily encrypting messages using a symmetric cipher, and chances are, anyone trying to interfere with your messages will have probably given up trying to guess the secret keys that have been used. At this point a potential attacker will start to explore the next avenue, which is tampering with the ciphertext and trying to fool the receiver.

Try It Out   **Tampering with an Encrypted Stream**

Look at the following example. Unlike previous examples, it is divided into three steps: the encryption step, a tampering step, and the decryption step. In the following case, it is assumed the attacker has some knowledge of the message format, and that you are using a streaming mode, which makes the XOR-based tampering easier to do.

```java
package chapter3;

import java.security.Key;
import java.security.SecureRandom;

import javax.crypto.Cipher;
import javax.crypto.spec.IvParameterSpec;

/**
 * Tampered message, plain encryption, AES in CTR mode
 */
public class TamperedExample
{
    public static void main(String[] args) throws Exception
    {
        SecureRandom     random = new SecureRandom();
        IvParameterSpec ivSpec = Utils.createCtrIvForAES(1, random);
        Key             key = Utils.createKeyForAES(256, random);
        Cipher          cipher = Cipher.getInstance("AES/CTR/NoPadding", "BC");
        String          input = "Transfer 0000100 to AC 1234-5678";

        System.out.println("input : " + input);

        // encryption step

        cipher.init(Cipher.ENCRYPT_MODE, key, ivSpec);

        byte[] cipherText = cipher.doFinal(Utils.toByteArray(input));

        // tampering step

        cipherText[9] ^= '0' ^ '9';

        // decryption step

        cipher.init(Cipher.DECRYPT_MODE, key, ivSpec);

        byte[] plainText = cipher.doFinal(cipherText);

        System.out.println("plain : " + Utils.toString(plainText));
    }
}
```

When you run the example, you should see the following output:

```
input : Transfer 0000100 to AC 1234-5678
plain : Transfer 9000100 to AC 1234-5678
```

How It Works

The cipher mode you are using is based not only on the use of the cipher but on encrypting the data by XORing the data with the output of the cipher. This allows you to reset some bits in the ciphertext knowing that the same bits will be changed in the plaintext when the ciphertext is decrypted.

Admittedly, the example is somewhat contrived, but it is designed to make the following point loudly: Given that an attacker has some knowledge of the structure of the message it is possible for the hacker to get up to all sorts of mischief. In this case, assuming the request represents an instruction for payment to the attacker's account, you can see that the amount in the decrypted message is considerably larger than the amount in the original message. Not so good!

This does not mean that you should avoid either streaming modes or stream ciphers like the plague. Using a different mode would increase the difficulty level of this style of attack, but even then, in less contrived situations the problem remains that you need to provide the receiver of the message with some way of verifying that the decrypted plaintext the receiver has generated is what you sent. To do this, you need some way of providing the receiver with a verification code that will allow the receiver to determine if the message has been tampered with. The basis of these codes is *symmetric ciphers* and *message digests*.

Let's look at message digests first.

Message Digests

Message digests compute a cryptographic hash, or secure checksum, for a particular message. They are of interest because of two properties that they have. Depending on the message size and the type of digest being used, the chances of generating the same message are extremely small. Second, changing a bit in an input message for which a digest has been computed will lead to an unpredictable change in the bits making up the new digest if the calculation is done again. This property of uniqueness and the lack of predictability make message digests a very useful part of any cryptographic toolbox.

Naturally, this also means that, like ciphers, message digest algorithms can come under a variety of attacks. In terms of what a successful attack constitutes, people trying to break digest algorithms look for two things: (1) the ease with which digests can be made to produce *collisions* — the same result for different inputs — with any data and (2) easy ways to produce collisions with minor changes to the input data. When this can be done, the digest algorithm has become little better, if at all, than a CRC.

I mention this specifically because, as this book was being written, some new weaknesses have been discovered in the very widely used algorithm SHA-1. Although they are not cause for immediate alarm, they do indicate that it is time to start migrating to some of the newer algorithms, and that researchers are becoming better at analyzing and attacking these algorithms. In the past, message digests have not been studied as well as ciphers, and this is changing, so you can probably expect some changes in the future.

Anyway, you will notice that SHA-1 is quite widely used in this book, as well as some of the newer algorithms, such as SHA-256. SHA-1 is used either because the algorithm being used requires it or because there are few implementations that support the use of other digests in that context. The principles are still the same, regardless of the digest being used, so the lessons can still be learned. Nonetheless, if you are planning on implementing a newer application, you should look at using the newer algorithms such as SHA-256 and SHA-512 where possible.

Try It Out   **Using a Message Digest**

The following example makes use of a message digest, in this case the NIST function SHA-1 described in FIPS PUB 180-1, in order to allow you to detect the tampering that was performed on the ciphertext when the decrypted, plaintext message is created. Note that the main change is simply the addition of the computed digest to the message payload before encryption and then the addition of a verification step when the message payload has been decrypted.

```java
package chapter3;

import java.security.Key;
import java.security.MessageDigest;
import java.security.SecureRandom;

import javax.crypto.Cipher;
import javax.crypto.spec.IvParameterSpec;

/**
 * Tampered message, encryption with digest, AES in CTR mode
 */
public class TamperedWithDigestExample
{
    public static void main(String[] args) throws Exception
    {
        SecureRandom      random = new SecureRandom();
        IvParameterSpec   ivSpec = Utils.createCtrIvForAES(1, random);
        Key               key = Utils.createKeyForAES(256, random);
        Cipher            cipher = Cipher.getInstance("AES/CTR/NoPadding", "BC");
        String            input = "Transfer 0000100 to AC 1234-5678";
        MessageDigest     hash = MessageDigest.getInstance("SHA-1", "BC");

        System.out.println("input : " + input);

        // encryption step

        cipher.init(Cipher.ENCRYPT_MODE, key, ivSpec);

        byte[] cipherText = new byte[cipher.getOutputSize(
                                    input.length() + hash.getDigestLength())];

        int ctLength = cipher.update(Utils.toByteArray(input), 0, input.length(),
                                                        cipherText, 0);

        hash.update(Utils.toByteArray(input));

        ctLength += cipher.doFinal(hash.digest(), 0, hash.getDigestLength(),
                                                cipherText, ctLength);

        // tampering step
```

```
cipherText[9] ^= '0' ^ '9';

// decryption step

cipher.init(Cipher.DECRYPT_MODE, key, ivSpec);

byte[] plainText = cipher.doFinal(cipherText, 0, ctLength);
int     messageLength = plainText.length - hash.getDigestLength();

hash.update(plainText, 0, messageLength);

byte[] messageHash = new byte[hash.getDigestLength()];
System.arraycopy(plainText, messageLength, messageHash,
                                        0, messageHash.length);

System.out.println("plain : " + Utils.toString(plainText, messageLength)
        + " verified: " + MessageDigest.isEqual(hash.digest(), messageHash));
    }
}
```

Running the previous program, you should see the following output.

```
input : Transfer 0000100 to AC 1234-5678
plain : Transfer 9000100 to AC 1234-5678 verified: false
```

This time, you can see there is something wrong with the decrypted ciphertext.

How It Works

The process used here is outlined in Figure 3-1. This time around, the message digest calculates a crypto-graphic hash of the plaintext as it should be. The hash is then appended to the message before encryption as an extra level of protection. On decryption, the hash is recomputed from the resulting plaintext. Because the plaintext has decrypted to a different value from before, the hash computation leads to a different value. The value does not match the expected one appended to the message, and you can therefore tell that tampering has occurred.

Although the fact that you can now tell that tampering is taking place is an improvement, you will see soon that you are not quite there yet. That being said, it would be worth pausing briefly to take a look at the new class that was introduced.

The MessageDigest Class

The java.security.MessageDigest class provides a general object to represent a variety of message digests. Like the KeyGenerator class, it uses the getInstance() factory pattern, and MessageDigest.getInstance() behaves exactly as other getInstance() methods in the JCA in the manner in which it follows precedence rules and finds algorithm implementations.

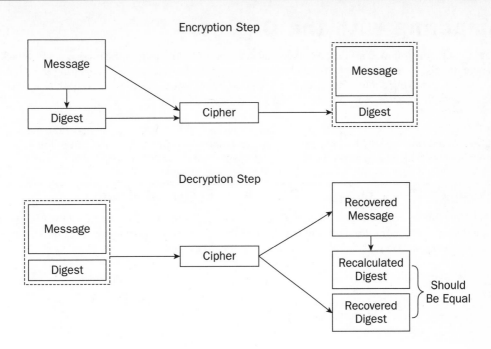

Combining a Cipher with a Message Digest

Figure 3-1

MessageDigest.update()

The update() method is used to feed data into the digest. There is no return value because the input data is just progressively mixed in to the digest function.

How much data you can feed safely into a hash function varies with the function you are using, and as a general rule the number of bits of security you get with a given digest function increases with the digest size. SHA-1, for example, produces a 160-bit digest, will handle 2^{64} bits and, in the light of recent results, is believed to offer 69 bits of security. SHA-512 (detailed in FIPS PUB 180-2), on the other hand, produces a 512-bit digest, will handle messages up to 2^{128} bits, and offers 256 bits of security.

MessageDigest.digest()

This closes off the progressive calculation and returns the final digest value. There are a couple of ways of using the digest() method: It will either return the byte array or will write the digest to a byte array that has the space required for the digest available. The space required for a digest is given by MessageDigest.getDigestSize().

MessageDigest.isEqual()

This is a static helper method that compares the two byte arrays passed to it and returns true if they are equal, false otherwise. These days, you would probably just use java.util.Arrays.equals(), but in this case, because you are trying to keep this flexible with regard to which JDK you are using, you should stick with MessageDigest.isEqual().

Tampering with the Digest

Previously, you assumed that the attacker was familiar with only part of the message. The attacker knew where the digits were and replaced the leading 0 with a 9, thus substantially changing the quantity the message was talking about. The example responded by introducing a message digest, which allowed you to spot the change. Now it is the attacker's turn to respond to you.

Still in a streaming mode, imagine the attacker is familiar with the entire contents of the message but cannot determine the key. This means the attacker cannot decrypt the message, but in this case knowing the contents of the message and the format of it means that the attacker does not have to.

Try It Out   **Tampering with a Digest in an Encrypted Stream**

Look at the following example; it is almost identical to the example that introduced the use of the message digest. The major differences are that not only are the message contents being altered, but the message digest tacked on to the end of the message is altered as well.

```java
package chapter3;

import java.security.Key;
import java.security.MessageDigest;
import java.security.SecureRandom;

import javax.crypto.Cipher;
import javax.crypto.spec.IvParameterSpec;

/**
 * Tampered message, encryption with digest, AES in CTR mode
 */
public class TamperedDigestExample
{
    public static void main(
        String[]      args)
        throws Exception
    {
        SecureRandom      random = new SecureRandom();
        IvParameterSpec ivSpec = Utils.createCtrIvForAES(1, random);
        Key             key = Utils.createKeyForAES(256, random);
        Cipher          cipher = Cipher.getInstance("AES/CTR/NoPadding", "BC");
        String          input = "Transfer 0000100 to AC 1234-5678";
        MessageDigest   hash = MessageDigest.getInstance("SHA-1", "BC");

        System.out.println("input : " + input);

        // encryption step

        cipher.init(Cipher.ENCRYPT_MODE, key, ivSpec);

        byte[] cipherText = new byte[cipher.getOutputSize(
                                    input.length() + hash.getDigestLength())];

        int ctLength = cipher.update(Utils.toByteArray(input), 0, input.length(),
                                                    cipherText, 0);
```

```
hash.update(Utils.toByteArray(input));

ctLength += cipher.doFinal(hash.digest(), 0, hash.getDigestLength(),
                                               cipherText, ctLength);

// tampering step

cipherText[9] ^= '0' ^ '9';

// replace digest

byte[] originalHash = hash.digest(Utils.toByteArray(input));
byte[] tamperedHash = hash.digest(
                Utils.toByteArray("Transfer 9000100 to AC 1234-5678"));

for (int i = ctLength - hash.getDigestLength(), j = 0;
                                     i != ctLength; i++, j++)
{
    cipherText[i] ^= originalHash[j] ^ tamperedHash[j];
}

// decryption step

cipher.init(Cipher.DECRYPT_MODE, key, ivSpec);

byte[] plainText = cipher.doFinal(cipherText, 0, ctLength);
int    messageLength = plainText.length - hash.getDigestLength();

hash.update(plainText, 0, messageLength);

byte[] messageHash = new byte[hash.getDigestLength()];
System.arraycopy(plainText, messageLength, messageHash,
                                       0, messageHash.length);

System.out.println("plain : " + Utils.toString(plainText, messageLength)
        + " verified: " + MessageDigest.isEqual(hash.digest(), messageHash));
    }
}
```

Try running the example; you should see the following output:

```
input : Transfer 0000100 to AC 1234-5678
plain : Transfer 9000100 to AC 1234-5678 verified: true
```

Unfortunately, the `verified: true` that appears at the end of the second line indicates that, using the current verification regime, your receiver could be fooled into thinking that what they decrypted is the message you sent.

How It Works

As with the previous Try It Out ("Tampering with an Encrypted Stream"), you have taken advantage of the fact the cipher is using XOR. This time around, the attacker has had to show more knowledge about the internals of the message structure so that they could compute the expected hash. This has allowed the attacker to zero out the one that was inserted originally and replace it with a new one, making the tampered stream appear as though it is internally consistent.

Note that the way the message digest is being altered demonstrates a big difference between a cryptographic hash and a normal checksum like CRC-32. The attacker has to be able to compute the full digest that the message already contains in addition to computing what the new digest value is meant to be. The reason is that, unlike CRC-32, the attacker cannot predict how a bit change in the message will affect the digest. This is a useful property that you are not taking full advantage of yet, but soon will.

However, there is still a problem, and although you would be forgiven for thinking otherwise, the problem is not with the choice of cipher and mode, but is more to do with how the digest function is being used.

MACs Based on Digests — the HMAC

The next example introduces the `Mac` class. In the following case, `Mac.getInstance()` is being used to produce a HMAC (a hash MAC), a message authentication code based on a cryptographic message digest, as detailed in RFC 2104. What makes a HMAC different from a regular message digest calculation is that it incorporates a secret key as well as some "under the hood" data into the calculation of the final hash. This reduces the problem of changing the HMAC used in the message to the problem of guessing the HMAC key as well as knowing the message contents.

Try It Out   **Using a HMAC**

Look at the example; you will see that the substitution of `MessageDigest` with a `Mac` is relatively straightforward.

```
package chapter3;

import java.security.Key;
import java.security.MessageDigest;
import java.security.SecureRandom;

import javax.crypto.Cipher;
import javax.crypto.Mac;
import javax.crypto.spec.IvParameterSpec;
import javax.crypto.spec.SecretKeySpec;

/**
 * Tampered message with HMac, encryption with AES in CTR mode
 */
public class TamperedWithHMacExample
{
    public static void main(String[] args) throws Exception
    {
        SecureRandom     random = new SecureRandom();
        IvParameterSpec ivSpec = Utils.createCtrIvForAES(1, random);
        Key             key = Utils.createKeyForAES(256, random);
        Cipher          cipher = Cipher.getInstance("AES/CTR/NoPadding", "BC");
        String          input = "Transfer 0000100 to AC 1234-5678";
```

```
         Mac                hMac = Mac.getInstance("HmacSHA1", "BC");
         Key                hMacKey = new SecretKeySpec(key.getEncoded(), "HmacSHA1");

     System.out.println("input : " + input);

     // encryption step

     cipher.init(Cipher.ENCRYPT_MODE, key, ivSpec);

     byte[] cipherText = new byte[cipher.getOutputSize(
                                    input.length() + hMac.getMacLength())];

     int ctLength = cipher.update(Utils.toByteArray(input), 0, input.length(),
                                                       cipherText, 0);

     hMac.init(hMacKey);
     hMac.update(Utils.toByteArray(input));

     ctLength += cipher.doFinal(hMac.doFinal(), 0, hMac.getMacLength(),
                                                   cipherText, ctLength);

     // tampering step

     cipherText[9] ^= '0' ^ '9';

     // replace digest

     // ?

     // decryption step

     cipher.init(Cipher.DECRYPT_MODE, key, ivSpec);

     byte[] plainText = cipher.doFinal(cipherText, 0, ctLength);
     int    messageLength = plainText.length - hMac.getMacLength();

     hMac.init(hMacKey);
     hMac.update(plainText, 0, messageLength);

     byte[] messageHash = new byte[hMac.getMacLength()];
     System.arraycopy(plainText, messageLength, messageHash,
                                            0, messageHash.length);

     System.out.println("plain : " + Utils.toString(plainText, messageLength)
           + " verified: " + MessageDigest.isEqual(hMac.doFinal(), messageHash));
   }
 }
```

Running this example yields the following output:

```
input : Transfer 0000100 to AC 1234-5678
plain : Transfer 9000100 to AC 1234-5678 verified: false
```

Apart from the fact that you are picking up the tampering again, you will also notice in the example that the step replacing the digest has been removed.

How It Works

By looking at Figure 3-2, you can see how the process you are now using is different from that used with a straight message digest. The reason the tampering is now "fool-proof" is the underlying assumption that the attacker does not know the secret key. Because the secret key is also being used for the HMAC, the attacker has no way of performing the replacement. The attacker can neither calculate the expected value after the change nor calculate the HMAC value that was in the original message; hence, the ? in the code—there isn't any code that can fill the spot. After all, if the attacker did know the secret key, it would be unnecessary to even bother with trying to tamper with the encrypted stream.

Another thing you will notice in the example is that the key being used for the HMAC is the same as the one being used for encryption. For the purposes of this example this is okay; it reduces the amount of code. In general you should avoid doing this. By having a different key for the HMAC object, you are at least safe in the knowledge that if an attacker does succeed in recovering the encryption key for the message, the attacker still has to recover another key before they can try to produce a message that your receiver will regard as authentic.

There are other ways of gaining this effect as well. You might also include a random IV in-line with the message data and create the effect of a HMAC by just using a digest. As long as the IV is secured along with the message content, an attacker will still be at a loss when it comes to trying to fiddle the digest. Of course, if the message is for long-term use, as soon as the message encryption key is compromised, a fake message can be generated. However, there are plenty of situations where messages might be generated and then thrown away after a single use where this method of keying the digest would be appropriate.

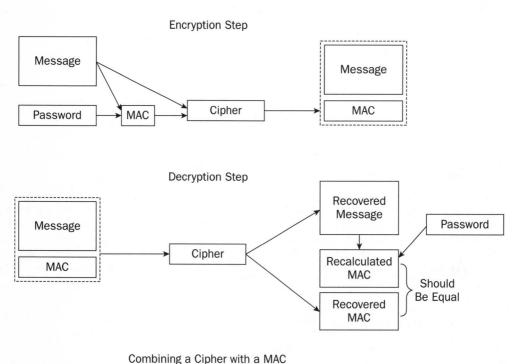

Combining a Cipher with a MAC

Figure 3-2

As for the `Mac` class introduced in the example, as you will see, it is basically like a `MessageDigest` but with an `init()` method.

The Mac Class

The `javax.crypto.Mac` class provides a general object to represent a variety of MAC algorithms. Like the `MessageDigest` class, it uses the `getInstance()` factory pattern, and `Mac.getInstance()` behaves exactly as other `getInstance()` methods in the JCE and JCA in the manner in which it follows precedence rules and finds algorithm implementations.

The JCA specifies a naming convention for HMAC objects: `HmacDigest`. It also specifies a naming convention for MACs based on password-based encryption (PBE), which is `PBEwithMac`, where `Mac` is the full name of the MAC being used. For example, a HMAC based on SHA-256 being used with PBE would be created using the following:

```
Mac     hMac = Mac.getInstance("PBEwithHmacSHA256");
```

Mac.init()

The `init()` method has two versions, one that just takes a key, which was used previously, and another that takes a key and an `AlgorithmParameterSpec` object.

In the case of a HMAC, the key should be at least the length of the MAC being produced. With MACs based on symmetric ciphers, which you will look at next, the key can be a suitable key for the cipher that the MAC algorithm is based on.

The second `init()` method is used because some MAC algorithms, like a cipher, can take parameters that affect the MAC calculation. MACs based on CBC mode ciphers can take initialization vectors to help hide key reuse with the same message, such as

```
mac.init(macKey, new IvParameterSpec(ivBytes));
```

You will take a closer look at MACs based on symmetric ciphers in the next section.

Mac.update()

As with the `MessageDigest` class, the `update()` method is used to feed data into the MAC. Again, depending on the size of the final MAC that is produced, you need to be careful that you are not expecting the particular MAC algorithm to deal with too much data. Feeding too much data into a `Mac.update()` will reduce the overall security you get from the MAC produced when you call `Mac.doFinal()`.

Mac.doFinal()

`Mac.doFinal()` simply produces the final MAC that is the result of the call to `Mac.init()` and `Mac.update()` and then resets the `Mac` object back to the state it was in when the last `Mac.init()` was called. You can treat it the same way as `MessageDigest.digest()`.

MACs Based on Symmetric Ciphers

Another, older method for calculating MACs is to use a symmetric cipher. NIST is in the process of reissuing standards for these in SP 800-38b, but algorithms for MAC calculation using DES were first published in FIPS PUB 81.

Try It Out   **Using a Cipher-Based MAC**

The following example shows you how to use DES in a MAC mode, via the `Mac` object.

```java
package chapter3;

import java.security.Key;
import java.security.MessageDigest;
import java.security.SecureRandom;

import javax.crypto.Cipher;
import javax.crypto.Mac;
import javax.crypto.spec.IvParameterSpec;
import javax.crypto.spec.SecretKeySpec;

/**
 * Message without tampering with MAC (DES), encryption AES in CTR mode
 */
public class CipherMacExample
{
    public static void main(String[] args) throws Exception
    {
        SecureRandom    random = new SecureRandom();
        IvParameterSpec ivSpec = Utils.createCtrIvForAES(1, random);
        Key             key = Utils.createKeyForAES(256, random);
        Cipher          cipher = Cipher.getInstance("AES/CTR/NoPadding", "BC");
        String          input = "Transfer 0000100 to AC 1234-5678";
        Mac             mac = Mac.getInstance("DES", "BC");
        byte[]          macKeyBytes = new byte[] {
                           0x01, 0x02, 0x03, 0x04, 0x05, 0x06, 0x07, 0x08 };
        Key             macKey = new SecretKeySpec(macKeyBytes, "DES");

        System.out.println("input : " + input);

        // encryption step

        cipher.init(Cipher.ENCRYPT_MODE, key, ivSpec);

        byte[] cipherText = new byte[cipher.getOutputSize(
                                        input.length() + mac.getMacLength())];

        int ctLength = cipher.update(Utils.toByteArray(input), 0, input.length(),
                                                            cipherText, 0);

        mac.init(macKey);
        mac.update(Utils.toByteArray(input));

        ctLength += cipher.doFinal(mac.doFinal(), 0, mac.getMacLength(),
                                                        cipherText, ctLength);
```

```
                    // decryption step

                    cipher.init(Cipher.DECRYPT_MODE, key, ivSpec);

                    byte[] plainText = cipher.doFinal(cipherText, 0, ctLength);
                    int    messageLength = plainText.length - mac.getMacLength();

                    mac.init(macKey);
                    mac.update(plainText, 0, messageLength);

                    byte[] messageHash = new byte[mac.getMacLength()];
                    System.arraycopy(plainText, messageLength, messageHash,
                                                          0, messageHash.length);

                    System.out.println("plain : " + Utils.toString(plainText, messageLength)
                          + " verified: " + MessageDigest.isEqual(mac.doFinal(), messageHash));
            }
        }
```

In this case, because there is no tampering, running the example demonstrates that the message will verify correctly, so you should see the following output:

```
    input : Transfer 0000100 to AC 1234-5678
    plain : Transfer 0000100 to AC 1234-5678 verified: true
```

How It Works

MACs based on ciphers do essentially the same job as MACs based on cryptographic hashes, so the principle that applies here is the same as before—a secret key is required to compute the MAC correctly and if you do not know the secret key, you can't compute the MAC again.

There are a variety of reasons why you might want to use a MAC based on a symmetric cipher, rather than using one based on a cryptographic hash. You, or perhaps the recipient of your messages, may have access to only one algorithm, the one used for encryption. A hash-based MAC might simply be too big. On the other hand, hash-based MACs, because they are larger, are less likely to have clashes for a given size of message. A MAC that is too small might turn out to be useless, as a variety of easy-to-generate messages might compute to the same MAC value, resulting in a collision. If there are enough of these collisions present, the usefulness of the MAC is reduced because being able to confirm a MAC tells you at best that the message is one of a set of possible messages, rather than, as you hope, the specific message that was sent.

It is really one of those situations where it depends on which issues are important and what the risks might be. Having said that, the general rule is that a bigger MAC value is a more secure one.

Digests in Pseudorandom Functions

You actually saw one example of the use of a digest as a source function for a pseudorandom function in Chapter 2, when you were reading about password-based encryption. In that case, the digest was used to mix the bits of the password and the salt together using some more general function and produce a string of bytes suitable for using as a key.

As you will see, digests can be used as the source functions for mask functions as well. The purpose of a mask function is to produce a pseudorandom byte (or octet if you want to be explicit) array that can then be XORed with the data you want to mask. The reason for masking is to prevent any patterns that might exist in the masked data from being visible.

You will look at some examples of PBE key generation functions and mask generation functions here so you can get a more general idea of how these are constructed, but the main thing to remember is that the functions take advantage of the fact that the changes in the output of an ideal digest function cannot be predicted by knowing any of the changes in its input.

PBE Key Generation

Two of the PKCS documents deal with password-based encryption. The first one is PKCS #5, which provides two schemes; the second is PKCS #12, which provides the basis for the scheme the PBE example was using in Chapter 2. All of them are based on the use of message digests. If you look at all three schemes, you will realize that they follow something of an evolutionary trail, and the best place to start is the beginning. Therefore, for the purposes of this book, I will just cover PKCS #5 Scheme 1, because it captures the basics of using a password, salt, and iteration count.

Try It Out   **Implementing PKCS #5 Scheme 1**

If you recall the discussion in Chapter 2 on the components of the `PBEKeySpec` and the `PBEParameterSpec`, the password is fed into a function that's based on a message digest and then mixed in some fashion together with the salt and the iteration count.

PKCS #5 Scheme 1 is such a function and provides a simple method for generation of keys up to 160 bits. Although it has been superseded by PKCS #5 Scheme 2 and the method detailed in PKCS #12, it is a good example of how a PBE key generation function can be put together. The algorithm used is simply

$$\text{Hash}(password \mid\mid salt)iterationCount$$

where `Hash()` is the message digest, *password* is an ASCII string that has been converted into a byte array, *salt* is a array of random bytes, and *iterationCount* is the iteration count value. The resulting array of bytes is referred to as the *derived key* and is then used for creating the encryption key and other things, such as an IV, if required.

It is fairly easy to express this in code, as you can see in the following sample implementation.

```
package chapter3;

import java.security.MessageDigest;

/**
 * A basic implementation of PKCS #5 Scheme 1.
 */
public class PKCS5Scheme1
{
    private MessageDigest digest;

    public PKCS5Scheme1(
```

```
            MessageDigest     digest)
    {
        this.digest = digest;
    }

    public byte[] generateDerivedKey(
        char[] password,
        byte[] salt,
        int     iterationCount)
    {
        for (int i = 0; i != password.length; i++)
        {
            digest.update((byte)password[i]);
        }

        digest.update(salt);

        byte[] digestBytes = digest.digest();
        for (int i = 1; i < iterationCount; i++)
        {
            digest.update(digestBytes);
            digestBytes = digest.digest();
        }

        return digestBytes;
    }
}
```

Having come up with a sample implementation, let's confirm that it works. You can do this by testing your implementation against the one used under the covers in the provider. You just need a PBE algorithm that uses PKCS #5 Scheme 1. One of these is PBEWithSHA1AndDES, which produces a key based on PKCS #5 Scheme 1 and then uses DES in CBC mode with PKCS #5 padding for doing the encryption.

Try running the following test for the PKCS5Scheme1 class; it uses PBEWithSHA1AndDES to do the encryption and then uses the new home-grown implementation with DES in CBC mode to do the decryption.

```
package chapter3;

import java.security.MessageDigest;

import javax.crypto.*;
import javax.crypto.spec.*;

/**
 * Basic test of the PKCS #5 Scheme 1 implementation.
 */
public class PKCS5Scheme1Test
{
    public static void main(
        String[] args)
        throws Exception
    {
```

```
            char[] password = "hello".toCharArray();
            byte[] salt = new byte[] { 1, 2, 3, 4, 5, 6, 7, 8, 9, 0 };
            byte[] input = new byte[] { 0x0a, 0x0b, 0x0c, 0x0d, 0x0e, 0x0f };
            int    iterationCount = 100;

            System.out.println("input  : " + Utils.toHex(input));

            // encryption step using regular PBE
            Cipher          cipher = Cipher.getInstance("PBEWithSHA1AndDES","BC");
            SecretKeyFactory fact = SecretKeyFactory.getInstance(
                                              "PBEWithSHA1AndDES", "BC");
            PBEKeySpec       pbeKeySpec = new PBEKeySpec(
                                              password, salt, iterationCount);

            cipher.init(Cipher.ENCRYPT_MODE, fact.generateSecret(pbeKeySpec));

            byte[] enc = cipher.doFinal(input);

            System.out.println("encrypt: " + Utils.toHex(enc));

            // decryption step - using the local implementation
            cipher = Cipher.getInstance("DES/CBC/PKCS5Padding");

            PKCS5Scheme1 pkcs5s1 = new PKCS5Scheme1(
                                     MessageDigest.getInstance("SHA-1", "BC"));

            byte[] derivedKey = pkcs5s1.generateDerivedKey(
                                        password, salt, iterationCount);

            cipher.init(Cipher.DECRYPT_MODE,
                              new SecretKeySpec(derivedKey, 0, 8, "DES"),
                              new IvParameterSpec(derivedKey, 8, 8));

            byte[] dec = cipher.doFinal(enc);

            System.out.println("decrypt: " + Utils.toHex(dec));
        }
    }
```

Running the test class should produce the following output:

```
input  : 0a0b0c0d0e0f
encrypt: af1c264c0946104d
decrypt: 0a0b0c0d0e0f
```

If you see this result, it means the home-grown implementation is producing the correct derived key, which allows you to initialize the decryption cipher correctly.

How It Works

The trick here is to know not only the means by which the PBE key is being generated but also which mode and padding is associated with the algorithm as well. The PKCS5Scheme1 class provides you with a correct implementation of the mixing function that uses the password, salt, and iteration count to produce a PBE key. By combining that with the correctly configured DES cipher, you are able to decrypt the output of the PBE cipher created with the provider.

Note that because the example uses DES in CBC mode, you also needed an IV and derivedKey is used as the source of this as well. Therefore, the example uses 16 of the 20 bytes generated: the first 8 for the DES key and the next 8 for the IV.

Mask Generation

As well as being used as a source function for key and IV generation in password-based encryption, message digests can also be used to generate pseudorandom streams of bytes to mask data that needs to be obfuscated. One such mask function can be found in PKCS #1 V2.1. The function name is MGF1.

The function is an interesting one to consider, because it is also very simple. The algorithm is simply, given T, which is initially an empty byte array; *seed*, which is a byte array containing a seed for the function; and the length of the message digest you are using as *hLen*, you can generate a mask in a byte array of *maskLength* length as follows:

1.   For *counter* from 0 to Ceiling(*maskLength* / *hLen*) – 1, do $T = T$ || Hash *(seed* || ItoOSP(*counter*)).

2.   Output the leading *maskLen* octets of T as the octet string *mask*.

The Ceiling() function is defined as Ceiling(x / y) and will return the smallest integer larger than or equal to the real number resulting from dividing x by y. Hash() is the function performed by the message digest you are using, and ItoOSP() is a function that converts an integer into a byte array, high byte first.

Try It Out   **Implementing MGF1**

Here is a sample implementation with a simple main() that generates a 20-byte mask. Try running it!

```java
package chapter3;

import java.security.MessageDigest;

/**
 * mask generator function, as described in PKCS1v2.
 */
public class MGF1
{
    private MessageDigest digest;

    /**
     * Create a version of MGF1 for the given digest.
     *
     * @param digest digest to use as the basis of the function.
     */
    public MGF1(
        MessageDigest digest)
    {
        this.digest = digest;
    }

    /**
     * int to octet string.
```

```
    */
    private void ItoOSP(
        int      i,
        byte[]   sp)
    {
        sp[0] = (byte)(i >>> 24);
        sp[1] = (byte)(i >>> 16);
        sp[2] = (byte)(i >>> 8);
        sp[3] = (byte)(i >>> 0);
    }

    /**
     * Generate the mask.
     *
     * @param seed source of input bytes for initial digest state
     * @param length length of mask to generate
     *
     * @return a byte array containing a MGF1 generated mask
     */
    public byte[] generateMask(
        byte[]   seed,
        int      length)
    {
        byte[]   mask = new byte[length];
        byte[]   C = new byte[4];
        int      counter = 0;
        int      hLen = digest.getDigestLength();

        while (counter < (length / hLen))
        {
            ItoOSP(counter, C);

            digest.update(seed);
            digest.update(C);

            System.arraycopy(digest.digest(), 0, mask, counter * hLen, hLen);

            counter++;
        }

        if ((counter * hLen) < length)
        {
            ItoOSP(counter, C);

            digest.update(seed);
            digest.update(C);

            System.arraycopy(digest.digest(), 0, mask, counter * hLen,
                                            mask.length - (counter * hLen));
        }

        return mask;
    }

    public static void main(String[] args) throws Exception
```

```
    {
        MGF1    mgf1 = new MGF1(MessageDigest.getInstance("SHA-1", "BC"));
        byte[]  source = new byte[] { 1, 2, 3, 4, 5, 6, 7, 8, 9, 10 };

        System.out.println(Utils.toHex(mgf1.generateMask(source, 20)));
    }
}
```

Running the class should produce the following 20 bytes of output:

```
e0a63d7c8c4d81cd1c0567bfab6c22ed2022977f
```

How It Works

The mask function can generate a stream of bytes suitable for obfuscation and masking of data from the seed, counter, and the message digest because of the property that an ideal message digest is supposed to have—namely, changes in the input to one lead to unpredictable changes to the output. The chances of different inputs leading to the same output is extremely small, providing the amount of data is not in excess of what the digest can handle. What constitutes too much data varies for a given digest, but if you look at PKCS #1 V2.1, you will see that MGF1 is restricted to generating masks of no more than 2^{32} bytes in size, as the digest it was initially designed for is SHA-1.

MGF1 is an interesting function to investigate; try a few different values and think about how it could be used. It is an interesting aspect of cryptography that you will often see similar techniques showing up in a variety of places, and in some respects, the process going on in MGF1 is very similar to the one you saw in CTR mode in Chapter 2. In Chapter 4, you will see MGF1 used with both techniques for RSA encryption and the generation of some types of RSA signatures.

There is still one aspect of use that I need to cover with message digests: Just as Java has I/O stream classes based on the `Cipher` class, there are also Java I/O stream classes based on `MessageDigest`.

Doing Digest-Based I/O

The JCA contains two classes for doing I/O involving message digests: `java.security` `.DigestInputStream` and `java.security.DigestOutputStream`. As with the cipher stream classes, you can use them anywhere you would use an `InputStream` or an `OutputStream`.

These stream classes are also a case where the usual factory pattern seen elsewhere in the JCA is not used. Instances of both `DigestInputStream` and `DigestOutputStream` are created using constructors, which take an `InputStream`, or `OutputStream`, to wrap, and a `MessageDigest` object to do the processing.

Look at the following example, which uses `DigestInputStream` and `DigestOutputStream`:

```
package chapter3;

import java.io.ByteArrayInputStream;
import java.io.ByteArrayOutputStream;
import java.security.DigestInputStream;
import java.security.DigestOutputStream;
import java.security.MessageDigest;
```

```
/**
 * Basic IO example using SHA1
 */
public class DigestIOExample
{
    public static void main(
        String[]    args)
        throws Exception
    {
        byte[]            input = new byte[] {
                            0x00, 0x01, 0x02, 0x03, 0x04, 0x05, 0x06, 0x07,
                            0x08, 0x09, 0x0a, 0x0b, 0x0c, 0x0d, 0x0e, 0x0f,
                            0x00, 0x01, 0x02, 0x03, 0x04, 0x05, 0x06 };;

        MessageDigest   hash = MessageDigest.getInstance("SHA1");

        System.out.println("input     : " + Utils.toHex(input));

        // input pass

        ByteArrayInputStream   bIn = new ByteArrayInputStream(input);
        DigestInputStream      dIn = new DigestInputStream(bIn, hash);
        ByteArrayOutputStream  bOut = new ByteArrayOutputStream();

        int     ch;
        while ((ch = dIn.read()) >= 0)
        {
            bOut.write(ch);
        }

        byte[] newInput = bOut.toByteArray();

        System.out.println("in digest : "
                            + Utils.toHex(dIn.getMessageDigest().digest()));

        // output pass

        bOut = new ByteArrayOutputStream();

        DigestOutputStream        dOut = new DigestOutputStream(bOut, hash);

        dOut.write(newInput);

        dOut.close();

        System.out.println("out digest: "
                            + Utils.toHex(dOut.getMessageDigest().digest()));
    }
}
```

Running the example, you should find that the digest produced on reading the input is the same as that produced on writing the reconstructed input. As a SHA-1 calculation on the same input should always lead to the same result, you should see the following output:

```
input      : 000102030405060708090a0b0c0d0e0f00010203040506
in digest  : 864ea9ee65d6f86847ba302ded2da77ad6c64722
out digest : 864ea9ee65d6f86847ba302ded2da77ad6c64722
```

One difference between the digest stream classes and the cipher stream classes is that, unlike a cipher, you can retrieve the state of the digest at any time via the `getMessageDigest()` method. Of course, if you do it in the manner used in the example, you will reset the message digest as a result of calling `MessageDigest.digest()`. `MessageDigest` objects are also cloneable, so if you wanted to take a sample of the current digest, but allow the digest to continue accumulating changes in the input, you could have instead written:

```
System.out.println("out digest: "
        + Utils.toHex(((MessageDigest)dOut.getMessageDigest().clone()).digest()));
```

This way, the `MessageDigest` object associated with the stream would not have been reset, allowing further writes to the stream to be accumulated on top of all the writes previously done, rather than having the digest start calculating from scratch.

Summary

In this chapter, you looked at methods for calculating cryptographic hashes, or message digests, on data using the `MessageDigest` class for the purpose of being able to tell if the data has been tampered with. You have also seen how secret keys can be incorporated into integrity testing using the `Mac` class.

Over the course of the chapter, you learned the following:

- ❑ Message digests are useful because it is not possible to predict the changes that will occur in the value of a calculated digest from the changes in the input to the digest calculation.

- ❑ In situations where a message digest is not enough, it is necessary to use a MAC, as it incorporates a secret key as well as the input data you are trying to protect.

- ❑ MACs can be based on symmetric ciphers or message digests.

- ❑ Digests can be used for PBE key generation and as a source of pseudorandom data.

- ❑ How to use the support for in-lining message digest calculation using the JCA classes that allow the mixing of message digests with input streams and output streams.

The shortcomings of the techniques you have looked at here are that, as with messages encrypted using symmetric key cryptography, MAC protection is meaningful only when the receiver of the message the MAC is for has access to the secret key. The question then becomes how you send the receiver the secret key, or is there another way of authenticating a message that does not require sending a secret key. You will find the answers to this in the next chapter, when you look at asymmetric key cryptography.

Exercises

1. Why are message digests and MACs a necessary part of sending a message using encryption?

2. You have been asked to implement a protocol that does not require encryption of the messages used in it, but it does require that the messages be tamperproof. How can you solve this problem while still allowing messages to be sent without encryption? What extra piece of information is now required when two parties want to communicate?

3. What is the primary limitation of the use of a MAC or message digest?

4. What is wrong with the following code?

```
cipher.init(Cipher.ENCRYPT_MODE, key);

String encrypted = new String(cipher.doFinal(input));

cipher.init(Cipher.DECRYPT_MODE, key);

byte[] decrypted = cipher.doFinal(encrypted.getBytes());
```

Asymmetric Key Cryptography

The problem posed with symmetric key ciphers, MACs, and HMACs is how to get the secret key to the recipient so that the recipient can decrypt the ciphertext when it is received. Asymmetric key cryptography is one answer. It is called asymmetric key cryptography because the keys used for performing encryption and decryption are different and are normally referred to as public and private keys.

This chapter introduces the concepts of asymmetric key cryptography, including how to use public and private keys for exchanging secret keys and creating digital signatures. Asymmetric algorithms come in a variety of shapes, and you will look at what parameters are required for key creation and what padding mechanisms are appropriate when messages are being encrypted. Unlike symmetric algorithms, asymmetric algorithms are not appropriate for bulk encryption, and you will see how asymmetric and symmetric cryptography is combined to achieve this.

By the end of this chapter, you should be able to

❑   Use and understand the most popular algorithms in use to date

❑   Understand the methods for performing key exchange and key agreement, as well as some of the pros and cons of using them

❑   Understand how to use padding mechanisms with asymmetric keys

❑   Create and verify digital signatures

Finally, you will also have a good knowledge of the various Java APIs that are in place for supporting the generation, manipulation, and use of asymmetric keys and ciphers.

Getting Started

This chapter extends the Utils class so that it also includes an implementation of SecureRandom, which will produce predictable output. Although this sounds insane from a cryptographic point of view, it will make it a lot easier for me to talk about the examples that use it, as you will be able to reproduce the output exactly.

Here is the class:

```
package chapter4;

import java.security.MessageDigest;
import java.security.SecureRandom;

/**
 * Utility class for chapter 4 examples
 */
public class Utils
    extends chapter3.Utils
{
    private static class FixedRand extends SecureRandom
    {
        MessageDigest    sha;
        byte[]           state;

        FixedRand()
        {
            try
            {
                this.sha = MessageDigest.getInstance("SHA-1", "BC");
                this.state = sha.digest();
            }
            catch (Exception e)
            {
                throw new RuntimeException("can't find SHA-1!");
            }
        }

        public void nextBytes(
            byte[] bytes)
        {
            int off = 0;

            sha.update(state);

            while (off < bytes.length)
            {
                state = sha.digest();

                if (bytes.length - off > state.length)
                {
                    System.arraycopy(state, 0, bytes, off, state.length);
                }
                else
                {
```

```
                    System.arraycopy(state, 0, bytes, off, bytes.length - off);
            }

            off += state.length;

            sha.update(state);
        }
    }
}

/**
 * Return a SecureRandom which produces the same value.
 * <b>This is for testing only!</b>
 * @return a fixed random
 */
public static SecureRandom createFixedRandom()
{
    return new FixedRand();
}
}
```

As you can see, it just builds on the idea of using a message digest to generate a pseudorandom stream of bytes. Type the new Utils class in to start off the chapter4 package and you are ready to begin.

The PublicKey and PrivateKey Interfaces

Any discussion on how asymmetric cryptography is done in Java needs to mention two interfaces: java .security.PublicKey and java.security.PrivateKey. All keys related to asymmetric encryption will implement one of these interfaces, and consequently, you will often see them as return values for methods on the various classes used to manipulate keys and key material.

The interfaces themselves directly extend java.security.Key but do not introduce any new methods — they simply provide type safety. You will see why this is the case as you look into the various algorithms in more detail. For the most part, each algorithm has its own set of key interfaces. This is because, unlike the case with symmetric key algorithms, which are basically one size fits all, every asymmetric algorithm is not only different in terms of how it behaves, but also in terms of the parameters required to construct a key.

This chapter starts by looking at regular encryption, but you will see that asymmetric cryptography also forms the foundation for key agreement and digital signatures.

The RSA Algorithm

The RSA algorithm was initially publicized in 1977 by Ronald Rivest, Adi Shamir, and Leonard Adleman. Recently declassified documents reveal that the method used by RSA was first discovered by Clifford Cocks in 1973 at GCHQ in Great Britain.

The algorithm gets its security from the difficulty of factoring large numbers. Essentially, the public and private keys are functions of a pair of large primes, and recovering the plaintext from a given ciphertext and the public key used to create it is believed to be equivalent to the problem of recovering the primes used to make the keys. How big a key has to be is an interesting question. The keys in the examples were chosen so they would be easy to type in and produce output that would fit on a line, not for reasons of security. In practice, the key size should be a minimum of 1,024 bits; double that if your application is required to keep messages protected for more than 10 years.

Although full derivation of the algorithm is well beyond the scope of this book, the algorithm itself is quite simple to express. Given two primes p and q, if you have other numbers n, e, and d such that:

$n = pq$

and

$ed \equiv 1 \bmod((p - 1)(q - 1))$

then, given a message m,

$c = m^e \bmod n$

$m = c^d \bmod n$

where c is the ciphertext. There are longer names for n, e, and d as well; they are the *modulus*, the *public exponent*, and the *private exponent*, respectively. In general, we choose the value of the public exponent so that the encryption step is computationally cheap to perform, and then generate the private exponent accordingly. As for n, p, and q: It is the size of n that determines how many bits the RSA key you have generated is said to have, so p and q need to have a bit length half that of the key size.

To make use of the algorithm, you need to make sure you can represent any message you want to encrypt as a positive big integer that is less than n. This is quite easy to do. In the case of Java, you just take the bytes making up the message and then create a positive `BigInteger` object from them.

Of course, in this case, because you are dealing with the JCE, you never have to convert a message into a `BigInteger` yourself. However, it is important to know that this is what is happening under the covers, as it does affect the way in which you can safely use the RSA algorithm. For example, I have already mentioned that the message m needs to have a value arithmetically less than n. The reason is that the arithmetic used in RSA is based on doing calculations mod n, or put another way, by dividing numbers by n and taking the remainder as the answer. The result is that any value greater than n will be reduced to that value mod n by the encryption process. You will see how you deal with large messages and RSA a bit later, but for the moment just remember that the fact you are doing everything using big-integer arithmetic means that the behavior of the algorithm is dictated by the underlying mathematics.

Try It Out   Basic RSA

As a starting point, try to run the following example. It will introduce you to the basic classes used for RSA, as well as show how the JCE allows you to take advantage of the common API even though the underlying implementation of RSA is very different from any algorithm you have encountered to date. The key size is 128 bits, one-eighth of the minimum recommended size, but it is big enough for the purposes here.

```
package chapter4;

import java.math.BigInteger;
import java.security.KeyFactory;
import java.security.interfaces.RSAPrivateKey;
import java.security.interfaces.RSAPublicKey;
import java.security.spec.RSAPrivateKeySpec;
import java.security.spec.RSAPublicKeySpec;

import javax.crypto.Cipher;

/**
 * Basic RSA example.
 */
public class BaseRSAExample
{
    public static void main(String[] args) throws Exception
    {
        byte[]          input = new byte[] { (byte)0xbe, (byte)0xef };
        Cipher          cipher = Cipher.getInstance("RSA/None/NoPadding", "BC");

        // create the keys
        KeyFactory      keyFactory = KeyFactory.getInstance("RSA", "BC");

        RSAPublicKeySpec pubKeySpec = new RSAPublicKeySpec(
                new BigInteger("d46f473a2d746537de2056ae3092c451", 16),
                new BigInteger("11", 16));
        RSAPrivateKeySpec privKeySpec = new RSAPrivateKeySpec(
                new BigInteger("d46f473a2d746537de2056ae3092c451", 16),
                new BigInteger("57791d5430d593164082036ad8b29fb1", 16));

        RSAPublicKey pubKey = (RSAPublicKey)keyFactory.generatePublic(pubKeySpec);
        RSAPrivateKey privKey = (RSAPrivateKey)keyFactory.generatePrivate(
                                                            privKeySpec);

        System.out.println("input : " + Utils.toHex(input));

        // encryption step

        cipher.init(Cipher.ENCRYPT_MODE, pubKey);

        byte[] cipherText = cipher.doFinal(input);

        System.out.println("cipher: " + Utils.toHex(cipherText));

        // decryption step

        cipher.init(Cipher.DECRYPT_MODE, privKey);

        byte[] plainText = cipher.doFinal(cipherText);

        System.out.println("plain : " + Utils.toHex(plainText));
    }
}
```

Chapter 4

When you run the example, you should see the following output:

```
input : beef
cipher: d2db15838f6c1c98702c5d54fe0add42
plain : beef
```

How It Works

In terms of how the `Cipher` class is used, the example is not that different from what you have seen before. What has changed is that the classes representing the key material for the keys in addition to the interfaces representing the keys themselves are now more specialized. Just from looking at the names given to them, it is evident that they are for RSA.

I will go into the details about the specification objects in more detail a bit later, but as you can see, the initialization of the RSA cipher involves defining some value objects that contain the numbers that define the RSA public and private keys. These are then converted into keys that are passed to the cipher object using a new factory class that deals with asymmetric keys — the `KeyFactory` class. After that, it looks like business as usual. The next step is to understand the `KeyFactory` class and what it does. Remember, as the `KeyFactory` class is an abstraction, what is said about it applies to all asymmetric algorithms.

The KeyFactory Class

The `java.security.KeyFactory` class provides the necessary abstraction layer to allow you to convert key specifications that you have created outside a provider's environment into `Key` objects that you can use within the provider, or take existing keys and convert them into specifications that you can then export. Like the `Cipher` class, it uses the `getInstance()` factory pattern, and `KeyFactory.getInstance()` behaves exactly as other `getInstance()` methods in the JCA in the manner in which it follows precedence rules and finds algorithm implementations.

The `KeyFactory` class has four conversion methods. Two of the methods convert key specifications into keys, `generatePublic()` and `generatePrivate()`. One method creates key specifications, `getKeySpec()`. The final method translates keys from one provider into keys suitable for use in another — the `translateKey()` method.

The two methods of most interest are the `generatePublic()` and `generatePrivate()` methods. In the example, you can see they are being used to convert the specification objects containing the key material for RSA keys into `Key` objects. Take a look at the specification objects and key interfaces now.

RSAPublicKeySpec and RSAPublicKey

As the suffix on the class name suggests, `RSAPublicKeySpec` is a value object that contains the necessary objects that can be used to create an RSA public key — the modulus and the public exponent.

Passing the `RSAPublicKeySpec` object to the `KeyFactory.generatePublic()` returns a `PublicKey` object. In this case, because it is RSA, the `KeyFactory` returns an object implementing `RSAPublicKey`, which has the same method signatures as `RSAPublicKeySpec`. There is a `getModulus()` method, which returns the `BigInteger` representing the modulus, and the `getPublicExponent()` method, which returns the `BigInteger` representing the public exponent.

RSAPrivateKeySpec and RSAPrivateKey

The `RSAPrivateKeySpec` is also a value object and in this case contains the objects that are required to create an RSA private key — the modulus and the private exponent.

Other than the fact you use `KeyFactory.generatePrivate()` to create the key object implementing `RSAPrivateKey`, and that you have a `getPrivateExponent()` method rather than a `getPublicExponent()`, the basic class and interface for dealing with RSA key material and RSA keys are essentially the same as their public key equivalents. You might expect this to be the case, because it follows from the symmetry inherent in the RSA algorithm.

Creating Random RSA Keys

You can also generate keys randomly, rather than having to have all the key material beforehand. As you have already seen, asymmetric algorithms require a public and a private key. Consequently, rather than using a `KeyGenerator` to generate a single `Key` object, you introduce `KeyPairGenerator` to generate a `KeyPair`.

You will look at these classes in more detail in a minute. A good way to understand them is to try using them first.

Try It Out   Creating Random RSA Keys

Try the following example. It creates an RSA key pair from a random source, encrypts a simple message with the pair's public key, and then recovers the message using the pair's private key to decrypt the ciphertext.

```java
package chapter4;

import java.security.Key;
import java.security.KeyPair;
import java.security.KeyPairGenerator;
import java.security.SecureRandom;

import javax.crypto.Cipher;

/**
 * RSA example with random key generation.
 */
public class RandomKeyRSAExample
{
    public static void main(String[] args) throws Exception
    {
        byte[]              input = new byte[] { (byte)0xbe, (byte)0xef };
        Cipher              cipher = Cipher.getInstance("RSA/None/NoPadding", "BC");
```

```
        SecureRandom        random = Utils.createFixedRandom();

        // create the keys
        KeyPairGenerator generator = KeyPairGenerator.getInstance("RSA", "BC");

        generator.initialize(256, random);

        KeyPair             pair = generator.generateKeyPair();
        Key                 pubKey = pair.getPublic();
        Key                 privKey = pair.getPrivate();
```

```
        System.out.println("input : " + Utils.toHex(input));

        // encryption step

        cipher.init(Cipher.ENCRYPT_MODE, pubKey, random);

        byte[] cipherText = cipher.doFinal(input);

        System.out.println("cipher: " + Utils.toHex(cipherText));

        // decryption step

        cipher.init(Cipher.DECRYPT_MODE, privKey);

        byte[] plainText = cipher.doFinal(cipherText);

        System.out.println("plain : " + Utils.toHex(plainText));
    }
}
```

Running the example produces the following output:

```
input : beef
cipher: 8274caf4a1f54b3b58f6798755d2cfce3e33f710a3f520865c0ccdca0a672601
plain : beef
```

Notice how as the key size goes up so does the size of the block of ciphertext. Even though at this point you are still only at a key size of 256 bits, one-fourth of what you would be using in an application, you can see that RSA is expanding the original 4-byte message substantially. There is no equivalent to CTR mode with RSA — you just have to accept the expansion as a necessary expense.

How It Works

As with BaseRSAExample, the example does look very similar to what you have seen before in Chapter 2; the only real difference being the use of KeyPair and KeyPairGenerator because you are now dealing with an asymmetric algorithm rather than a symmetric one. To really understand the example, you just need to understand the classes involved in the public and private key generation.

The KeyPair Class

The java.security.KeyPair class serves as a holder for a private key and its associated public key. It is a simple value object with two methods. The getPrivate() and getPublic() methods return the private and public keys making up the key pair.

The KeyPairGenerator Class

The `java.security.KeyPairGenerator` is like the `KeyFactory` class in the manner in which it is created, via the call to `KeyPairGenerator.getInstance()`, and in how calls to `getInstance()` are resolved by the JCA framework in terms of the precedence rules and which provider is chosen if one is not specified.

The class itself is very simple to use. There are four `initialize()` methods, two that take an integer key size — one with a user-specified source of randomness — and two `initialize()` methods that take `AlgorithmParameterSpec` objects instead. You will see as you go further that the `AlgorithmParameterSpec` versions are the most powerful, as often with asymmetric algorithms the key size is only one of several parameters that can be specified and often not the only one you want to control.

Finally, there are the actual methods that return the key pair that the class generates: `KeyPairGenerator.generateKeyPair()` and `KeyPairGenerator.genKeyPair()`. These methods are functionally equivalent; which one you use really depends on whether you prefer `gen` to `generate`.

As it turns out, there is an `AlgorithmParameterSpec` class specific to RSA, the `RSAKeyGenParameterSpec` class. It is also one of the simplest you will run into, so take a look at it next.

The RSAKeyGenParameterSpec Class

As mentioned earlier, when generating RSA key pairs, you normally try to choose a value for the public exponent and allow the private exponent to be derived from that accordingly. The JCA allows you to specify both the key size you want and the public exponent for RSA key pairs generated by `KeyPairGenerator` object by using the `KeyPairGenerator.initialize()` method that takes an `AlgorithmParameterSpec` object as a parameter. The class you use for this is `java.security.spec.RSAKeyGenParameterSpec`, which appeared in JDK 1.3. It is very simple to use, just taking a key size and a public exponent in its constructor.

For example, if you wanted to specify one of the standard public exponents such as the value F4, recommended in X.509, and the default for the Bouncy Castle provider, you could change the call to the `initialize()` method on the `generator` object to the following:

```
generator.initialize(
            new RSAKeyGenParameterSpec(256, RSAKeyGenParameterSpec.F4), random);
```

All RSA public keys generated by the `generator` object would have the public exponent set to the value represented by F4 — the integer 0x10001.

Improving RSA Performance

A cursory examination of the first RSA example shows that the private exponent of the private key is considerably larger than the public exponent. This is the reason why use of an RSA private key is so much slower than the use of the public key. The reasons for the difference make sense; it means that encrypting data is quick, which can be very useful if you are using a client with limited CPU power, and also, as you will see later, that digital signature verification is quick as well.

Can you speed up use of the private key? As it turns out, you can. It requires knowledge of the primes used to create the modulus, which you should be keeping to yourself, but because you should be keeping the details of the private exponent secret anyway, adding a few more things to keep with the same secret is not such a big issue. The reason that knowledge of the primes is so important is that knowing them means you can take advantage of the Chinese Remainder Theorem.

Chinese Remainder Theorem

Discovered by a first century Chinese mathematician Sun Tse, the Chinese Remainder Theorem, briefly, says the following:

"Given a number n that has a prime factorization of $p1*p2* \ldots *pi$, the system of simultaneous congruencies of the form:

$$(x \bmod p_j) \equiv a_j, j = 1,2,\ldots,i$$

has a unique solution modulo n."

Or put another way, a number less than n can be uniquely identified by the results of taking the number mod each of the primes making up n.

I am not going to go into the mathematics of this in more detail, as it is covered in other publications, but the important point is that the theorem means that you can perform the calculations involving the private exponent using a different formula to that used for the public exponent. Because the calculation involves using much smaller big integers than the modulus, the calculation will be substantially faster.

In Chapter 4, I mention that using Chinese Remainder Theorem (CRT) involves keeping the prime factors of the modulus (referred to in the theorem as n). It turns out that in the implementation of CRT, there are several other values that you can precompute and keep that will further improve the speed of the calculation. For this reason, you will see that the `RSAPrivateCrtKey` and `RSAPrivateCrtKeySpec` classes have methods for extracting eight values rather than two.

RSAPrivateCrtKeySpec and RSAPrivateCrtKey

`java.security.spec.RSAPrivateCrtKeySpec` is a value object that provides the key material for a RSA private key that can take advantage of CRT.

In exactly the same manner as for an `RSAPrivateKeySpec`, you can pass an `RSAPrivateCrtKeySpec` to a `KeyFactory` object that was created for RSA, and you should get back a key that implements `java.security.interfaces.RSAPrivateCrtKey`, which extends `RSAPrivateKey`. If you get back a key that implements only `RSAPrivateKey` after passing in an `RSAPrivateCrtKeySpec`, it probably indicates that the underlying provider does not implement CRT. If private key operations with RSA seem very slow, this may well be the reason.

`RSAPrivateCrtKeySpec` and `RSAPrivateCrtKey` have the same method signatures. The methods available on both allow you to retrieve the values making up the CRT key. They are as follows:

❑ `getModulus()` returns the value of the modulus n.

❑ `getPrivateExponent()` returns the value of the private exponent d.

❑ `getPrimeP()` returns the value of the prime p.

❑ `getPrimeQ()` returns the value of the prime q.

Finally, the `getPrimeExponentP()`, `getPrimeExponentQ()`, and `getCrtcoefficient()` methods all return values based on *p* and *q*, which are precomputed in order to further speed up use of the RSA private key.

In the case of the Bouncy Castle provider, `RSAPrivateCrtKey` objects are returned by the underlying `KeyPairGenerator` implementation, but if you want to get some idea of how expensive private key operations are without CRT, you can always roll your own `RSAPrivateKeySpec` by taking the equivalent values it requires from an `RSAPrivateCrtKey`.

Multi Prime Chinese Remainder Theorem

If you recall the initial discussion about CRT, it relies on having access to the primes used to generate the modulus. The interesting thing about it is that the theorem does not say there has to be two primes for generating a modulus, nor does RSA. You could have four primes instead; so, for example, if you were using a 2,048-bit key, rather than having two primes of 1,024 bit involved in the generation of the key and the subsequent use of the private key, you could have four primes of 512 bits involved in the generation of the key and the calculations involving the private key. Issues about the changes in the difficulty of factoring that the presence of more than two primes in the generation of the modulus makes notwithstanding, private key operations in the four prime case will be substantially faster than the corresponding operations in the two prime case.

The interface `java.security.interfaces.RSAMultiPrimePrivateCrtKey` and the classes `java.security.spec.RSAMultiPrimePrivateCrtKeySpec` and `java.security.spec .RSAOtherPrimeInfo` are provided to support this method of calculation. I will not discuss it in more detail here, as currently there is no implementation of it in the Bouncy Castle provider, and the method is subject to patents as well. However, if you would like to know more about it, have a look at the JavaDoc and the associated standard RSA Security's PKCS #1. You will find that it follows quite naturally from what I discussed initially about CRT.

At this point, you have more or less covered the mechanics of the RSA algorithm itself. Now you can look at the mechanisms that are ultimately used to convert the bytes you want to encrypt into a big integer that can be used in the algorithm.

RSA Padding Mechanisms

The big difference between RSA and a regular symmetric cipher can be demonstrated by replacing the line:

```
byte[]              input = new byte[] { (byte)0xbe, (byte)0xef };
```

with the line:

```
byte[]              input = new byte[] { 0x00, (byte)0xbe, (byte)0xef };
```

Doing this produces the following output instead:

```
input : 00beef
cipher: 09d9c77b2e43a0b6c0b1114523dd4458a7b68b0eee381da2c22895e7a4f44c96
plain : beef
```

There are two things you probably noticed here. The most glaring is that the plaintext is not the same as the ciphertext — the leading zero has disappeared. The second is that the ciphertext with the new input is the same as the ciphertext with the old input. Although this might explain why the plaintext generated does not have the leading zero, you still might be left wondering what happened between providing the input data and the encryption process that stripped it off. Does this mean that RSA, or at least the implementation, is broken?

Fortunately, both the RSA algorithm and the implementation are fine. Think back to the explanation of how the algorithm works at the start of this section and you will realize that the byte array provided as input is converted into a big integer so that the algorithm can be applied. It is this process of conversion to a big integer where the leading zeros are dropped — in the world of numbers, leading zeros are not meaningful.

Of course, in this case, leading zeros are meaningful, so including extra padding that allows you to preserve them makes sense. Padding does not just serve the purpose of allowing you to maintain leading zeros. Try changing the example now so that the public exponent is F0 (the value 0x3) rather than F4 (the value 0x100001). You can do this by importing `java.security.spec.RSAKeyGenParameterSpec` and changing the call to `generator.initialize()` as follows:

```
generator.initialize(
        new RSAKeyGenParameterSpec(256, RSAKeyGenParameterSpec.F0), random);
```

Making this change and running the example again should produce something like this:

```
input : 00beef
cipher: 00.00000000000000000000000000000000000000000000000006a35ddd3c9cf
plain : beef
```

It is one thing to lose the leading zero, but something worse has happened here. The data you have encrypted can now be recovered by simply taking the cube root of the ciphertext. The reason is that the input data, when converted to a big integer and raised to the power of the public exponent, is actually less than the modulus. So rather than further complicating the life of someone trying to recover the original message, doing the mod step in the calculation has returned the original number raised to a power. As you can see, padding the message so that it becomes a big integer closer in size to the modulus before it is raised to the public exponent serves more than just the purpose of protecting leading zeros.

I already mentioned PKCS #1 in the context of detailing methods of using Chinese Remainder Theorem. As it turns out, PKCS #1 also details padding mechanisms for use with the RSA algorithm. Originally, it only specified one mechanism, which is the reason for the naming convention you are about to see. However, it has since been revised and now specifies some other padding mechanism as well. The convention in Java is to refer to the original padding mechanism that was specified in PKCS #1 version 1.5 as `PKCS1Padding`. The extra padding mechanisms created since then are referred to by the names given in PKCS #1 instead. Let's consider the original mechanism first.

PKCS #1 V1.5 Padding

PKCS #1 originally just described a mechanism with three types of padding modes for a block to be encrypted. The first, type 0, is to use nothing but zeros, equivalent to `NoPadding` in the JCE. The second, type 1, is used when the RSA algorithm is applied to the data to be encrypted using the public key. The third, type 2, is used when the algorithm is being applied to the data using the private key. These second and third techniques are referred to as PKCS1Padding in the JCE.

Type 1 PKCS #1 padding is quite simple to apply. Given a message M the padded message M_p will be

$$M_p = \text{0x00} \parallel \text{0x01} \parallel F \parallel \text{0x00} \parallel M$$

where F is a string of bytes of the value 0xFF. The $\parallel$ is a concatenation operator. There are some restrictions on how big M can be. F must be at least at least 8 bytes long, so M can be no longer than the length of the key in bytes less 11.

Type 2 PKCS #1 padding is also quite simple. Given a message M the padded message M_p will be

$$M_p = \text{0x00} \parallel \text{0x02} \parallel R \parallel \text{0x00} \parallel M$$

where R is a string of pseudorandom bytes, which must again be at least 8 bytes long.

The interesting difference between these two mechanisms is that while both will produce big integers that are within a byte or so of the size of the key being used, type 1 guarantees that the same value of M encrypted with the same key will always produce the same ciphertext. Type 2, on the other hand, guarantees the opposite. It is highly unlikely a type 2 padded message will ever encrypt to the same ciphertext. For this reason, type 1, as you will see later, is used with signatures, which are created by processing using the private key. Imagine that the same document signed with the same key might produce the same signature. Type 2, on the other hand, is what the `Cipher` object uses when it is created using the padding mode `"PKCS1Padding"`, and a public key is used for the encryption step.

Try It Out   PKCS #1 V1.5 Padding

Try the following example. Note that the data now has a leading zero on it and `PKCS1Padding` has been specified. Because it uses the public key to encrypt with, the padding is type 2 and would normally uses random data. I have therefore passed in a fixed random generator in order to reliably reproduce the output.

```java
package chapter4;

import java.security.Key;
import java.security.KeyPair;
import java.security.KeyPairGenerator;
import java.security.SecureRandom;

import javax.crypto.Cipher;

/**
 * RSA example with PKCS #1 Padding.
 */
public class PKCS1PaddedRSAExample
{
    public static void main(String[] args) throws Exception
    {
        byte[]              input = new byte[] { 0x00, (byte)0xbe, (byte)0xef };
        Cipher              cipher = Cipher.getInstance("RSA/None/PKCS1Padding","BC");
```

```
SecureRandom      random = Utils.createFixedRandom();

// create the keys
KeyPairGenerator generator = KeyPairGenerator.getInstance("RSA", "BC");

generator.initialize(256, random);

KeyPair          pair = generator.generateKeyPair();
Key              pubKey = pair.getPublic();
Key              privKey = pair.getPrivate();

System.out.println("input : " + Utils.toHex(input));

// encryption step

cipher.init(Cipher.ENCRYPT_MODE, pubKey, random);

byte[] cipherText = cipher.doFinal(input);

System.out.println("cipher: " + Utils.toHex(cipherText));

// decryption step

cipher.init(Cipher.DECRYPT_MODE, privKey);

byte[] plainText = cipher.doFinal(cipherText);

System.out.println("plain : " + Utils.toHex(plainText));
    }
}
```

You should see the following output demonstrating that the padding has allowed the leading zero to be maintained:

```
input : 00beef
cipher: 01fce4a90b326bb1c3ebc2f969a84024d157499038f73ee03635c4e6ffb3377e
plain : 00beef
```

Try the modification given earlier to change the public exponent to the value F0. You will see that the padding is not just helping preserve the original plaintext but helping protect it as well.

How It Works

The difference, of course, is that the leading zero is preserved because the original message has first had the padding added, and then the result string of octets is converted into a big integer. Before, with no padding, just the message was converted into a big integer.

The other effect of this is that now you are dealing with a big integer that is much closer to the size of the modulus. Therefore, even when you are using a small public exponent like the value F0, or 3, the mod arithmetic is able to make its presence felt and make the RSA process meaningful.

OAEP Padding

Optimal Asymmetric Encryption Padding, or OAEP, is the latest method of padding specified in PKCS #1. It was originally outlined by Mihir Bellare and Phillip Rogaway in 1994 and has since been adopted as a method in PKCS #1 under the full name RSAES-OAEP. OAEP has the advantage that it is provably secure in the random oracle model, or put another way, that if the hash functions OAEP is based on are ideal, the only way to break an OAEP-encoded encrypted RSA message is to break RSA itself. Before you continue with what OAEP actually looks like on the wire, it's worth having a look at exactly what this last statement means.

In this context, an oracle is essentially a black box that you can prod for information. It might be something that decrypts the older PKCS #1 formatted messages, for example. Say you want to know what a particular message decrypts to and you can get the oracle to return the result of decrypting a message. It is possible, as outlined in the "Million Message Attack" discussed in RFC 3218 and originally detailed in Daniel Bleichenbacher's paper "Chosen Ciphertext Attacks Against Protocols Based on the RSA Encryption Standard PKCS #1," to generate a number of transforms of the ciphertext you are trying to decrypt and then use the information you get back from the oracle when you try to get it to decrypt the transformed messages to slowly recover the plaintext of the ciphertext.

You can do this because there are some things in the structure of a PKCS #1 type 2 message that you can predict. An OAEP message, on the other hand, will always come back not only looking completely random, but while a correctly decrypted one will have internal consistency, OAEP makes use of a masking function based on a cryptographic hash. This means that you cannot actually check the message for consistency until you have XORed it with a stream of bytes generated by a function whose output you cannot predict, because you are not sure you have the right input. In a similar way to the use of the hash function in key agreement, the combined effect of the hash and masking function here is to deprive an attacker of the capability to take advantage of the mathematical properties of the underlying algorithm. The oracle, or black box, available to you will, at best, be sending back "random" noise.

> You can find more information on the random oracle model in Bellare and Rogaway's paper "Random Oracles Are Practical: A Paradigm for Designing Efficient Protocols." While there is still some controversy about how good a method of proving security the random oracle approach is, it would be fair to say it is an improvement.

Having gone through all that, although it is recommended that new applications use OAEP wherever possible, the message here is not necessarily the case that traditional PKCS #1 padding is insecure. The real message is you should always try to avoid giving anything intelligible away when rejecting a message: Take as long to handle a rejection as an acceptance and give out only the minimal amount of information—none if you can get away with it. Avoid leaks!

So how does OAEP actually work? As I have already alluded to, it involves a cryptographic hash function, H(), and a mask function, Mask(), based on the hash function. Broadly speaking, it breaks down into the following three steps, given a message M, a parameter string P, and a random seed S:

1. $M_1 = \text{Mask}((H(P) \,||\, PS \,||\, 0x01 \,||\, M), S)$

2. $M_2 = \text{Mask}(S, M_1)$

3. $M_p = 0x00 \,||\, M_2 \,||\, M_1$

where PS is a pad string of zeros, $||$ is concatenation, and M_p is the resulting masked and padded message. The mask function operates by using its second argument as a seed to a pseudorandom octet generator, which is then used to mask the octets making up the first one. I will not discuss the mask function here in detail, as it is detailed in PKCS #1, other than to mention the name of it—MGF1. You will see that MGF1 is used in a number of other places later. The parameter string P is defined by default as the empty string, so, as you will see in the example that follows, normally there is no need to specify it.

A cursory glance at the equations shows that the masked and padded message M_p is a concatenation of two masked messages, one hiding the seed for masking the message you are trying to protect, and the other masking the padded message itself. It also reveals that using this padding mechanism has a substantial overhead, as you need space for the seed as well as space for the hash of the parameter string P. As the seed is the same size as the hash, if $hLen$ is the length of the hash in octets and $kLen$ is the size of the key in octets, this gives the maximum size for the messages you can encrypt as:

$MaxLen = kLen - 2hLen - 2$

Unlike in traditional PKCS #1 padding, the pad string PS can be of zero length.

Try It Out   OAEP Padding

Compare the following example to the PKCS1PaddedRSAExample class you looked at earlier. You will note that, even though the message being encrypted is the same size as before, the key size has had to expand from 256 to 384 bits in order to provide the minimum required space for the padding to fit.

```
package chapter4;

import java.security.Key;
import java.security.KeyPair;
import java.security.KeyPairGenerator;
import java.security.SecureRandom;

import javax.crypto.Cipher;

/**
 * RSA example with OAEP Padding and random key generation.
 */
public class OAEPPaddedRSAExample
{
    public static void main(
        String[]     args)
        throws Exception
    {
        byte[]          input = new byte[] { 0x00, (byte)0xbe, (byte)0xef };
        Cipher          cipher = Cipher.getInstance(
                                "RSA/None/OAEPWithSHA1AndMGF1Padding", "BC");
        SecureRandom    random = Utils.createFixedRandom();

        // create the keys
        KeyPairGenerator generator = KeyPairGenerator.getInstance("RSA", "BC");

        generator.initialize(386, random);

        KeyPair         pair = generator.generateKeyPair();
        Key             pubKey = pair.getPublic();
```

```
Key                privKey = pair.getPrivate();

System.out.println("input : " + Utils.toHex(input));

// encryption step

cipher.init(Cipher.ENCRYPT_MODE, pubKey, random);

byte[] cipherText = cipher.doFinal(input);

System.out.println("cipher: " + Utils.toHex(cipherText));

// decryption step

cipher.init(Cipher.DECRYPT_MODE, privKey);

byte[] plainText = cipher.doFinal(cipherText);

System.out.println("plain : " + Utils.toHex(plainText));
    }
}
```

In this case, running the example should produce the following output with the expanded ciphertext:

```
input : 00beef
cipher: 020692d99b7b73e8284134590f1f04dbdbdfeee627d3da72a18acf244e41da4a012a834c
1c890213a8508f5406816ef74b
plain : 00beef
```

Of course, 384 bits is well below an acceptable key size, so in practice the extra overhead OAEP requires is not generally an issue. The main thing to remember is that it does not give you as much room in an RSA block as the older PKCS #1 padding mechanism specified in PKCS #1 V1.5.

How It Works

Of course, the trick here is that you have simply included a different padding string in the cipher name passed to `Cipher.getInstance()`. The JCE then does the rest for you.

One thing to note about what is happening under the covers: Look at the format given for the name of the cipher's padding string, it really reads "OAEPWithDigestAndMaskFunctionPadding". This naming convention is outlined in "Java Cryptography Architecture API Specification and Reference," which is provided in the standard Java documentation hierarchy and allows for the specification of a range of digests and masking functions. So, for example, to do OAEP-encoded based on SHA-256 with its default parameters, the padding string you would use would be "OAEPwithSHA256andMGF1Padding"; likewise for any other digest algorithm or mask function that might be supported by the provider you are using.

The previous example should work in any JCE with the BC provider installed. However, if you are using JDK 1.5 or later, a number of classes were added to the JCE to better support OAEP, and as it is now the padding mode of choice, you can expect to make use of them.

The PSource Class

The `javax.crypto.PSource` class is used to specify a source for the *P* parameter that appears in the equations above for creating the padded string. Currently there is only one type of parameter that can be supported and this is provided by a public extension of `PSource`, `PSource.PSpecified`. This parameter takes a byte array for its constructor; by default, this is of zero length, so defining a default `PSource` equivalent to the object `PSource.PSpecified.DEFAULT` for use with an OAEP padding parameter specification would look like:

```
PSource defaultPSource = new PSource.PSpecfied(new byte[]);
```

Ordinarily you would not change this; however, if you wanted to explicitly label every OAEP-encoded message encrypted with a given key from a given server with a message number you might use instead

```
PSource labeledPSource = new PSource.PSpecified(msgNumber);
```

where `msgNumber` is a byte array representing the message number of the encrypted block been sent. Any message decrypted without the correct *P* parameter set will be rejected.

In terms of `get` methods, `PSource` has only one method on it, `PSource.getAlgorithm()`, which returns the algorithm name. The extension class `PSource.PSpecified` adds one more method, `PSource.PSpecified.getValue()`, which simply returns the byte array that it was constructed with. For the most part, the `get` methods associated with `PSource` and `PSource.PSpecified` are only used by the underlying JCE provider you are using.

The MGF1ParameterSpec Class

The `java.security.spec.MGF1ParameterSpec` class is used to represent the standard mask generation function MGF1. It also takes only one parameter for its constructor — the name of the message digest function used to drive the masking function.

For example, the default digest for MGF1 is SHA-1, so a default definition for the `MGF1ParameterSpec` in regular OAEP looks like:

```
MGF1ParameterSpec defaultMGF1 = new MGF1ParameterSpec("SHA-1");
```

The class also has a number of default value objects: `MGF1ParameterSpec.SHA1`, `MGFParameterSpec.SHA256`, `MGFParameterSpec.SHA384`, and `MGFParameterSpec.SHA512`, which allow you to define versions of MGF1 for SHA-1, SHA-256, SHA-384, and SHA-512.

The `MGFParameterSpec` method has a single `get` method, `MGFParameterSpec.getDigestAlgorithm()`, which returns the name of the digest algorithm the MGF1 function is based on.

The OAEPParameterSpec Class

Putting it all together, you have `java.security.spec.OAEPParameterSpec`. Like the `PSource.PSpecified` class, it also has a default value that can be used: `OAEPParameterSpec.DEFAULT`. Defining the default value for the `OAEPParameterSpec` long hand, you would end up with the following definition:

```
OAEPParameterSpec  defaultOAEPSpec = new OAEPParameterSpec(
        "SHA-1", "MGF1", MGF1ParameterSpec.SHA1, PSource.PSpecified.DEFAULT);
```

As you can see, the construction of the OAEPParameterSpec object follows from the original equations describing the padding mechanism. The first argument is the hash function H, the second argument is the name of the mask function Mask, and then the parameters of the mask function are given, in the default case, a parameter specification object for the MGF1 function based on SHA-1. Finally the parameter string P is given, in this case an empty byte array.

Ordinarily, you will use this object so you can set the parameter string P. When you are using it, the only rule you need to be aware of with constructing an OAEPParameterSpec is that it is recommended in PKCS #1 that the same hash algorithm is used for both the function H and the mask generation function. So, for example, if you wanted to use SHA-256 for H, you should have a definition that looks something like this:

```
OAEPParameterSpec  sha256OAEPSpec = new OAEPParameterSpec(
        "SHA-256", "MGF1", MGF1ParameterSpec.SHA256, PSource.PSpecified.DEFAULT);
```

although you might want to have a different value passed for the parameter string P. Currently, MGF1 is the only mask generation function supported. Follow PKCS #1 and IEEE P1361 if you are interested in further developments in this area.

The OAEPParameterSpec class has get methods on it that allow you to retrieve the values it was constructed with, as with PSource, and MGF1ParameterSpec the get() methods are really of most relevance inside the provider you are using.

Which brings me to the last point. Having created an OAEPParameterSpec, how do you use it? As you would expect, it is just passed to Cipher.init(), so using the sha256OAEPSpec as an example you could write

```
Cipher c = Cipher.getInstance("RSA/None/OAEPWithSHA256AndMGF1Padding");

c.init(Cipher.ENCRYPT_MODE, publicKey,
                        sha256OAEPParameterSpec, new SecureRandom());
```

Wrapping RSA Keys

You saw in Chapter 2 that it was possible to use symmetric keys to wrap other symmetric keys. You can achieve the same effect for wrapping asymmetric keys using exactly the same API.

Try It Out   Wrapping an RSA Private Key

Look at the following example. Note that, unlike the example in Chapter 2, you are now using Cipher.PRIVATE_KEY to tell the wrapping cipher what kind of key you are expecting. If you had wrapped a public key (strange I will admit), you would need to pass Cipher.PUBLIC_KEY.

```
package chapter4;

import java.security.Key;
import java.security.KeyPair;
```

```java
import java.security.KeyPairGenerator;
import java.security.SecureRandom;

import javax.crypto.Cipher;

public class AESWrapRSAExample
{
    public static void main(String[] args) throws Exception
    {
        Cipher        cipher = Cipher.getInstance("AES/ECB/PKCS7Padding", "BC");
        SecureRandom random = new SecureRandom();

        KeyPairGenerator fact = KeyPairGenerator.getInstance("RSA", "BC");
        fact.initialize(1024, random);

        KeyPair       keyPair = fact.generateKeyPair();
        Key           wrapKey = Utils.createKeyForAES(256, random);

        // wrap the RSA private key
        cipher.init(Cipher.WRAP_MODE, wrapKey);

        byte[] wrappedKey = cipher.wrap(keyPair.getPrivate());

        // unwrap the RSA private key
        cipher.init(Cipher.UNWRAP_MODE, wrapKey);

        Key key = cipher.unwrap(wrappedKey, "RSA", Cipher.PRIVATE_KEY);

        if (keyPair.getPrivate().equals(key))
        {
            System.out.println("Key recovered.");
        }
        else
        {
            System.out.println("Key recovery failed.");
        }
    }
}
```

Try running the example and you should be rewarded with the message Key recovered.

How It Works

Just as with the example in Chapter 2, internally the Cipher object doing the wrapping calls the Key.getEncoded() method on the PrivateKey object passed in to the Cipher.wrap() method. This produces an encrypted byte stream containing the wrapped key. Likewise, unwrapping the key is a matter of passing the encrypted bytes to the Cipher.unwrap() method. A feature of using wrapping is that if the provider being used is based on a hardware adapter that will not expose the contents of private keys in the clear, the internal equivalent of the getEncoded() method and the accompanying encryption can be carried out in the confines of the hardware adapter.

It is interesting to note that you do not need to use a specific wrapping mechanism here. Unlike the situation with symmetric keys where the getEncoded() method returns just the bytes making up the key, in the case of an asymmetric key, there is quite a lot of structural information in the encoding of the key in addition to the key material. If you attempt to use unwrap() on an asymmetric key with the wrong secret key, it will fail quite badly, as the unwrapping mechanism will not be able to put the key back together.

Secret Key Exchange

As you have seen, using RSA limits the size of the message you can encrypt to what fits within a single block. Often this space will be further restricted because you also have to make use of padding. The question then remains: How do you make use of this technology to safely encrypt larger amounts of data? You could try breaking the data into chunks, but depending on the number of chunks required, this might be very slow. In some cases, if an attacker has some knowledge of the data you are trying to encrypt, breaking it into chunks might further compromise the private key of the person you are encrypting the data for.

The answer, as it turns out, is quite simple.

Try It Out   **Secret Key Exchange**

Try the following example program:

```
package chapter4;

import java.io.ByteArrayOutputStream;
import java.io.IOException;
import java.security.Key;
import java.security.KeyPair;
import java.security.KeyPairGenerator;
import java.security.SecureRandom;

import javax.crypto.Cipher;
import javax.crypto.spec.IvParameterSpec;
import javax.crypto.spec.SecretKeySpec;

/**
 * RSA example with OAEP Padding and random key generation.
 */
public class RSAKeyExchangeExample
{
    private static byte[] packKeyAndIv(
        Key             key,
        IvParameterSpec ivSpec)
        throws IOException
    {
        ByteArrayOutputStream   bOut = new ByteArrayOutputStream();

        bOut.write(ivSpec.getIV());
        bOut.write(key.getEncoded());

        return bOut.toByteArray();
    }
```

```java
    private static Object[] unpackKeyAndIV(
        byte[]    data)
{
    byte[]    keyD = new byte[16];
    byte[]     iv = new byte[data.length - 16];

    return new Object[] {
        new SecretKeySpec(data, 16, data.length - 16, "AES"),
        new IvParameterSpec(data, 0, 16)
    };
}

public static void main(String[] args) throws Exception
{
    byte[]            input = new byte[] { 0x00, (byte)0xbe, (byte)0xef };
    SecureRandom      random = Utils.createFixedRandom();

    // create the RSA Key
    KeyPairGenerator generator = KeyPairGenerator.getInstance("RSA", "BC");

    generator.initialize(1024, random);

    KeyPair           pair = generator.generateKeyPair();
    Key               pubKey = pair.getPublic();
    Key               privKey = pair.getPrivate();

    System.out.println("input              : " + Utils.toHex(input));

    // create the symmetric key and iv
    Key             sKey = Utils.createKeyForAES(256, random);
    IvParameterSpec sIvSpec = Utils.createCtrIvForAES(0, random);

    // symmetric key/iv wrapping step
    Cipher            xCipher = Cipher.getInstance(
                                "RSA/NONE/OAEPWithSHA1AndMGF1Padding", "BC");

    xCipher.init(Cipher.ENCRYPT_MODE, pubKey, random);

    byte[]            keyBlock = xCipher.doFinal(packKeyAndIv(sKey, sIvSpec));

    // encryption step
    Cipher            sCipher = Cipher.getInstance("AES/CTR/NoPadding", "BC");

    sCipher.init(Cipher.ENCRYPT_MODE, sKey, sIvSpec);

    byte[] cipherText = sCipher.doFinal(input);

    System.out.println("keyBlock length  : " + keyBlock.length);
    System.out.println("cipherText length: " + cipherText.length);

    // symmetric key/iv unwrapping step
    xCipher.init(Cipher.DECRYPT_MODE, privKey);
```

```
          Object[] keyIv = unpackKeyAndIV(xCipher.doFinal(keyBlock));

          // decryption step
          sCipher.init(Cipher.DECRYPT_MODE, (Key)keyIv[0],
                                            (IvParameterSpec)keyIv[1]);

          byte[] plainText = sCipher.doFinal(cipherText);

          System.out.println("plain                : " + Utils.toHex(plainText));     }
}
```

Running the example, you should get the following output:input   : 00beef
keyBlock length : 128
cipherText length: 3
plain   : 00beef

As you can see, the technique is not without overhead; on the other hand, it does remove most limits on how much data you can actually send and gives you the full advantage of the greater speed that you can get from the use of symmetric key algorithms.

How It Works

The trick, of course, is in the wrapping of the key of the symmetric cipher using xCipher and encrypting the data using the symmetric key using sCipher. If you look at Figure 4-1, you can see that you send both the encrypted data and the encrypted key to the receiver, who then recovers the symmetric key using a private key and then recovers the data by decrypting it using the secret key.

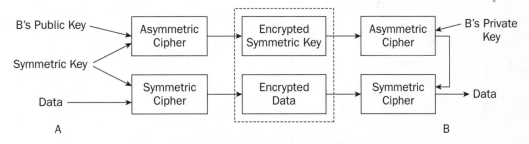

A Sends B Encrypted Data Using Key Exchange

Figure 4-1

You can use RSA as you have above, or as you will see, El Gamal, to provide this sort of encryption. The overall process has a good feel to it. The asymmetric algorithm is used for what it is best at, and the symmetric algorithm is used for what it is best at—everything in the right place.

Note that there is one element missing from the example. We have not done anything about providing a means of verifying the integrity of the data that was encrypted. Remember, it is important to include a MAC, a digest, or some other verifying information so that the decrypted data can be verified.

Key Agreement

Key agreement algorithms do not make it possible to encrypt messages in the same way as one can with an algorithm such as RSA. What they do offer is a means for two, or in some cases, more parties to agree on a common secret key with which they can then encrypt messages that they want to pass between each other.

The Diffie-Hellman Algorithm

The Diffie-Hellman algorithm takes it name from Whitfield Diffie and Martin Hellman, who invented the algorithm in 1976. GCHQ in Britain has also declassified documents showing that the algorithm dates back to 1974, when it was developed by Malcolm Williamson. Like RSA, the algorithm uses modulus arithmetic. Unlike RSA, the algorithms security relies on the difficulty of solving the discrete logarithm problem and the Diffie-Hellman Problem. The two problems are related and essentially boil down to the difficulty of finding a number x for a given y such that $G^x = y$, where G is a generator for numbers in the group covered by P, a large prime number. It turns out that this is difficult enough, at least at the moment, to be regarded as intractable.

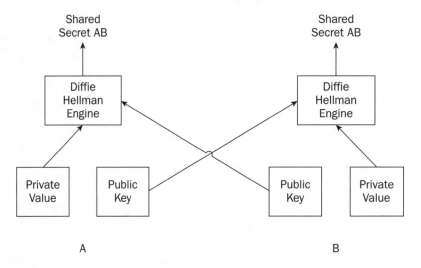

Diffie-Hellman Between Two Parties

Figure 4-2

Although the process cannot be used for regular encryption, it does allow two parties to arrive at the same secret key through a series of calculations. If you compare Figure 4-2 to Figure 4-1, you can see the process is quite different. The algorithm is quite simple: Given a large prime number P, a generator G for the group over P, party A chooses a private number U and party B chooses a private number V. Then:

1. A sends B G^U mod P (A's public key).
2. B sends A G^V mod P (B's public key).
3. Communication is then carried out using a session key based on G^{UV} mod P.

One more piece of notation you need to be familiar with: The private value associated with a given party is normally referred to as X, and the public value, $G^X \bmod P$, is normally referred to as Y.

The algorithm does not seem too complicated; fortunately, the code is not complicated either.

Try It Out   **Diffie-Hellman Key Agreement**

Try the following example:

```java
package chapter4;

import java.math.BigInteger;
import java.security.KeyPair;
import java.security.KeyPairGenerator;
import java.security.MessageDigest;

import javax.crypto.KeyAgreement;
import javax.crypto.spec.DHParameterSpec;

public class BasicDHExample
{
    private static BigInteger g512 = new BigInteger(
            "153d5d6172adb43045b68ae8e1de1070b6137005686d29d3d73a7"
          + "749199681ee5b212c9b96bfdcfa5b20cd5e3fd2044895d609cf9b"
          + "410b7a0f12ca1cb9a428cc", 16);
    private static BigInteger p512 = new BigInteger(
            "9494fec095f3b85ee286542b3836fc81a5dd0a0349b4c239dd387"
          + "44d488cf8e31db8bcb7d33b41abb9e5a33cca9144b1cef332c94b"
          + "f0573bf047a3aca98cdf3b", 16);

    public static void main(String[] args) throws Exception
    {
        DHParameterSpec  dhParams = new DHParameterSpec(p512, g512);
        KeyPairGenerator keyGen = KeyPairGenerator.getInstance("DH", "BC");

        keyGen.initialize(dhParams, Utils.createFixedRandom());

        // set up
        KeyAgreement aKeyAgree = KeyAgreement.getInstance("DH", "BC");
        KeyPair      aPair = keyGen.generateKeyPair();
        KeyAgreement bKeyAgree = KeyAgreement.getInstance("DH", "BC");
        KeyPair      bPair = keyGen.generateKeyPair();

        // two party agreement
        aKeyAgree.init(aPair.getPrivate());
        bKeyAgree.init(bPair.getPrivate());

        aKeyAgree.doPhase(bPair.getPublic(), true);
        bKeyAgree.doPhase(aPair.getPublic(), true);

        //      generate the key bytes
        MessageDigest    hash = MessageDigest.getInstance("SHA1", "BC");
        byte[] aShared = hash.digest(aKeyAgree.generateSecret());
        byte[] bShared = hash.digest(bKeyAgree.generateSecret());
```

```
            System.out.println(Utils.toHex(aShared));
            System.out.println(Utils.toHex(bShared));
    }
}
```

Running the program shows you that you get the following shared secret on each side:

```
98f2669e0458195dece063e99f0b355598eb096b
98f2669e0458195dece063e99f0b355598eb096b
```

As far as generation of key pairs go, the program looks like any other. A slightly deeper look reveals that there are a number of consequences from the use of Diffie-Hellman and key agreement in general.

The first consequence, as you can see from the fact that the fixed random allows you to fix the value of the final shared secret, is that if you reuse the keys used in a key agreement, you will get the same shared secret as a result. The same shared secret means the same shared symmetric key. This gives rise to the following maxim about the keys used by the KeyAgreement class and their lifetime:

> **Keys used for key agreement should have a lifetime no longer than the lifetime you give the symmetric key they are used to generate. Keys used by the KeyAgreement class should be temporary in nature.**

The second consequence, perhaps not as obvious, is that if you imagine a situation where the agreement was not taking place in the safety of a single file, you could instead imagine the agreement was being done in a situation where attackers might be able to introduce a phase or two of their own — the so-called man-in-the-middle attack, shown in Figure 4-3. There is nothing in the previous code that tells you how to verify the origins of the key the other party has sent you.

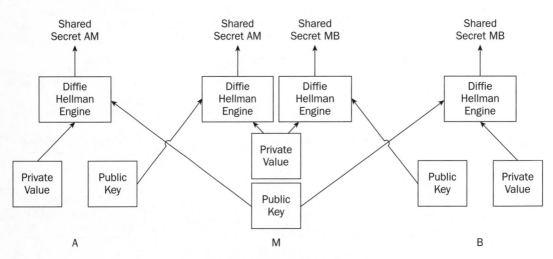

If A and B are not sure they are getting the right
Public Keys, M is able to become a
"Man in the Middle"

Figure 4-3

> If you use `KeyAgreement`, it is important to use it in conjunction with an authentication mechanism in order to prevent a man-in-the-middle attack.

As mentioned earlier, the setup for the program looks very similar to that used for RSA. However, other than the use of the string DH in the selection of the key pair generator, there are some other classes provided by the JCE for supporting Diffie-Hellman. You will look at those classes in the next sections.

The DHParameterSpec Class

The `javax.crypto.spec.DHParameterSpec` class is a value object that contains the two, or three, parameters. As you can see from the example, the standard constructor takes the values P and G, the prime and the generator for the group represented by the prime, respectively.

There is also a second constructor that you can use to speed up the key exchange process. The second constructor takes a bit length for the private value and will limit the size of the value generated. By default, the private value generated as part of the key generation process will be less than P but with 8 bits of its size. With a P value that is 1,024 bits long, this will make the calculation of the public key for the key agreement slower than it probably needs to be. Depending on the application, you might decide that a private value of no greater than 512 bits is adequate, in which case, given p1024 and g1024 being a 1,024-bit prime and its generator, you might construct a `DHParameterSpec` as follows:

```
DHParameterSpec dhSpec = new DHParameterSpec(p1024, g1024, 512);
```

`DHParameterSpec` objects can also be generated using the provider. You will see how a bit later, in the section dealing with the `AlgorithmParametersGenerator` class.

Specification Objects for Diffie-Hellman Keys

The JCE also provides objects for carrying key and parameter material for Diffie-Hellman keys in a provider-independent manner. These objects can be used to carry around material related to keys for any of the Diffie-Hellman-based algorithms. The two classes used for this purpose are `javax.crypto.spec.DHPrivateKeySpec` and `javax.crypto.spec.DHPublicKeySpec`.

`DHPrivateKeySpec` takes the private value X and the P and G values that are required to use it, as in:

```
DHPrivateKeySpec dhPrivateSpec = new DHPrivateKeySpec(x, p, g);
```

`DHPublicKeySpec` takes the public value Y and the P and G values that it was created with. As a code example simply:

```
DHPublicKeySpec dhPublicSpec = new DHPublicKeySpec(y, p, g);
```

Like other key specification classes both `DHPrivateKeySpec` and `DHPublicKeySpec` are simple value objects, so the only functionality they offer consists of `get()` methods for recovering the values they were constructed with.

Interfaces for Diffie-Hellman Keys

In the previous example, you relied on the `Key` class. If you need greater type safety, the JCE does provide `javax.crypto.interfaces.DHPrivateKey`, `javax.crypto.interfaces.DHPublicKey`, and a parent class for both of them that extends `Key`, namely, `javax.crypto.interfaces.DHKey`.

`DHKey` provides a single method, `DHKey.getParams()`, which returns the `DHParameterSpec` associated with the public and private keys.

`DHPrivateKey` also has a single method, called `DHPrivateKey.getX()`, which returns the private value that is not transmitted as part of the agreement process.

`DHPublicKey` also has a single method called `DHPublicKey.getY()`. The value returned by `getY()` is G^X mod P, where X is the value return by the corresponding private key's `getX()` method and G and P are the values of the associated `DHParameterSpec` object.

Diffie-Hellman with Elliptic Curve

The capability to perform key agreement is not just restricted to traditional Diffie-Hellman; it is also possible to use elliptic curve cryptography to perform it.

Elliptic curve cryptography is built using the properties of finite fields. As a cryptographic method it was originally proposed in 1985 by two people, quite independently: Neal Koblitz at the University of Washington and Victor Miller at IBM.

A *field* is basically a mathematical group that provides operations for addition, subtraction, multiplication, and division that always produce results in the field. I use the term *finite* when referring to the previous fields because the fields have a limited number of members. It is this property of being finite that makes it possible to do cryptography with the curves that exist over the fields. Two particular field constructions are of most interest here: F_p contains curves over the prime finite field p, and F_{2^m} is a field made up of curves that can be derived from what is referred to as an optimal normal basis representation or a polynomial representation derived from m-bit strings. F_{2^m} is an interesting space because being binary, it can be handled very efficiently by computers. It is also an area covered by a number of patents, so, at least for your purposes, you will concentrate on curves over F_p. You will see from looking at the examples that whether a curve is over F_{2^m} or F_p, from the JCE/JCA point of view, it is pretty much the same to deal with.

The method derives its security from the difficulty of the Elliptic Curve Discrete Logarithm Problem, which could be summed up as follows:

Given two points on a curve, P and Q, find a number k such that $kP = Q$.

It turns out that for a sufficiently large value of k, solving this problem is a very lengthy process. Looking at how elliptic curve derives its security also gives you some idea of how it works.

Imagine A and B agree on a curve and some fixed point G. This information does not need to be secret. In order for A and B to communicate, as with the original Diffie-Hellman, A and B choose two secret numbers x and y.

1. A sends B *xG* (A's public key).

2. B sends A *yG* (B's public key).

3. Communication is then carried out using a session key based on *xyG*, which both A and B are now able to calculate.

The next important thing is to have a well-formed curve. Fortunately, a large number of these have already been published in publications like X9.62 and FIPS PUB 186-2. The curve in the following example is one such standard.

Try It Out   Diffie-Hellman with Elliptic Curve

Have a look at the following example:

```
package chapter4;

import java.math.BigInteger;
import java.security.KeyPair;
import java.security.KeyPairGenerator;
import java.security.MessageDigest;
import java.security.spec.ECFieldFp;
import java.security.spec.ECParameterSpec;
import java.security.spec.ECPoint;
import java.security.spec.EllipticCurve;

import javax.crypto.KeyAgreement;

public class BasicECDHExample
{
    public static void main(String[] args) throws Exception
    {
        KeyPairGenerator keyGen = KeyPairGenerator.getInstance("ECDH", "BC");
        EllipticCurve    curve = new EllipticCurve(
           new ECFieldFp(new BigInteger(
                   "fffffffffffffffffffffffffffffffeffffffffffffffff", 16)),
           new BigInteger("fffffffffffffffffffffffffffffffefffffffffffffffc", 16),
           new BigInteger("64210519e59c80e70fa7e9ab72243049feb8deecc146b9b1", 16));

        ECParameterSpec  ecSpec = new ECParameterSpec(
          curve,
          new ECPoint(
            new BigInteger("188da80eb03090f67cbf20eb43a18800f4ff0afd82ff1012", 16),
            new BigInteger("f8e6d46a003725879cefee1294db32298c06885ee186b7ee", 16)),
          new BigInteger("ffffffffffffffffffffffff99def836146bc9b1b4d22831", 16),
          1);

        keyGen.initialize(ecSpec, Utils.createFixedRandom());

        // set up
        KeyAgreement aKeyAgree = KeyAgreement.getInstance("ECDH", "BC");
        KeyPair      aPair = keyGen.generateKeyPair();
        KeyAgreement bKeyAgree = KeyAgreement.getInstance("ECDH", "BC");
        KeyPair      bPair = keyGen.generateKeyPair();
```

```
                // two party agreement
                aKeyAgree.init(aPair.getPrivate());
                bKeyAgree.init(bPair.getPrivate());

                aKeyAgree.doPhase(bPair.getPublic(), true);
                bKeyAgree.doPhase(aPair.getPublic(), true);

                // generate the key bytes
                MessageDigest    hash = MessageDigest.getInstance("SHA1", "BC");
                byte[] aShared = hash.digest(aKeyAgree.generateSecret());
                byte[] bShared = hash.digest(bKeyAgree.generateSecret());

                System.out.println(Utils.toHex(aShared));
                System.out.println(Utils.toHex(bShared));
        }
    }
```

Running the example should produce the following output:

```
5ea61569aed14f67b67377dc6ca223e7ab013844
5ea61569aed14f67b67377dc6ca223e7ab013844
```

The example manages to generate the same key on both sides as expected.

How It Works

Looking at the example, you can see that other than the setup parameters of the key generator and the fact the KeyAgreement.getInstance() method is passed "ECDH" rather than "DH", it is identical to the original example using Diffie-Hellman. Very different math, but at the level the JCE abstraction layer sits at, essentially the same to use.

So what about the differences? Have a look at how the parameters are constructed; it will tell you a bit more about how the method works and how the objects used in the previous example relate to the discussion at the beginning of this section.

ECField, ECFieldFp, and ECFieldF2m

The interface java.security.interfaces.ECField is the base interface for elliptic curve finite fields. Both java.security.spec.ECFieldFp and java.security.spec.ECFieldFm implement it. ECField has a single method, ECField.getFieldSize(), which returns the size of the finite field — in the case of ECFieldFp, the bit length of the prime p, or in the case of ECFieldF2m, the bit length of m.

ECFieldFp serves as the holder for the prime number that distinguishes the field over which a curve constructed with it is operating. It has a single constructor, which takes a prime, and a single get method, ECFieldFp.getP(), which returns it.

ECFieldF2m, as its name implies, serves as the holder for the distinguishing information for the field over which any curve created with it is operating. In terms of construction, it has more variations than ECFieldFp, because it allows for $F_2{}^m$ curves to be constructed over both a normal basis and a polynomial basis. Likewise, its get methods may return null depending on what kind of basis it was constructed for. If you want to fully understand this one, you really need to read up on elliptic curves first.

Having said that, from your point of view, the important thing to remember is that, like ECFieldFp, it just serves to distinguish the field.

Having established the field over which the curve will operate, the next step is to specify the curve.

The EllipticCurve Class

As its name suggests, java.security.spec.EllipticCurve is a holding class for the values that describe an elliptic curve. As expected, it has get() methods for retrieving the objects associated with its component parts. It is the construction of the object, however, that is of more interest.

To understand how an EllipticCurve is put together, you need to be aware that the typical equation that the kind of elliptic curve you are interested in follows, with minor variations:

$$y^2 = x^3 + ax^2 + b$$

with the values x and y restricted to a particular finite field and the values a and b being constants.

Take another look at the construction of the curve used in the previous example, using the base constructor for the EllipticCurve class.

```
EllipticCurve    curve = new EllipticCurve(
    new ECFieldFp(new BigInteger(
            "fffffffffffffffffffffffffffffffffffffffffeffffffffffffffff", 16)),
    new BigInteger("fffffffffffffffffffffffffffffffffffffffffeffffffffffffffffc", 16),
    new BigInteger("64210519e59c80e70fa7e9ab72243049feb8deecc146b9b1", 16));
```

Comparing it to the requirements of the equation, you can see the first argument is the field, in this case based on the prime number represented by the BigInteger passed in to the constructor of ECFieldFp. The second and third arguments are just the values of the constants a and b, as expected from the equation.

The second constructor for the elliptic curve object also takes a seeding value.

Now that you've specified a curve, the other piece of published information you need is a fixed point on the curve that you can then use to calculate the public keys.

The ECPoint Class

The java.security.spec.ECPoint class provides the containing object for the coordinates of a point on an elliptic curve, and consequently the space it operates in.

There is not much to say about this class. It is constructed from the (X, Y) coordinates of the point, both of which are BigInteger objects, and ECPoint.getAffineX() and ECPoint.getAffineY() return the X and Y coordinate values, respectively. The one thing to remember about it is that it does contain Java's idea of the infinite point, ECPoint.POINT_INFINITY, which returns null for both its get() methods.

The ECParameterSpec Class

The java.security.spec.ECParameterSpec class serves to bring everything together so you can use the elliptic curve for cryptography.

The class has a single constructor that takes the curve you want to use, a base point, the order of the base point, and what is referred to as a *cofactor*. You have already read about the curve parameter and what makes up the base point, or generator, as it is referred to in the ECParameterSpec class. The only two parameters you still need to look at are the order and the cofactor. It would help at this time to have another look at a definition of the class, so here is an extract of use from the previous example.

```
ECParameterSpec  ecSpec = new ECParameterSpec(
  curve,
  new ECPoint(
   new BigInteger("188da80eb03090f67cbf20eb43a18800f4ff0afd82ff1012", 16),
   new BigInteger("f8e6d46a003725879cefee1294db32298c06885ee186b7ee", 16)),
  new BigInteger("ffffffffffffffffffffffff99def836146bc9b1b4d22831", 16),
  1);
```

The order is the last BigInteger appearing in the constructor. It and the cofactor, which is 1 in this case, relate some properties that the base point has to the curve it is being used with. The order is a large prime, and when multiplied by the cofactor, it gives the number of points available on the curve. For efficiency reasons it is better to keep the cofactor as small as possible, so you will normally see curves with cofactors in the range of 1 to 4.

Used together, these values allow you to calculate your private value and the point on the curve that you can then publish to people you want to interact with, be it by key agreement or so they can verify digital signatures you have created.

The ECGenParameterSpec Class

As mentioned earlier, there are a large number of predefined, or *named*, curves with reference points already described. Typically, they appear in documents such as X9.62 and FIPS PUB-186-2. Depending on which curves your provider supports, you can take advantage of these named curves and point parameters by using the java.security.spec.ECGenParameterSpec.

As it happens, the curve used in the BasicECDHExample is called prime192v1 and is specified in X9.62. Consequently, if you wanted to, rather than specify the curve and parameter specification as

```
EllipticCurve    curve = new EllipticCurve(
  new ECFieldFp(new BigInteger(
            "fffffffffffffffffffffffffffffffffefffffffffffffff", 16)),
  new BigInteger("fffffffffffffffffffffffffffffffffefffffffffffffffc", 16),
  new BigInteger("64210519e59c80e70fa7e9ab72243049feb8deecc146b9b1", 16));

ECParameterSpec  ecSpec = new ECParameterSpec(
  curve,
  new ECPoint(
   new BigInteger("188da80eb03090f67cbf20eb43a18800f4ff0afd82ff1012", 16),
   new BigInteger("f8e6d46a003725879cefee1294db32298c06885ee186b7ee", 16)),
  new BigInteger("ffffffffffffffffffffffff99def836146bc9b1b4d22831", 16),
  1);
```

you could have just imported java.security.spec.ECGenParameterSpec and said this instead:

```
ECGenParameterSpec ecSpec = new ECGenParameterSpec("prime192v1");
```

Try making the change; you will see it produces exactly the same result.

The named elliptic curve parameters supported by the Bouncy Castle provider are listed in Appendix B. If you are using a different provider, you should find a list of the curves supported in the documentation associated with it.

Elliptic Curve Cryptography Before JDK 1.5

Prior to JDK 1.5, there was no explicit support for elliptic curve cryptography in Java. If you are trying to use a version of Java that predates 1.5, the APIs used were always particular to the provider you were using. Appendix B has a description of how to do elliptic curve cryptography prior to JDK 1.5 using the Bouncy Castle API. These classes are similar to, but not quite the same as, those provided by the JCA today, and you will probably find this applies to most providers. Having said that, if you are planning to use a lot of elliptic curve cryptography in Java, these days it is worth moving to JDK 1.5 — there is a lot to be said for having to write something only once.

Diffie-Hellman for More Than Two Parties

An interesting feature of Diffie-Hellman key agreement is that the traditional implementation can be used to generate an agreed key between more than two parties. This is the reason that KeyAgreement .doPhase() is capable of returning a key.

Try It Out   Three-Party Diffie-Hellman

You can modify the previous BaseDHExample program to generate an agreed key between three parties by making a few simple changes. The first change involves adding a third KeyAgreement object to take part in the process and create a key for the object as follows:

```
KeyAgreement cKeyAgree = KeyAgreement.getInstance("DH", "BC");
KeyPair      cPair = keyGen.generateKeyPair();
```

Next, you need to initialize the KeyAgreement object in the same fashion as the other KeyAgreement objects were:

```
cKeyAgree.init(cPair.getPrivate());
```

At this point the process you follow changes. Before the KeyAgreement objects are invoked with the lastPhase parameter set to true, you introduce an extra step where KeyAgreement.doPhase() is called with the lastPhase parameter set to false. This step gives you three intermediate keys that you'll use in the next phase (you will need to add an import for java.security.Key as well).

```
Key ac = aKeyAgree.doPhase(cPair.getPublic(), false);
Key ba = bKeyAgree.doPhase(aPair.getPublic(), false);
Key cb = cKeyAgree.doPhase(bPair.getPublic(), false);
```

Taking the intermediate keys, you replace the calls representing the last phase of the agreement with these three lines:

```
aKeyAgree.doPhase(cb, true);
bKeyAgree.doPhase(ac, true);
cKeyAgree.doPhase(ba, true);
```

At this point, all three KeyAgreement objects should now be in such a state that calls to KeyAgreement .generateSecret() will return the same value in all three cases. You can show this by adding the following line to the end of the modified example before you run it.

```
byte[] cShared = hash.digest(cKeyAgree.generateSecret());
System.out.println(Utils.toHex(cShared));
```

And, assuming you are still using the fixed random from the Utils class, you will get the following output:

```
dd602f60ae382db7b435dd71b0674f5ab64bbb7b
dd602f60ae382db7b435dd71b0674f5ab64bbb7b
dd602f60ae382db7b435dd71b0674f5ab64bbb7b
```

How It Works

As you can see, despite its age, Diffie-Hellman is still a useful algorithm. Imagine instead trying to use the RSA algorithm to do a three-way agreement. In the most naïve case, where each party would have to exchange keys with every other party, setting up a three-way conversation could take as many as six RSA key exchanges. Also, each party would be left with the added problem that it would have to keep track of which key to use depending on who it was sending a message to or receiving one from, or another round of negotiation would have to be added to allow the parties to then agree on a common key. In a case where a common key between multiple parties is useful, key authentication issues not withstanding, Diffie-Hellman key agreement is still the simplest approach.

The El Gamal Algorithm

El Gamal is a variant on Diffie-Hellman and derives its security from the same ideas. Although in some ways it is not as "neat" as the RSA algorithm, El Gamal is still very widely used — it is still the algorithm of choice for most keys used for encryption in Open PGP (RFC 2440).

In El Gamal, to send a message to another party whose public key is $G^y \bmod P$, you create a temporary public key, $G^x \bmod P$, encrypt the message by multiplying it by $G^{xy} \bmod P$, the multiplication also being modulo P, and send the temporary public key and the enciphered message as a single block. Although it works, as you will see, it does have the effect of making the ciphertext twice the size of the key.

Try It Out   **El Gamal Encryption**

Following is an example of random key generation and encryption using El Gamal. You will find it runs a lot slower than the equivalent RSA example. You will read about the reasons for this a bit later, but if you run it first, you will get a much better idea of what is meant by "a lot slower."

```
package chapter4;

import java.security.Key;
import java.security.KeyPair;
import java.security.KeyPairGenerator;
import java.security.SecureRandom;
```

```
import javax.crypto.Cipher;

/**
 * El Gamal example with random key generation.
 */
public class RandomKeyElGamalExample
{
    public static void main(String[] args) throws Exception
    {
        byte[]           input = new byte[] { (byte)0xbe, (byte)0xef };
        Cipher           cipher = Cipher.getInstance(
                                           "ElGamal/None/NoPadding", "BC");
        KeyPairGenerator generator = KeyPairGenerator.getInstance("ElGamal", "BC");
        SecureRandom     random = Utils.createFixedRandom();

        // create the keys

        generator.initialize(256, random);

        KeyPair          pair = generator.generateKeyPair();
        Key              pubKey = pair.getPublic();
        Key              privKey = pair.getPrivate();

        System.out.println("input : " + Utils.toHex(input));

        // encryption step

        cipher.init(Cipher.ENCRYPT_MODE, pubKey, random);

        byte[] cipherText = cipher.doFinal(input);

        System.out.println("cipher: " + Utils.toHex(cipherText));

        // decryption step

        cipher.init(Cipher.DECRYPT_MODE, privKey);

        byte[] plainText = cipher.doFinal(cipherText);

        System.out.println("plain : " + Utils.toHex(plainText));
    }
}
```

Running the program produces the following:

```
input : beef
cipher: 8c2e699772c14496bc82400d11decae4f662fe90864e8c553b78136679fcdfaa60c378b5
69083525c021fcf77e40f661525da56ed4133df92848aaba2459dff5
plain : beef
```

How It Works

Overall, there is not much to say here about the use of the algorithm itself. As far as using the public key for encryption, El Gamal is pretty much like RSA; because it is based on math, you will have trouble with leading zeros if you do not use padding. The big difference you will notice when comparing the output to that of the RSA example is that the block of ciphertext produced is twice the size of the key—unlike RSA, where it is the same size as the key. Whether this is important to you really depends on the constraints of your application, but the larger cipher block size is one of the reasons El Gamal is not favored.

The biggest problem, at least in this case, is the speed of the key generation. As you saw previously, the generation of an El Gamal key pair requires Diffie-Hellman parameters, and calculating these values from scratch is very expensive. Internally, when initialized only with a key size, the `KeyPairGenerator` has to first generate the P and G values before it can generate the key pair. You will find, at least in the case of the Bouncy Castle provider, that this is a one-off cost—generating successive key pairs is much quicker because the P and G values calculated for the first key pair can be reused. Not surprisingly, you will also find that the Diffie-Hellman key pair generator exhibits the same behavior.

Can you pre-generate a `DHParameterSpec` so that you can pass in parameters like you did with Diffie-Hellman? As it turns out, you can; you just need to use an `AlgorithmParametersGenerator` object to create them.

The AlgorithmParameterGenerator Class

Like other classes in the JCA, `java.security.AlgorithmParameterGenerator` is created using the `getInstance()` factory pattern, and further, in keeping with classes like `MessageDigest`, it follows the same rules with regard to the precedence rules used if the Java runtime encounters more than one implementation for a given algorithm. The methods on `AlgorithmParameterGenerator` that are of most of interest to you are the `init()` methods, of which there are four, and the `generateParameters()` method, which is used to retrieve the generated `AlgorithmParameters` object.

AlgorithmParameterGenerator.init()

The `init()` method comes in two flavors: two that just take a size value with an optional source of randomness and two that take `AlgortihmParameterSpec` objects for situations where it may be necessary to pass parameters other than the size to the generator. It depends on what you are generating as to what suits best. For something like Diffie-Hellman/ElGamal, the size attribute is enough to generate the prime P and the generator G that will provide the basic parameters. Then again, you want to create a parameters object for Diffie-Hellman that takes advantage of the ability to limit the size of the private value—in this case just the size will not be enough, and you will need an `AlgorithmParameterSpec` object to pass the necessary information in.

Take a look at examples of both over the next two sections.

AlgorithmParameterGenerator.generateParameters()

This returns the `AlgorithmParameters` that you want to generate. I already covered the `AlgorithmParameters` object in Chapter 2, so there's no need to go into too much detail here, other than to mention, as you have probably guessed, `AlgorithmParameters` is used everywhere.

Enough background though. You can now try using the class.

Try It Out   El Gamal Using AlgorithmParameterGenerator

Have a look at the following example and compare it with the `RandomKeyElGamalExample`. Try running the example and then read on.

```
package chapter4;

import java.security.AlgorithmParameterGenerator;
import java.security.AlgorithmParameters;
import java.security.Key;
import java.security.KeyPair;
import java.security.KeyPairGenerator;
import java.security.SecureRandom;
import java.security.spec.AlgorithmParameterSpec;

import javax.crypto.Cipher;
import javax.crypto.spec.DHParameterSpec;

/**
 * El Gamal example with random key generation.
 */
public class AlgorithmParameterExample
{
    public static void main(String[] args) throws Exception
    {
        byte[]            input = new byte[] { (byte)0xbe, (byte)0xef };
        Cipher            cipher = Cipher.getInstance(
                                        "ElGamal/None/NoPadding", "BC");
        SecureRandom      random = Utils.createFixedRandom();

        // create the parameters
        AlgorithmParameterGenerator apg = AlgorithmParameterGenerator.getInstance(
                                                "ElGamal", "BC");

        apg.init(256, random);

        AlgorithmParameters     params = apg.generateParameters();
        AlgorithmParameterSpec  dhSpec = params.getParameterSpec(
                                                DHParameterSpec.class);

        // create the keys
        KeyPairGenerator generator = KeyPairGenerator.getInstance("ElGamal", "BC");

        generator.initialize(dhSpec, random);

        KeyPair           pair = generator.generateKeyPair();
        Key               pubKey = pair.getPublic();
        Key               privKey = pair.getPrivate();

        System.out.println("input : " + Utils.toHex(input));

        // encryption step

        cipher.init(Cipher.ENCRYPT_MODE, pubKey, random);

        byte[] cipherText = cipher.doFinal(input);
```

119

```
            System.out.println("cipher: " + Utils.toHex(cipherText));

            // decryption step

            cipher.init(Cipher.DECRYPT_MODE, privKey);

            byte[] plainText = cipher.doFinal(cipherText);

            System.out.println("plain : " + Utils.toHex(plainText));
        }
    }
```

Because of the fixed seed used in the "random" number generator, you should see that this prints the same results as the original `RandomKeyElGamalExample`. The reason is that the process that takes place internally to the provider, at least in Bouncy Castle's case, is exactly the same as the process you have made explicit in the code.

How It Works

In the new example, you are generating the parameters for the *P* and *G* values and then passing them to the key pair generator class explicitly, rather than letting it create them based on the key size. This relieves the key pair generator of the need to generate its own set of parameters.

Although it is probably hard to tell the difference in speed just from running the examples, if you add some timing code around the key pair generation in `RandomKeyElGamalExample` and `AlgorithmParameterExample`, you will see that the time spent in `KeyPairGenerator` `.generateKeyPair()` is substantially less in the later case.

You read in earlier discussion that the `AlgorithmParameterGenerator` class can also take an `AlgorithmParameterSpec` object on its `init()` methods. As it happens, there is an `AlgorithmParameterSpec` class that is applicable to parameter generation for Diffie-Hellman type parameters — the `DHGenParameterSpec` class.

The DHGenParameterSpec Class

As you read earlier, an optimization to Diffie-Hellman is to limit the size of the private value associated with a public key. As you also learned, you can construct a `DHParameterSpec` that will limit the size of the private values it generates when used with a suitable `KeyPairGenerator` object. It would be useful to be able to incorporate this information into our generated parameters as well, so the JCE provides a class that allows us to configure an `AlgorithmParameterGenerator` object created for Diffie-Hellman algorithms — `javax.crypto.spec.DHGenParameterSpec`. So rather than simply specifying a size for the prime *P*, as you do on the line:

```
        apg.init(256, random);
```

if you wanted to limit the private value to, say, 200 bits, you could have instead said

```
        apg.init(new DHGenParameterSpec(256, 200), random);
```

where the arguments to the constructor of `DHGenParameterSpec` are the size of the prime *P* in bits and the maximum size in bits of the private value *Y*. This would then produce `DHParameterSpec` objects with the `DHParameterSpec.getL()` method returning 200 thus limiting the private values to 200 bits.

Digital Signatures

The utility of digital signatures relies on the fact that a digital signature is created using some secret known only to the creator of signature, and the digital signature can be verified using public information published by the signature creator. In addition to being authentic, digital signatures are non-reputable. If a signature is put forward by a particular creator, then for the creator to deny making it, the secret would have to have been compromised, or the creator is not telling the truth.

The other thing about digital signature algorithms is they are all based on the use of cryptographic hashes, or message digests. This is due to the limitations in size that asymmetric algorithms impose on the messages they can process. This leads to an important point: It is the size of input restrictions on the message digest used in the signature that determines the amount of data it is safe to sign with a given algorithm. The key size serves only to protect the digest. If the data you are signing is larger than the maximum allowable for a particular digest algorithm, increasing the key size will not help.

> **The input size restrictions on the message digest used in a digital signature scheme determines how much data it is safe to sign with that scheme.**

There are two processes that are associated with digital signatures: signature construction and signature verification. As you will see, these are not quite the same as the two processes associated with ciphers, encryption, and decryption. A user only has to be able to verify a signature; there is no requirement that users can read its contents, and in Java the two processes required for the creation and manipulation of digital signatures are encapsulated in the class `Signature`.

The Signature Class

Objects that provide the underlying functionality offered by `java.security.Signature` are created using the `getInstance()` factory pattern like other classes of a similar kind in the JCA. Accordingly, `Signature.getInstance()` will obey whatever precedence rules that have been configured in your Java runtime if you fail to specify a provider. Unlike the `Cipher` class, the `Signature` class does not have static integers to represent its various modes, but instead goes into a particular mode depending on which one of two methods are called. The methods are `Signature.initSign()` and `Signature.initVerify()`, and they put the `Signature` object into a state for signature creation or signature verification, respectively.

Using the Signature Class in Signature Creation Mode

There are two variations of the method `Signature.initSign()` that can be called to put a `Signature` object in signature creation mode. Both take a private key, which is the most important bit, and one `initSign()` method also gives you the option of passing in a source of randomness.

After the `Signature` object is initialized for signing, the use of it is then very similar to what you saw with the `MessageDigest` class. There is a set of `Signature.update()` methods that are then used to feed data into the `Signature` object, and when all the data has been fed in, `Signature.sign()` is called. Depending on which version is called, it will either return the digital signature as a byte array or load it into a passed in byte array.

Using the Signature Class in Signature Verification Mode

There are also two variations of the method `Signature.initVerify()`. Unlike with the `initSign()` method, the second variation, which takes a `Certificate` as its argument, is simply a convenience version of the first `initVerify()` method, which takes a public key.

Feeding data into the `Signature` object as part of the verification process is identical to that of the signature creation process; you just use the `update()` methods. The actual verification step itself, however, is slightly different. Once all the data used in the original signature generation is fed into the `Signature` class using the `update()` methods, the boolean method `Signature.verify()` is called with the byte array representing the signature being checked passed in as an argument. If the `verify()` method returns `true`, the signature is okay; if it returns `false`, the data and the signature do not match.

Signature.setParameter() and Signature.getParameters()

In the same way as `Cipher`, or `KeyPairGenerator`, objects can use `AlgorithmParameterSpec` objects to provide extra information or return an `AlgorithmParameters` object that tells you what extra information would be required if you needed to repeat the operation being performed by the `Cipher`, or `KeyPairGenerator`, object, so too can `Signature` objects. As you would expect, `Signature.getParameters()` returns the `AlgorithmParameterSpec` object associated with the current operation. However, there is a difference with the passing in of the `AlgorithmParameterSpec` object. In the case of the `Signature` class, rather than passing the `AlgorithmParameterSpec` as part of the object's initialization, you use `Signature.setParameter()`. The `setParameter()` method will throw an `InvalidAlgorithmParameterException` if the passed in parameters are inappropriate for the signature implementation.

You will see an example of dealing with parameters when you deal with the RSA PSS digital signature type a bit later. First, have a look at an algorithm that was purpose-built only for the job of signature creation and verification.

The Digital Signature Algorithm

The Digital Signature Algorithm (DSA) was originally proposed by the U.S. National Institute of Standards and Technology (NIST) in August 1991. DSA then became the first digital signature scheme to be recognized by a government with the publication FIPS PUB 186, which described the Digital Signature Standard (DSS). You will occasionally see the algorithm referred to under both titles, although they are not quite the same, as DSS specifically requires the use of the SHA-1 message digest.

The interesting thing about DSA is that it cannot be used for encryption. If you look at Figure 4-4, you will see that the algorithm is designed only to allow verification of a signature via a calculation using the public key that does not expose the data used to create the signature in the first place.

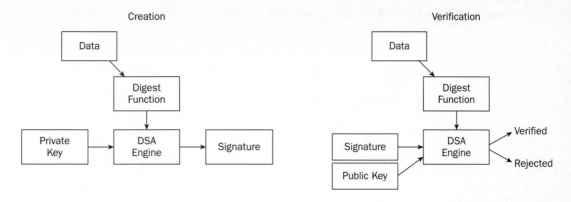

DSA Signature Processes

Figure 4-4

Regular DSA

Traditional DSA, like Diffie-Hellman, derives its security from the discrete logarithm problem. To use it, you need the following:

❑ A prime number Q, such that $2^{159} < Q < 2^{160}$

❑ A prime P with the property that Q divides $(P-1)$

❑ A generator G for a unique cyclic group of order Q in the field of P

I will not go into the math required to calculate the generator here. The important point is that having acquired values for P, Q, and G, you can then create a public key by choosing a private value X, where $1 \le X \le Q$, and compute a public value Y, which is G^X mod P. The public key then becomes the values Y, P, Q, and G. The private key is represented by the value X, P, Q, and G.

Having created public and private keys, you then need to be able to create signatures and verify them. Unlike with the RSA algorithm where public and private key operations can be done using the same method, DSA uses one set of calculations for creating a signature and a different set for verifying one.

Given a hash function H() — SHA-1, if you are following the DSS — creating a signature in DSA for a message M goes through the following steps:

1. Choose a random secret integer K, such that $0 < K < Q$.

2. Calculate $R = (G^K \bmod P) \bmod Q$.

3. Calculate $S = ((K^{-1} \bmod Q)(H(M) + XR)) \bmod Q$.

The signature is then represented by the numbers R and S.

In the case of verification of a signature, you start with the public key of the signer, the values R and S, and perform the following steps:

1. Verify $0 < R < Q$, and $0 < S < Q$, rejecting the signature otherwise.

2. Calculate $A = S^{-1} \bmod Q$, $B = (AH(M)) \bmod Q$, and $C = (RA) \bmod Q$.

3. Compute $V = (G^B Y^C \bmod P) \bmod Q$.

If V is equal to R, accept the signature; reject the signature otherwise.

I am not going to dwell further on the math here, as you can find more in depth discussions in books referred to in Appendix D, such as in *Handbook of Applied Cryptography* by Menezes, van Oorschot, and Vanstone. What is really more relevant to you is how much of this do you have to worry about if you are using Java and the `Signature` class?

Try It Out   DSA

Here is an example of doing DSA and your first use of the `Signature` class as well. As you can see, not withstanding the need to at least know the algorithm name, the `Signature` class hides all the underlying calculations and reduces the use of DSA to just dealing with the results of the creation and verification process.

```java
package chapter4;

import java.security.KeyPair;
import java.security.KeyPairGenerator;
import java.security.SecureRandom;
import java.security.Signature;

public class BasicDSAExample
{
    public static void main(String[] args) throws Exception
    {
        KeyPairGenerator keyGen = KeyPairGenerator.getInstance("DSA", "BC");

        keyGen.initialize(512, new SecureRandom());

        KeyPair             keyPair = keyGen.generateKeyPair();
        Signature           signature = Signature.getInstance("DSA", "BC");

        // generate a signature
        signature.initSign(keyPair.getPrivate(), Utils.createFixedRandom());

        byte[] message = new byte[] { (byte)'a', (byte)'b', (byte)'c' };

        signature.update(message);

        byte[]  sigBytes = signature.sign();

        // verify a signature
        signature.initVerify(keyPair.getPublic());

        signature.update(message);
```

```
        if (signature.verify(sigBytes))
        {
            System.out.println("signature verification succeeded.");
        }
        else
        {
            System.out.println("signature verification failed.");
        }
    }
}
```

Run the example and you should see the output:

```
signature verification succeeded.
```

How It Works

As with any asymmetric algorithm, you start by creating a key pair for the algorithm you want to use. After that, you initialize the `signature` object to use your private key in the following line:

```
signature.initSign(keyPair.getPrivate(), Utils.createFixedRandom());
```

If you remember back to the description of the DSA algorithm, a random number is required to generate a signature, so you are using the `initSign()` method that takes a random number source as well as a private key. If you had not included the random number source, a default one would have been created for you by the provider.

The next step is to feed the data you want to sign into the `signature` object, which you do by calling the `update()` method. After using `update()`, you then calculate the signature retrieving a byte array representation of it using the `sign()` method.

The last half of the example just verifies the signature you created in the first half. You use the `initVerify()` method, passing in the public key of the signer; do another call to the `update()` method to feed the data you believe the signature is based on into the `signature` object; and then call the `verify()` method, passing it the byte array representation of the signature. If the signature is valid for the data, as it should be in the case of the example, `verify()` returns `true`. In the event that the signature was not valid for the data, `verify()` would have returned `false`.

If you look at the use of `KeyPairGenerator`, there is no sign of the parameters that were discussed earlier because they were passed before key creation was done. This is because you are playing the same game as you were originally with El Gamal — the `KeyPairGenerator` instance you are using is creating the parameters for you. As with Diffie-Hellman and El Gamal, it is possible for you to calculate parameters beforehand and use them. To carry these parameters around, the JCA provides the `DSAParameterSpec` class.

The DSAParameterSpec Class

The `java.security.spec.DSAParameterSpec` object serves as the holding class for the DSA parameters discussed previously. It has a single constructor that takes the P, Q, and G values used in the key generation process and three `get()` methods that allow the values to be retrieved.

As with objects of the type `DHParameterSpec`, `DSAParameterSpec` objects can also be generated using the `AlgorithmParameterGenerator` class. So if you wanted to create a `DSAParameterSpec` object for 512-bit keys like the ones you are using previously, the following code could be used to create the parameter object:

```
AlgorithmParameterGenerator apg = AlgorithmParameterGenerator.getInstance(
                                                          "DSA", "BC");

apg.init(512, new SecureRandom());

AlgorithmParameters        params = apg.generateParameters();
AlgorithmParameterSpec     dsaSpec = params.getParameterSpec(
                                              DSAParameterSpec.class);
```

Having created the parameter object, you could then use it for generation of your key pairs by passing it to an instance of the `KeyPairGenerator` class when you call `KeyPairGenerator.initialize()`.

Of course, rather than generating keys randomly, you might want to produce them using a `KeyFactory` class. To make this possible, the JCA also provides specification classes for carrying key material for DSA keys.

Specification Objects for DSA Keys

The JCA also provides objects for carrying key and parameter material for DSA keys, and they can be used to create simple value objects that can then be used to pass around key material for DSA keys. The two classes used for this purpose are `java.security.spec.DSAPrivateKeySpec` and `java.security.spec.DSAPublicKeySpec`.

`DSAPrivateKeySpec` has a single constructor that just takes the private value X and the parameters used to create the public value from it P, Q, and G — the values in the `DSAParameterSpec` object. An example of use might look as follows:

```
DSAPrivateKeySpec dsaPrivateSpec = new DSAPrivateKeySpec(x, p, q, g);
```

`DSAPublicKeySpec` also has a single constructor that takes the public value Y and the parameters that were used to create it, P, Q, and G, leading to usage like:

```
DSAPublicKeySpec dsaPublicSpec = new DSAPublicKeySpec(y, p, q, g);
```

As usual with the other key specification value objects, the only methods on `DSAPrivateKeySpec` and `DSAPublicKeySpec` are `get()` methods for retrieving the various values used to construct them.

Interfaces for DSA Keys

In the `BasicDSAExample` program, you just used the `KeyPair` class directly after generating the keys. If you need greater type safety, the JCA does provide `java.security.interfaces.DSAPrivateKey`, `java.security.interfaces.DSAPublicKey`, and a parent class for both of them that extends `Key`, namely, `java.security.interfaces.DSAKey`, which you can use to distinguish DSA keys from other asymmetric keys you are using.

`DSAKey` provides a single method, `DSAKey.getParams()`, which returns the `DSAParameterSpec` associated with the public and private keys.

DSAPrivateKey also has a single method on it, DSAPrivateKey.getX(), which returns the private value that is not transmitted as part of the agreement process.

DSAPublicKey also has a single method on it, DSAPublicKey.getY(). The value returned by getY() is G^X mod P, where X is the value return by the corresponding private keys getX() method and G and P are the values of the associated DSAParameterSpec object.

Elliptic Curve DSA

There is also an algorithm for doing DSA signing using elliptic curve cryptography rather than the algorithm described in the DSS. The algorithm is referred to as ECDSA, and in the same manner as Diffie-Hellman using elliptic curve is similar to the original Diffie-Hellman using primes, DSA with elliptic curve also involves creating a signature that consists of the two numbers, R and S. Likewise, the signature is verified by calculating a number V from the signature and the signer's public key and confirming that it is equal to R.

Other than that, ECDSA is described in detail in X9.62 and requires some knowledge of the fundamentals of elliptic curve cryptography, so I will not go into the methodology further here. As you will see, the differences in the underlying math that make ECDSA work are completely hidden when you are using it in Java.

Try It Out   DSA with Elliptic Curve

Have a look at the following example and compare it with the BasicDSAExample class you looked at earlier. You create a different KeyPairGenerator object as you would expect, but after that the only difference is the "ECDSA" parameter passed to Signature.getInstance(). The mechanics of both signing and verifying are identical to before.

```java
package chapter4;

import java.security.KeyPair;
import java.security.KeyPairGenerator;
import java.security.SecureRandom;
import java.security.Signature;
import java.security.spec.ECGenParameterSpec;

/**
 * Simple example showing signature creation and verification using ECDSA
 */
public class BasicECDSAExample
{
    public static void main(
        String[]    args)
        throws Exception
    {
        KeyPairGenerator keyGen = KeyPairGenerator.getInstance("ECDSA", "BC");
        ECGenParameterSpec ecSpec = new ECGenParameterSpec("prime192v1");

        keyGen.initialize(ecSpec, new SecureRandom());

        KeyPair             keyPair = keyGen.generateKeyPair();
        Signature           signature = Signature.getInstance("ECDSA", "BC");
```

```
        // generate a signature
        signature.initSign(keyPair.getPrivate(), Utils.createFixedRandom());

        byte[] message = new byte[] { (byte)'a', (byte)'b', (byte)'c' };

        signature.update(message);

        byte[]  sigBytes = signature.sign();

        // verify a signature
        signature.initVerify(keyPair.getPublic());

        signature.update(message);

        if (signature.verify(sigBytes))
        {
            System.out.println("signature verification succeeded.");
        }
        else
        {
            System.out.println("signature verification failed.");
        }
    }
}
```

Run the example and you should get the message `signature verification succeeded.`

How It Works

As I mentioned earlier, the magic is in the abstraction layer provided by the JCA. With relatively minor changes, it is possible to change code to use a completely different implementation.

One thing worth noting in this example is that it is using the `ECGenParameterSpec` that you discussed earlier, so you could move to a completely different curve and key size by just changing the string passed to `ECGenParameterSpec`'s constructor. For example, if you wanted to move from 192 to a 239 bit key size, you could change

```
ECGenParameterSpec ecSpec = new ECGenParameterSpec("prime192v1");
```

to

```
ECGenParameterSpec ecSpec = new ECGenParameterSpec("prime239v1");
```

RSA-Based Signature Algorithms

Signatures are created using the RSA algorithm by applying the RSA algorithm using the private key and then distributing the result as the signature. Because of the way the RSA algorithm works, this means the signature can be decrypted using the public key, giving you the process you see in Figure 4-5. The reason it works so well is that if a signature decrypts successfully with a given public key, then it *must* have been created with the corresponding private key.

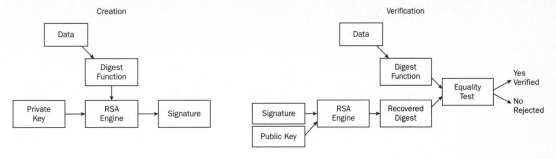

RSA Signature Processes

Figure 4-5

As with padding modes, the most popular methods for using RSA with signatures are outlined in PKCS #1. After the same fashion as padding modes, there are two types, an earlier one based on PKCS #1 version 1.5 and a more recent one that appeared in PKCS1 version 2.

PKCS #1 1.5 Signatures

PKCS #1 version 1.5 signatures use type 1 PKCS1 padding. To rehash the discussion before, type 1 PKCS #1 padding is when, given a message M, the padded message M_p is

$$M_p = 0x00 \ || \ 0x01 \ || \ F \ || \ 0x00 \ || \ M$$

where F is a string of octets of the value 0xFF and $||$ is the concatenation operator. F must be at least 8 octets long, so M can be no longer than the length of the key in octets less 11.

Try It Out   RSA Signature Generation

Try running the following example; you will see that once again the changes are quite minor.

```
package chapter4;

import java.security.KeyPair;
import java.security.KeyPairGenerator;
import java.security.SecureRandom;
import java.security.Signature;

public class PKCS1SignatureExample
{
    public static void main(String[] args) throws Exception
    {
        KeyPairGenerator keyGen = KeyPairGenerator.getInstance("RSA", "BC");

        keyGen.initialize(512, new SecureRandom());

        KeyPair             keyPair = keyGen.generateKeyPair();
        Signature           signature = Signature.getInstance("SHA1withRSA", "BC");

        // generate a signature
```

```
        signature.initSign(keyPair.getPrivate(), Utils.createFixedRandom());

        byte[] message = new byte[] { (byte)'a', (byte)'b', (byte)'c' };

        signature.update(message);

        byte[]  sigBytes = signature.sign();

        // verify a signature
        signature.initVerify(keyPair.getPublic());

        signature.update(message);

        if (signature.verify(sigBytes))
        {
            System.out.println("signature verification succeeded.");
        }
        else
        {
            System.out.println("signature verification failed.");
        }
    }
}
```

Once again you should see the message `signature verification succeeded`.

How It Works

Once again you see that if you change the call to `Signature.getInstance()` and provide the appropriate key pair, everything else just falls into place.

One thing you can see in this example that you have not seen before with the `Signature` class is that the name of signature algorithm appears to have an underlying structure to it. As it turns out, it does, and the structure is described in the standard naming conventions outlined in the JCA documentation as well. The format is *DigestwithEncryption*", so if you were going to use SHA-224, the name string would be "`SHA224withRSA`", SHA-256 would be "`SHA256withRSA`", and so on.

PSS Signatures

RSASSA-PSS, or PSS for short, is similar in function to OAEP, and is outlined in PKCS #1 version 2. Like a traditional signature method, it involves using a hash function H() to create calculate a digest of the message to be signed. Creating the signature involves creating a padded data block containing the digest and masking it with mask function Mask, based on the hash function H() and a random salt S. The padded data block is then encrypted using the private key of the signer.

To create a signature M_s for a message M and the key K you perform the following steps:

1. $M_1 = 0x00 \,||\, 0x00 \,||\, 0x00 \,||\, 0x00 \,||\, 0x00 \,||\, 0x00 \,||\, 0x00 \,||\, 0x00 \,||\, H(M) \,||\, S$

2. $M_2 = P \,||\, 0x01 \,||\, S$

3. $M_3 = Mask(M_2, H(M_1)) \,||\, H(M_1) \,||\, 0xBC$

4. $M_s = RSAEncrypt(K, M_3)$

P in this case is pad string of octets of the value 0x00. The length of P given by:

$kLen - sLen - hLen - 2$

where $kLen$ is usually the block size in octets, $sLen$ is the length of S in octets, and $hLen$ is the length of the hash in octets.

Verification of a PSS signature is simply a matter of decrypting the signature using the public key, extracting the salt, and then reconstructing $H(M_1)$ from the data that was signed. If the reconstructed value is the same as that found in the decrypted block, the signature is valid for the data. Otherwise, it should be rejected.

Note that unlike the older method the presence of the random salt means that two signatures generated from the same input data and the same private key will not have produced the same byte arrays. To allow for this possibility, it is possible to have a salt of zero length, meaning the calculation will always produce the same result for the same data and the same private key.

As you can see, PSS is very different from the older PKCS #1 signature encoding; however, since PSS is also based on RSA, you can create an example of using PSS by changing only a single line in the code for `PKCS1SignatureExample`.

Try replacing the line:

```
Signature    signature = Signature.getInstance("SHA1withRSA", "BC");
```

with the line:

```
Signature    signature = Signature.getInstance("SHA1withRSAandMGF1", "BC");
```

and you are now using PSS.

Like the previous PKCS #1 mechanism, you can see that the PSS signature algorithm name also has a specific structure. The structure reflects the fact that PSS is related to OAEP and goes "*Digest*withRSAand*MaskFunction*". Although MGF1 is currently the only mask function available, a variety of digests such as SHA-256, SHA-384, and SHA-512 can be used in place of SHA-1. If you try one of the other digests remember the hyphen (-) is left out of the digest name — for instance, SHA-256 becomes SHA256.

Like OAEP, PSS signatures can also have parameters; you will look at the parameter class now.

The PSSParameterSpec Class

The `java.security.spec.PSSParameterSpec` class first appeared in JDK 1.4, where it could be used to change the size of the salt associated with the signature. More recently, in JDK 1.5, it now allows setting all the available parameters for the PSS signature mechanism. This gives you two ways of constructing a PSSParameterSpec depending on what you want to set. As the older constructor is really a subset of the newer constructor, you will have a look at the newer constructor first.

The `PSSParameterSpec` class provides a default value, which is `PSSParameterSpec.DEFAULT`. Coded the long way it looks like this:

```
PSSParameterSpec defaultSpec = new PSSParameterSpec(
                           "SHA-1", "MGF1", MGF1ParameterSpec.SHA1, 20, 1);
```

Used with the `signature` object in the example that was modified to use PSS, you would pass it in as follows:

```
signature.setParameter(defaultSpec);
```

Comparing the constructor for the `PSSParameterSpec` to the `OAEPParameterSpec` you saw earlier, the similarities between the two are obvious. The first parameter is the message digest to be used, the second parameter is the mask generation function to be used, and the third is the algorithm parameter specification for the mask generation function. The only different ones are the fourth and the fifth.

The fourth parameter is the value that can be passed to the older single parameter constructor; it gives the size of the salt that is to be used in the signature generation.

The fifth parameter is what is referred as the *trailer field*. This tells the signature generator what trailer byte to put at the end of the signature. At the moment only one value for the trailer field has been specified, the value 1, which maps to a trailer byte in the signature of 0xBC. You will have a closer look at how this mapping is done in the next chapter, but for the moment you will have to take my word for it.

Finally, the `PSSParameterSpec` class, as its name implies, is a simple value object, so the only methods on it are `get()` methods for retrieving the values an instance of `PSSParameterSpec` was constructed with.

Summary

This brings you to the end of looking at the basics of asymmetric cryptography. You have now covered the fundamentals for asymmetric encryption, symmetric key exchange, key agreement, and the creation of digital signatures, as well as the algorithm parameters that they might require. You have also looked at the encryption algorithms RSA and El Gamal, the key agreement algorithms Diffie-Hellman and elliptic curve Diffie-Hellman, as well as digital signature algorithms based on RSA, DSA, and elliptic curve DSA.

Over the course of this chapter, you learned how to

❑   Create asymmetric keys from key specification objects using the KeyFactory class.

❑   Create random asymmetric keys using the `KeyPairGenerator` class.

❑   Do asymmetric encryption with the `Cipher` class.

❑   Do key agreement using the `KeyAgreement` class.

❑   Create digital signatures with the `Signature` class.

❑   Use `AlgorithmParameters` objects with `Cipher` and `Signature` classes.

❑   Use the `AlgorithmParameterGenerator` class to create `AlgorithmParameters` objects.

Finally, you also saw how to use an asymmetric key to encrypt, or wrap, a symmetric key and how to wrap asymmetric keys using secret key objects.

I mentioned earlier that encoded asymmetric keys include a large amount of structural information in addition to the key material. The same also applies to algorithm parameters and the contents of some signatures. This structural information is built upon a language that is also the foundation for X.509 certificates and many protocols surrounding cryptography and certificate management. So before you can go much farther, it would be good to have a basic understanding of how this language for describing structures works. This is what you will look at next.

Exercises

1. A colleague is attempting to use RSA for key exchange, and the implementation is failing whenever the leading byte of the key happens to be zero. What will be causing this problem? How do you fix it?

2. The maximum amount of data that can be encrypted with RSA or El Gamal is normally limited by the size of the key, less any padding overhead that might exist. If you wanted to use either of these algorithms to help encrypt an arbitrarily large amount of data, how would you do it?

3. Key agreement is different from key exchange in that it makes it possible for two or more people to arrive at the same key independently. What is the important thing to combine with a key agreement scheme if you are going to use one safely?

4. You saw previously that it was possible to use a MAC to authenticate data but that it had the disadvantage that it required a shared secret between all the parties wishing to check the same MAC. What asymmetric technique can you use instead that avoids this problem? What is it about it that makes it easier?

Object Description in Cryptography Using ASN.1

At this point one thing probably has become obvious to you. There are a number of areas in cryptography that, in order for communication to take place, require two implementations to have the same idea about how algorithms are implemented as well as have a common language for exchanging required parameter information for those algorithms.

This chapter introduces ASN.1, which is a language designed for just this purpose. By the end of this chapter, you should

❑ Have enough knowledge to read and understand most ASN.1 modules related to cryptography

❑ Understand the basic ASN.1 types and the relevant ASN.1 binary encoding rules

❑ Understand how ASN.1 binary encoding can be used with the Java APIs for encoding `AlgorithmParameters`

❑ Understand how public and private keys can be encoded as ASN.1 objects and re-created later

Finally, you will see how to use the `EncryptedPrivateKeyInfo` class defined in the JCE, as well as see what is taking place when it does its job.

What Is ASN.1?

Abstract Syntax Notation 1, or ASN.1, came out of the standards developed by ISO and CCITT (renamed ITU-T at the start of the 1990s) when work was being done on Open Systems Interconnection (OSI) standards. Work on OSI started in the early 1980s when, reputedly, hundreds of people used to attend the standards meetings. The primary design goal for ASN.1 was to provide a standard notation for use in specifying protocols that was concise in its encoding. Prior to the rise of the Internet, its use was mainly in the area of telecommunication standards, but we now see it in widespread use for describing key encodings, secure protocols, and algorithm parameters. The main standard defining it is X.680, and there are an additional six standard documents that build on X.680: X.681, X.682, X.683, X.684, X.691, and X.693. You'll find details of these listed in Appendix D, but as you can see, put briefly, ASN.1 is big!

It is not an easy thing to sum up in a few pages either. Most people who write about it tend to sprinkle quotes from H. P. Lovecraft's *The Mountains of Madness* into the commentary, as well as biblical offerings from the story of the *Tower of Babel*, in an attempt to help their readers work through the mysteries of ASN.1 and how it is used. True, it can be baroque, almost unfathomable in places, but it has a long history and has actually solved a lot of the problems associated with the building of universal protocols. So, while I doubt it is the final word on the problem of universal communication, it definitely has a lot to offer.

More importantly, in the case of cryptography, almost every standard you are likely to make use of, such as the PKCS standards and the PKIX RFCs, uses ASN.1 somewhere. Although this does not mean you have to understand ASN.1 in depth, it does mean you need some knowledge of it and how it works. Understanding something about it also gives you insight into some of the design decisions that were made when the Java cryptography APIs were developed and why various classes work together the way they do.

Still, as I have mentioned, both ASN.1 and its syntax can seem kind of weird and it is best approached with a sense of humor. To put you into the right frame of mind, I would remind you of Chancellor Gorkon's claim in *Star Trek VI: The Undiscovered Country*: "You have not experienced Shakespeare until you have read him in the original Klingon." I would not go as far as comparing most cryptographic standard documents to Shakespeare, but ASN.1 is definitely the original Klingon!

Getting Started

It is not necessary to add any new functionality to the Utils class for this chapter. However, as I will be extending it again in later chapters and to keep the examples regular, I'll define a new version of the Utils class to start the chapter5 package with. This new version is simply an extension of the one used in Chapter 4 and looks as follows:

```
package chapter5;

/**
 * Chapter 5 Utils
 */
public class Utils extends chapter4.Utils
{

}
```

Create the new chapter5 package and type the Utils class in.

Now you are ready to proceed.

Basic ASN.1 Syntax

The underlying syntax of ASN.1, or at least the bit you have to deal with, is quite simple. There are three things you need to be able to recognize when you are trying to read an ASN.1 module:

- ❏ Comment syntax
- ❏ Object identifiers
- ❏ The module structure

Comment Syntax

As with Java, there are two commenting styles used in ASN.1, one for block comments, which are delimited by /* and */, and one for single-line comments, which start with "--" and end with "--".

Unlike Java, ASN.1 block comments can contain other block comments. The block comment syntax is newer than the line comment syntax, so for historical reasons, you will often see multiple lines of line comments used where a block comment could have been used otherwise.

Object Identifiers

Object identifiers, often referred to as OIDs for short, provide a unique handle for an object or ASN.1 module in the ISO/ITU-T universe. They were introduced into ASN.1 to make it possible to construct a globally unique namespace, which also made it easy for organizations to be allocated part of that namespace, which they could then extend as required. For this reason, the best way to think of the structure of an OID is like it is a path, or arc, through a tree.

For example, the RSA Security algorithm that you are using when you call `Signature.getInstance()` with `"SHA256withRSA"` has an object identifier associated with it that goes like this:

```
iso(1) member-body(2) us(840) rsadsi(113549) pkcs(1) pkcs-1(1) 11
```

with the leftmost end representing where you start at the root of the tree. In its short form, this OID would be seen as "1.2.840.113549.1.1.11", and looking at the OID definition, you can see that RSA Security was assigned the OID "1.2.840.113549" by the U.S. branch of ISO. After that, RSA Security started its own branch, assigning the OID "1.2.840.113549.1" to its PKCS standards, and then further assigning OID "1.2.840.113549.1.1" to PKCS #1 and finally getting to the algorithm, which has simply been given the number 11, resulting in the OID for SHA-256 with RSA encryption: "1.2.840.113549.1.1.11". You can see another way of looking at the assignments that were done up to RSA Security in Figure 5-1.

There are three primary branches, or *arcs*, on the object identifier tree, all of which you will see used from time to time. The assignments are the ITU-T — the number 0, ISO — the number 1, and joint ISO/ITU-T organizations with the number 2. After that how the space is carved up becomes quite arbitrary, as the primary arc owners allocated numbers at the next level down to other organizations as they needed to. That said, despite the apparently arbitrary nature of how an OID gets created, the numbers are globally unique and serve the purpose of providing identification for ASN.1 modules, data types, algorithms, and just about anything else you can imagine. The only complication is that, because OIDs are based around organization rather than subject, in some cases you will notice the same cryptographic algorithm will be referred to by different OIDs.

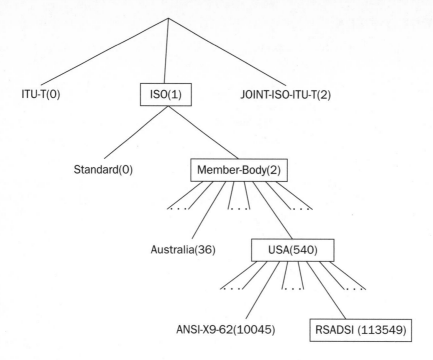

Another View of the Arc to RSA Security

Figure 5-1

The Module Structure

A module is typically structured along the following lines:

```
ModuleName { ObjectIdentifier }
DEFINITIONS Tagging TAGS ::=
BEGIN
EXPORTS export_list ;
IMPORTS import_list ;

body

END
```

`ModuleName` and `ObjectIdentifier` have values that are used to identify the module being described. For example, the module defined in RFC 3161 (Time-Stamp Protocol) starts as follows:

```
PKIXTSP {iso(1) identified-organization(3) dod(6) internet(1)
         security(5) mechanisms(5) pkix(7) id-mod(0) id-mod-tsp(13)}
```

This tells you the name of the module is `PKIXTSP` and that it is associated with an object identifier, which in its basic form will be `1.3.6.1.5.5.7.0.13`.

Tagging tells you the tagging environment for the module. You will read about tagging in more detail a bit later, but you can expect to see one of IMPLICIT, EXPLICIT, or AUTOMATIC. If no tagging environment is specified, as in the TAGS : := is missing altogether, you can assume tagging is EXPLICIT. In the case of RFC 3161, you will see the following:

```
DEFINITIONS IMPLICIT TAGS ::=
```

This means the default tagging type for the module is IMPLICIT. The ": :=" symbol looks a bit like an assignment but more correctly reads as "is defined as." Later you will see that definitions can follow it, but in this case nothing follows it, as everything between the BEGIN and END is included.

The *export_list* is the list of types that this module defines that other ASN.1 modules can import. If EXPORTS is missing altogether, it means that everything defined in the module can be imported by another one. If you see the export list missing — that is, you just see EXPORTS ; — it means nothing is available for export.

The *import_list* is the list of types that are being imported into the module and where they are from. This is the thing that is of the most interest to you. If you are trying to implement a particular protocol or algorithm suite and are using an ASN.1 module as your reference, the *import_list* tells you where to look for definitions that are not in the module you are using as your primary reference point. An example of an import list, also from RFC 3161, is as follows:

```
IMPORTS

    Extensions, AlgorithmIdentifier
    FROM PKIX1Explicit88 {iso(1) identified-organization(3)
    dod(6) internet(1) security(5) mechanisms(5) pkix(7)
    id-mod(0) id-pkix1-explicit-88(1)}

    GeneralName FROM PKIX1Implicit88 {iso(1)
    identified-organization(3) dod(6) internet(1) security(5)
    mechanisms(5) pkix(7) id-mod(0) id-pkix1-implicit-88(2)}

    ContentInfo FROM CryptographicMessageSyntax {iso(1)
    member-body(2) us(840) rsadsi(113549) pkcs(1) pkcs-9(9)
    smime(16) modules(0) cms(1)}

    PKIFreeText FROM PKIXCMP {iso(1) identified-organization(3)
    dod(6) internet(1) security(5) mechanisms(5) pkix(7) id-mod(0)
    id-mod-cmp(9)} ;
```

As you can see, the component imports just follow a format of

```
    import_item FROM source
```

where *import_item* is the type, or value, being imported and *source* is the name and OID for the module where *import_item* has been defined. Note the semicolon on the end of the collection of imports; it terminates the IMPORTS statement. Anything you read after the semicolon is a local definition. Of course, if the IMPORTS statement is missing, you should have all the information you need in the ASN.1 module in front of you.

Now consider *body*. It is terminated by the keyword END and it is the *body* where all the type and value definitions that the ASN.1 module provides are. Here are some examples taken from the body of the module defined in RFC 3161:

```
id-ct-TSTInfo  OBJECT IDENTIFIER ::= { iso(1) member-body(2)
                    us(840) rsadsi(113549) pkcs(1) pkcs-9(9) smime(16) ct(1) 4}


TSAPolicyId ::= OBJECT IDENTIFIER
```

The first line defines a value. In this case, it is saying id-ct-TSTInfo is of the type OBJECT IDENTIFIER and has the OID value 1.2.840.113549.1.9.16.1.4. Looking at the line also gives you the basic syntax for ASN.1 value definitions:

```
name type ::= value
```

where *name* is the name you want to refer to *value* with, *type* is the type of the value, and then *value* is specified in whatever notation is appropriate for the particular type given by *type*.

The second definition defines a new type that can be used in the module. What it is saying is that where you see TSAPolicyId, you are looking at a special case of OBJECT IDENTIFIER. As you can probably see, the basic syntax is

```
newType ::= type
```

where *newType* is the new type being created and *type* is the existing type it is based on. As with other languages, types you define can be used to build other types and definitions.

ASN.1 names can consist of upper- and lowercase letters, numbers, and dashes (the "-" character). Like any language, there are also a couple of conventions for creating names. Module names and type names all start with uppercase letters, whereas names for everything else start with lowercase letters.

A lot more can go into an ASN.1 module, but this gives you enough to make sense of the various RFCs, PKCS documents, and other standards—so I will stop here. The next thing you need to do is look at the basic types that are available.

ASN.1 Types

Broadly speaking, ASN.1 types fall into three categories: simple types, string types, and structured types. The string types are further subdivided into two more categories, those that just deal with raw bits and those that represent specific character encodings. The structured types consist of two container types— SEQUENCE and SET—that allow you to build complex structures using all the categories of type.

I will start with the simple types, which are used to represent fundamental values such as booleans, integers, and dates. I will then deal with the string and structured types.

Simple Types

The simple types in ASN.1 are

❏   BOOLEAN

❏   ENUMERATED

❑   INTEGER

❑   NULL

❑   OBJECT IDENTIFIER

❑   UTCTime

❑   GeneralizedTime

There are no real surprises with most of these:

BOOLEAN encodes a true or false value.

ENUMERATED is a special case of INTEGER that can be used to represent signed integers of any magnitude. Note that I said *signed* — INTEGER values are encoded as two's-complement numbers, high byte first in "big endian" format.

You can think of NULL in a similar way to the Java null, although there is a slight twist, as it is ASN.1's way of distinguishing a value set to nothing, rather than absent, which you will see later is also a possibility.

You have already learned what object identifiers are in the section on basic ASN.1 syntax. Not surprisingly, OBJECT IDENTIFIER is the type they are given.

UTCTime and GeneralizedTime are two that deserve some special attention; both are used to define a "Coordinated Universal Time," but UTCTime has only a two-digit year. GeneralizedTime has a four-digit year. Both objects represent time as strings of ASCII, with major differences being that GeneralizedTime has a four-digit year and can represent seconds to an arbitrary precision, whereas UTCTime has a two-digit year and cannot go any lower than seconds in its resolution. Although it should be obvious how a GeneralizedTime is used, a question remains: How do you deal with the two-digit year in UTCTime?

One interpretation of UTCTime is that the two-digit year is interpreted as spanning the century starting from 1950 to 2049, but others are also used. A UTCTime can also be interpreted as going from 1900 to 1999, or as being on a sliding window, as in if it's 2005, the digits 55 to 99 are interpreted as indicating 1955 to 1999, and 0 to 55 is interpreted as meaning 2000 to 2055. How you work this one out depends on the standard you are working with, but you will be relieved to know that for the most part people have settled on the meaning that maps 50 to 99 as 1950 to 1999, and 00 to 49 as 2000 to 2049.

Bit String Types

The two bit string types are BIT STRING and OCTET STRING.

BIT STRING allows you to store an arbitrary string of bits of an arbitrary length. For this reason there are two components to a bit string: The first is a string of octets that contains the actual string of bits and 0 to seven pad bits to make the string a multiple of 8 bits in length, and the second is a pad count that records how many pad bits were added. A bit string can be of zero length.

OCTET STRING allows you to store a string of octets and maps quite nicely onto a Java byte array.

Character String Types

ASN.1 has many character string types, almost all of which appear in some standard or another. The character string types are as follows:

- ❏ BMPString
- ❏ GeneralString
- ❏ GraphicString
- ❏ IA5String
- ❏ NumericString
- ❏ PrintableString
- ❏ TeletexString (T61String)
- ❏ UniversalString
- ❏ UTF8String
- ❏ VideotexString
- ❏ VisibleString

As you go through the different character string types, you will see that the distinctions made between each type are all based on what characters can be in a string of the particular type being considered, as the character range goes from a restricted 7-bit character set to a full 32-bit character set. Once you have had the experience of looking at a range of ASN.1 modules, you will probably realize that the use of a particular character string type is as much a reflection of the hardware and software that was available when the module was being written as it is a reflection of the mind of the module writer.

The BMPString takes its name from the "Basic Multilingual Plane," which contains all the characters associated with the "living languages," with a fixed 16 bits per character. Its character set is the one represented by ISO 10646, the same set represented by the Unicode standard. It is quite a natural fit with the Java programming language and now sees extensive use.

The GeneralString and the GraphicString are actually related, so I will discuss them together. Both string types are related to the character sets described in the International Register of Coded Character Sets detailed in ISO 2375. The GraphicString can contain any one of the printing characters that appear in the register, but not the control characters. A GeneralString can contain control characters as well. Since the arrival of Unicode, use of these two types is becoming rarer and rarer.

The IA5String takes its name from an old ITU-T recommendation "International Alphabet 5." ASCII is actually a variant of this alphabet, and these days the type is considered to cover the whole of ASCII with its character set.

The NumericString can contain the digits 0 to 9 and the space character.

The PrintableString can contain a limited range of ASCII characters, which consists of the uppercase letters "A" to "Z", the lowercase letters "a" to "z", the digits "0" to "9", and the following other characters: " "(space), " ' " (apostrophe), "(,)" (comma in parentheses), "+", "," (comma), "-", ".", ":", "=", and "?".

The `TeletexString` was originally known as the `T61String`, as it was originally based on the character set specified in CCITT Recommendation T.61 for Teletex. It is an 8-bit-per-character type, but there is the added feature that the ASCII ESC character starts an escape sequence that changes which actual characters are represented by the character stream that follows. The way this works is that each escape sequence should cause a display device to change the lookup table used for interpreting characters to the one indicated by the escape sequence. This allows the `TeletexString` to be used to support a wide range of languages, but it also makes it very difficult to interpret if you are on the receiving end of one.

The `UniversalString` is another update for internationalization. It was added to ASN.1 in 1994 to allow for the representation of strings made up of 32-bit characters. It is very rare to see one of these, as most modern languages are built on Unicode so there is not a lot of native support. Nonetheless, you will run into them occasionally; just hope you will not have to display the contents of an arbitrary `UniversalString` using Java just yet.

The `UTF8String` takes its name from "Universal Transformation Format, 8 bit," the same encoding that is often discussed with Java. This character string type works nicely with Unicode while still allowing the representation of the full character set possible in a `UniversalString`. It is the recommended string type for full internationalization, so you will see these used increasingly.

The `VideotexString` was designed to accommodate characters that can be used to build simple images. The strings are a mixture of pixel information and control codes, where an 8-bit character is typically considered to contain a 3×2 array of pixels. Fortunately, the type was designed for use with videotext systems, and, to date, I have never had to deal with one of these in a standards document involving cryptography.

The `VisibleString` could originally contain only characters that appeared in ISO 646, and occasionally you will even see it referred to as an `ISO646String`. Since 1994 it has been interpreted as containing plain ASCII, but unlike an `IA5String`, it includes only the printing characters plus space. No control characters are allowed.

Reading through this list you have probably realized that the broad coverage of character sets that some of these string types purport to represent makes them, for want of a better phrase, simply scary. Fortunately, it is very unusual to encounter the more bizarre ones, largely due to the standardization of some of the simpler string types on variants of ASCII and the growth of Unicode. So take a deep breath, relax, and read on.

Structured Types

ASN.1 has two structured types: SEQUENCE and SET.

You will also see these used as SEQUENCE OF and SET OF. When you see the OF keyword, the SET or SEQUENCE will only contain ASN.1 objects of the type specified afterwards. For example:

```
Counters ::= SEQUENCE OF INTEGER
```

indicates that an object of type `Counters` contains only 0, or more, ASN.1 objects of type INTEGER.

As for the difference between a SEQUENCE and a SET: A SEQUENCE specifies the order of its components in its declaration, whereas a SET is an unordered collection. For example:

```
DigestInfo ::= SEQUENCE {
            digestAlgorithm  AlgorithmIdentifier,
            digest OCTET STRING }
```

tells you that an ASN.1 object of type `DigestInfo` is a sequence with two elements, the first of which is an `AlgorithmIdentifier`, the second an `OCTET STRING`. On the other hand, if you created a similar example for a `SET`, as in:

```
InfoSet ::= SET {
                digestAlgorithm  AlgorithmIdentifier,
                digest OCTET STRING }
```

it just means you will find the two component types in the `SET`, but not necessarily in that order. For the most part, uses of `SET` will look like this:

```
attrValues SET OF AttributeValue
```

which is considerably easier to make sense of.

Type Annotations

Two annotations can be applied to types. One is `OPTIONAL`, which when applied to a field means it can be left out totally. The other is `DEFAULT`, which specifies the value for field if it is not present.

You will see both of these in the context of `SEQUENCE` and `SET` objects, for example:

```
VersionedData ::= SEQUENCE {
                version INTEGER DEFAULT 0,
                data OCTET STRING OPTIONAL }
```

`DEFAULT` tells you that the value may be left out of the encoding of the `SEQUENCE`. If it is, you should set the value of the `version` field in whatever Java object you are representing your `VersionedData` object with the value 0.

The `data` field, however, is marked as `OPTIONAL`, which means it can be left out. As you might also have an encoding that has not included the `version` field because it is set to its default value of 0, the possible lengths of a `SEQUENCE` representing a `VersionedData` object are as follows:

❑   0 — Version field is default value and absent, data field is also absent.

❑   1 — Version field is default value and absent, data field is present, or version field is present, data field is absent.

❑   2 — Version field is present, data field is present.

Note that being `OPTIONAL` and absent is not the same as setting the field to `NULL`. In fact you cannot use `NULL` here anyway, as the field has to contain a type of `OCTET STRING`. As I hinted at earlier, unlike in Java, where `null` is a value you can assign to any extension of `Object`, `NULL` in ASN.1 is a specific value.

Tagging

Every encoding of a standard ASN.1 type has a default tag value of one octet already, which serves the purpose of allowing someone parsing a byte stream containing ASN.1-encoded objects to work out how to interpret the bytes following. You can see the tag values for some of the common types that are specified for BER encoding in Table 5-1. The default tag value occupies the lower five bits (bits 5-1) of the available eight in the octet, and there are modifiers that can be applied to the default tag value.

Base Type	Tag Value	Base Type	Tag Value	Base Type	Tag Value
BOOLEAN	0x01	ENUMERATED	0x0a	IA5String	0x16
INTEGER	0x02	UTF8String	0x0c	UTCTime	0x17
BIT STRING	0x03	SEQUENCE	0x10	GeneralizedTime	0x18
OCTET STRING	0x04	SET	0x11	VisibleString	0x1a
NULL	0x05	NumericString	0x12	UniversalString	0x1c
OBJECT IDENTIFIER	0x06	PrintableString	0x13	BMPString	0x1e

The most important of these modifiers for you is bit 6, which if set means the type is a constructed type. What this means is that the byte stream following will be made up of other ASN.1 objects that need to be assembled to make up the object being parsed. I'll deal with this in more detail when you look at BER encoding, but for now it's enough to know that SEQUENCE and SET are always marked with the constructed bit. Therefore, although the tag value for SEQUENCE is 0x10 and SET is 0x11, the encoded values you will encounter will be 0x30 to indicate a SEQUENCE follows and 0x31 to indicate a SET, because both these types are composed of one or more other ASN.1 objects.

Bits 8 and 7 specify the *class* of the tag. As I'm currently talking about default types, these bits will both be zero, which indicates they are in the UNIVERSAL class, which generally means the actual tag value is for one of the predefined ASN.1 types. The other tag classes are CONTEXT-SPECIFIC, PRIVATE, and APPLICATION. The bit values associated with each class are as follows:

Class	Bit 8	Bit 7
UNIVERSAL	0	0
APPLICATION	0	1
CONTEXT-SPECIFIC	1	0
PRIVATE	1	1

You can ignore PRIVATE and APPLICATION because, as their names suggest, they are used in specific ASN.1 modules designed for specific applications. So at least in the case of the ASN.1 modules you deal with in cryptography for open standards, you will never run into them, and if you did, interpreting them would be dependent on the documentation accompanying the module. CONTEXT-SPECIFIC, on the other hand, is the default class of tagging and by far the most common, so I will concentrate on the CONTEXT-SPECIFIC class of tags here.

In addition to the predefined tag values, ASN.1 also allows the users to specify their own tag values. The syntax used to specify a tagged type in ASN.1 follows the pattern:

```
[(class) number] (TagStyle) Type
```

where the parameters in (), *class* and *TagStyle*, are optional and *Type* is the type that the tag in this context now represents. If *class*, which can be one of APPLICATION, CONTEXT-SPECIFIC, or PRIVATE, is left out, it is considered to be the default, that is, CONTEXT-SPECIFIC. So, if you see something like

```
encodedKey [1] OCTET STRING
```

you can tell that encodedKey is an OCTET STRING, which has the CONTEXT-SPECIFIC tag of value 1, done using the default style of tagging for the module. If the IMPLICIT or EXPLICIT keywords appear for *TagStyle*, then they override the tag style for the module, for that tag only, to be either IMPLICIT or EXPLICIT. The tag style for the module is determined by the tagging environment that has been specified in the DEFINITIONS block of the ASN.1 module, and as I mentioned earlier, it can be one of three tagging possibilities: AUTOMATIC, EXPLICIT, and IMPLICIT.

For small value tags, from 0 to 30, the actual value of the tag is stored in the bottom five bits, where the value associated with a normal ASN.1 tag goes otherwise. For tag values from 31 to 127, the bottom five bits are all set to 1 and the next octet is used to contain the tag number. If the number is higher than 127, the top bit of the next octet is set to 1 and the number is stored in seven-bit chunks, with the top bit of each octet being set to 1 if there is another chunk to follow.

By way of example, if you ignore whether bit 6 gets set for the moment, an ASN.1 object that has been given a 0 tag, as in has [0] in front of its type, will be the byte 0x80. If it has been tagged with [32], the tag will take two bytes — 0x9f to indicate a tag greater than 31, and 0x20 to give the actual value of the tag. Finally, if it has been tagged with "[128]' there will be three bytes of tag — 0x9f, 0x81 to give the first seven bits of the value with the bit 8 set to indicate another byte follows, and 0x00 to give the next seven bits of the value with bit 8 not set to indicate it is the last seven bits of the tag value.

The next sections review the three tagging environments, EXPLICIT, IMPLICIT, and AUTOMATIC, in the context of tags created in the CONTEXT-SPECIFIC class.

EXPLICIT Tagging

If you see nothing in the definition's block of an ASN.1 module, or you see

```
DEFINITIONS EXPLICIT TAGS ::=
```

then the default tagging style for that module is EXPLICIT. You might also see something like this:

```
encodedKey [1] EXPLICIT OCTET STRING
```

which means regardless of the default tagging for the module, encodedKey is an explicitly tagged OCTET STRING with the tag value 1.

EXPLICIT tagging actually wraps the underlying encoding, so it is the easiest to interpret. By "wrap" I mean that an explicitly tagged object has another object around it that serves the purpose of carrying the tag value. The easiest way to understand this is to start looking at the actual bytes produced during an encoding. For example, looking at the encodedKey definition again, assuming you started with 32-byte array when you made it, printing one in hex might give you the following bytes in the header:

```
a1 22 04 20...
```

where `0xa1` tells you that you have a constructed (bit 6 is set), context-specific (bit 8 is set), tagged object with the tag value 1 (the bottom five bits) with a body of length 34 bytes (0x22). The body then starts with 0x04, a universal tag that is for an OCTET STRING, and the OCTET STRING also has a body of length 32 bytes (0x20), which is the bytes that you started with.

Note that the constructed bit (bit 6) is set in the byte starting the tag header — it is what tells you there is another encoding wrapped in the encoding of the tagged encoding. You will see how important the constructed bit becomes in interpreting tagged objects when you look at IMPLICIT tagging next.

IMPLICIT Tagging

Often you will see

```
DEFINITIONS IMPLICIT TAGS ::=
```

at the start of an ASN.1 module. If you see this, it means that the tagging style in the module is IMPLICIT. You may also see a declaration like

```
keyEncoded [1] IMPLICIT OCTET STRING
```

This also indicates that you are looking at an IMPLICIT tag.

The IMPLICIT tag style takes its name from the fact that the original tag value associated with the object it tags is overridden so the original tag value is now only *implicit* from the context in which the encoding is interpreted. As you will see, this can also introduce a certain amount of ambiguity.

Once again, the best way to deal with this is to look at the bytes produced in the header. This time the 32 byte value for the octets making up the encoded key gives the following header:

```
81 20 ...
```

This time you have a tagged object, with the tag value 1, which is 32 bytes in length. What happened to the OCTET STRING tag? Yes, it is gone. It has been replaced with the tag number you specified (0x01), marked in the tag byte as CONTEXT-SPECIFIC (0x80), thus giving you 0x81.

Without getting into a debate about the merits of this tagging style, you can see how important it is to handle it correctly. Just how vital this is becomes obvious when you look at what can happen with the encoding for an ASN.1 structure that might be defined as follows:

```
TroublesomeSequence ::= SEQUENCE {
                    encoding1 OCTET STRING,
                    encoding2 [0] OCTET STRING OPTIONAL
}
```

which is used in the following context:

```
troublesome [1] TroublesomeSequence
```

Now imagine that you encode a value for `troublesome` with both `encoding1` and `encoding2` created using 32-byte octet strings. The header for `troublesome` will look as follows:

```
a1 44 04 20 ...
```

Note that this time the byte starting the header—0xa1—has bit 6 set indicating that the value is constructed. This has happened because the `IMPLICIT` tag is overriding the tag value of a constructed type, in this case a `SEQUENCE`. After the tag byte, you then have a length byte and you can see the 0x04 indicating your first octet string. So far, so good.

Now make it more interesting. The `encoding2` field in `TroublesomeSequence` is `OPTIONAL`, meaning it can be left out. So I will now look at the header for the encoding of `troublesome`, where only `encoding1` has been set to a 32-byte value and `encoding2` has been left out. Doing this gives the following bytes in the header:

```
a1 22 04 20 ...
```

Now look back at the example for `EXPLICIT` tagging and see if you can find a difference. Yes, there is no difference. It is not possible to tell the difference between a particular ASN.1 base type with a tag of type `EXPLICIT` and a tagged `SEQUENCE`, or `SET`, of type `IMPLICIT` containing only one member that is of the same base type as used in the `EXPLICIT` case.

This leaves you with the following general rule, which you will be reminded of again later.

> **When interpreting encodings containing ASN.1 objects with `IMPLICIT` tagging, you must write code to interpret each `IMPLICIT` tag explicitly.**

AUTOMATIC Tagging

You will see this only in the `DEFINITIONS` section of the module. In the particular world you are looking at, `AUTOMATIC` is very rare—if you do see it, it means that everything in a `SEQUENCE` or `SET` is automatically tagged, with the first element tagged as 0. The tags are added using the `IMPLICIT` style unless the item that would be tagged is already tagged, or is a `CHOICE` item.

This one is almost better left to using an ASN.1 tool for dealing with it. If you have to deal with one by hand, the best way is to print the module out and then record what the tag values should be by hand. After that, cross your fingers and hope that you haven't missed one or tagged a `CHOICE` item by mistake.

CHOICE

The `CHOICE` type indicates that the ASN.1 field, or variable, will be one of a group of possible ASN.1 types or structures. If you are looking for another equivalent, the `CHOICE` type is very similar to a union in C or Pascal, the difference being that tagging is normally used to resolve any possible ambiguities. For example, looking at

```
SignerIdentifier ::= CHOICE {
                issuerAndSerialNumber IssuerAndSerialNumber,
                subjectKeyIdentifier [0] SubjectKeyIdentifier }
```

you can see that a `SignerIdentifier` can be either of the type `IssuerAndSerialNumber` or an object with a 0 tag of the underlying type `SubjectKeyIdentifier`.

The zero tag will be applied with the `IMPLICIT` style — that is, it will override the default tag value for whatever type makes up a `SubjectKeyIdentifier`. This leads to an interesting issue about choice types that was touched on in the discussion on the `AUTOMATIC` style of tagging. Because choice types contain tag values that are used to distinguish which item in the `CHOICE` is represented, any object of type `CHOICE` is never tagged using the `IMPLICIT` style. I will repeat this as well; it is important!

> **A tag applied to an ASN.1 object of type `CHOICE` is always applied using the `EXPLICIT` style of tagging.**

CLASS

The `CLASS` type was introduced in 1994 because of problems with the `ANY` syntax and ASN.1 macros, partly a result of the ambiguities they made possible in definitions, and also because the syntax was almost impossible to deal with properly if you were trying to write an automated tool. Strictly speaking, the `ANY` type is no longer supported, although as you will see, it still lives on. It represents the one non-backward-compatible change made in ASN.1's history, and even 10 years on, we still seem to be coming to terms with it.

The effect is that prior to 1994, where you would have written

```
AlgorithmIdentifier ::= SEQUENCE {
                    algorithm OBJECT IDENTIFIER,
                    parameters ANY DEFINED BY algorithm OPTIONAL }
```

you now write

```
ALGORITHM-IDENTIFIER ::= CLASS {
                        &id OBJECT IDENTIFIER UNIQUE,
                        &Type OPTIONAL
}
WITH SYNTAX { OID &id [PARAMETERS &Type] }

AlgorithmIdentifier { ALGORITHM-IDENTIFIER:InfoObjectSet } ::= SEQUENCE {
        algorithm ALGORITHM-IDENTIFIER.&id({InfoObjectSet}),
        parameters ALGORITHM-IDENTIFIER.&Type({InfoObjectSet}{@.algorithm}) OPTIONAL
}
```

You'll see the definition using `CLASS` in PKCS #1. The definition using `ANY` appeared in X.509. The `{@.algorithm}` in the second definition provides the equivalent to the `DEFINED BY algorithm`. It tells you that for a given value of the `algorithm` field, the `parameters` field is constrained to the associated parameter value in `InfoObjectSet`.

Now look at the parameterization in the definition of `AlgorithmIdentifier`, the actual structure that contains ASN.1 values, as in:

```
AlgorithmIdentifier { ALGORITHM-IDENTIFIER:InfoObjectSet } ::= SEQUENCE {
```

The purpose behind this is to make the following definition possible in PKCS #1:

```
DigestInfo ::= SEQUENCE {
                 digestAlgorithm DigestAlgorithm,
                 digest OCTET STRING
}

DigestAlgorithm ::= AlgorithmIdentifier { {PKCS1-v1-5DigestAlgorithms} }
```

where `PKCS1-v1-5DigestAlgorithms` is defined as:

```
PKCS1-v1-5DigestAlgorithms ALGORITHM-IDENTIFIER ::= {
                         { OID id-md2 PARAMETERS NULL }
                       | { OID id-md5 PARAMETERS NULL }
                       | { OID id-sha1 PARAMETERS NULL }
                       | { OID id-sha256 PARAMETERS NULL }
                       | { OID id-sha384 PARAMETERS NULL }
                       | { OID id-sha512 PARAMETERS NULL }
}
```

or, in common language, the possible values for a PKCS #1 digest algorithm identifier.

I have glossed over the fact that if you look at the actual PKCS #1 document, you will see that `id-md2`, `id-md5`, and so on are defined with the type `OBJECT IDENTIFIER`, but you now have the general idea.

Encoding Rules

There are currently five encoding methods recognized for encoding ASN.1 objects into streams of bytes:

- ❑ BER encoding includes the Basic Encoding Rules.
- ❑ DER encoding includes the Distinguished Encoding Rules.
- ❑ CER encoding includes the Canonical Encoding Rules.
- ❑ PER encoding includes the Packed Encoding Rules.
- ❑ XER encoding includes the XML Encoding Rules.

I mention all of them for completeness, as you can see the number of methods indicates that people have had a few goes at producing encoding methods to date and there is probably still more to be written. Fortunately, the only two methods of interest are BER encoding and DER encoding.

BER Encoding

BER stands for Basic Encoding Rules. As you've probably guessed from the example encodings you've seen so far, BER encoding follows the tag-length-value (TLV) convention. A tag is used to identify the type, a value defining the length of the content is next, and then the actual value of the content follows.

BER encoding offers three methods for encoding an ASN.1 object:

- ❏ Primitive definite-length
- ❏ Constructed definite-length
- ❏ Constructed indefinite-length

Simple types employ the primitive definite-length, bit and character string types will employ whatever method is most expedient, and structured types employ one of the constructed methods. If an object is tagged with the IMPLICIT style, the encoding used is the same as that used for the type of the object being tagged. If an object is tagged with the EXPLICIT style, one of the constructed methods will be used to encode the tagging.

How is it decided which method is most expedient? Strictly speaking, the decision is made on the basis of whether you know how long the encoding of the object will be when you start writing it out. However, in some cases, standards do specify BER indefinite-length, so in situations like that, you will end up with objects that are indefinite-length encoded regardless of whether it would have been possible to hold the object in memory. To fully understand what this means, you need to take a look at the three methods in more detail.

The Primitive Definite-Length Method

The definite-length methods all require that you know the length of what you are trying to encode in advance. The primitive definite-length method is appropriate for any nonstructured type, or implicitly tagged versions of the same, and an encoding of this type is created by first encoding the tag assigned to the object, encoding the length, and then writing out the encoding of the body.

You'll look at how the bodies are encoded in more detail later, but how the encoding of the length is done is worth looking at here. If the length is less than or equal to 127, a single octet is written out containing the actual length as a 7-bit number. If the length is greater than 127, the first octet written out has bit 8 set and bits 7–1, represent the number of octets following that contain the actual length. The length is then written out, one octet at a time, high order octet first.

For example, a length of 127 will produce a length encoding with 1 byte of the value 0x7f, a length of 128 will produce a 2-byte encoding with the values 0x81 and 0x80, and a length of 1,000 will produce a 3 byte encoding — 0x82, 0x03, and 0xe8. This is the simplest method of encoding and, as you will see, is required for DER encodings.

The Constructed Definite-Length Method

Length octets in this case are generated the same way as for the primitive definite-length method, but the initial byte in the tag associated with any object encoded in this fashion will have bit 6 set, indicating the encoding is of the constructed type.

As you would imagine, the regular structured types such as SEQUENCE and SET, or implicitly tagged objects derived from them, are still encoded as the concatenation of the BER encoding of the objects that make them up. Likewise, explicitly tagged objects are encoded using the BER encoding of the object that was tagged. Where this does become different is when bit string and character string types, or implicit types derived from them, are encoded using the constructed definite-length method.

When this happens, the original bit string, or character string, is encoded as a series of substrings that are of the same base type as the constructed string. For example, if you are trying to encode a byte array using the constructed definite-length method as an OCTET STRING, the encoding will start with an OCTET STRING tag with bit 6 set indicating that it is constructed. Then, after the length octets, the body of the encoding will be made up a series of smaller OCTET STRING encodings using the primitive definite-length method, the sum of which will be the byte array that you were originally trying to encode.

You might use this method where you have several values that make up a single ASN.1 type that exist separately prior to creating an encoding of the ASN.1 type. For example, an e-mail address may be defined as a single ASN.1 type but be assembled from parts "name" + "@" + "domain" prior to encoding, which can be encoded as substrings of a constructed string representing the full address.

The Constructed Indefinite-Length Method

Unlike the previous two methods, the constructed indefinite-length method does not require you to know the length of the encoding you are trying to construct in advance. With this method, the encoding of the tag value follows the same procedure as for the constructed definite-length method; however, the length is written out as the single octet of the value 0x80, and instead of being able to use the length of the encoding to determine when you reach the end of the contents in the body of the encoding, there is an end-of-contents marker—two octets of the value 0x00, which actually equate to tag 0, length 0. Other than the requirement for and the presence of the end-of-contents marker, encoding of objects is handled in much the same way as for constructed definite-length.

This method of encoding is useful where the length of the value is not known at the time the tag and length for the value is encoded. This method is common when encodings are very large and memory or efficiency constraints prevent the entire value being buffered to determine its length before encoding it.

DER Encoding

The Distinguished Encoding Rules, or DER, are so called because they make identical data within identical ASN.1 definitions reduce to identical binary encodings. This is particularly important in security applications where the binary data will be digitally signed. There is also an interesting covert channel made possible with BER encodings where equivalent, but different BER encodings can be used to transmit extra information. For example, an octet string representing encrypted data could be represented using a constructed method where the length of the substrings making up the encrypted data could be used to leak information about either the data itself or the key used to encrypt it. As DER always reduces a value to the same encoding no matter what, such a covert channel is not possible.

DER adds the following restrictions to BER encoding to make this possible:

- ❑ Only definite-length is allowed.

- ❑ Only SEQUENCE, SET, implicitly tagged objects derived from SEQUENCE and SET, and all tags of EXPLICIT type use constructed definite-length.

- ❑ The length of the encoding must be encoded in the minimum number of bytes possible. For example, no leading zeros that add length but do not change the value of the item being encoded are included.

- ❑ Fields that are set to their default value are not included in the encoding.

- ❑ The objects contained in a SET are sorted.

DER encoding is the most common form of encoding you will encounter, and it is also the simplest to perform. The only area of complication is the sorting of the objects contained in SET objects. A DER-encoded SET is sorted by ordering the objects inside it according to their encoded value in ascending order. Encodings are compared by padding them with trailing zeros so they are all the same length, with the result that a DER-encoded SET will be ordered on the tag value of each object. Be careful about relying on this, though. A BER-encoded SET is not necessarily sorted, so if you are trying to write code to handle both BER- and DER-encoded SET objects, it is a mistake to rely on the ordering taking place.

The Bouncy Castle ASN.1 API

The Bouncy Castle ASN.1 API evolved to deal with the ASN.1 binary encoding and binary decoding requirements of the other Bouncy Castle APIs and the provider implementation. As such, although it does not represent a full implementation of ASN.1, it does cover most of the issues that seem to arrive when dealing with cryptographic protocols and structures.

The main package for the API is org.bouncycastle.asn1, and there are a variety of packages off org.bouncycastle.asn1 that contain classes for assisting with the implementation of various message and data formats. For example, org.bouncycastle.asn1.pkcs has classes for use with the PKCS standards, org.bouncycastle.asn1.cms has classes for supporting the ASN.1 objects in RFC 3852, and org.bouncycastle.asn1.x509 has classes for supporting the ASN.1 objects used in X.509.

The org.bouncycastle.asn1 package has a few simple ideas underlying it to support the encoding requirements you run into with cryptographic protocols. The following conventions apply:

❑   Objects whose names start with DER encode in DER format.

❑   Objects whose names start with BER prefer to encode in BER format but can encode in DER format.

❑   Objects that support both BER and DER inherit from a parent object starting with ASN1.

❑   ASN1InputStream is the class that should be used for reading encoded streams.

❑   ASN1OutputStream and BEROutputStream will write classes out in both DER and BER format, depending on what their preferred encoding is.

❑   DEROutputStream will force objects to encode in DER.

The need for having the DEROutputStream behave the way that it does is quite important. Two common issues arise when you are working with other implementations of protocols and also in the general sense when you are generating hashes and signatures.

The general issue of being compatible with other implementations is that a lot of implementations seem to ignore the requirement to support BER encoding even when it is specified in the documentation for the standard that is apparently being implemented. So on more than one occasion, you may find yourself having to convert an object that is BER encoded into one that is only DER encoded. The property DEROutputStream has of forcing DER encoding makes this conversion quite simple.

For example, imagine you have a BER-encoded object in a byte array called *berData* that you want to convert to a DER-encoded object in a byte array that you will call *derData*. Using the Bouncy Castle ASN.1 API, you can achieve the conversion to DER with the following lines:

```
ASN1InputStream       aIn = new ASN1InputStream(berData);
ByteArrayOutputStream bOut = new ByteArrayOutputStream();
DEROutputStream       dOut = new DEROutputStream(bOut);

dOut.writeObject(aIn.readObject());

derData = bOut.toByteArray();
```

If you run into a problem where, say, you have a PKCS #12 file from one product that refuses to import into another, there is a good chance it is the inability of the second product to deal with BER encoding that is the problem.

In a similar vein, standards that specify methods for calculating digital signatures, hashes, or MACs on ASN.1-encoded data will often specify that it must be calculated on the DER encoding of the objects. You can use virtually the same technique to do the conversion, depending on how you have everything set up. The only difference might be that you need to iterate on aIn.readObject() if berData contains more than one object.

Creating the Basic ASN.1 Types

The object hierarchy in the ASN.1 base package works as follows. The root object for all the simple types, bit string types, and structured and tagged types is DERObject. As it turns out, a better name would have been ASN1Object, but originally, it seemed you might be able to get away without dealing with BER, so when you see the name you can think of it as a chance to learn from example. There is no escaping it!

At the moment, a number of types have both BER and DER encoding implementations, and they have parent implementations that following the convention of starting with ASN.1. Most types produce DER-compatible encodings. Currently the following implementations are associated with the following ASN.1 types:

- ❑ BIT STRING—DERBitString

- ❑ BMPString—DERBMPString

- ❑ BOOLEAN—DERBoolean

- ❑ ENUMERATED—DEREnumerated

- ❑ GeneralizedTime—DERGeneralizedTime

- ❑ GeneralString—DERGeneralString

- ❑ IA5String—DERIA5String

- ❑ INTEGER—DERInteger

- ❑ NULL—ASN1Null, BERNull, DERNull

- ❑ NumericString—DERNumericString

- ❑ OBJECT IDENTIFIER—DERObjectIdentifier

- ❑ OCTET STRING—ASN1OctetString, BERConstructedOctetString, DEROctetString

- ❑ PrintableString—DERPrintableString

- ❑   SEQUENCE—ASN1Sequence, BERSequence, DERSequence

- ❑   SET—ASNSet, BERSet, DERSet

- ❑   TeletexString(T61String)—DERT61String

- ❑   UniversalString—DERUniversalString

- ❑   UTCTime—DERUTCTime

- ❑   UTF8String—DERUTF8String

- ❑   VisibleString—DERVisibleString

All these objects provide implementations of Object.equals() and Object.hashCode().

Only the object names starting with DER or BER provide constructors, and these are pretty much what you would expect. The constructors for classes corresponding to the bit string types can take byte arrays, with DERBitString also being able to take the number of pad bits. There are constructors for the classes corresponding to the character string types that can take String objects, except for DERUniversalString, which will only take a byte array, because Java is not able to represent 32-bit characters directly. There are constructors for the time-based classes that take Date objects. A DERObjectIdentifier can be constructed from a String representation of an OBJECT IDENTIFIER; the constructor for DERBoolean simply takes true or false. DERInteger and DEREnumerated both take int and BigInteger. The constructors for the tagged object types take a tag number, a flag specifying whether the tagging is explicit or not, and the object to be tagged.

Finally, the BER and DER types supporting SEQUENCE and SET can be either constructed as structures that have a single object inside them by using a constructor that takes a single encodable object or as structures that contain multiple objects by using an ASN.1 API equivalent to Vector or ArrayList, the ASN1EncodableVector class.

You will also notice that the base classes for each type usually have two getInstance() methods on them. The getInstance() methods come in two flavors. The first simply takes an object and returns whatever the base type is. This is a convenient method to enable you to avoid casting and other conversions that can be necessary when manipulating ASN.1 objects. The other method takes an ASN1TaggedObject and a boolean argument, the purpose of which is to say whether the tagging present on the ASN1TaggedObject is explicit, in which case the boolean is true, or implicit, in which case the boolean is false. It is this getInstance() pattern that is used throughout the ASN.1 API to deal with the complications that might arise due to implicit tagging with the various types.

Dealing with Tagging

The main issue with tagging, as you saw earlier, is that if an object is implicitly tagged, the actual tag the object is meant to have is implicit from the context in which its encoding appears. For the most part, without knowledge of what has been encoded originally, the best you can tell from the actual encoded information is that you have a tag value associated with a bunch of bytes. The exception to this is if the tag is marked as constructed, but even then the best you can do is tell you have a bunch of objects, or possibly just one object, which may in fact be inside an explicitly tagged SET or SEQUENCE.

From the point of view of programming this, a few simple examples would help. For example, say you created a BIT STRING from a byte array that represented a string of bits that was a multiple of 8, and then wanted to create an implicitly tagged version of it with the tag value 1. You could do this with the following code:

```
              DERBitString     bits = new DERBitString(byteArray, 0);
              ASN1TaggedObject taggedBits = new DERTaggedObject(false, 1, bits);
```

To recover `bits` from the tagged object you would then use the following:

```
              bits = DERBitString.getInstance(taggedBits, false);
```

Likewise if `bits` was actually wrapped in a SEQUENCE because you were trying to encode the following structure:

```
       WrappedBits ::= SEQUENCE {
                       bits BIT STRING }
```

and you were trying to implicitly tag the outer sequence as well with a tag value of 1. You might end up with the following fragment instead:

```
              DERBitString     bits = new DERBitString(byteArray, 0);
              ASN1Sequence     wBits = new DERSequence(bits);
              ASN1TaggedObject taggedWBits = new DERTaggedObject(false, 1, wBits);
```

and this time recovering it from the tagged object would be as follows:

```
              wBits = ASN1Sequence.getInstance(taggedWBits, false);
              bits = (DERBitString)wBits.getObjectAt(0);
```

As I mentioned earlier, it is the use of `false` that tells the API that it is dealing with an implicitly tagged object. If, instead, the tagging used in the code fragments was explicit, you would replace every occurrence of `false` with `true`.

So that covers the basics. Before you go on to look at some real examples, you'll try creating an ASN.1 structure of your own.

Defining Your Own Objects

Imagine you are trying to create a Java object implementing the following ASN.1 structure using DER encoding:

```
MyStructure ::= SEQUENCE {
                version INTEGER DEFAULT 0,
                created GeneralizedTime,
                baseData OCTET STRING,
                extraData [0] UTF8String OPTIONAL,
                commentData [1] UTF8String OPTIONAL }
```

The first thing you can notice is the presence of tagging. In this case the tagging is not specified in the actual structure, so you need to know what tagging environment you are in. You therefore look at the DEFINITIONS block in the module the structure appears in and see this:

```
DEFINITIONS IMPLICIT TAGS ::=
```

So you know tags have to be handled implicitly.

The other thing you can notice is the use of a DEFAULT. As mentioned earlier, in a DER-encoded object, a field that's set to its default value must be left out of the encoding. In a BER-encoded object it may or may not be present. In this case, you are using DER, so you must ensure that you do not include the version field in the encoding if it is set to its default value. In general, though, it is a good idea to adopt the following policy for BER as well.

> **A field set to its specified default is left out of the encoding.**

The final thing to note is the use of OPTIONAL. You have to take into account that one of, or both of, extraData and commentData might not be present in the encoding, and that, while they have the same base types, the tagging is used to distinguish them.

So now that you know what you are up against, take a look at the code.

Try It Out   Implementing an ASN.1-Based Java Object

This example is quite large, so I'll go through it in stages. The first step is to provide the necessary imports and to extend the general-purpose class that the API uses for creating ASN.1 objects— org.bouncycastle.asn1.ASN1Encodable. So here is the basic class header:

```
package chapter5;

import java.util.Date;

import org.bouncycastle.asn1.*;

/**
 * Implementation of an example ASN.1 structure.
 * <pre>
 * MyStructure ::= SEQUENCE {
 *                  version INTEGER DEFAULT 0,
 *                  created GeneralizedTime,
 *                  baseData OCTET STRING,
 *                  extraData [0] UTF8String OPTIONAL,
 *                  commentData [1] UTF8String OPTIONAL }
 * <pre>
 *
 */
public class MyStructure extends ASN1Encodable
{
    private DERInteger          version;
    private DERGeneralizedTime  created;
    private ASN1OctetString     baseData;
    private DERUTF8String       extraData = null;
    private DERUTF8String       commentData = null;
```

Now you need at least one constructor that will allow you to create the object from an ASN1Sequence that you might have just read from an ASN1InputStream. Note that doing this is a little involved, because any one of three fields in the actual sequence may be missing from the encoding. If the `version` field was its default value, it will be left out, and the `extraData` and `commentData` fields are optional, so they may be missing as well. What follows is a simple way of dealing with the optional fields; in some circumstances, you might want to include code that confirms the order the optional fields appear in the sequence as well, rather than simply recognizing them.

```java
/**
 * Constructor from an ASN.1 SEQUENCE
 */
public MyStructure(
    ASN1Sequence    seq)
{
    int index = 0;

    // check for version field
    if (seq.getObjectAt(0) instanceof DERInteger)
    {
        this.version = (DERInteger)seq.getObjectAt(0);
        index++;
    }
    else
    {
        this.version = new DERInteger(0);
    }

    this.created = (DERGeneralizedTime)seq.getObjectAt(index++);
    this.baseData = (ASN1OctetString)seq.getObjectAt(index++);

    // check for optional fields
    for (int i = index; i != seq.size(); i++)
    {
        ASN1TaggedObject    t = (ASN1TaggedObject)seq.getObjectAt(i);

        switch (t.getTagNo())
        {
        case 0:
            extraData = DERUTF8String.getInstance(t, false);
            break;
        case 1:
            commentData = DERUTF8String.getInstance(t, false);
            break;
        default:
            throw new IllegalArgumentException(
                        "Unknown tag " + t.getTagNo() + " in constructor");
        }
    }
}
```

Having written a constructor to get you from the ASN.1 world to the Java world, you now also need a constructor to get you from the Java world into a form where you can produce an ASN.1 binary encoding. The following is just a basic one, as you can imagine you might write convenience constructors depending on how you, or your fellow developers, were likely to use the class. As you might also imagine, this constructor is simpler than the one that builds from an `ASN1Sequence`, although you are still checking for the presence, or not, of optional fields.

Note that you are also creating the internal objects so they will encode in DER format, regardless of whether the object is written to a `DEROutputStream` or an `ASN1OutputStream`.

```
/**
 * Constructor from corresponding Java objects and primitives.
 */
public MyStructure(
    int     version,
    Date    created,
    byte[]  baseData,
    String  extraData,
    String  commentData)
{
    this.version = new DERInteger(version);
    this.created = new DERGeneralizedTime(created);
    this.baseData = new DEROctetString(baseData);

    if (extraData != null)
    {
        this.extraData = new DERUTF8String(extraData);
    }

    if (commentData != null)
    {
        this.commentData = new DERUTF8String(commentData);
    }
}
```

I have skipped the `get()` methods altogether, as they are obvious. The last fragment you need to look at is the implementation of the abstract `ASN1Encodable.toASN1Object()` method and the end of the class. When `ASN1OutputStream.writeObject()` is called, the `toASN1Object()` method is invoked to produce an object that can then be encoded on the stream. You should note that while the code again checks for the presence of the optional fields before adding them to the `ASN1EncodableVector`, which will be used to create the `DERSequence` object, you must also check the value of the `version` field and only include it if it is not its default value.

```
/*
 * Produce an object suitable for writing to an ASN1/DEROutputStream
 */
public DERObject toASN1Object()
{
    ASN1EncodableVector    v = new ASN1EncodableVector();

    if (version.getValue().intValue() != 0)
    {
        v.add(version);
    }

    v.add(created);
    v.add(baseData);

    if (extraData != null)
    {
        v.add(new DERTaggedObject(false, 0, extraData));
```

```
            }

        if (commentData != null)
        {
            v.add(new DERTaggedObject(false, 1, commentData));
        }

        return new DERSequence(v);
    }
}
```

Now you can try a simple test class. The test class dumps the ASN.1 binary encoding that is generated for each version of `MyStructure` you create to the screen as hex. It does this by using the convenience method `ASN1Encodable.getEncoded()` that `MyStructure` inherits to generate the byte encoding. See what you get.

```
package chapter5;

import java.util.Date;

/**
 * Test for MyStructure
 */
public class MyStructureTest
{
    public static void main(String[] args)
        throws Exception
    {
        byte[] baseData = new byte[5];
        Date    created = new Date(0); // 1/1/1970

        MyStructure     structure = new MyStructure(
                                    0, created, baseData, null, null);

        System.out.println(Utils.toHex(structure.getEncoded()));
        if (!structure.equals(structure.toASN1Object()))
        {
            System.out.println("comparison failed.");
        }

        structure = new MyStructure(0, created, baseData, "hello", null);

        System.out.println(Utils.toHex(structure.getEncoded()));
        if (!structure.equals(structure.toASN1Object()))
        {
            System.out.println("comparison failed.");
        }

        structure = new MyStructure(0, created, baseData, null, "world");

        System.out.println(Utils.toHex(structure.getEncoded()));
        if (!structure.equals(structure.toASN1Object()))
        {
            System.out.println("comparison failed.");
```

```
        }

        structure = new MyStructure(0, created, baseData, "hello", "world");

        System.out.println(Utils.toHex(structure.getEncoded()));
        if (!structure.equals(structure.toASN1Object()))
        {
            System.out.println("comparison failed.");
        }

        structure = new MyStructure(1, created, baseData, null, null);

        System.out.println(Utils.toHex(structure.getEncoded()));
        if (!structure.equals(structure.toASN1Object()))
        {
            System.out.println("comparison failed.");
        }
    }
}
```

And here is the output:

```
3018180f3139373030313031303030303030305a04050000000000
301f180f3139373030313031303030303030305a0405000000000000800568656c6c6f
301f180f3139373030313031303030303030305a04050000000000008105776f726c64
3026180f3139373030313031303030303030305a04050000000000000800568656c6c6f8105776f726c64
301b020101180f3139373030313031303030303030305a04050000000000
```

I have highlighted every second object's encoding with bold so that it is easier to see where the encoding of one object starts and finishes. You will look at this in more depth in the following section.

How It Works

There have been a few of steps to make all this happen. The first is you have extended ASN1Encodable to create an object suitable for passing to an ASN1OutputStream and you have implemented the toASN1Object() method to construct a DERSequence object that contains the primitive types you want to encode. The second is that you have written a constructor that allows you to take the types that you normally use in Java programming and convert them into their ASN.1 counterparts. Likewise, you provided a constructor to get you from the ASN.1 view of the MyStructure object, where it exists only as a sequence, back to the Java viewpoint. The only thing missing are the get() methods, and in this case you would just add whatever was appropriate to the application you were trying to develop.

Having a closer look at the output of the example also gives you more of an insight into what is going on when the encoding is being generated.

Starting at the beginning, you can see the tag for a SEQUENCE—0x10—Ored together with the value indicating a constructed type 0x20 (bit 6), giving you the value 0x30. The next byte is the length byte, and after that the values making up the internals of the SEQUENCE start to appear. Looking at the first four lines, you can see that the first encoding appearing in the sequence is that of a GeneralizedTime, which starts with a tag of 0x18. This has happened because, in the first four cases, the version field has its default value so is left out. On the fifth line, you can see the first object in the sequence is an INTEGER, tag 0x02, and this has happened because the version field is now 1—a value different from its default of 0.

As you would expect, the `GeneralizedTime` is always present, and you also see the OCTET STRING (tag 0x04) making up the `baseData` field. Then you come to the UTF8Strings, which would normally start with a tag of 0x0c. However, because of implicit tagging, it starts with 0x80 in the case of the `extraData` field, which has a tag value of 0, and 0x81 in the case of the `commentData` field, which has a tag value of 1. The easiest place to see this is to look at the difference at the end of the encoding on lines 2 and 3 where, on line 2 the `commentData` field is absent, and on line 3 the `extraData` field is absent.

At this point you should have a basic understanding of what is happening when an ASN.1 structure you have seen the definition for is encoded. Before you go on to look at some real-world structures, I will just diverge briefly to mention the classes that can be used to examine structures for which you only have the encoded object.

Analyzing an Unknown Encoded Object

The API also provides a general-purpose class that allows you to get a, more or less, human-readable dump of an ASN.1-encoded object. You can find it in the package `org.bouncycastle.asn1.util`; it is called `ASN1Dump`. It has a single method on it called `ASN1Dump.dumpAsString()`, which takes a single ASN.1 encodable object and returns the hierarchy it contains as a `String` object.

There is also an associated utility class called `Dump` in the same package. It contains a main method, which takes a single argument being a file that you want to run the `ASN1Dump` class over. Running a command like this:

```
java org.bouncycastle.asn.util.Dump id.p12
```

will dump out every ASN.1 object found in the file `id.p12`.

Try It Out   Using ASN1Dump

Let's try a simple example that builds on the work you did in the last section and see what `ASN1Dump` produces:

```
package chapter5;

import java.util.Date;

import org.bouncycastle.asn1.util.ASN1Dump;

/**
 * Example for ASN1Dump using MyStructure.
 */
public class ASN1DumpExample
{
    public static void main(String[] args)
        throws Exception
    {
        byte[] baseData = new byte[5];
        Date   created = new Date(0); // 1/1/1970

        MyStructure     structure = new MyStructure(
```

```
                                        0, created, baseData, "hello", "world");

        System.out.println(ASN1Dump.dumpAsString(structure));

        structure = new MyStructure(1, created, baseData, "hello", "world");

        System.out.println(ASN1Dump.dumpAsString(structure));
    }
}
```

When you run the example, you should expect to see the two structures get dumped out as follows:

```
DER Sequence
    GeneralizedTime(19700101000000GMT+00:00)
    DER Octet String[5]
    Tagged [0] IMPLICIT
        UTF8String(hello)
    Tagged [1] IMPLICIT
        UTF8String(world)

DER Sequence
    Integer(1)
    GeneralizedTime(19700101000000GMT+00:00)
    DER Octet String[5]
    Tagged [0] IMPLICIT
        UTF8String(hello)
    Tagged [1] IMPLICIT
        UTF8String(world)
```

As you can see, you have two SEQUENCE objects, both of which conform to the structure outlined in the previous section.

How It Works

ASN1Dump takes an object that extends ASN1Encodable and traverses its structure, building up an indented tree view of the internals of the object.

There is one thing a little odd about the output, though. As I have said previously, correctly working out what an implicitly tagged object is requires knowledge of the structure being parsed. In the previous output, the ASN1Dump class has correctly identified what is contained in the tagged objects. What is going on?

The answer, of course, is that it's cheating. As the tagged object has been constructed from the real objects involved, ASN1Dump can tell what type it is. Try adding the following lines to the example and running it again (you will need to import org.bouncycastle.asn1.ASN1InputStream as well):

```
        ASN1InputStream aIn = new ASN1InputStream(structure.getEncoded());

        System.out.println(ASN1Dump.dumpAsString(aIn.readObject()));
```

You will see the following extra lines of output:

```
DER Sequence
    Integer(1)
    GeneralizedTime(19700101000000GMT+00:00)
    DER Octet String[5]
    Tagged [0] IMPLICIT
        DER Octet String[5]
    Tagged [1] IMPLICIT
        DER Octet String[5]
```

This makes more sense. As the implicit tagging has overridden the tag for the UTF8String, the best the ASN1Dump class can do is recognize the implicitly tagged objects as being of the type OCTET STRING. Still, the ASN1Dump class is doing the best it can, and it does provide you with a basic analysis tool for dealing with ASN1-encoded messages. Having come this far, it is time to look at how ASN.1 applies to real-world situations in the JCA and JCE.

Using ASN.1 in Java: Some Real Examples

I have already mentioned objects of the type AlgorithmParameters as usually having an ASN.1 equivalent. As it happens, public and private keys that return "X.509" and PKCS#8 as their formats also return encodings created using ASN.1 when their Key.getEncoded() method is called and it is an ASN.1 object that is inside a PKCS #1 V1.5 signature when it is encrypted using an RSA private key.

Because these are all Java objects you are already familiar with, and you are going to be dealing with more ASN.1-based objects later in this book, now have a look at what goes on with these objects from the point of their ASN.1 binary encoding.

Some Basic ASN.1 Structures

There are a couple of structures that show up frequently enough in the ASN.1 modules associated with cryptography that they deserve mentioning before you start looking at some examples. The first is called AlgorithmIdentifier and originally appeared in X.509; the second is Attribute and originally appeared in the ISO/ITU-T useful definitions module. You will have a look at these common structures first, because they will provide you with some background when it comes to dealing with the examples.

The AlgorithmIdentifier Structure

The AlgorithmIdentifier structure serves simply to hold an object identifier representing a particular algorithm and an optional parameters structure that holds the parameters required. You will encounter a few variations of the structure, as some people define it for themselves, but even the variations usually boil down to this basic ASN.1 structure:

```
AlgorithmIdentifier ::= SEQUENCE {
                    algorithm OBJECT IDENTIFIER,
                    parameters SomeASN1Type OPTIONAL }
```

Pre-1994 the *SomeASN1Type* would have been ANY DEFINED BY algorithm. These days, of course, you will see a CLASS definition to show the linkage between the OBJECT IDENTIFIER representing the algorithm and the parameters field's actual type. This tells you that any ASN.1 structure can occupy that field and that the value you find there will depend on the value of the algorithm field.

One further thing you need to know: For historical reasons, the optional parameters field is often set to NULL instead of being left out, so you will often see a standard that specifies that the parameters field must be set to NULL rather than being left out. This happened because when the 1988 syntax for AlgorithmIdentifier was translated to the 1997 one, the OPTIONAL somehow got left out. Although this was later fixed via a defect report, whatever you do, if you are creating an AlgorithmIdentifier and you see parameters are NULL, make sure you include the NULL. Empty is not the same as NULL.

The Attribute Structure

The Attribute structure is another general structure that you will see a lot. The following definition is from RFC 3852:

```
Attribute ::= SEQUENCE {
            attrType OBJECT IDENTIFIER,
            attrValues SET OF AttributeValue
}

AttributeValue ::= ANY
```

Astute readers will remember that in the earlier discussion on the basics of ASN.1, support for ANY was withdrawn in 1994. The fact that RFC 3852 was published in 2004, some 10 years later, stands as a testimonial to how much of an upheaval that withdrawal caused. Versions of Attribute based on the use of the CLASS type and parameterization are starting to appear as well; see the ASN.1 module for PKCS #7 V1.6 as an example. However, the definition from RFC 3852 will be sufficient for the purposes here.

As you can see, the Attribute structure is basically a tagged SET, the content of which is determined by the OBJECT IDENTIFIER in the attrType field.

Encoding an IV

In the case of most block ciphers, such as AES in CBC mode, the only parameter value that is likely to be required in the parameters field of an AlgorithmIdentifier representing an encoding is the IV, and for most algorithms, it is defined as:

```
IvParam ::= OCTET STRING
```

So how do you convert an IV into its ASN.1 binary encoding using the JCA? Let's take a look at one approach.

Try It Out   Encoding an IV with ASN.1

Here is a basic example that uses an IvParameterSpec and an AlgorithmParameters object to create an ASN.1 binary encoding of an IV. Try running it.

```
package chapter5;

import java.security.AlgorithmParameters;
```

```
import javax.crypto.spec.IvParameterSpec;

import org.bouncycastle.asn1.ASN1InputStream;
import org.bouncycastle.asn1.util.ASN1Dump;

/**
 * Example showing IV encoding
 */
public class IVExample
{
    public static void main(String[] args) throws Exception
    {
        // set up the parameters object
        AlgorithmParameters  params = AlgorithmParameters.getInstance(
                                                        "AES", "BC");

        IvParameterSpec      ivSpec = new IvParameterSpec(new byte[16]);

        params.init(ivSpec);

        // look at the ASN.1 encodng.
        ASN1InputStream      aIn = new ASN1InputStream(params.getEncoded("ASN.1"));

        System.out.println(ASN1Dump.dumpAsString(aIn.readObject()));
    }
}
```

When you run the example, you should see the following output:

```
DER Octet String[16]
```

This output conforms to the ASN.1 description you saw for an IV earlier.

How It Works

The `AlgorithmParameters` class is the key to generating ASN.1 binary encodings for parameters. In this case, you have initialized the `params` object with an `IvParameterSpec` containing the IV you want to produce an encoding for. Then you called `AlgorithmParameters.getEncoded()`, explicitly requesting an ASN.1 binary encoding.

As you have already seen, you can also recover the `AlgorithmParameters` object for a particular cipher you have just used by calling `Cipher.getParameters()`, which will return an object that is already initialized. Likewise, this returned object's `getEncoded()` method will also return the ASN.1 binary encoding for the parameters. You will see an example of this a bit later.

Inside a PKCS #1 V1.5 Signature

I mentioned in the last chapter that PKCS #1 V1.5 signatures also included a structure around the hash, in addition to the padding that was applied. Like the IV parameters, the structure is very simple and is known as a `DigestInfo` object. It holds details of the message digest algorithm used to create the hash in the signature, as well as the actual bytes making up the hash that was calculated during the signing process. When a signature is sealed with a private key, the hash it contains is exported as the DER encoding of a `DigestInfo` structure. It is this encoded string of bytes that then has padding applied before encryption with the private key produces the final signature.

Earlier in this chapter, you looked at the `DigestInfo` structure when I was discussing the use of the ASN.1 `CLASS` type in the definition of `AlgorithmIdentifier`. The structure was defined as follows:

```
DigestInfo ::= SEQUENCE{
                    digestAlgorithm  DigestAlgorithm,
                    digest OCTET STRING }

DigestAlgorithm ::= AlgorithmIdentifier { {PKCS1-v1-5DigestAlgorithms} }
```

As you can see, the `DigestAlgorithm` type is an `AlgorithmIdentifier`. There is one twist here, though; the extra bit at the end in the braces, namely:

```
{ {PKCS1-v1-5DigestAlgorithms} }
```

told you something about this particular extension of `AlgorithmIdentifier`. Its set of possible values comes from another structure called `PKCS1-v1-5DigestAlgorithms`, which consists of a list of object identifiers, parameter pairs that represent the current range of PKCS #1 V1.5 signature types supported by PKCS #1. I won't repeat the possible values here, as you can find them in the original discussion on the `CLASS` type; however, I will mention that is the encoded form of the possible values listed in `PKCS1-v1-5DigestAlgorithms`, which you will find inside the plaintext of PKCS #1 V1.5 signatures. So much for the background; you'll see now if that is the case.

Try It Out   **Looking Inside a PKCS #1 V1.5 Signature**

Try the following example. As you can see, it uses the regular `Signature` class to create a byte array containing a signature created using SHA-256 and RSA. However, in the verification part, it uses a `Cipher` to unlock the signature and then parses the structure contained in the decrypted block, checking the section containing the hash that was calculated when the signature was created against one generated for the same data using SHA-256.

```java
package chapter5;

import java.security.*;

import javax.crypto.Cipher;

import org.bouncycastle.asn1.ASN1InputStream;
import org.bouncycastle.asn1.ASN1OctetString;
import org.bouncycastle.asn1.ASN1Sequence;
import org.bouncycastle.asn1.util.ASN1Dump;

/**
 * Basic class for exploring PKCS #1 V1.5 Signatures.
 */
public class PKCS1SigEncodingExample
{
    public static void main(String[] args) throws Exception
    {
        KeyPairGenerator keyGen = KeyPairGenerator.getInstance("RSA", "BC");

        keyGen.initialize(512, new SecureRandom());

        KeyPair          keyPair = keyGen.generateKeyPair();
```

```
Signature          signature = Signature.getInstance("SHA256withRSA", "BC");

// generate a signature
signature.initSign(keyPair.getPrivate());

byte[] message = new byte[] { (byte)'a', (byte)'b', (byte)'c' };

signature.update(message);

byte[]  sigBytes = signature.sign();

// verify hash in signature
Cipher     cipher = Cipher.getInstance("RSA/None/PKCS1Padding", "BC");

cipher.init(Cipher.DECRYPT_MODE, keyPair.getPublic());

byte[]  decSig = cipher.doFinal(sigBytes);

// parse the signature
ASN1InputStream    aIn = new ASN1InputStream(decSig);
ASN1Sequence       seq = (ASN1Sequence)aIn.readObject();

System.out.println(ASN1Dump.dumpAsString(seq));

// grab a digest of the correct type
MessageDigest      hash = MessageDigest.getInstance("SHA-256", "BC");

hash.update(message);

ASN1OctetString    sigHash = (ASN1OctetString)seq.getObjectAt(1);
if (MessageDigest.isEqual(hash.digest(), sigHash.getOctets()))
{
    System.out.println("hash verification succeeded");
}
else
{
    System.out.println("hash verification failed");
}
    }
}
```

Running the example, you should see the following:

```
DER Sequence
    DER Sequence
        ObjectIdentifier(2.16.840.1.101.3.4.2.1)
        NULL
    DER Octet String[32]

hash verification succeeded
```

So you found the correct hash value and the signature hash verified as expected. Looking at the dump, you can see the OBJECT IDENTIFIER value for SHA-256 and then a 20-byte OCTET STRING, which is the actual SHA-256 hash that was calculated.

How It Works

As I mentioned earlier, the byte array that gets padded during signature calculation is actually a DER encoding of a `DigestInfo` object. The signature is then a representation of the padded DER encoding that has been encrypted with the private key. Decrypting the signature with the public key gives you back this DER-encoded stream, and if you look at the section of the output representing the ASN.1 dump, you can see that stream produces at the top level a single sequence that contains two objects, the first of which is itself a sequence.

If you look back at the definition for an `AlgorithmIdentifier`, you can see that the OBJECT IDENTIFIER giving the value for `algorithm` field is `2.16.840.1.101.3.4.2.1`. If you look it up in a registry of identifiers, you will discover this is for the algorithm SHA-256. The other thing you can tell from the dump is that the `parameters` field in the `AlgorithmIdentifier` is the value NULL, which you would expect, as the digest does not require any input other than the data it is supposed to verify. Of course, it could have been left out altogether because the field is optional, but this is another one of those moments where you have to allow for history.

Encoding PSS Signature Parameters

Although PSS signatures themselves do not contain an ASN.1 structure, they do have algorithm parameters. PSS algorithm parameters are interesting to look at, because it possible for every field in their corresponding ASN.1 structure to be set to their default values. The structure used for PSS parameters is defined in PKCS #1 and, after some simplifying, looks something like this:

```
RSASSA-PSS-params ::= SEQUENCE {
                      hashAlgorithm [0] HashAlgorithm DEFAULT sha1,
                      maskGenAlgorithm [1] MaskGenAlgorithm DEFAULT mgf1SHA1,
                      saltLength [2] INTEGER DEFAULT 20,
                      trailerField [3] TrailerField DEFAULT trailerFieldBC }


HashAlgorithm ::= AlgorithmIdentifier


MaskGenAlgorithm ::= AlgorithmIdentifier


TrailerField ::= INTEGER
```

I won't go into the specifics of the default values here, but they are also the ones represented by `PSSParameterSpec.DEFAULT`, so you would expect that creating a PSS signature with the default parameter set and retrieving its `AlgorithmParameters` would produce an empty SEQUENCE in its ASN.1 binary encoding.

Try It Out   Encoding PSS Parameters

Here is a simple example using parameters with the `Signature` class that allows you to have a look at the encodings being produced. Strictly speaking, the setting of the default parameters is not necessary, as the `Signature.getInstance()` method returns a `Signature` object that already has parameters set. However, it does show how the use of algorithm parameters is different with the `Signature` class compared to the `Cipher` class. Have a look at the example, run it, and see what it produces.

```
package chapter5;

import java.security.AlgorithmParameters;
import java.security.Signature;
import java.security.spec.PSSParameterSpec;

import org.bouncycastle.asn1.ASN1InputStream;
import org.bouncycastle.asn1.util.ASN1Dump;

/**
 * Example showing PSS parameter recovery and encoding
 */
public class PSSParamExample
{
    public static void main(String[] args) throws Exception
    {
        Signature  signature = Signature.getInstance("SHA1withRSAandMGF1", "BC");

        // set the default parameters
        signature.setParameter(PSSParameterSpec.DEFAULT);

        // get the default parameters
        AlgorithmParameters params = signature.getParameters();

        // look at the ASN.1 encodng.
        ASN1InputStream    aIn = new ASN1InputStream(params.getEncoded("ASN.1"));

        System.out.println(ASN1Dump.dumpAsString(aIn.readObject()));
    }
}
```

Running the example produces the following output:

```
DER Sequence
```

indicating you have an empty sequence.

How It Works

The call to `Signature.getParameters()` returns an `AlgorithmParameters` object that is set to contain the default parameters for creating a PSS signature. As they are default parameters, you would expect none of the fields in the RSASSA-PSS-params to be included in the encoding, and consequently the SEQUENCE will be empty, which is what the output indicates.

An interesting thing to do here is to change one of the parameters and see how the encoding changes. In Chapter 4 I mentioned that PSS signatures can be created with a zero salt size. You can configure the `Signature` object used in the example by changing the call to `setParameter()` from

```
        signature.setParameter(PSSParameterSpec.DEFAULT);
```

to

```
        signature.setParameter(new PSSParameterSpec(0));
```

You should see the following output:

```
DER Sequence
    Tagged [2]
        Integer(0)
```

This output indicates that the sequence is no longer empty. It is now carrying a 0 value for the `saltLength` field, which has a default value of 20.

Encoding Public and Private Keys

I have already touched on the fact that the encoded forms of public and private keys contain a considerable amount of structure in them, and as it happens, the language used for describing these structures is ASN.1. Looking at it in the same manner as with other Java specification objects, an encoded form of a key is simply a value object, so as you would imagine, the JCA provides wrapping objects that can wrap the encoded forms and then be used to convert them back into keys using the `KeyFactory` class.

Because there are different ASN.1 structures built for handling public and private keys, the JCA provides two classes for wrapping key encodings. The first one you will look at, used for wrapping public key encodings, is the `X509EncodedKeySpec`. The second one, used for wrapping private key encodings, is the `PKCS8EncodedKeySpec`.

The X509EncodedKeySpec Class

The `java.security.spec.X509EncodedKeySpec` class takes its name from the origins of the structure used to wrap public keys. It has a single constructor on it that takes a byte array that should contain a DER encoding of the structure that appears in the key block of an X.509 certificate. This is the encoding that should be returned by a public key that has a return value for `Key.getFormat()` of `X.509`.

The structure for representing a public key was also defined in X.509 and is named `SubjectPublicKeyInfo`. In ASN.1 it appears as follows:

```
SubjectPublicKeyInfo ::= SEQUENCE {
                    algorithm AlgorithmIdentifier,
                    subjectPublicKey BIT STRING }
```

You can see it has two elements: an `AlgorithmIdentifier`, which in this case is used to signify what algorithm the key is for, and then a `BIT STRING`, which is used to store an encoding of the key material.

The reason for the `BIT STRING` is that, as you have seen already, asymmetric keys generally require different parameters depending on the algorithm, and as it should be possible to use the same basic structure to wrap anything from elliptic curve to RSA keys, a `BIT STRING` was settled on as the most general object to use. So, while the examples that follow will deal only with RSA keys, the principles can be applied to the encoding of any public key. It is just a matter of knowing what underlying structure goes in the `subjectPublicKey` field.

So, how do you deal with RSA public keys? As it turns out, X.509 also defined a structure for RSA public keys, which is also included in PKCS1. The ASN.1 definition is

```
RSAPublicKey ::= SEQUENCE {
                modulus INTEGER,
                publicExponent INTEGER }
```

and the `subjectPublicKey` field in a `SubjectPublicKeyInfo` structure is simply a `BIT STRING` wrapping a DER encoding of the previous structure.

This leaves you with the `algorithm` field. You need a specific `AlgorithmIdentifier` to indicate that the content of the `subjectPublicKey` field is an RSA public key. In the case of RSA, the `OBJECT IDENTIFIER` you use in the `algorithm` field of the `AlgorithmIdentifier` is

```
rsaEncryption OBJECT IDENTIFIER ::= {
                iso(1) member-body(2) us(840) rsadsi(113549) pkcs(1) pkcs-1(1) 1
}
```

and the parameters are defined as having the value `NULL`. (Remember, this is very different from empty; this means the parameters field is expected to have the `NULL` value in it.) Using the Bouncy Castle APIs, the Java equivalent for the `AlgorithmIdentifier` would be

```
AlgorithmIdentifier rsaKey = new AlgorithmIdentifier(
                PKCSObjectIdentifiers.rsaEncryption, new DERNull());
```

So when `Key.getEncoded()` is called on an RSA public key, the key material is encoded into the ASN.1 `RSAPublicKey` structure, the DER encoding of the structure is then converted into a `BIT STRING`, and the resulting `BIT STRING` and the RSA-specific `AlgorithmIdentifier` are then used to assemble the `SubjectPublicKeyInfo` object. The `SubjectPublicKeyInfo` object is then written out as a DER-encoded stream and returned in a byte array.

So having retrieved the byte array from `Key.getEncoded()`, how do you convert it back into a public key? You will find out now.

Try It Out   Using the X509EncodedKeySpec

Try the following example. It generates a small RSA key pair and then takes the output of `Key.getEncoded()` for the public key and uses it to create an `X509EncodedKeySpec`, which is then used to regenerate the original key. Along the way, it uses Bouncy Castle's ASN.1 package to dump out the underlying structure, so you can compare what gets generated to the previous discussion.

```
package chapter5;

import java.security.*;
import java.security.spec.X509EncodedKeySpec;

import org.bouncycastle.asn1.ASN1InputStream;
import org.bouncycastle.asn1.util.ASN1Dump;
import org.bouncycastle.asn1.x509.SubjectPublicKeyInfo;

/**
 * Simple example showing use of X509EncodedKeySpec
 */
public class X509EncodedKeySpecExample
{
    public static void main(String[] args) throws Exception
    {
        // create the keys
```

```
            KeyPairGenerator generator = KeyPairGenerator.getInstance("RSA", "BC");

            generator.initialize(128, Utils.createFixedRandom());

            KeyPair              pair = generator.generateKeyPair();

            // dump public key
            ASN1InputStream       aIn = new ASN1InputStream(
                                            pair.getPublic().getEncoded());
            SubjectPublicKeyInfo  info = SubjectPublicKeyInfo.getInstance(
                                            aIn.readObject());

            System.out.println(ASN1Dump.dumpAsString(info));
            System.out.println(ASN1Dump.dumpAsString(info.getPublicKey()));

            // create from specification
            X509EncodedKeySpec   x509Spec = new X509EncodedKeySpec(
                                            pair.getPublic().getEncoded());
            KeyFactory            keyFact = KeyFactory.getInstance("RSA", "BC");
            PublicKey             pubKey = keyFact.generatePublic(x509Spec);

            if (pubKey.equals(pair.getPublic()))
            {
                System.out.println("key recovery successful");
            }
            else
            {
                System.out.println("key recovery failed");
            }
        }
    }
```

You should see something like the following output:

```
DER Sequence
    DER Sequence
        ObjectIdentifier(1.2.840.113549.1.1.1)
        NULL
    DER Bit String[26, 0]

DER Sequence
    Integer(193768625448396182147878757503948840199)
    Integer(65537)

key recovery successful
```

As you can see from the ASN.1 dump information, the SubjectPublicKeyInfo structure (the first sequence) and the ASN.1 RSAPublicKey structure (the second sequence) are what we expected. Recreating the key has worked as well.

How It Works

You used the org.bouncycastle.asn1.x509.SubjectPublicKeyInfo object in the example to make life easier for yourself in reconstructing the encoded public key so you can print its contents. Like any class in the `org.bouncycastle.asn1.x509` package, it is simply a value object. The main reason you use it here is that it has a convenient method called `SubjectPublicKeyInfo.getPublicKey()` that reconstructs the ASN.1 object encoded in the `subjectPublicKey` field of the ASN.1 structure.

The next step in the example is the creation of the `X509EncodedKeySpec` from the same encoded information that you just dumped. As you did with the other key specification objects for asymmetric algorithms, you simply create a `KeyFactory` of the right type and call the `KeyFactory.generatePublic()` method to create the public key.

The string representation of the object identifier can also be used to create the `SecretKeyFactory`. For example, rather than creating the `SecretKeyFactory` with the line:

```
KeyFactory          keyFact = KeyFactory.getInstance("RSA", "BC");
```

you could have instead written

```
KeyFactory          keyFact = KeyFactory.getInstance(
                        info.getAlgorithmId().getObjectId().getId(), "BC");
```

This can be very useful if you do not know the name of the algorithm beforehand, or in situations where you may have a variety of different types of encoded key types and you are trying to minimize the amount of code required to handle them.

The PKCS8EncodedKeySpec Class

Like the `X509EncodedKeySpec` class, the `java.security.spec.PKCS8EncodedKeySpec` class also takes its name from the standard responsible for it. RSA Security's PKCS #8 entitled "Private Key Information Syntax" deals with encoding private keys, both with and without encryption, and the `PKCS8EncodedKeySpec` is designed to deal with private keys that have not been encrypted.

`PrivateKeyInfo` is the name of the structure for dealing with encoded private keys that have not been encrypted. Calling `Key.getEncoded()` on an object representing a private key that returns `PKCS#8` if you call `Key.getFormat()` will return the DER encoding of a `PrivateKeyInfo` structure representing the material required to construct the private key.

The full definition of `PrivateKeyInfo`, defined in PKCS #8, reads as follows:

```
PrivateKeyInfo ::= SEQUENCE {
                    version Version,
                    privateKeyAlgorithm PrivateKeyAlgorithmIdentifier,
                    privateKey PrivateKey,
                    attributes [0] IMPLICIT Attributes OPTIONAL }

Version ::= INTEGER {v1(0)}
PrivateKeyAlgorithmIdentifier ::= AlgorithmIdentifier
PrivateKey ::= OCTET STRING
Attributes ::= SET OF Attribute
```

A look through the ASN.1 tells you a few things: The version number is currently always zero; the type `PrivateKeyAlgorithmIdentifier` is a renaming of `AlgorithmIdentifier`, which in this case is a similar structure to the one you are used to; and the `privateKey` field contains an OCTET STRING.

Note that the attributes field is implicitly tagged with the value zero. Assuming you had an ASN1Sequence object, called seq, that represented a PrivateKeyInfo object, you would need to take the implicit tagging into account, and the optional nature of the field with some code like this:

```
if (seq.size() == 4)
{
    attributes = ASN1Set.getInstance(
                            (ASN1TaggedObject)seq.getObjectAt(3), false);
}
```

First you check if the attributes field is present. If it is, you recover the ASN1Set that the attributes field represents by using the static ASN1Set.getInstance() method for tagged objects and set the second argument, which determines the type of tagging to use, to false. The false parameter indicates implicit tagging. As I mentioned before, this is important because if the attributes field has only one element in its SET, attempting to parse the field assuming explicit tagging will make the field appear to be an explicitly tagged version of the structure represented by the element. The fact it is meant to be a SET containing that element will disappear.

So take a look at what happens when you try to wrap an RSA private key in a PrivateKeyInfo structure. First, the privateKeyAlgorithm field holds the same contents as the algorithm field in the SubjectPublicKeyInfo field for an RSA public key(you use the OBJECT IDENTIFIER rsaEncryption with the parameters field set to NULL. As with the RSA public key, there needs to be another structure to provide a DER-encoded object to go in the OCTET STRING represented by the privateKey field of the PrivateKeyInfo structure. In the case of an RSA private key, PKCS #1 defines a structure called RSAPrivateKey, which looks as follows:

```
RSAPrivateKey ::= SEQUENCE {
                    version Version,
                    modulus INTEGER,
                    publicExponent INTEGER,
                    privateExponent INTEGER,
                    prime1 INTEGER,
                    prime2 INTEGER,
                    exponent1 INTEGER,
                    exponent2 INTEGER,
                    coefficient INTEGER,
                    otherPrimeInfos OtherPrimeInfos OPTIONAL }

Version ::= INTEGER { two-prime(0), multi(1) }
(CONSTRAINED BY {-- version must be multi if otherPrimeInfos present --})

OtherPrimeInfos ::= SEQUENCE SIZE(1..MAX) OF OtherPrimeInfo

OtherPrimeInfo ::= SEQUENCE {
                    prime INTEGER,
                    exponent INTEGER,
                    coefficient INTEGER }
```

The structure is pretty close to what you would expect. You have a collection of INTEGER objects representing a regular RSA private key that uses Chinese Remainder Theorem and an optional extra field for a sequence of extra values on the end in case the key is a multi-prime one. The value MAX is application-dependent, but you can expect in most provider implementations it will be big enough for the number of OtherPrimeInfo structures held by any encoded keys you are using.

More formally, a look at the comment in the constraints on the `Version` value tells us that a call to `Key.getEncoded()` on a Java object implementing `RSAPrivateCrtKey` should produce a two-prime version with the `version` field set to 0. An `RSAMultiPrimePrivateCrtKey`, on the other hand, will produce a multiversion with the `version` field set to 1 with the extra coefficients for a multi-prime RSA private key in the sequence represented by `otherPrimeInfos`. If it was a multi-prime key, you will find that the `OtherPrimeInfo` structures making up the sequence have the values corresponding to those in the `RSAOtherPrimeInfo` objects associated with the Java instance of the key.

So, how do you use this knowledge in Java? The first thing you should look at is the mechanism for creating a private key using a `KeyFactory`. As you would expect, it is just the same as for a public key. Given a Java object `privKey`, which implements the `RSAPrivateKey` interface, you can create a `PKCS8EncodedKeySpec` by writing

```
PKCS8EncodedKeySpec    pkcs8Spec = new PKCS8EncodedKeySpec(privKey.getEncoded());
```

Having created the `pkcs8Spec` object, you can then re-create the private key as follows:

```
KeyFactory  keyFact = KeyFactory.getInstance("RSA", "BC");
PrivateKey  priv = keyFact.generatePrivate(pkcs8Spec);
```

The Bouncy Castle APIs also provide a wrapper class that allows you to dump the internals of the structure returned by the encoding of a private key. You can find the class in the `org.bouncycastle.asn1.pkcs` package and its name is `PrivateKeyInfo`. If you wanted to try dumping the contents of `Key.getEncoded()` for an object implementing the `PrivateKey` interface, you could use the following code fragment:

```
ASN1InputStream    aIn = new ASN1InputStream(priv.getEncoded());
PrivateKeyInfo     info = PrivateKeyInfo.getInstance(aIn.readObject());

System.out.println(ASN1Dump.dumpAsString(info));
System.out.println(ASN1Dump.dumpAsString(info.getPrivateKey()));
```

and you should see the contents of the `PrivateKeyInfo` structure printed out, followed by the contents of the structure encoded in the string of octets contained in the `privateKey` field of the `PrivateKeyInfo` structure.

When you are exporting private keys, the normal reason is to make them available to another application, or perhaps persist them on disk. Given that it is a private key you are dealing with in this case, you will often want to encrypt the DER-encoded data representing the private key as well. PKCS #8 also provides a structure for putting together an encrypted coding for a key. It builds on the `PrivateKeyInfo` object, and the JCE provides a class that allows you to construct and manipulate the encrypted coding directly. The class you use for this is the `EncryptedPrivateKeyInfo` class.

The EncryptedPrivateKeyInfo Class

The `javax.security.EncryptedPrivateKeyInfo` class allows you to package encrypted private key data with details of the encryption algorithm used to create it. The class takes its name from a structure of the same name defined in PKCS #8, where it is defined as follows:

```
EncryptedPrivateKeyInfo ::= SEQUENCE {
                            encryptionAlgorithm AlgorithmIdentifier,
                            encryptedData EncryptedData }

EncryptedData ::= OCTET STRING
```

Other than the fact that the octets held in the `encryptedData` field represent an encrypted encoding of a `PrivateKeyInfo` object, this is a very simple structure. You have the `encryptionAlgorithm` field, which contains an `AlgorithmIdentifier` describing the algorithm used for encryption and any parameters that might need to be passed to another cipher trying to implement the same algorithm, and then you have the encrypted data enclosed in an `OCTET STRING`.

You'll now review some of the methods on the `EncryptedPrivateKeyInfo` class so you can see how it is built on top of the PKCS #8 `EncryptedPrivateKeyInfo` structure.

EncryptedPrivateKeyInfo()

The `EncryptedPrivateKeyInfo` class has three constructors on it. One is used to create the object from a byte array that contains an ASN.1-encoded PKCS #8 `EncryptedPrivateKeyInfo` structure. The other two are used for creating an `EncryptedPrivateKeyInfo` object that will be used to produce the ASN.1 binary encoding of the structure in PKCS #8.

EncryptedPrivateKeyInfo.getAlgParameters()

This method returns an `AlgorithmParameters` object, which carries the parameters information that is needed, together with the key to initialize the cipher used to decrypt the private key. As you have probably already guessed, this is the same information that is carried in the `parameters` field of the `AlgorithmIdentifier` in the PKCS #8 `EncryptedPrivateKeyInfo` structure.

EncryptedPrivateKeyInfo.getKeySpec()

The `getKeySpec()` method takes an appropriately initialized cipher and returns a `PKCS8EncodedKeySpec` that contains the encoding for the PKCS #8 `PrivateKeyInfo` object that was encrypted when the `EncryptedPrivateKeyInfo` object was created. You can then pass the key specification to a `KeyFactory` and create a private key suitable for use with the provider you are using.

EncryptedPrivateKeyInfo.getEncoded()

This method returns the ASN.1 binary encoding of the `EncryptedPrivateKeyInfo` structure defined in PKCS #8 as a byte array. If you are exporting one of these objects, the data returned by this method is the one you want to use. Do not confuse `getEncoded()` with the `EncryptedPrivateKeyInfo` `.getEncryptedData()` method. That method only returns the value of the `encryptedData` field, so, as you would expect, it does not include any of the information about the encryption algorithm used.

Now take a look at how this all goes together.

| Try It Out | Using EncryptedPrivateKeyInfo and PBE |

The following example builds not only on the discussion of the `PKCS8EncodedKeySpec` and the `EncryptedPrivateKeyInfo` class, but also on the previous discussion about the `AlgorithmParameters` class and password-based encryption. Try running it and then read on.

```
package chapter5;

import java.security.*;
import java.security.spec.PKCS8EncodedKeySpec;

import javax.crypto.Cipher;
import javax.crypto.EncryptedPrivateKeyInfo;
import javax.crypto.SecretKeyFactory;
```

```java
import javax.crypto.spec.PBEKeySpec;

/**
 * Simple example showing how to use PBE and an EncryptedPrivateKeyInfo object.
 */
public class EncryptedPrivateKeyInfoExample
{
    public static void main(String[] args) throws Exception
    {
        // generate a key pair
        KeyPairGenerator kpg = KeyPairGenerator.getInstance("RSA", "BC");
        kpg.initialize(128, Utils.createFixedRandom());

        KeyPair pair = kpg.generateKeyPair();

        // wrapping step
        char[]             password = "hello".toCharArray();
        byte[]             salt = new byte[20];
        int                iCount = 100;
        String             pbeAlgorithm = "PBEWithSHAAnd3-KeyTripleDES-CBC";
        PBEKeySpec         pbeKeySpec = new PBEKeySpec(password, salt, iCount);
        SecretKeyFactory   secretKeyFact = SecretKeyFactory.getInstance(
                                                      pbeAlgorithm, "BC");
        Cipher             cipher = Cipher.getInstance(pbeAlgorithm, "BC");

        cipher.init(Cipher.WRAP_MODE, secretKeyFact.generateSecret(pbeKeySpec));

        byte[]             wrappedKey = cipher.wrap(pair.getPrivate());

        // create carrier
        EncryptedPrivateKeyInfo pInfo = new EncryptedPrivateKeyInfo(
                                      cipher.getParameters(), wrappedKey);

        // unwrapping step - note we only use the password
        pbeKeySpec = new PBEKeySpec(password);

        cipher = Cipher.getInstance(pInfo.getAlgName(), "BC");

        cipher.init(Cipher.DECRYPT_MODE,
            secretKeyFact.generateSecret(pbeKeySpec), pInfo.getAlgParameters());

        PKCS8EncodedKeySpec pkcs8Spec = pInfo.getKeySpec(cipher);
        KeyFactory          keyFact = KeyFactory.getInstance("RSA", "BC");
        PrivateKey          privKey = keyFact.generatePrivate(pkcs8Spec);

        if (privKey.equals(pair.getPrivate()))
        {
            System.out.println("key recovery successful");
        }
        else
        {
            System.out.println("key recovery failed");
        }
    }
}
```

Assuming all went according to plan, running the example will produce the message:

```
key recovery successful
```

As usual, the RSA key size is absurdly small for reasons that it will fit better when you look at the ASN.1 structures a bit further on. Other than that, after the key generation, there is a lot going on. Therefore, you will work through the example step-by-step.

How It Works

The first stage is familiar from the discussion in Chapter 2 about password-based encryption and the discussion on key wrapping in Chapter 4. You set up a PBEKeySpec, create a SecretKeyFactory to handle it using the PKCS #12 algorithm PBEWithSHAAnd3-KeyTripleDES-CBC. The PBE algorithm uses a mixing function similar to the one you looked at in Chapter 3 and SHA-1 to create three DES keys and an IV, which are then used to initialize a Triple-DES cipher operating in CBC mode.

Having initialized the Cipher object appropriately with the key generated by the SecretKeyFactory, you then used the Cipher.wrap() method to create the byte array that contains the encrypted version of the encoding of the private key. Next, you construct the EncryptedPrivateKeyInfo in the following manner:

```
EncryptedPrivateKeyInfo pInfo = new EncryptedPrivateKeyInfo(
                                    cipher.getParameters(), wrappedKey);
```

As you saw earlier, Cipher.getParameters() returns an AlgorithmParameters object. One feature of this object is that it has an AlgorithmParameters.getEncoded() method on it that returns an encoded form of the parameters it contains. In this case, the getEncoded() method returns the DER encoding of the following structure, which is defined in PKCS #12:

```
pkcs-12PbeParams ::= SEQUENCE {
                        salt OCTET STRING,
                        iterations INTEGER
}
```

The pkcs-12PbeParams structure carries the salt and the iteration count that you initialized the PBEKeySpec object, pbeKeySpec, with. It is the SEQUENCE represented by the pkcs-12PbeParams structure that serves as the parameters field in the AlgorithmIdentifier contained in the encryptionAlgorithm field of the PKCS #8 EncryptedPrivateKeyInfo object. You can dump out this structure by adding

```
System.out.println(ASN1Dump.dumpAsString(
        new ASN1InputStream(cipher.getParameters().getEncoded()).readObject())));
```

which will produce the following extra output:

```
DER Sequence
    DER Octet String[20]
    Integer(100)
```

As you can see the iteration count is 100, and if you dumped out the contents of the OCTET STRING, you would find it contained the bytes making up the salt that you passed in to the PBEKeySpec originally.

The only apparently missing ingredient is the OBJECT IDENTIFIER that is required to populate the algorithm field contained in the AlgorithmIdentifier inside the encryptionAlgorithm field. Funnily enough if you were to add

```
System.out.println(cipher.getParameters().getAlgorithm());
```

to the line after the call to cipher.wrap() in the example, you would see the following extra line printed in the output:

```
1.2.840.113549.1.12.1.3
```

which happens to be the value of the OBJECT IDENTIFIER defined in PKCS #12 for PBEWithSHAAnd3-KeyTripleDES-CBC. This last piece of information then allows the EncryptedPrivateKeyInfo object you are creating to fill in the encryptionAlgorithm field of the ASN.1 structure it contains.

The last step in the example is where you recover the encrypted private key that is stored in pInfo, our EncryptedPrivateKeyInfo object. In this case, you only have to initialize the PBEKeySpec as follows:

```
pbeKeySpec = new PBEKeySpec(password);
```

as the other parameters are stored in the AlgorithmParameters object that is extracted from the EncryptedPrivateKeyInfo object. After the pbeKeySpec is converted to a key and the cipher is initialized for decryption, a PKCS8EncodedKeySpec is retrieved from the EncryptedPrivateKeyInfo object and the original private key is recovered. As you would expect adding the following lines:

```
ASN1InputStream    aIn = new ASN1InputStream(pkcs8Spec.getEncoded());
PrivateKeyInfo     info = PrivateKeyInfo.getInstance(aIn.readObject());

System.out.println(ASN1Dump.dumpAsString(info));
System.out.println(ASN1Dump.dumpAsString(info.getPrivateKey()));
```

after the point where pkcs8Spec is set produces the following extra output:

```
DER Sequence
    Integer(0)
    DER Sequence
        ObjectIdentifier(1.2.840.113549.1.1.1)
        NULL
    DER Octet String[100]

DER Sequence
    Integer(0)
    Integer(19376862544839618214787875750394884019 9)
    Integer(65537)
    Integer(176280162144807927893221216887705181313)
    Integer(16432478544733070881)
    Integer(11791807603515952679)
    Integer(5879506071310035233)
    Integer(6852660091055565157)
    Integer(6468103171312594380)
```

The first ASN.1 dump is that of the PrivateKeyInfo structure, and it contains an AlgorithmIdentifier structure whose algorithm field has been set to the OBJECT IDENTIFIER for

RSA encryption, indicating that the `PrivateKeyInfo` structure contains an RSA key. The second ASN.1 dump is the private key encoded as a version 0 `RSAPrivateKey` structure from PKCS #1, which simply contains the value making up the private key in much the same way as the `RSAPrivateCrtKeySpec` class does.

There is one thing in the example worth further discussion. When you created the encrypted byte array to initialize the `EncryptedPrivateKeyInfo` object with, you did the following:

```
cipher.init(Cipher.WRAP_MODE, secretKeyFact.generateSecret(pbeKeySpec));

byte[]      wrappedKey = cipher.wrap(pair.getPrivate());
```

which returns a byte array containing the encrypted form of the ASN.1-encoded `PrivateKeyInfo` object that was returned by the private key's `Key.getEncoded()` method. You could have used the following instead:

```
cipher.init(Cipher.ENCRYPT_MODE, secretKeyFact.generateSecret(pbeKeySpec));

byte[]      wrappedKey = cipher.doFinal(pair.getPrivate().getEncoded());
```

The reason this was not done is to draw attention to the fact that if you were using a provider based on a hardware cryptographic device and the device has been set up not to publish private keys outside of it — often the very reason for having one — `Key.getEncoded()` on the private key might actually return `null` because the device forbids the operation. The reason this might happen is that the provider will be expecting developers to use the wrapping mechanism instead, as it allows the provider to encrypt the private key information before it leaves the safety of the device.

Summary

This chapter looked at ASN.1, its binary encodings, and how they are used by a variety of classes in the JCA and JCE to allow you to pass data structures around in an application-independent manner. Building on this, you have also had a closer look at how public and private keys are encoded and how to make use of the `EncryptedPrivateKeyInfo` class.

Over the course of the chapter, you learned

- ❑   What ASN.1 is, what types it has, how structures are built in it, and how they encode

- ❑   How to read and understand the ASN.1 modules related to cryptography

- ❑   How ASN.1 binary encoding is utilized for encoding `AlgorithmParameters` and how you can reconstruct parameters from an ASN.1 binary encoding

- ❑   How the `X509EncodedKeySpec` and the `PKCS8EncodedKeySpec` are used to carry ASN.1-encoded public and private keys and how the `KeyFactory` class is used to convert them to Java objects

- ❑   How to create encrypted encodings of private keys

ASN.1 has uses that go well beyond just the encoding of algorithm parameters and asymmetric keys. It is also used to provide messaging formats and provides the method for encoding X.509 certificates, which are a fundamental part of most public key infrastructure (PKI) solutions. The next chapter looks at how X.509 certificates are constructed, as well as how to use the JCA classes that support them.

Exercises

1. What happens to fields set to their default values when the ASN.1 structure that contains them is encoded using DER?

2. How would you implement the following ASN.1 type using the Bouncy Castle ASN.1 API?

```
MyChoice ::= CHOICE {
            message UTF8String,
            id      INTEGER }
```

3. What is meant by the word IMPLICIT in respect to a style of tagging? Think of a simple example of how it would be done using one of the classes representing an ASN.1 primitive in the Bouncy Castle API. What implication does the IMPLICIT style have for items that are derived from the CHOICE type?

4. What are the two classes used to hold the DER encodings of public and private keys, respectively? What class is used to convert the encodings back into actual keys?

5. What does an EncryptedPrivateKeyInfo object contain?

Distinguished Names and Certificates

Asymmetric encryption provides ways of allowing you to distribute keys with relative safety that other people can use to send encrypted messages or verify signatures you have created. The problem, however, is that from the point of view of the people you are distributing the public keys to, the simple presence of a public key is not enough for someone to determine whether it is the public key they have or even if the use they are being asked to put it to is one that you intended. Distinguished names and the certificates that carry them were created to solve this problem.

This chapter introduces distinguished names, certificates, and certification requests. Distinguished names contain information about the owner of a public key carried by a certificate. Certification requests provide a mechanism by which you can ask some other party, presumably trusted by the people you want to give the certificate to, to issue you with a certificate that can also be trusted. In general, this is done by issuing a certificate that can be verified using another certificate issued by the trusted party that is already in the hands of the people who you want to accept your new certificate.

By the end of this chapter, you should

- ❑ Understand what an X.500 name is
- ❑ Understand what a public key certificate is, most particularly those that use X.509
- ❑ Be able to make use of the Java classes representing X.500 name and certificates
- ❑ Be able to generate your own certification requests and certificates
- ❑ Be able to create a certificate from a certificate request
- ❑ Be able to form multiple certificates into a certificate chain, or path

Finally, you should understand how to make use of the certificate storage class in Java and how to selectively retrieve certificates from it.

Getting Started

For this chapter, you need to add some more functionality to the Utils class: the capability to create a random RSA key pair.

Here is the Utils class for this chapter:

```java
package chapter6;

import java.security.KeyPair;
import java.security.KeyPairGenerator;
import java.security.SecureRandom;

/**
 * Chapter 6 Utils
 */
public class Utils extends chapter5.Utils
{
    /**
     * Create a random 1024 bit RSA key pair
     */
    public static KeyPair generateRSAKeyPair()
        throws Exception
    {
        KeyPairGenerator kpGen = KeyPairGenerator.getInstance("RSA", "BC");

        kpGen.initialize(1024, new SecureRandom());

        return kpGen.generateKeyPair();
    }
}
```

As you can see, it has one new method on it that generates an RSA key pair. Nothing mysterious here! Type the class in to start the chapter6 package off, and you are ready to proceed.

Distinguished Names

The distinguished name, or DN, was originally proposed in X.501 in OSI to describe the X.500 directory structure. The idea of the directory structure was that it would form a hierarchy, similar to the one in Figure 6-1, with each level down a particular branch being identified by a relative distinguished name, or RDN, with the full path being described by a distinguished name, or DN, which is made up of a collection of the RDNs traversed.

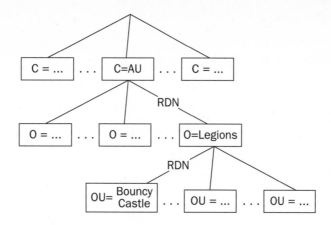

The X.500 Directory Structure

Figure 6-1

The two ASN.1 types that make up a distinguished name are as follows:

```
DistinguishedName ::= RDNSequence

RDNSequence ::= SEQUENCE OF RelativeDistinguishedName

RelativeDistinguishedName ::= SET SIZE (1..MAX) OF AttributeTypeAndValue

AttributeTypeAndValue ::= SEQUENCE {
                            type  OBJECT IDENTIFIER,
                            value ANY }
```

So what can go into an RDN? As you can see, the definition is so broad that it led to a famous quote by Bob Jueneman on the IETF-PKIX mailing list: " . . . there is nothing in any of these standards that would prevent me from including a 1-gigabit MPEG movie of me playing with my cat as one of the RDN components of the DN in my certificate." For this reason, a number of other standards such as SET and RFC 2253 define restrictions that can be placed on the OID values used for the type field, the actual structures that can be put in the value field, and even the number of elements that can be in the RDN and DN.

The most common DN you are likely to have seen is a character string equivalent like the following:

```
"CN=www.bouncycastle.org, OU=Bouncy Castle, O=Legions, C=AU"
```

Each of the "X=some value" pairs making up the previous distinguished name, or DN, is what goes into a RelativeDistinguishedName, and as the ASN.1 structure of a DistinguishedName suggests, the String representation of a DN is simply a comma-separated list of "X=some value" pairs. These are commonly based on RFC 2253, although, as mentioned, you will find that not everybody agrees on what ASN.1 string type a given field should be.

As you have probably guessed, the *X* referred to in the last paragraph gets converted into an OBJECT IDENTIFIER. Common values for the string versions of *X* and their details are as follows:

❏   CN — commonName, OID "2.5.4.3", limited to 64 characters

❏   OU — organizationalUnitName, OID "2.5.4.11", limited to 64 characters

❏   O — organizationName, OID "2.5.4.10", limited to 64 characters

❏   C — country, OID "2.5.4.6", limited to 2 characters

❏   L — localityName, OID "2.5.4.7", limited to 64 characters

❏   ST — stateOrProvinceName, OID "2.5.4.8", limited to 64 characters

For the most part the *"some value"* gets converted to one of a PrintableString or UTF8String unless it has been defined as something else. For example, another common RDN type EMAILADDRESS is defined in PKCS #9 as being of the type IA5String. Strictly speaking, an e-mail address has no place in a DN, as it isn't part of any directory structure that the DN might otherwise be trying to describe. I'll discuss this further when you look at how to do it correctly using certificate extensions.

The main way to define a DN in Java is using the X500Principal class that can be used to create a Java object representing an X.500 DN from an encoding, or from a character string.

The X500Principal Class

The javax.security.auth.x500.X500Principal class was introduced in JDK 1.4. It has constructors that allow you to make one from either an ASN.1-encoded stream, byte array, or a String. In the case of the String constructor, the class constructs itself using the format defined in RFC 2253 and RFC 1779. The string parser used by the String constructor will also recognize RDN types that are defined in RFC 2459. The class also provides implementations of Object.equals() and Object.hashCode() and provides two methods for retrieving the DN contained in the object as either a byte array, using getEncoded(), or a string using getName().

X500Principal.getEncoded()

The getEncoded() method returns the X500Principal's DER encoding. This method, together with the override of Object.equals() and Object.hashCode(), are the three principal methods to use on the class. As you will see when I discuss getName() in more detail, converting a DN from a string back into an encoding is a lot harder than you might imagine. So whenever possible, you are better manipulating the byte array.

X500Principal.getName()

The getName() method returns a String representing the DN. It comes in two flavors, one that takes no parameters and returns the DN as a String, the other that takes a format name as a String and attempts to return the DN formatted according to the format specified. Although this is very useful, if a human needs to read a DN, there is a problem if you want to try to take a random X500Principal out of, say, a certificate, and get back the same encoding by just relying on the String representation.

As you might recall from Chapter 5, there are a number of ways of representing a character string in ASN.1, a few of which will print quite nicely in Java. The problem arises that if the encoding used to create the value for the RDN is easily displayable, but not what is expected, then converting a DN to a `String` and then back to an ASN.1 encoding may result in a different encoding being produced. Of course, if everyone was just following a single standard, this would not be an issue, but it is quite common to find `PrintableString`, `UTF8String`, `BMPString`, and `IA5String` in an encoding and then discover that this actually matters to some other piece of software you are using. Unfortunately, none of this encoding information will generally be carried along by a `X500Principal` when a `getName()` is called. This is not the fault of the class either; this issue is not an easy one to solve without forcing people to write their own parsers of `String`-based DNs for every occasion. The trick is to try to avoid using the `Strings` for anything other than display where possible and simply manipulate the object and save it in its encoded form.

> **Converting an encoded X.500 name to a string and back to an** `X500Principal` **may mean that the** `getEncoded()` **method on the** `X500Principal` **does not return the original encoding. Avoid having to do such conversions when possible.**

Public Key Certificates

Certificates, or to be more specific, *public key* certificates, provide a mechanism that allows a third party, or issuer, to vouch for the fact that a particular public key is linked with a particular owner, or subject. Every certificate has a private key associated with it, and a chain of certificates is a list of certificates where each certificate other than the first one and the last one have had its private key used to sign the next certificate after it. The first certificate, the root certificate, is normally self-signed; you have to accept it as trusted for the certificate chain to be valid. The last certificate, or the end entity certificate, simply provides you with a public key you are interested in, which, assuming you accept the root certificate, you can regard as authentic. The entity responsible for issuing the certificates is referred to as a *certificate authority*, or more commonly, a CA.

Support for public key certificates was added into Java with JDK 1.1, with further work being done in JDK 1.2, as experience from JDK 1.1 showed that some of the ideas behind the `java.security` API for certificates were becoming problematic. As of JDK 1.2, the classes for supporting certificates in the JCA can now be found in the package `java.security.cert`, and the first of these you need to understand is the `Certificate` class.

The Certificate Class

The `java.security.cert.Certificate` class provides the basic support for public key certificates. It provides the methods for extracting the public key stored in the certificate, identifying the certificate's type, verifying the signature contained in the certificate, and getting an encoded version of the certificate.

Certificate.getType()

The `getType()` method returns a `String` indicating the underlying certificate type. For the most part, you can expect this method to return `"X.509"`, which indicates that the certificate is an X.509 certificate and will probably also be implemented using the extension class `java.security.cert.X509Certificate`. I will discuss the `X509Certificate` class a bit later.

Certificate.getPublicKey()

The getPublicKey() method returns the public key that the certificate is carrying.

The key should be suitable for use with whatever provider you used to create the certificate, but your mileage will vary if you try mixing public key certificates created with one provider with encryption or signature algorithms implemented with another. In a case where you do need to mix providers, you may need to use a KeyFactory created for the algorithm provider to transform the key retrieved from the certificate into something that will work with the algorithm provider.

Certificate.verify()

The verify() method checks that the signature contained in the certificate can be verified using the public key of the entity that was supposed to have signed the certificate. There are two versions of the verify() method, one that just takes the public key to use for verification as a parameter, and another that takes the public key to use and a provider name.

Unlike Signature.verify(), Certificate.verify() is a void and can throw one of five exceptions when it is called. The most likely one, when the public key is the wrong value, is a SignatureException indicating the signature did not match what was expected. The other four exceptions that can be thrown are as follows:

❏   NoSuchProviderException if no provider can be found

❏   NoSuchAlgorithmException if the signature algorithm used in the certificate is not recognized

❏   InvalidKeyException if the public key passed in is for the wrong algorithm

❏   CertificateException if there is a problem encoding the certificate in order to calculate any hash required as part of signature verification

Certificate.getEncoded()

The getEncoded() method returns a byte array containing an encoding of a certificate. What this contains depends on the return value of the getType() method, but in the case of an X.509 certificate, the byte array returned by getEncoded() will normally contain the certificate as a DER encoding of its ASN.1 structure.

X.509 Certificates

X.509 certificates, covered here, have their origins in the same OSI standards that produced X.500 and in a lot of ways follow the demise of the original X.500 directory concept. Originally with version 1, introduced in 1988, it was assumed that you could use the Issuer DN of a given certificate to build the certificate chain going back to the root; so given a collection of certificates, you would be able to easily sort them into a chain starting at a root and going to the end entity. This turned out to be too restrictive, and in 1993, version 2 introduced the concepts of *unique identifiers* for both the issuer and the subject to allow for reuse of DNs but still maintained the directory structure. Finally, the whole "enterprise" collapsed, and the concept of *certificate extensions* was introduced in version 3 in 1996. This introduced concepts like key usage and completely removed the restriction that a certificate chain had to follow the directory structure, allowing for both a hierarchical approach and a *web of trust* approach where there is no clear hierarchy, but a lot of cross dependencies.

Of the three different types, you will probably not see any version 2 certificates, or certificates using the unique identifiers that were added in version 2, as the use of the unique identifiers added in version 2 was discourage with the release of version 3. There are still a lot of X.509 version 1 certificates in use, especially for self-signed root certificates. You will find version 3 certificates for virtually all other applications.

Back in the Java world, support for X.509 certificates was explicitly added with the introduction of the java.security.cert package in JDK 1.2. The fundamental classes are the X509Certificate class and the X509Extension interface that's implemented by the X509Certificate class. The X509Extension interface supports the use of version 3 extensions. You'll look at the X509Certificate class first and then move onto the X509Extension interface and the methods on X509Certificate that derive from it.

The X509Certificate Class

The java.security.cert.X509Certificate class provides the basic support for X.509 certificates. The design of the class and the interfaces it implements is based on the following ASN.1 structures published in X.509:

```
Certificate  ::=  SEQUENCE  {
    tbsCertificate          TBSCertificate,
    signatureAlgorithm      AlgorithmIdentifier,
    signatureValue          BIT STRING  }
```

As you can see, an X.509 certificate is simply a sequence with three fields in it. As you have probably also guessed, most of the detail is in the tbsCertificate field, which contains the data that was used to generate the signature represented in the signatureValue field using the algorithm given by the details contained in the AlgorithmIdentifier in the signatureAlgorithm field. As you will see in a minute, the TBSCertificate structure contains the details of the issuer of the certificate as well as information on who it was issued for(the subject. The AlgorithmIdentifier structure is the same one you saw in Chapter 5.

I will start by detailing the TBSCertificate structure and going through the relevant methods on the X509Certificate class so that you can see how the ASN.1 structures relate to the class. Apart from giving you extra insight into the way the certificate class works, referring to the ASN.1 structure will also help explain some of the strange problems you may encounter when dealing with X.509 certificates.

X509Certificate.getTBSCertificate()

The getTBSCertificate() method returns the bytes making up the ASN.1 encoding of the TBSCertificate structure. These are the bytes that are used as the input data for calculating the signature the certificate carries, so if you wanted to verify a certificate signature using the Signature class, you could do so using the public key of the certificate issuer and the bytes returned by getTBSCertificate(). The actual structure contained in the ASN.1 encoding that getTBSCertificate() returns is defined in X.509 as follows:

```
TBSCertificate  ::=  SEQUENCE  {
    version         [0]  EXPLICIT Version DEFAULT v1,
    serialNumber         CertificateSerialNumber,
    signature            AlgorithmIdentifier,
    issuer               Name,
```

```
        validity              Validity,
        subject               Name,
        subjectPublicKeyInfo  SubjectPublicKeyInfo,
        issuerUniqueID   [1]  IMPLICIT UniqueIdentifier OPTIONAL,
                              -- If present, version shall be v2 or v3
        subjectUniqueID  [2]  IMPLICIT UniqueIdentifier OPTIONAL,
                              -- If present, version shall be v2 or v3
        extensions       [3]  EXPLICIT Extensions OPTIONAL
                              -- If present, version shall be v3 }

  Name ::= CHOICE { RDNSequence }
```

and most of the get() methods that follow provide access to fields in this structure. I will ignore the extensions field for the moment, as I will cover it when in the discussion of the X509Extension interface.

X509Certificate.getVersion()

The getVersion() method returns the version of the TBSCertificate structure that was used to create the certificate. The ASN.1 definition of Version is defined as follows:

```
  Version  ::=  INTEGER {  v1(0), v2(1), v3(2)  }
```

Ideally, X.509 certificates will always be encoded so that if extensions is present, the version will be v3; if issuerUniqueID and subjectUniqueID are present and extensions is not the version will be v2; and if none of extensions, issuerUniqueID, and subjectUniqueID are present, the version will be v1. However, if you are importing certificates from a variety of possibly unknown sources, the truth is that you cannot rely on the fact that

```
  boolean v3 = (x509Cert.getVersion() == 3);
```

setting v3 to true means the extensions field is present, as some organizations have issued certificates that purport to be version 3 but could really be accommodated using version 1.

The getVersion() method diverts from what is in the encoded certificate in that it returns 3 if the certificate is type v3, 2 if it is of type v2, and 1 if it is of type v1. This is different from the actual version number stored in the TBSCertificate structure, since, as you can see from the ASN.1, the numbering starts with 0. In fact, as the TBSCertificate structure is generally DER encoded, in the case of a version 1 certificate, the actual version number will not be present. Therefore, if you need to process the contents of a TBSCertificate structure by hand, be prepared to deal with the version field being missing.

X509Certificate.getSerialNumber()

The getSerialNumber() returns a BigInteger representing the value of the serialNumber field in the TBSCertificate structure. You can see from the definition of TBSCertificate that this is of the type CertificateSerialNumber, which is defined as follows:

```
  CertificateSerialNumber  ::=  INTEGER
```

It is very rare for these values to be represented as anything other than a BigInteger, so don't assume you can represent them as an int or a long.

Something else that's also rare, but is possible, is that the serial number will be negative. While the definition allows for it, it seems a bit odd that this happens. The likelihood is that some CAs are written forgetting that an ASN.1 INTEGER is a signed number and the certificate generation code does not allow for a leading zero in the case where the encoding of their internal, probably unsigned, representation has its top bit set. Avoid using negative serial numbers, because there are some applications out there that assume serial numbers are always positive; likewise, avoid assuming the serial number will always be positive. The issuer information, which you will look at next, and the serial number serve to uniquely identify the certificate, but any search based on this will most likely fail or return the wrong certificate if the serial number is negative and you have changed its sign.

X509Certificate.getIssuerX500Principal()

As you saw in the definition of the TBSCertificate structure, the issuer is simply a Name structure, so you use getIssuerX500Principal() to retrieve the DN of the issuer of the certificate. Combined with the serial number, the principal representing the issuer should uniquely identify the certificate.

You have already looked at DNs and the Name structure at the start of the chapter; however, I will make one further comment. Originally, prior to JDK 1.4, there was only X509Certificate.getIssuerDN(), which returned an object representing the X.500 name associated with the issuer of the certificate. The major problem was that it meant the only obvious provider-independent way to get access to the DN was via the Object.toString() method(something you have already seen that is, at best, quite hazardous. Now you can use getIssuerX500Principal(), which returns a X500Principal object, a DN, which has a precise defined behavior, and better yet, a getEncoded() method, so that for the most part, you can avoid converting the DN into a String whenever possible.

If you are using JDK 1.3 or earlier, the Bouncy Castle API also provides a helper class in the org.bouncycastle.jce package called PrincipalUtil, which returns a Bouncy Castle–specific object, X509Principal, an equivalent to the X500Principal class. You can use the PrincipalUtil.getIssuerX509Principal() to extract the issuer from a certificate, and the object you get back will allow you to avoid having to convert the issuer principal into a String in order to do processing on it.

X509Certificate.getNotBefore() and X509Certificate.getNotAfter()

The getNotBefore() and getNotAfter() methods are derived from the validity field in the TBSCertificate structure. The validity field has a type Validity, which is defined as follows:

```
Validity ::= SEQUENCE {
     notBefore      Time,
     notAfter       Time }

Time ::= CHOICE {
     utcTime        UTCTime,
     generalTime    GeneralizedTime }
```

The notBefore field represents the time at which the certificate starts to be valid, and the getNotBefore() method returns it as a Date object. The notAfter field represents the last time at which the certificate will be valid, and the getNotAfter() method returns it as a Date object.

Note that the Time type can be a UTCTime, which has a two-digit year. You are unlikely to run into a new certificate carrying UTCTime these days. However, if you expect to be using certificates, say, from a legacy application, make sure the provider you are using for loading the certificates is handling the conversion from a two- to a four-digit year correctly. Otherwise, you may find certificates expiring before their time, or staying valid much longer than they should be.

X509Certificate.checkValidity()

There are two versions of the checkValidity() method.

Called without parameters, the method checks the certificate's notBefore and notAfter times against the current time and throws an exception if the certificate is not yet valid or has expired.

Called with a single date parameter, the method checks the notBefore and notAfter times against the time represented by the date passed in and throws an exception if the certificate was not yet valid at that date or the certificate had already expired at that date.

The exceptions that will be thrown by checkValidity() if there is a problem with the time checking can be one of two. CertificateNotYetValidException is thrown if the time being checked is prior to the notBefore time, and CertificateExpiredException is thrown if the time being checked is after the notAfter date.

X509Certificate.getSubjectX500Principal()

The subject field, representing the owner of the public key in the certificate, is also defined in the TBSCertificate structure as a Name, and the getSubjectX500Principal() method returns the DN for the key owner as a X500Principal. In a similar manner to getIssuerX500Principal(), originally this was often done using X509Certificate.getSubjectDN() with the same resultant problems. Whenever possible, avoid the use of getSubjectDN(). If you are using JDK 1.3 or earlier, you can use the Bouncy Castle helper class PrincipalUtil to retrieve the subject principal instead. After the same fashion as the issuer principal, you can call PrincipalUtil.getSubjectX509Principal() to return an object, which will give you more options with processing of the certificate's subject principal.

X509Certificate.getIssuerUniqueID()

You saw earlier that the issuerUniqueID field was defined as:

```
issuerUniqueID  [1]  IMPLICIT UniqueIdentifier OPTIONAL,
```

The ASN.1 definition of UniqueIdentifier is defined as:

```
UniqueIdentifier  ::=  BIT STRING
```

In the case of Java, the easiest match for an arbitrary bit string is an array of booleans, so the getissuerUniqueID() method returns a boolean array matching the BIT STRING that was in the issuerUniqueID field if it is present — a very rare occurrence; you will normally only see one in a version 2 certificate.

X509Certificate.getSubjectUniqueID()

Like the issuerUniqueID, the subjectUniqueID is defined as:

```
subjectUniqueID [2]  IMPLICIT UniqueIdentifier OPTIONAL,
```

and the getSubjectUniqueID() returns an array of booleans representing the BIT STRING value that was present in the subjectUniqueID field, if the field is present. Once again, you would only expect to see this value set in version 2 certificates.

X509Certificate.getSignature()

The getSignature() method returns the bytes making up the signature stored in the BIT STRING contained in the signatureValue field. These bytes are suitable for verification with a java.security.Signature class.

X509Certificate.getSigAlgOID() and X509Certificate.getSigAlgParams()

The getSigAlgOID() method returns the value of the OBJECT IDENTIFIER in the algorithm field of the AlgorithmIdentifier structure in the signatureAlgorithm field in the Certificate structure. The getSigAlgParams() returns a byte array that represents the DER encoding of the parameters field in the AlgorithmIdentifier structure in the signatureAlgorithm field.

You would have noticed there is a signature field in the TBSCertificate structure that's also of the type AlgorithmIdentifier. The purpose of this is to provide a cross-check against the unsigned signatureAlgorithm field in the Certificate structure. The contents of the signatureAlgorithm field and the signature field will always be equal in a valid certificate.

X509Certificate.getSigAlgName()

The getSigAlgName() method will return a more (hopefully) human-friendly version of the name that is associated with the signature algorithm used(for example, SHA1withDSA rather than the 1.2.840.10040.4.3 that getSigAlgOID() would return.

Try It Out   **Creating a Self-Signed Version 1 Certificate**

This actually gives you enough to look at the process of creating a version 1 X.509 certificate. There is not any support for doing certificate creation directly in the JCA; however, the Bouncy Castle APIs have X.509 certificate generators in the org.bouncycastle.x509 package. Look at the following example using the org.bouncycastle.x509.X509V1CertificateGenerator:

```
package chapter6;

import java.math.BigInteger;
import java.security.*;
import java.security.cert.X509Certificate;
import java.util.Date;

import javax.security.auth.x500.X500Principal;

import org.bouncycastle.x509.X509V1CertificateGenerator;

/**
 * Basic X.509 V1 Certificate creation.
 */
public class X509V1CreateExample
{
    public static X509Certificate generateV1Certificate(KeyPair pair)
        throws InvalidKeyException, NoSuchProviderException, SignatureException
    {
        // generate the certificate
```

```
          X509V1CertificateGenerator   certGen = new X509V1CertificateGenerator();

          certGen.setSerialNumber(BigInteger.valueOf(System.currentTimeMillis()));
          certGen.setIssuerDN(new X500Principal("CN=Test Certificate"));
          certGen.setNotBefore(new Date(System.currentTimeMillis() - 50000));
          certGen.setNotAfter(new Date(System.currentTimeMillis() + 50000));
          certGen.setSubjectDN(new X500Principal("CN=Test Certificate"));
          certGen.setPublicKey(pair.getPublic());
          certGen.setSignatureAlgorithm("SHA256WithRSAEncryption");

          return certGen.generateX509Certificate(pair.getPrivate(), "BC");
      }

      public static void main(String[] args) throws Exception
      {
          // create the keys
          KeyPair           pair = Utils.generateRSAKeyPair();

          // generate the certificate
          X509Certificate cert = generateV1Certificate(pair);

          // show some basic validation
          cert.checkValidity(new Date());

          cert.verify(cert.getPublicKey());

          System.out.println("valid certificate generated");
      }
  }
```

Running the example should produce the line

```
valid certificate generated
```

on standard output.

How It Works

The heart of the example is the generator method(generateV1Certificate(). Going through the setting up of the X509V1CertificateGenerator object, you can see that the set() methods called correspond to the setting of the fields you have just looked at in the TBSCertficate structure and are closely equivalent to the names used in the get() methods implemented by the X509Certificate class. There are a few things worth noting, so I will go through the use of the generator class step-by-step.

First off, the serial number for the certificate is set on the following line:

```
certGen1.setSerialNumber(BigInteger.valueOf(System.currentTimeMillis()));
```

The best way to create serial numbers is largely up to the environment you are working in. The main thing is they need to be positive and unique for a given issuer value. Keep in mind that, because it is a BigInteger, you have a few bits you can work with, so it should always be possible to come up with an algorithm that will make sure the numbers are unique.

The next thing that is done is that the issuer of the certificate is assigned. As you would expect, this is simply an X.500 name, so I used an `X500Principal` to do this.

```
certGen1.setIssuerDN(new X500Principal("CN=Test Certificate"));
```

After the issuer, the `notBefore` and `notAfter` fields are set.

```
certGen1.setNotBefore(new Date(System.currentTimeMillis() - 50000));
certGen1.setNotAfter(new Date(System.currentTimeMillis() + 50000));
```

The generator object uses a `GeneralizedTime` to represent these dates, so the certificate you are producing will have a four-digit year on it. You can see from the `Date` objects being used that while the certificate will be valid when the program finishes, it has a total lifetime of only 100 seconds, 50 of which have already gone when it is created.

After setting the dates, you set the subject. Like the issuer this is also an `X500Principal` and, because the certificate is self-signed, has the same value as the issuer.

```
certGen1.setSubjectDN(new X500Principal("CN=Test Certificate"));
```

In the normal case, where the subject, or owner of the public key, is a different entity from the entity issuing the certificate, you would expect the `X500Principal` passed to the `setSubjectDN()` method to be different from that passed to `setIssuerDN()`.

Next, the example sets the public key that will be carried in the certificate:

```
certGen1.setPublicKey(pair.getPublic());
```

After this, you specify the signature algorithm that will be used to sign the certificate. In this case you are using SHA-256 with RSA with the signature format, as outlined in PKCS #1 version 1.5.

```
certGen1.setSignatureAlgorithm("SHA256WithRSAEncryption");
```

Finally, you generate the certificate, providing a private key to sign it with and the name of the provider you want to use:

```
return certGen1.generateX509Certificate(pair.getPrivate(), "BC");
```

Because this certificate is self-signed, it just uses the private key that corresponds to the public key on the certificate. As you will see a bit later when you read about certification requests, you would normally be using a completely different private key to sign a certificate with(the private key you would use would be the one corresponding to the public key on the CA certificate that you issued for yourself so that people could check that certificates claiming to be issued by you really were.

X.509 Extensions

The extensions field in the `TBSCertificate` structure was added with the release of X.509 version 3. As you can see from the original definition of `TBSCertificate`, it is optional, explicitly tagged, and of the type `Extensions`. The ASN.1 definition of `Extensions` is as follows:

```
Extensions  ::=  SEQUENCE SIZE (1..MAX) OF Extension

Extension  ::=  SEQUENCE  {
    extnID       OBJECT IDENTIFIER,
    critical     BOOLEAN DEFAULT FALSE,
    extnValue    OCTET STRING  }
```

MAX, of course, is implementation-dependent, but will normally always be big enough for the purposes of accommodating any certificates you have to deal with.

You can see that the actual Extension type is a three-member sequence. First, there is the extnID field, which identifies what extension is contained in an Extension structure and how to interpret the bytes in the extnValue field. Next, there is the critical field, which determines whether or not an implementation trying to process a X.509 certificate must be able to understand the extension if it is to process the certificate correctly. Finally, there is the extnValue field, which contains a DER encoding of the type associated with an extension associated with the identifier stored in the extnID field.

X.509 does not cover all the possibilities for extensions. Getting coverage on this is dependent on what *profile* the certificate is being created for. The signature on a certificate being valid is one thing, but you also need to know that the certificate is being valid for the use it is being presented to you for, and this is where the profile comes in. In the case of certificates, a profile tells you which extensions should be critical, what the allowed values of some of the certificates extensions might be, what extensions might have to be present, and which criteria must be met for a certificate chain to be recognized as valid. For example, I may trust an individual enough to sign a certificate for you to allow you to send signed e-mail, but it is another thing completely to trust someone to the level where I would expect another party to accept an executable signed with a certificate I had issued and think I had verified that the executable was not going to cause mischief. A profile provides the guidelines that allow someone that has been presented with a certificate to decide not only whether a particular CA signed the certificate, but also whether the certificate is being presented for a use that the CA issued it for.

There are now quite a few profiles, the most prevalent one probably being the Internet profile, also known as PKIX, which is covered in RFC 3280. Most providers will endeavor to conform to the PKIX profile, but which profile you should be using will also depend a lot on what environment you are working in, as many national standards bodies now have their own idea of what constitutes a good profile, and not all of them are in agreement.

That completes the background information on the outside world's view of extensions. Now you will have a look at the Java support for extensions.

The X509Extension Interface

The X509Extension interface provides some basic methods for investigating the extensions that are present in an X.509 certificate. It allows you to find out which extensions are critical and which are not, to get the value for a particular extension, and, finally, to check if there are any extensions that are unsupported by the profile the extension was created in.

X509Extension.getCriticalExtensionsOIDs()

The `getCriticalExtensionsOIDs()` method returns a possibly empty set of `String` objects representing the object identifiers related to the extensions marked as critical — that is, with the critical field set to `TRUE` — in the implementing certificate. If there are no extensions present in the implementing certificate, the method returns `null`.

X509Extension.getExtensionValue()

The `getExtensionValue()` method takes a string representing the object identifier of the extension you are interested in getting the value for. The method returns a byte array containing the DER-encoded `OCTET STRING` that is present in the `extnValue` field in the `Extension` structure associated with the passed in OID, or `null` if an extension related to that OID is not present.

Note the words "the method returns the `OCTET STRING` stored in the `extnValue` field." If you need to do further examinations on the structure associated with the extension, you will need to do something like the following to convert the byte array you get back from the method into the type that is indicated by the extension's OID:

```
ASN1InputStream     aIn = new ASN1InputStream(
                                 x509Cert.getExtensionValue(extensionOID));
ASN1OctetString     extnValue = (ASN1OctetString)aIn.readObject();

aIn = new ASN1InputStream(extnValue.getOctets());

DERObject           extensionType = aIn.readObject();
```

The value `extensionType` will then contain the ASN.1 predefined types making up the structure that is associated with the object identifier indicated by *extensionOID*.

X509Extension.getNonCriticalExtensionOIDs()

The `getCriticalExtensoinsOIDs()` method returns a possibly empty set of `String` objects representing the object identifiers related to the extensions not marked as critical — that is, with the critical field set to the default value of `FALSE` — in the implementing certificate. If there are no extensions present in the implementing certificate, the method returns `null`.

X509Extension.hasUnsupportedCriticalExtension()

The `hasUnsupportedCriticalExtension()` method returns `true` if the certificate contains an extension that is marked as critical but that is not expected as a critical extension by the profile the certificate was created for; otherwise, the method returns `false`.

It's actually hard to see what real use this method has now, since from JDK 1.4, an API for doing certificate path validation was introduced. In general, if you are using it, you will probably find it conforms to the PKIX profile; however, if you are serious about checking your certificates, you should use the CertPath API, which is discussed in Chapter 7.

Extensions Supported Directly by X509Certificate

Some of the more common extensions are supported directly by the X509Certificate class. You'll have a look at them here. The directly supported extensions help give you some idea of how the path validation APIs get the information they need to do their job, as well as how usage restrictions can be placed on version 3 certificates.

The common extensions are defined as part of X.500, which has the object identifier "2.5", being off the joint ISO/ITU-T branch. X.500 then assigned arc 29 to certificate extensions, giving it the name id-ce. You will also find these extensions among those documented in RFC 3280.

X509Certificate.getKeyUsage()

The KeyUsage extension is simply a BIT STRING and is associated with the object identifier id-ce-keyUsage, which has the value "2.5.29.15". The extension's ASN.1 definition looks as follows:

```
KeyUsage ::= BIT STRING {
        digitalSignature        (0),
        nonRepudiation          (1),
        keyEncipherment         (2),
        dataEncipherment        (3),
        keyAgreement            (4),
        keyCertSign             (5),
        cRLSign                 (6),
        encipherOnly            (7),
        decipherOnly            (8) }
```

The getKeyUsage() method returns these as an array of booleans. In the event that not all bits are set in the BIT STRING, the array of booleans is always padded out to eight elements, with the missing elements being set to false.

The presence of a particular bit indicates what roles the issuer of the certificate had in mind when the certificate was generated. The name of the bits and their meanings are as follows:

❑ digitalSignature — The key can be used with signature mechanisms other than those involving certificate signing.

❑ nonRepudiation — The key can be used for verifying signatures used to provide a nonrepudiation service.

❑ keyEncipherment — The key can be used to encrypt other keys.

❑ dataEncipherment — The key can be used to encrypt data other than cryptographic keys.

❑ keyAgreement — The key can be used for key agreement.

❑ keyCertSign — The key may be used for verifying other certificates.

❑ cRLSign — The key can be used to verify a signature on a CRL, or certificate revocation list. You will have closer look at CRLs in Chapter 7.

❑ encipherOnly — This bit is only meaningful if the KeyAgreement bit is set. If both it and the KeyAgreement bit are set, key agreement can be carried out only for the purpose of encrypting data.

❑ decipherOnly — This bit is only meaningful if the KeyAgreement bit is set. If both it and the KeyAgreement bit are set, key agreement can be carried out only for the purpose of decrypting data.

X509Certificate.getSubjectAlternativeNames()

In addition to the details of the subject name provided by the getSubjectX500Principal(), a certificate can also carry other names that the owner of the public key in the certificate can be known by. This is done using the SubjectAltName extension, which allows a range of alternatives to be included for identifying the subject. If you want to include the e-mail of a subject in a certificate, this is really the place to do it, rather than use the older PKCS #9 e-mail address field in the DN.

The SubjectAltName extension is indicated by the presence of the OID "2.5.29.17" (id-ce-subjectAltName). The value of the extension is a GeneralNames structure, which is defined as follows and has the following ASN.1 definition:

```
SubjectAltName ::= GeneralNames

GeneralNames ::= SEQUENCE SIZE (1..MAX) OF GeneralName

GeneralName ::= CHOICE {
                otherName                    [0]     AnotherName,
                rfc822Name                   [1]     IA5String,
                dNSName                      [2]     IA5String,
                x400Address                  [3]     ORAddress,
                directoryName                [4]     Name,
                ediPartyName                 [5]     EDIPartyName,
                uniformResourceIdentifier    [6]     IA5String,
                iPAddress                    [7]     OCTET STRING,
                registeredID                 [8]     OBJECT IDENTIFIER }

AnotherName ::= SEQUENCE {
                type-id    OBJECT IDENTIFIER,
                value      [0] EXPLICIT ANY DEFINED BY type-id }

EDIPartyName ::= SEQUENCE {
                nameAssigner           [0]     DirectoryString OPTIONAL,
                partyName              [1]     DirectoryString }

DirectoryString ::= CHOICE {
        teletexString     TeletexString,
        printableString   PrintableString,
        bmpString         BMPString,
        universalString   UniversalString,
        uTF8String        UTF8String }
```

I'll show you how to construct a SubjectAltName extension in the example a bit later. Meanwhile, when it comes to reading one using the getSubjectAlternativeNames() method, the method returns null if the extension is not present, or if it is present, it returns an immutable collection representing the GeneralNames structure.

The mechanism for constructing the collection is as follows. Each entry in the GeneralNames structure is turned into a two-element list, the first element being an integer representing the tag associated with that `GeneralName`, and the second element being an object representing the value of the `GeneralName`. The various values are returned either as Java `String` objects or as byte arrays that contain the DER encoding of the name value. The tags returned as `String` objects are those for `rfc822Name`, `dNSName`, `uniformResourceIdentifier`, `iPAddress`, `directoryName`, and `registeredID`. IP addresses are converted into strings using dotted quad notation in the case of IPv4 and for IPv6 in the form "a1:a2: . . . :a8", where a1 to a8 each represent one part of the eight 16-bit pieces making up the address. Directory name objects are converted into `String` objects using RFC 2253 string format. In the case of the others, the DER-encoded value of the choice item is returned in a byte array.

Note, the conversion of directory names to RFC 2253 strings may not always have the desired result. If you need to process directory names in the `SubjectAltName` extension, you may need to unpack the extension by hand instead using `X509Extension.getExtensionValue()`.

X509Certificate.getIssuerAlternativeNames()

The `IssuerAltName` extension is indicated by the presence of the OID "2.5.29.18" (`id-ce-issuerAltName`). It is defined in the same way as the `SubjectAltName` extension, as a `GeneralNames` structure, and consequently also returns a collection that has been formatted according to the rules outlined for `getSubjectAlternativeNames()`.

X509Certificate.getBasicConstraints()

The `BasicConstraints` extension is indicated by the presence of the OID "2.5.29.19" (`id-ce-basicConstraints`). The `getBasicConstraints()` method returns an int value, and to understand why, you need to look at the ASN.1 definition of the `BasicConstraints` structure that is as follows:

```
BasicConstraints ::= SEQUENCE {
     cA                  BOOLEAN DEFAULT FALSE,
     pathLenConstraint   INTEGER (0..MAX) OPTIONAL }
```

The return value of the method is derived from the value of the `pathLenConstraint`, which is meaningful only if the `cA` field is set to `TRUE`, meaning that the subject of the certificate is a certificate authority. If the `cA` field is `FALSE`, then the extension indicates that the certificate is an end entity certificate and should not be used to sign another one.

When `pathLenConstraint` is meaningful it indicates how many certificates can follow the one that contains the extension. For example, if the value is 0, then any certificate verifiable by the certificate containing the extension must be an end entity certificate. If `pathLenConstraint` is left out and the `cA` field is `TRUE`, then any number of CA certificates can follow the certificate containing the extension.

So in respect of the `getBasicConstraints()` method: If the `cA` field is `TRUE` and the `pathLenConstraint` has been set, then the value returned is the int representing the value in `pathLenconstraint`; if `pathLenConstraint` is not present, then `Integer.MAX_VALUE` is returned instead. If the `cA` field is `FALSE`, then `getBasicConstraints()` returns -1, indicating the certificate containing the extension can only come at the end of the chain.

X509Certificate.getExtendedKeyUsage()

The `ExtendedKeyUsage` extension was created when it turned out a more flexible arrangement than the one offered by the `KeyUsage` extension was required. It is associated with the object identifier "2.5.29.37" (`id-ce-extKeyUsage`) and its ASN.1 definition is as follows:

```
ExtKeyUsageSyntax ::= SEQUENCE SIZE (1..MAX) OF KeyPurposeId

KeyPurposeId ::= OBJECT IDENTIFIER
```

As you can see, the type encoded in the `extnValue` field is just a sequence of OIDs, so unlike the `KeyUsage` extension, the `ExtendedKeyUsage` allows the certificate issuer to use object identifiers to determine what the public key in the certificate can be used for. The greater customization this extension allows in certificate purpose has resulted in it becoming increasingly popular, with a number of organizations and companies publishing lists of object identifiers that can be used as a `KeyPurposeId`.

The PKIX profile described in RFC 3280 describes a number of these, which are for supporting some of the more standard uses a certificate key can be put to. The current list includes the following:

- ❑ `anyExtendedKeyUsage`, OID "2.5.29.37.0", key can be used for any purpose.
- ❑ `id-kp-serverAuth`, OID "1.3.6.1.5.5.7.3.1", key can be used for SSL/TLS server authentication.
- ❑ `id-kp-clientAuth`, OID "1.3.6.1.5.5.7.3.2", key can be used for SSL/TLS client authentication.
- ❑ `id-kp-codeSigning`, OID "1.3.6.1.5.5.7.3.3", key can be used for signing executable code.
- ❑ `id-kp-emailProtection`, OID "1.3.6.1.5.5.7.3.4", key can be used for e-mail encryption/signing.
- ❑ `id-kp-timeStamping`, OID "1.3.6.1.5.5.7.3.8", key can be used for creating timestamps.
- ❑ `id-kp-OCSPSigning`, OID "1.3.6.1.5.5.7.3.9", key can be used for signing OCSP (RFC 2560) messages.

As you may have guessed from the "1.3.6.1.5.5.7.3", also known as `id-kp`, is an object identifier that marks an arc reserved for PKIX extended key purpose object identifiers.

Both `KeyUsage` and `ExtendedKeyUsage` extensions can appear in the same certificate, so it is acceptable to include both if you are creating a certificate that contains both, or evaluating one that contains both, just make sure they are consistent with each other. For example, it does not make sense to have a `KeyUsage` extension with only the `dataEncipherment` bit set and have an `ExtendedKeyUsage` extension with the `id-kp-codeSigning` OID present.

Try It Out   Creating a Self-Signed Version 3 Certificate

Creation of a version 3 certificate is very similar to a version 1 certificate — the only difference is the presence of extensions. This section creates a version 3 certificate with a couple of the extensions covered in the last section.

Choice of extensions is largely dictated by the purpose the certificate is for, although you will also see in Chapter 7 that extensions exist that serve to provide references to how to verify the certificate is still valid, what other certificate can be used to verify it, and extra information on the public key contained in the certificate. In the example here I'll generate a self-signed certificate marked for use with SSL using the `ExtendedKeyUsage` extension, as well as set the appropriate bits in the `KeyUsage` extension. The certificate will also be marked as unsuitable for use as a CA cert by using the `BasicConstraints` extension, and finally I'll include an e-mail address for the certificate's subject using the `SubjectAltName` extension.

```
package chapter6;

import java.math.BigInteger;
```

```java
import java.security.*;
import java.security.cert.X509Certificate;
import java.util.Date;

import javax.security.auth.x500.X500Principal;

import org.bouncycastle.asn1.x509.BasicConstraints;
import org.bouncycastle.asn1.x509.ExtendedKeyUsage;
import org.bouncycastle.asn1.x509.GeneralName;
import org.bouncycastle.asn1.x509.GeneralNames;
import org.bouncycastle.asn1.x509.KeyPurposeId;
import org.bouncycastle.asn1.x509.KeyUsage;
import org.bouncycastle.asn1.x509.X509Extensions;
import org.bouncycastle.x509.X509V3CertificateGenerator;

/**
 * Basic X.509 V3 Certificate creation with TLS flagging.
 */
public class X509V3CreateExample
{
    public static X509Certificate generateV3Certificate(KeyPair pair)
        throws InvalidKeyException, NoSuchProviderException, SignatureException
    {
        // generate the certificate
        X509V3CertificateGenerator  certGen = new X509V3CertificateGenerator();

        certGen.setSerialNumber(BigInteger.valueOf(System.currentTimeMillis()));
        certGen.setIssuerDN(new X500Principal("CN=Test Certificate"));
        certGen.setNotBefore(new Date(System.currentTimeMillis() - 50000));
        certGen.setNotAfter(new Date(System.currentTimeMillis() + 50000));
        certGen.setSubjectDN(new X500Principal("CN=Test Certificate"));
        certGen.setPublicKey(pair.getPublic());
        certGen.setSignatureAlgorithm("SHA256WithRSAEncryption");

        certGen.addExtension(X509Extensions.BasicConstraints, true,
                                            new BasicConstraints(false));

        certGen.addExtension(X509Extensions.KeyUsage, true,
                new KeyUsage(KeyUsage.digitalSignature | KeyUsage.keyEncipherment));

        certGen.addExtension(X509Extensions.ExtendedKeyUsage, true,
                            new ExtendedKeyUsage(KeyPurposeId.id_kp_serverAuth));

        certGen.addExtension(X509Extensions.SubjectAlternativeName, false,
                    new GeneralNames(
                        new GeneralName(GeneralName.rfc822Name, "test@test.test")));

        return certGen.generateX509Certificate(pair.getPrivate(), "BC");
    }

    public static void main(String[] args) throws Exception
    {
        // create the keys
        KeyPair         pair = Utils.generateRSAKeyPair();

        // generate the certificate
```

```
X509Certificate cert = generateV3Certificate(pair);

        // show some basic validation
        cert.checkValidity(new Date());

        cert.verify(cert.getPublicKey());

        System.out.println("valid certificate generated");
    }
}
```

How It Works

As you can see, this is example is very similar to the last one, so the basics of the certificate construction are essentially what was described earlier. The difference in this case is the use of the X509V3CertificateGenerator class and that you are now adding some extensions to the certificate.

Looking at the example, note that each call to the X509V3CertificateGenerator.addExtension() method takes three parameters reflecting the three fields required in an extension that you saw in the ASN.1 definition earlier:

```
Extension  ::=  SEQUENCE  {
     extnID       OBJECT IDENTIFIER,
     critical     BOOLEAN DEFAULT FALSE,
     extnValue    OCTET STRING  }
```

The first and second parameters, representing extnID and critical, are self-explanatory. The last parameter, which is used to fill in the extnValue field, needs a bit more examination, though. For example, take the adding of a KeyUsage extension, which is done on the following lines:

```
certGen.addExtension(X509Extensions.KeyUsage, true,
            new KeyUsage(KeyUsage.digitalSignature | KeyUsage.keyEncipherment));
```

The last parameter is an ASN1Encodable object representing the value of the extension. What happens internally to the generator is that the value is encoded as a DER-encoded byte array, which is then used to create an OCTET STRING. It is this OCTET STRING that is then assigned as the value of the extnValue field. Likewise, if you were to add

```
byte[] usageExt = cert.getExtensionValue(X509Extensions.KeyUsage.getId());
```

the byte array usageExt would represent the DER encoding of the OCTET STRING, and the octets contained in the OCTET STRING would represent the DER encoding of KeyUsage.

One further point of interest about the example is the choice of whether or not to make a particular extension critical by passing true as the value for the critical field. As mentioned earlier, this largely depends on the profile that the certificate is being created for. In the case of the example, the choices have been based on the PKIX profile detailed in RFC 3280. If you look up RFC 3280, you will see that BasicConstraints in an end entity certificate may be marked as critical; in the example I have taken the option of doing so. KeyUsage, on the other hand, should be marked as critical, so it is. ExtendedKeyUsage may also be critical; however, if it is, the key can be used only for the purpose allowed by the extension, and the purpose given in the extension must also correspond with the purposes allowed by the KeyUsage extension if it is present. In my case, I wanted to assert the purpose of the certificate key strongly, so I have marked `ExtendedKeyUsage` as critical. Finally, I added the `SubjectAltName` extension, which in this case has a purely informational role and so is marked as noncritical.

Reading and Writing Certificates

There are two principal encodings used for reading and writing individual certificates: native DER format and the PEM format, which is described in some early RFCs on securing e-mail, RFC 1421 to RFC 1424, which were about Privacy Enhanced E-mail. The PEM format is basically a base 64-encoded version of the DER encoding with an ASCII header and footer attached.

Getting the DER encoding of a certificate is easy — just call the `Certificate.getEncoded()` method on the certificate object. Writing PEM-encoded certificates is not directly supported in the JCA, but the Bouncy Castle APIs include a class for generating them called the `PEMWriter`, which lives in the `org.bouncycastle.openssl` package. I will show you examples of using both these methods of writing certificates in the discussion of the class you use for reading certificate streams — the `CertificateFactory` class.

The CertificateFactory Class

Like other classes in the JCA, objects of the type `java.security.cert.CertificateFactory` are not created directly but are instead created using the `getInstance()` factory pattern, and as with other factory-based classes, the return value of `getInstance()` follows the provider precedence rules that the Java runtime has been set up with.

The `CertificateFactory` class has a number of methods on it for reading in certificates, certificate revocation lists, and certificate paths. For the moment you will just look at the methods for reading certificates, because certificate revocation lists and certificate paths are covered in the next chapter.

CertificateFactory.generateCertificate()

The `generateCertificate()` method takes an `InputStream` as a parameter and proceeds to read certificates from it. If more than one certificate is present in the stream, and the stream supports `InputStream.mark()` and `InputStream.reset()`, `generateCertificate()` will return one certificate per invocation until it runs out of certificates, at which stage it returns `null`. If there is trailing data, however, a `CertificateException` will be thrown.

CertificateFactory.generateCertificates()

The `generateCertificates()` method also takes an `InputStream` as a parameter but, in this case, reads the entire stream and returns a, possibly empty, `Collection` class containing the certificates that were read. Like the `generateCertificate()` method, a `CertificateException` is thrown in the event of a parsing error.

Try It Out   **Using the CertificateFactory Class**

This example reads a single certificate defined in an `InputStream`. It uses the earlier Try It Out ("Creating a Self-Signed Version 1 Certificate") to provide the source data, but you could just as easily get the data from a file.

```
package chapter6;

import java.io.*;
import java.security.*;
import java.security.cert.CertificateFactory;
import java.security.cert.X509Certificate;

/**
 * Basic example of using a CertificateFactory.
 */
public class CertificateFactoryExample
{
    public static void main(String[] args) throws Exception
    {
        // create the keys
        KeyPair           pair = Utils.generateRSAKeyPair();;

        // create the input stream
        ByteArrayOutputStream bOut = new ByteArrayOutputStream();

        bOut.write(X509V1CreateExample.generateV1Certificate(pair).getEncoded());

        bOut.close();

        InputStream in = new ByteArrayInputStream(bOut.toByteArray());

        // create the certificate factory
        CertificateFactory fact = CertificateFactory.getInstance("X.509","BC");

        // read the certificate
        X509Certificate x509Cert = (X509Certificate)fact.generateCertificate(in);

        System.out.println("issuer: " + x509Cert.getIssuerX500Principal());
    }
}
```

Running the example should produce the line:

```
issuer: CN=Test Certificate
```

on standard output.

How It Works

An InputStream for the CertificateFactory is created using a byte array primed with the DER encoding of a X.509 certificate, and the certificate is then recovered using the generateCertificate() method.

One interesting modification you could try is to change the example so that it writes the certificate data in PEM format instead. You can do this using the Bouncy Castle org.bouncycastle.openssl.PEMWriter class, and after adding the appropriate import statement, replace the line

```
        bOut.write(X509V1CreateExample.generateV1Certificate(pair).getEncoded());
```

with the lines

```
PEMWriter                  pemWrt = new PEMWriter(new OutputStreamWriter(bOut));

pemWrt.writeObject(X509V1CreateExample.generateV1Certificate(pair));

pemWrt.close();
```

You should see that the certificate still reads okay; however, if you add the line

```
System.out.println(Utils.toString(bOut.toByteArray()));
```

after the call to bOut.close(), you will see that you now have a base 64-encoded version of the certificate between the headers "-----BEGIN CERTIFICATE-----" and "-----END CERTIFICATE-----".

Try It Out   Reading Multiple Certificates

As mentioned earlier, the CertificateFactory also allows you to retrieve more than one certificate from a stream. The following example shows how to this by looping; in the How It Works section I'll discuss the method that returns a Collection. Try running it and then read on.

```
package chapter6;

import java.io.*;
import java.security.*;
import java.security.cert.CertificateFactory;
import java.security.cert.X509Certificate;
import java.util.*;

/**
 * Basic example of reading multiple certificates with a CertificateFactory.
 */
public class MultipleCertificateExample
{
    public static void main(String[] args) throws Exception
    {
        // create the keys
        KeyPair          pair = Utils.generateRSAKeyPair();

        // create the input stream
        ByteArrayOutputStream bOut = new ByteArrayOutputStream();

        bOut.write(X509V1CreateExample.generateV1Certificate(pair).getEncoded());
        bOut.write(X509V3CreateExample.generateV3Certificate(pair).getEncoded());

        bOut.close();

        InputStream in = new ByteArrayInputStream(bOut.toByteArray());

        // create the certificate factory
        CertificateFactory fact = CertificateFactory.getInstance("X.509","BC");

        // read the certificate
```

```
       X509Certificate      x509Cert;
       Collection           collection = new ArrayList();

       while((x509Cert = (X509Certificate)fact.generateCertificate(in)) != null)
       {
           collection.add(x509Cert);
       }

       Iterator it = collection.iterator();
       while (it.hasNext())
       {
           System.out.println("version: " +
                                     ((X509Certificate)it.next()).getVersion());
       }
   }
}
```

Running the example, you should see it print the version numbers for the certificates it finds; in this case, the output will read

```
version: 1
version: 3
```

indicating that the factory managed to read the two certificates that were written.

How It Works

This example follows from the discussion after the previous example using the CertificateFactory class. The only difference this time is that you have primed the byte array used for InputStream generation with two certificates rather than one and then looped, adding each certificate to a collection as you read it.

There are a couple of points that do need to be covered about it, though. The first one is that in the case you are looking at here, you can use the fact.generateCertificate() method in a loop because a ByteArrayInputStream supports the InputStream.mark() and InputStream.reset() methods. If this was not the case, you would need to add the line

```
       in = new BufferedInputStream(in);
```

prior to entering the while loop.

The second point is that rather than using the loop, you could have just used the CertificateFactory. generateCertificates() method, which returns a Collection class containing all the certificates it found in the InputStream. You can try that as an alternative by replacing the lines

```
       Collection           collection = new ArrayList();

       while((x509Cert = (X509Certificate)fact.generateCertificate(in)) != null)
       {
           collection.add(x509Cert);
       }
```

with the single line

```
Collection          collection = fact.generateCertificates(in);
```

and you will see that the example produces the same result. As you can imagine, this is likely to be less trouble, as otherwise you have make sure whatever stream you are reading from can support the `mark()` and `reset()` methods on `InputStream`.

If the purpose of reading multiple certificates is to read a certificate path, or chain, there is a good chance you should be using the `CertPath` API instead and the `CertificateFactory` methods that are relevant to it. You look at how to do this in Chapter 7; for now the next thing to look at is how to request a certificate from a CA so you can actually build a certificate chain in the first place.

Certification Requests

A certification request is a structure that is supplied to a CA, giving the CA the details that a key owner wants to appear in a certificate the owner wants the CA to create. Certification requests need to accommodate a couple of needs. Obviously, they need to contain the public key and some identifying information for the person who owns it. They also need to be tamper-proof so that the CA can be confident that the information that the CA is about to include in a certificate generated in response to the request is valid.

A variety of vendors have, from time to time, produced their own format for creating certification requests, but by far the most common and supported structure is the format defined by RSA Security in the standards document PKCS #10.

```
CertificationRequest ::= SEQUENCE {
                         certificationRequestInfo  CertificationRequestInfo,
                         signatureAlgorithm        AlgorithmIdentifier,
                         signature                 BIT STRING }

CertificationRequestInfo ::= SEQUENCE {
                             version        INTEGER,
                             subject        Name,
                             subjectPKInfo  SubjectPublicKeyInfo,
                             attributes     [0] Attributes }


Attributes ::= SET OF Attribute
```

The `CertificationRequest` structure looks very similar to that of a X.509 certificate. It consists of a block of signed data; an `AlgorithmIdentifier` identifying the signature algorithm used and a `BIT STRING` containing the actual signature that was created using the DER encoding of the `CertificationRequestInfo` structure as input. This is not especially surprising, as it is doing a similar job. The big difference is that a `CertificationRequest` is always self-signed — that is, the public key contained in the `subjectPKInfo` object inside the `CertificationRequestInfo` structure is always the key that is used to verify the signature. This means the owner of the private key corresponding to the public key in the `CertificationRequestInfo` structure must have been the one who created the signed request.

The `CertificationRequestInfo` structure is considerably simpler than the `TBSCertificate` structure, however. Apart from a version number, the structure consists of the `subject` field, which contains the

X.500 name that is to appear as the subject in the issued certificate. Then there is the `subjectPKInfo` field, which contains the public key that is to appear in the certificate. Finally, there is an `attributes` field, which is a set of `Attribute` structures.

The `Attribute` structure is the same one that you have seen before; the only special note required is that, in the case of PKCS #10, the legitimate attribute types are defined in PKCS #9. There are two of them: the `challengePassword` attribute and the `extensionRequest` attribute.

The `challengePassword` attribute is used to send the CA a password that can be used to request revocation of the certificate being issued. The OID associated with the `attrType` field for `challengePassword` is `pkcs-9-at-challengePassword`, which has the value "1.2.840.113549.1.9.7". The SET assigned to the `attrValues` field in the `challengePassword` can only contain one entry, which is of the type `DirectoryString`, the same type you saw in the description of the `GeneralName` type. What is actually put in the `DirectoryString` is then up to the CA. If you need to use this attribute, you will find the requirements are likely to vary from place to place.

The `extensionRequest` attribute is used to request specific extensions to be added to the certificate when it is issued. The `attrType` value for `extensionRequest` is `pkcs-9-at-extensionRequest` — the OID value "1.2.840.113549.1.9.14". Unlike the `challengePassword`, the contents of the `attrValues` field is more rigorously defined. There can only be one entry in the SET, and it is an `Extensions` structure. It is the same one you saw as part of the `TBSCertificate` structure in the X.509 certificate definition, so the use of this attribute is uniform across CAs.

You will look at the use of the `extensionRequest` attribute a bit later, but at this point I would like you to look at an example of how to create a basic certification request.

Try It Out   Creating a Certification Request

A good place to start with certification requests is to just create a basic one. Have a look at the following example. It creates a certification request that is suitable for creating a basic certificate — one that simply provides a common name in the subject.

```
package chapter6;

import java.io.OutputStreamWriter;
import java.security.KeyPair;
import java.security.KeyPairGenerator;

import javax.security.auth.x500.X500Principal;

import org.bouncycastle.jce.PKCS10CertificationRequest;
import org.bouncycastle.openssl.PEMWriter;

/**
 * Generation of a basic PKCS #10 request.
 */
public class PKCS10CertRequestExample
{
    public static PKCS10CertificationRequest generateRequest(
        KeyPair pair)
        throws Exception
```

```
    {
        return new PKCS10CertificationRequest(
                "SHA256withRSA",
                new X500Principal("CN=Requested Test Certificate"),
                pair.getPublic(),
                null,
                pair.getPrivate());
    }

    public static void main(String[] args) throws Exception
    {
        // create the keys
        KeyPairGenerator kpGen = KeyPairGenerator.getInstance("RSA", "BC");

        kpGen.initialize(1024, Utils.createFixedRandom());

        KeyPair          pair = kpGen.generateKeyPair();

        PKCS10CertificationRequest request = generateRequest(pair);

        PEMWriter    pemWrt = new PEMWriter(
                                        new OutputStreamWriter(System.out));

        pemWrt.writeObject(request);

        pemWrt.close();
    }
}
```

Running the example produces a PEM-encoded certification request, which should look as follows:

```
-----BEGIN CERTIFICATE REQUEST-----
MIIBYjCBzAIBADAlMSMwIQYDVQQDExpSZXF1ZXN0ZWQgVGVzdCBDZXJ0aWZpY2F0
ZTCBnzANBgkqhkiG9w0BAQEFAAOBjQAwgYkCgYEAsO4slP/KdZQsZyYn3asTWDtX
E1YN+QQbbHELK7boPQa91YHv5DV/SgucThoXXCtSA45d3dQhrEbZ2+HRBarZIylk
Nc+VmcV1qFX5KsD9wCYPMtdAYYog6jz259yCOKPDXPm787Q5t9h2zV3Ml1i0eWhC
cdRYiWHQ5g20W4Bq3GsCAwEAATANBgkqhkiG9w0BAQsFAAOBgQBGzajsmJyWULew
wXlAqC4RcaaNnSxGv25DRSmRyUcngWhTe/T8JEi5HN5s8ELQUQ62/Y7XLyUyd/g6
h/DHjuSDg6W6NdxdOV61L+mFnlck6XJsevvm8DANvKiEQxPCegwIeUoyhYLw0Mip
K0SnuvXv52WLd9Mv7TP8VHAtmfqRng==
-----END CERTIFICATE REQUEST-----
```

As mentioned earlier, the PEM encoding is simply a base 64 encoding of the DER encoding of the certification request structure between a header and footer. One thing to watch out for: There are two variations on what should be in the header and footer in a certification request. OpenSSL uses "CERTIFICATE REQUEST," but other applications also use "NEW CERTIFICATE REQUEST."

How It Works

The basic information required to go into a certification request is the public key it is meant to contain and the X.500 name of the owner of the public key. The request needs to be signed using the private key corresponding to the public key, and a signature algorithm needs to be specified. All this is encapsulated in the following lines:

```
        return new PKCS10CertificationRequest(
                "SHA256withRSA",
                new X500Principal("CN=Test Certificate"),
                pair.getPublic(),
                null,
                pair.getPrivate());
```

Having created the request, you need to turn it into a format suitable for passing onto a CA so they can issue a certificate based on it. This example uses PEM, which is a format suitable for sending through e-mail or cutting and pasting into a Web form. In cases where the CA can accept the request directly as a DER-encoded object, you might have simply written the request out to a file.

This will get you a basic certificate with whatever default extensions the CA adds to it. What do you do if you need to request a particular extension rather than the default ones, or just add extra information to the certificate that the CA is willing to include? The answer is to make use of the extensionRequest attribute. Take a look at how that is done now.

Try It Out   Adding Extensions to a Certification Request

Here is a modified version of the last example. It adds a SubjectAltName extension to the certification request. You add this to the attributes section of the certification request by using the extensionRequest attribute. The idea is that the CA picks up the attribute as part of processing the certification request.

Have a look at the example and try running it.

```
package chapter6;

import java.io.OutputStreamWriter;
import java.security.KeyPair;
import java.security.KeyPairGenerator;
import java.util.Vector;

import javax.security.auth.x500.X500Principal;

import org.bouncycastle.asn1.DEROctetString;
import org.bouncycastle.asn1.DERSet;
import org.bouncycastle.asn1.pkcs.Attribute;
import org.bouncycastle.asn1.pkcs.PKCSObjectIdentifiers;
import org.bouncycastle.asn1.x509.GeneralName;
import org.bouncycastle.asn1.x509.GeneralNames;
import org.bouncycastle.asn1.x509.X509Extension;
import org.bouncycastle.asn1.x509.X509Extensions;
import org.bouncycastle.jce.PKCS10CertificationRequest;
import org.bouncycastle.openssl.PEMWriter;

/**
 * Generation of a basic PKCS #10 request with an extension.
 */
public class PKCS10ExtensionExample
{
    public static PKCS10CertificationRequest generateRequest(
        KeyPair pair)
        throws Exception
    {
```

```
        // create a SubjectAlternativeName extension value
        GeneralNames  subjectAltName = new GeneralNames(
                new GeneralName(GeneralName.rfc822Name, "test@test.test"));

        // create the extensions object and add it as an attribute
        Vector  oids = new Vector();
        Vector  values = new Vector();

        oids.add(X509Extensions.SubjectAlternativeName);
        values.add(new X509Extension(false, new DEROctetString(subjectAltName)));

        X509Extensions  extensions = new X509Extensions(oids, values);

        Attribute  attribute = new Attribute(
                            PKCSObjectIdentifiers.pkcs_9_at_extensionRequest,
                            new DERSet(extensions));

        return new PKCS10CertificationRequest(
                "SHA256withRSA",
                new X500Principal("CN=Requested Test Certificate"),
                pair.getPublic(),
                new DERSet(attribute),
                pair.getPrivate());
    }

    public static void main(String[] args) throws Exception
    {
        // create the keys
        KeyPairGenerator kpGen = KeyPairGenerator.getInstance("RSA", "BC");

        kpGen.initialize(1024, Utils.createFixedRandom());

        KeyPair          pair = kpGen.generateKeyPair();

        PKCS10CertificationRequest  request = generateRequest(pair);

        PEMWriter         pemWrt = new PEMWriter(
                                        new OutputStreamWriter(System.out));

        pemWrt.writeObject(request);

        pemWrt.close();
    }
}
```

You should get the following lines:

```
-----BEGIN CERTIFICATE REQUEST-----
MIIBkDCB+gIBADAlMSMwIQYDVQQDExpSZXF1ZXN0ZWQgVGVzdCBDZXJ0aWZpY2F0
ZTCBnzANBgkqhkiG9w0BAQEFAAOBjQAwgYkCgYEAsO4slP/KdZQsZyYn3asTWDtX
E1YN+QQbbHELK7boPQa91YHv5DV/SgucThoXXCtSA45d3dQhrEbZ2+HRBarZIylk
Nc+VmcV1qFX5KsD9wCYPMtdAYYog6jz259yCOKPDXPm787Q5t9h2zV3Ml1i0eWhC
```

```
cdRYiWHQ5g20W4Bq3GsCAwEAAaAsMCoGCSqGSIb3DQEJDjEdMBswGQYDVR0RBBIw
EIEOdGVzdEB0ZXN0LnRlc3QwDQYJKoZIhvcNAQELBQADgYEAZGPA0Jyw49cHPJjG
bloqKAPN1BO200AiRFsHnkOQ1DopJff3mW+FdszAc9g6rTB4/YAiM4r0E314e0vm
XSlW2q8sp+c2XJO7PUIdJIuAUnvSmMb/uwXFP2SzLdjLcmymMsnFfjvwkht0K2it
O5HuUDuhLnxEimGlUEBrfkdrsH0=
-----END CERTIFICATE REQUEST-----
```

Note how the output is very similar to that of the last example; the only change is toward the end where the encoding of the attribute data for the certification request has been added.

How It Works

I mentioned earlier that the `extensionRequest` attribute was defined in PKCS #9 and that the attribute value associated with it was defined as follows:

```
ExtensionRequest ::= Extensions
```

where the `Extensions` structure is the same one you saw defined for the `TBSCertificate` structure earlier.

Now if you look back at the example you will see that the lines

```
Vector   oids = new Vector();
Vector   values = new Vector();

oids.add(X509Extensions.SubjectAlternativeName);
values.add(new X509Extension(false, new DEROctetString(subjectAltName)));

X509Extensions   extensions = new X509Extensions(oids, values);
```

are creating the `Extensions` structure referred to previously, and then an appropriately labeled `Attribute` structure is created to carry the `Extensions` structure in the lines

```
Attribute   attribute = new Attribute(
                          PKCSObjectIdentifiers.pkcs_9_at_extensionRequest,
                          new DERSet(extensions));
```

This is then passed into the constructor for the `PKCS10CertificationRequest` object wrapped in a `DERSet` object so that the resulting value can be used to fill in the `attributes` field in the PKCS #10 `CertificationRequestInfo` structure.

Of course, in real life, a CA would probably do more than just run some code to perform this operation. The CA should at least make sure the person requesting the additional extensions has the right to have them in place and that any identifying information included in extensions such as the `SubjectAltName` extension is actually correct. However, from the point of view of the technology, you can see how it is done.

Now that you know how to create certification requests and add attributes to them as required, it is time to look at how the process works in full, and how certificate chains are created as a result of it. I'll discuss that now as you look at writing a basic CA.

Writing a Simple Certificate Authority

Now you will look at taking a certification request and using it and an existing root certificate to generate a new certificate. As you can see from Figure 6-2, this is essentially what a certificate authority does in its most basic form.

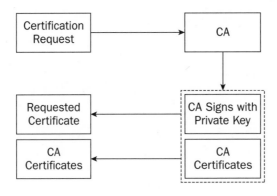

Converting a Certification Request into a Certificate
with Associated Validation Certificates

Figure 6-2

Creating a certificate with a signature that can be verified by another certificate creates a relationship between the two certificates that is normally expressed in terms of a certificate path or a certificate chain, and the validation of these certificate paths is one of the things that various profiles concern themselves with. In Java terms the simplest way to think of a certificate path is as an array of certificates, with the first certificate in the array being the end entity certificate, whose signature can be verified by the next certificate in the array, and the last certificate in the array is the root certificate, which is normally self-signed and has to be accepted on trust.

In X.509 terms there are a couple of steps to finding out which certificate has signed which. First you would expect if one certificate can be used to verify another one, that same certificate will have a subject that is equal to the issuer on the certificate being verified. Second, you would obviously expect that, given that the subject of any certificate is the issuer of another, the key on the first certificate will validate the signature on the second. Of course, an issuer may have issued several certificates, so another two extensions are provided with X.509 version 3, which can be used to make it easier to work out, given an unordered set of certificates, what order the certificates are meant to be in. The extensions are the `AuthorityKeyIdentifier` and the `SubjectKeyIdentifier`.

The OID and value of the `AuthorityKeyIdentifier` extension are defined as follows:

```
id-ce-authorityKeyIdentifier OBJECT IDENTIFIER ::=  { id-ce 35 }

AuthorityKeyIdentifier ::= SEQUENCE {
    keyIdentifier             [0] KeyIdentifier            OPTIONAL,
    authorityCertIssuer       [1] GeneralNames             OPTIONAL,
    authorityCertSerialNumber [2] CertificateSerialNumber OPTIONAL   }

KeyIdentifier ::= OCTET STRING
```

As you can see, the kind of information contained in the `AuthorityKeyIdentifier` is what you would imagine would be associated with the issuer of the certificate it is attached to. For example, setting the `authorityCertIssuer` and `authorityCertSerialNumber` to the issuer and serial number of the verifying certificate is usually enough to identify the issuer's certificate uniquely. The `keyIdentifier` field allows the issuer's certificate to be identified in another way as well — by associating an `OCTET STRING` with the key that is in the verifying certificate. You can make use of this information to find the issuer's certificate if the issuer's certificate includes the `SubjectKeyIdentifier` extension.

The OID and value of the `SubjectKeyIdentifier` extension are defined as follows:

```
id-ce-subjectKeyIdentifier OBJECT IDENTIFIER ::= { id-ce 14 }

SubjectKeyIdentifier ::= KeyIdentifier
```

This value can be anything, but two currently recommended approaches are as follows:

❑   Calculate the 160-bit SHA-1 hash of the value of the `BIT STRING` field `subjectPublicKey`, excluding the tag value, length, and number of pad bits.

❑   Perform the same operation as previously; however, use only the least significant 60 bits of the SHA-1 value and prepend the bit string `"0100"` to the start of it, giving a 64-bit number.

People also use other ways of generating the bytes, such as a sequence of monotonically increasing integers; it doesn't really matter. The important thing is that a clash is highly unlikely, and if the `keyIdentifier` field in an `AuthorityKeyIdentifier` is used, it is taken from the value of the `SubjectKeyIdentifier` of the issuer certificate corresponding to the `AuthorityKeyIdentifier`.

The PKIX profile, described in RFC 3280, specifies that while neither of these extensions should be marked as critical, they should be included in any certificate generated. As you can see, used properly, the two extensions provide essentially the same facility as pointers, but in an X.509 landscape, and make building certificate chains on the fly a lot easier.

Try It Out   Creating a Certificate from a Certification Request

This example takes the process one step farther and creates a certificate. In it two key pairs get created: one that is used to create a certification request using the same method as the last example; the other that is used to create a root certificate using use a method defined in an earlier example ("Try It Out: Creating a Self-Signed Version 1 Certificate"). The certificate that gets created from the certification request is a version 3 certificate containing the extensions used in the version 3 creation Try It Out ("Creating a Self-Signed Version 3 Certificate") plus two more. The extra extensions are the `AuthorityKeyIdentifier` and the `SubjectKeyIdentifier`, which, as you have read, are required for RFC 3280 compliance.

```
package chapter6;

import java.io.OutputStreamWriter;
import java.math.BigInteger;
import java.security.KeyPair;
import java.security.cert.X509Certificate;
import java.util.Date;
import java.util.Enumeration;

import org.bouncycastle.asn1.ASN1Set;
import org.bouncycastle.asn1.DERObjectIdentifier;
```

```java
import org.bouncycastle.asn1.pkcs.Attribute;
import org.bouncycastle.asn1.pkcs.PKCSObjectIdentifiers;
import org.bouncycastle.asn1.x509.BasicConstraints;
import org.bouncycastle.asn1.x509.ExtendedKeyUsage;
import org.bouncycastle.asn1.x509.KeyPurposeId;
import org.bouncycastle.asn1.x509.KeyUsage;
import org.bouncycastle.asn1.x509.X509Extension;
import org.bouncycastle.asn1.x509.X509Extensions;
import org.bouncycastle.jce.PKCS10CertificationRequest;
import org.bouncycastle.openssl.PEMWriter;
import org.bouncycastle.x509.X509V3CertificateGenerator;
import org.bouncycastle.x509.extension.AuthorityKeyIdentifierStructure;
import org.bouncycastle.x509.extension.SubjectKeyIdentifierStructure;

/**
 * An example of a basic CA.
 */
public class PKCS10CertCreateExample
{
    public static X509Certificate[] buildChain() throws Exception
    {
        // create the certification request
        KeyPair           pair = Utils.generateRSAKeyPair();

        PKCS10CertificationRequest  request =
                                PKCS10ExtensionExample.generateRequest(pair);

        // create a root certificate
        KeyPair           rootPair = Utils.generateRSAKeyPair();
        X509Certificate   rootCert =
                        X509V1CreateExample.generateV1Certificate(rootPair);

        // validate the certification request
        if (!request.verify("BC"))
        {
            System.out.println("request failed to verify!");
            System.exit(1);
        }

        // create the certificate using the information in the request
        X509V3CertificateGenerator  certGen = new X509V3CertificateGenerator();

        certGen.setSerialNumber(BigInteger.valueOf(System.currentTimeMillis()));
        certGen.setIssuerDN(rootCert.getSubjectX500Principal());
        certGen.setNotBefore(new Date(System.currentTimeMillis()));
        certGen.setNotAfter(new Date(System.currentTimeMillis() + 50000));
        certGen.setSubjectDN(request.getCertificationRequestInfo().getSubject());
        certGen.setPublicKey(request.getPublicKey("BC"));
        certGen.setSignatureAlgorithm("SHA256WithRSAEncryption");

        certGen.addExtension(X509Extensions.AuthorityKeyIdentifier,
                        false, new AuthorityKeyIdentifierStructure(rootCert));

        certGen.addExtension(X509Extensions.SubjectKeyIdentifier,
```

```
                    false, new SubjectKeyIdentifierStructure(request.getPublicKey("BC")));

        certGen.addExtension(X509Extensions.BasicConstraints,
                                        true, new BasicConstraints(false));

        certGen.addExtension(X509Extensions.KeyUsage,
         true, new KeyUsage(KeyUsage.digitalSignature | KeyUsage.keyEncipherment));

        certGen.addExtension(X509Extensions.ExtendedKeyUsage,
                      true, new ExtendedKeyUsage(KeyPurposeId.id_kp_serverAuth));

        // extract the extension request attribute
        ASN1Set attributes = request.getCertificationRequestInfo().getAttributes();

        for (int i = 0; i != attributes.size(); i++)
        {
            Attribute    attr = Attribute.getInstance(attributes.getObjectAt(i));

            // process extension request
            if (attr.getAttrType().equals(
                        PKCSObjectIdentifiers.pkcs_9_at_extensionRequest))
            {
                X509Extensions extensions = X509Extensions.getInstance(
                                        attr.getAttrValues().getObjectAt(0));

                Enumeration e = extensions.oids();
                while (e.hasMoreElements())
                {
                    DERObjectIdentifier oid = (DERObjectIdentifier)e.nextElement();
                    X509Extension        ext = extensions.getExtension(oid);

                    certGen.addExtension(oid, ext.isCritical(),
                                            ext.getValue().getOctets());
                }
            }
        }

        X509Certificate  issuedCert = certGen.generateX509Certificate(
                                            rootPair.getPrivate());

        return new X509Certificate[] { issuedCert, rootCert };
    }

    public static void main(String[] args) throws Exception
    {
        X509Certificate[]    chain = buildChain();

        PEMWriter        pemWrt = new PEMWriter(
                                    new OutputStreamWriter(System.out));

        pemWrt.writeObject(chain[0]);
        pemWrt.writeObject(chain[1]);

        pemWrt.close();
    }
}
```

Run this and you should see the program print out the two PEM-encoded certificates. The first one will be much larger, being the issued certificate and carrying the necessary extensions to indicate its usage and origins. The second one will appear a lot smaller, as it is a version 1 certificate with no extensions attached.

How It Works

The example proceeds through a number of steps. The `createChain()` method starts out pretending it is a client and then starts to behave as a CA instead.

First, in "client mode," a certification request is created; then, in "CA mode," a root certificate is created.

Next, still in CA mode, the certification request is validated and then the client certificate is created. This step introduces a couple of new classes as well: `AuthorityKeyIdentifierStructure` and `SubjectKeyIdentifier` structure, both of which are defined in the `org.bouncycastle.x509.extension` package.

The `AuthorityKeyIdentifierStructure` class is a helper class that allows you to create the necessary structure for the value field in an `AuthorityKeyIdentifier` extension. Like the other extension objects you looked at previously, it generates an `ASN1Encodable` object, which is then encoded as an `OCTET STRING` internally and added to the certificate. The `SubjectKeyIdentifierStructure` object is also a helper class and calculates a `KeyIdentifier` for the passed in public key using the SHA-1 method and returns it wrapped in an `OCTET STRING` suitable for re-encoding into a `SubjectKeyIdentifier` extension value. You add the `AuthorityKeyIdentifier` extension so you have a link with the certificate that can be used to verify you. The `SubjectKeyIdentifier` gets added in case anyone needs to create a link back to your certificate in the future.

Once the `AuthorityKeyIdentifier`, `SubjectKeyIdentifier`, and other extensions have been added, the example then extracts the attributes from the certification request and looks for an `extensionRequest` attribute. If it finds one, it then creates an `X509Extensions` object by extracting the value from the attribute set and iterates through it, retrieving each extension as an `org.bouncycastle.asn1.x509.X509Extension` object and adding it to the certificate generator using the `addExtension()` method that takes a DER-encoded byte array. Too easy!

Well, in some ways it is too easy. In real life you would probably want to do a bit more. To start with, the CA code isn't checking that it is overwriting one of its own extensions when it adds one from the user. Nor is any validation being done on the contents of the extension being added. As mentioned earlier with extensions that contain identifying information on the owner of the certificate, it is worth making sure the identifying information is for the person you think it is and that the information inserted is only what is acceptable. For example, you might allow your local users to add their e-mail addresses to their certificates if they want to. So the first form of validation you would want to do on the `SubjectAltName` extension is make sure the only value in it is an `rfc822Name`, and then you would want to check that it is an e-mail address that makes sense. If you are running a business, you probably don't want to issue certificates to your staff that tell people that the staff member's private business e-mail address is `evil@evil_competitor.com`, do you?

After the extensions are parsed and added in the certification request, the resulting certificate chain, consisting of the root certificate and the client certificate, is printed out. In the normal course of events this is what would be sent by the CA to the client; the only difference is that in the real world, clients would never need to expose their private keys. The CA would also normally use the same private key and root certificate for signing a number of certificates and may have a number of intermediate certificates resulting in a certificate path, or chain, similar to the one seen in Figure 6-3.

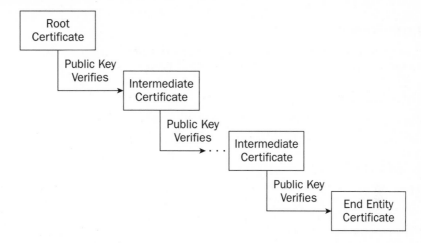

The Linkage between Certificates in a Certificate Path, or Chain

Figure 6-3

Certificate Paths and Stores

Dealing with collections of certificates that are dependent on each other in some ways is the rule rather than the exception, and the JCA has two classes that can help you read, manipulate, and analyze collections of certificates. The first one, the `CertPath` class, provides you with a more useful alternative to using arrays for representing certificate chains that supports encoding and can be used with the path validation classes. The other one, the `CertStore` class, provides you with a collection class that can be searched in a variety of ways using implementations of a selection interface `CertSelector`.

The CertPath Class

The `java.security.cert.CertPath` class provides a carrier for certificate chains, or paths. Objects of the class are not created directly; instead, you use one of the `CertificateFactory.generateCertPath()` methods. The `CertPath` class also provides overrides for the `Object.equals()` and `Object.hashCode()` methods, which allow `CertPath` objects representing the same certificate paths to be meaningfully compared and categorized.

There are three `generateCertPath()` methods on the `CertificateFactory` class. The first one takes an `InputStream` as a parameter and expects the stream to contain the certificate path encoded in whatever the default encoding is for the factory. The second allows you to specify an alternative encoding if the factory object supports it. The third one simply takes a list of certificates.

You can find out what encodings are supported for reading and writing certificate paths by calling the `CertificateFactory.getCertPathEncodings()` method on the factory object you are using. The method returns an `Iterator` of the names of the available encodings, with the first encoding in the `Iterator` being the default one.

CertPath.getType()

The `getType()` method returns the type of the certificate contained in the `CertPath`. In this situation you would expect this to be `"X.509"`, but there are other proposals out there, so this may change.

CertPath.getCertificates()

The `getCertificates()` method returns an immutable, possibly empty, list of certificate objects representing the certificates making up the certificate path.

CertPath.getEncoded()

There are two `getEncoded()` methods. The first takes no parameters and simply returns a byte array representing the certificate path using the default encoding for the `CertPath` object. The second takes a `String` representing an encoding format name as a parameter and returns a byte array containing the certificate path encoded using the requested format if it is available. The `getEncoded()` methods can throw a `CertificateEncodingException` if a problem occurs during the encoding or the requested encoding format is not available.

CertPath.getEncodings()

The `getEncodings()` method returns an `Iterator` containing `String` objects giving the names of the encoding methods supported by the `CertPath` object. Typically names are "PKIPATH," "PEM," or "PKCS7."

Now check out an example using the PEM format.

Try It Out   Writing a CertPath

Look at the following example. You are already familiar with the PEM format, as it was used in the last Try It Out ("Creating a Certificate from a Certification Request"). This example produces the same encoding for the certificate path, but by using the `CertPath` class instead.

```
package chapter6;

import java.io.ByteArrayInputStream;
import java.security.cert.CertPath;
import java.security.cert.CertificateFactory;
import java.security.cert.X509Certificate;
import java.util.Arrays;

/**
 * Basic example of creating and encoding a CertPath.
 */
public class CertPathExample
{
    public static void main(String[] args) throws Exception
```

```
    {
    X509Certificate[]    chain = PKCS10CertCreateExample.buildChain();

        // create the factory and path object
    CertificateFactory  fact = CertificateFactory.getInstance("X.509", "BC");
    CertPath            certPath = fact.generateCertPath(Arrays.asList(chain));

    byte[] encoded = certPath.getEncoded("PEM");

    System.out.println(Utils.toString(encoded));

    // re-read the CertPath
    CertPath            newCertPath = fact.generateCertPath(
                                    new ByteArrayInputStream(encoded), "PEM");

    if (newCertPath.equals(certPath))
    {
            System.out.println("CertPath recovered correctly");
        }
    }
}
```

Running the example will print the two certificates out as it did for the create example, showing you that a PEM-encoded path has been created. After the certificates are listed it should then print

```
CertPath recovered correctly
```

This output shows that the certificate path was re-created correctly from the encoded form.

How It Works

The example is quite simple. As you can see, both CertPath classes are created using the generateCertPath() method on the CertificateFactory class. In the first case you are just converting the array generated by PKCS10CertCreateExample.buildChain() into a list and then passing it to the generateCertPath() method to get back a CertPath object.

After that you encode the certificate path into "PEM" format, print the result, and then build a new CertPath object by using the generateCertPath() method that takes an InputStream and an encoding. The recovered CertPath is then compared with the original one using Object.equals(). As the message is printed, you can see that Object.equals() has been overridden, and you know that the path has been reconstructed correctly.

As you will see in Chapter 7, this is not the final word on the CertPath class; however, the next thing you will look at is another useful class for manipulating individual certificates — the CertStore class.

The CertStore Class

One of the purposes of the CertStore class is used as a means to provide access to certificates through the provider-based architecture in the JCA. Creating a CertStore involves using a similar getInstance() factory pattern used by other classes in the JCA, and the CertStore.getInstance() follows the same precedence rules as other JCA getInstance() methods if the provider is not specified. In addition to the type of `CertStore` to create and an optional provider, the `CertStore.getInstance()` method also takes parameters that are used to initialize the `CertStore`. You'll look at how the parameters object is typically created in the next example.

The feature of the `CertStore` class I will concentrate on here is that the `getCertificates()` method provides a mechanism for arbitrarily searching for and retrieving certificates from a `CertStore` object. The `getCertificates()` method is used by invoking it with an object implementing the `CertSelector` interface as a parameter. It is the object implementing `CertSelector` that is used by the `CertStore` to determine which certificates are being searched for.

The `CertSelector` interface carries two methods on it. One is `Object.clone()`, so any implementation of a `CertSelector` should be cloneable. The other is a `match()` method that takes a single certificate as a parameter and returns `true` or `false` depending on whether the code in the `match()` methods implementation decides the certificate is one of those it is looking for. As X.509 certificates are so commonplace, the JCA provides an implementation of `CertSelector` that can be used for retrieving `X509Certificate` objects from a `CertStore`. The class that provides this implementation is the `X509CertSelector` class.

The X509CertSelector Class

The `java.security.cert.X509CertSelector` class provides an implementation of the `CertSelector` interface that allows you to search a `CertStore` for certificates that match on a variety of X.509-related fields. It has a variety of `set()` methods on it that allow you to specify criteria for matching an X.509 certificate that might be present in a `CertStore` object.

The `X509CertSelector` works by offering a range of `set()` methods, each of which can be used to provide values to be matched against in a X.509 certificate. If no `set()` methods are called, an `X509CertSelector` will match every certificate in the store. If more than one `set()` method is called, the `X509CertSelector` will only match certificates for whichever criteria specified via a `set()` method is matched.

I'll describe the most basic methods here; however, if you look at the JavaDoc for the class, you will see that the `X509CertSelector` also allows you to search on a variety of certificate extensions, including, but not limited to, `SubjectKeyIdentifier`, `AuthorityKeyIdentifier`, `KeyUsage`, `SubjectAltName`, and `IssuerAltName`.

X509CertSelector.setCertificate()

The `setCertificate()` method allows you to set up the selector so that it matches only the passed-in certificate. This is very useful if you want to easily tell if a given certificate is present in a `CertStore`.

X509CertSelector.setIssuer()

The `setIssuer()` method allows you to match certificates with the `issuer` field of the `TBSCertificate` structure set to the passed-in issuer. If the method is set to `null`, it matches any issuer.

There are two versions of `setIssuer()` worth using. The first takes an `X500Principal` directly but is only available in JDK 1.5 and later. The other one takes a byte array representing the DER encoding of the X.500 name you are looking for. If you are using a JVM earlier than JDK 1.5, the latter method is the one you should use.

X509CertSelector.setSerialNumber()

The setSerialNumber() takes a BigInteger as a parameter and will match any certificate with the same value in the serialNumber field of the TBSCertificate structure. If passed a null (the default), it will match any serial number.

X509CertSelector.setSubject()

The setSubject() method allows you to match certificates with the subject field of the TBSCertificate structure set to the passed-in subject. If the method is set to null, it matches any subject. The setSubject() method offers the same alternatives as setIssuer() in terms of possible parameters, with the same restrictions on JVM version.

Try It Out   **Using a CertStore and a X509CertSelector**

This example shows the use of a basic CertStore and a X509CertSelector. It uses the PKCS10CreateExample.createChain() method to generate the certificates again, but in this case it uses the certificate array to create a CertStore, which it then searches using an X509CertSelector.

```
package chapter6;

import java.security.cert.CertStore;
import java.security.cert.CollectionCertStoreParameters;
import java.security.cert.X509CertSelector;
import java.security.cert.X509Certificate;
import java.util.Arrays;
import java.util.Iterator;

import javax.security.auth.x500.X500Principal;

/**
 * Example using a CertStore and a CertSelector
 */
public class CertStoreExample
{
    public static void main(String[] args)
        throws Exception
    {
        X509Certificate[]   chain = PKCS10CertCreateExample.buildChain();

        // create the store
        CollectionCertStoreParameters params = new CollectionCertStoreParameters(
                                                    Arrays.asList(chain));
        CertStore store = CertStore.getInstance("Collection", params);

        // create the selector
        X509CertSelector selector = new X509CertSelector();
        selector.setSubject(
                new X500Principal("CN=Requested Test Certificate").getEncoded());

        // print the subjects of the results
        Iterator certsIt = store.getCertificates(selector).iterator();
        while (certsIt.hasNext())
```

```
    {
        X509Certificate cert = (X509Certificate)certsIt.next();

        System.out.println(cert.getSubjectX500Principal());
    }
  }
}
```

Running the example should just produce the following output:

```
CN=Requested Test Certificate
```

indicating, as you would expect, that the end entity certificate in the chain has been matched by the selector.

How It Works

Like the previous example this one also follows a simple formula. The certificate chain is created and used to create a list. The list is turned into a suitable parameters object and used to create a CertStore object. A X509CertSelector is then created with a specific subject set on it and is used to retrieve one of the certificates present in the CertStore.

The parameters object you are using in this case, an instance of a CollectionCertStoreParameters class, is the simplest case for creating a CertStore. The CollectionCertStoreParameters class implements the java.security.cert.CertStoreParameters interface and just serves as a carrier for a collection of certificates, and possibly CRLs, into the underlying provider to create the CertStore. The CertStoreParameters interface is basically a marker interface. It also adds Cloneable, and it is this marker interface that the construction process for a CertStore looks for when it is receiving parameters. This flexibility is required, as a CertStore may have a database or a server process behind it, not just a collection of in memory certificates. For another example of CertStoreParameters, for use with an LDAP server if supported by the provider, have a look at java.security.cert.LDAPCertStoreParameters. You can probably imagine other ways to implement the CertStoreParameters interface so that it works with your favorite database instead.

This brings you to the end of the basics for dealing with certificates, most especially those defined in X.509 and used in the Internet PKIX profile as described in RFC 3280.

Summary

In this chapter, you looked at the fundamentals for understanding and using public key certificates based around the X.509 standard. You saw how certificate extensions are used and studied one of the mechanisms used for creating certificate requests, detailed in PKCS #10. In addition, you saw how dependencies can exist between certificates and how these are represented using certificate paths.

Over the course of this chapter you have learned the following:

❑   What an X.500 name is and how it relates to the X500Principal class

❑   What a public key certificate is, most particularly ones that use X.509

❑   How to make use of the Java classes and interfaces relating to certificates

❑   How to generate your own PKCS #10 certification requests and X.509 certificates using the Bouncy Castle APIs

❑   How to create PEM encodings of ASN.1-encoded objects

❑   How to interpret a PKCS #10 certification request and create a certificate from it, as well as some of the issues that need to be considered when you are doing so

❑   How to create `CertPath` objects and use them to compare and encode certificate paths

Finally, you also saw how to make use of the `CertStore` API and use implementations of `CertSelector` to selectively retrieve certificates from a `CertStore`.

Certificates provide you with a mechanism of publishing your identity, and by allowing for certificate chains, or paths, you are able to get others to vouch that a certificate you want them to accept is recognized by someone they trust. The problem then becomes what do you do if the private key on the certificate you have issued is compromised? Perhaps it turns out with another certificate you have signed, the signature was gained by deception. How do you have that certificate revoked? Having allowed for revocation, how do you then tell that a certificate you have obtained from someone else is still valid? If one of the certificates in the path from the root certificate you trust to the end certificate you want to trust is no longer valid, how would you know? I will answer these questions in the next chapter, which discusses certificate revocation and path validation.

Exercises

1.   What is the biggest danger of trying to manipulate X.500 names as `String` objects in Java?

2.   How do you add an e-mail address for a certificate subject to a version 3 X.509 certificate?

3.   How do you request the CA to add a certificate extension when you issue a certification request?

4.   What is a certificate path, or chain? What roles do the root certificate and the end entity certificates play, respectively?

5.   What is the easiest way to generate a particular type of encoding for a certificate path?

Certificate Revocation and Path Validation

X.509 digital certificates provide you with standardized formats that allow you to link public keys with particular entities in an otherwise device-independent fashion. Certificate paths, or chains, provide a mechanism that allow you to recognize a given entity as trusted providing you trust the parties involved in creating the validation certificates leading up to that of the entity.

This is not the end of the problem. Certificates can be used to validate a variety of things, including timestamps, other certificates, executable code, and so on. The question then becomes, if the signature on the certificate you want to use is valid, is the use the certificate is being presented to you for the one the issuer of the certificate authorized when the issuer signed it? Even then, if it is being presented for an apparently legitimate use, how do you know the issuer has not since decided to revoke the authorization the issuer has extended?

This chapter introduces some of the common mechanisms both for finding out if an issuer has since withdrawn authorization for the use of a certificate and also what mechanisms are available in Java to validate a certificate path so you can tell that not only is the end entity certificate legitimate, but that every certificate between it and the one you really trust is legitimate as well.

By the end of this chapter you should

- ❑ Understand what a certificate revocation list is

- ❑ Know how to create and interpret X.509 certificate revocation lists

- ❑ Understand what Online Certificate Status Protocol (OCSP) is and how it differs from standard certificate revocation list processing

- ❑ Know how to use the Bouncy Castle APIs to implement OCSP

- ❑ Know what certificate path validation is and how it is done in the JCA

- ❑ Know how to introduce your own forms of path validation using the JCA APIs

Finally, you will also know how to take a random collection of certificates, and possibly certificate revocation lists, in a `CertStore` and create a certificate path that is valid for a certificate of interest to you.

Getting Started

At this point, you are starting to cover some bigger issues in certificate handling — or at least the implementations that surround them. To do this, you need a ready supply of certificates, so let's further extend the `Utils` class to add the necessary functionality.

For the purposes of looking at certificate revocation and path validation, you need at least three certificates. The reasons for this will become obvious as you look further into the chapter, but for the moment I'll just go through the three methods to be added, quickly reviewing some of the ground you have already covered. Although the additions are rather long, they are not complex, and I will break the class up rather than presenting it as one chunk so I can better comment on it.

The first step, of course, is the class header and the initial declaration, given here:

```
package chapter7;

import java.math.BigInteger;
import java.security.*;
import java.security.cert.X509Certificate;
import java.util.Date;

import javax.security.auth.x500.X500Principal;

import org.bouncycastle.asn1.x509.*;
import org.bouncycastle.x509.*;
import org.bouncycastle.x509.extension.*;

/**
 * Chapter 7 Utils
 */
public class Utils extends chapter6.Utils
{
    private static final int VALIDITY_PERIOD = 7 * 24 * 60 * 60 * 1000; // one week
```

The first certificate you need is the CA root certificate. You can use a self-signed version 1 certificate in this position, so as they are the simplest to make, I'll define the `generateRootCert()` method to create one of those as follows:

```
    /**
     * Generate a sample V1 certificate to use as a CA root certificate
     */
    public static X509Certificate generateRootCert(KeyPair pair)
        throws Exception
    {
        X509V1CertificateGenerator  certGen = new X509V1CertificateGenerator();

        certGen.setSerialNumber(BigInteger.valueOf(1));
        certGen.setIssuerDN(new X500Principal("CN=Test CA Certificate"));
        certGen.setNotBefore(new Date(System.currentTimeMillis()));
        certGen.setNotAfter(
                new Date(System.currentTimeMillis() + VALIDITY_PERIOD));
        certGen.setSubjectDN(new X500Principal("CN=Test CA Certificate"));
```

```
        certGen.setPublicKey(pair.getPublic());
        certGen.setSignatureAlgorithm("SHA1WithRSAEncryption");

        return certGen.generateX509Certificate(pair.getPrivate(), "BC");
    }
```

The next certificate you need is an intermediate certificate. You'll usually see one or more of these in a certificate chain, because they not only reduce the number of certificates that have to be signed using the root certificates private key (a good thing), but they also allow the same root to be used as the origin of specialized chains validated for use only for particular applications. This has to be a version 3 certificate, because at the least it should identify itself as a CA certificate using the basic constraints extension.

Here is the code for the generateIntermediateCert() method that will provide the intermediate certificates:

```
/**
 * Generate a sample V3 certificate to use as an intermediate CA certificate
 */
public static X509Certificate generateIntermediateCert(
    PublicKey intKey, PrivateKey caKey, X509Certificate caCert)
    throws Exception
{
    X509V3CertificateGenerator  certGen = new X509V3CertificateGenerator();

    certGen.setSerialNumber(BigInteger.valueOf(1));
    certGen.setIssuerDN(caCert.getSubjectX500Principal());
    certGen.setNotBefore(new Date(System.currentTimeMillis()));
    certGen.setNotAfter(
                new Date(System.currentTimeMillis() + VALIDITY_PERIOD));
    certGen.setSubjectDN(
                        new X500Principal("CN=Test Intermediate Certificate"));
    certGen.setPublicKey(intKey);
    certGen.setSignatureAlgorithm("SHA1WithRSAEncryption");

    certGen.addExtension(X509Extensions.AuthorityKeyIdentifier,
                        false, new AuthorityKeyIdentifierStructure(caCert));
    certGen.addExtension(X509Extensions.SubjectKeyIdentifier,
                            false, new SubjectKeyIdentifierStructure(intKey));
    certGen.addExtension(X509Extensions.BasicConstraints,
                                        true, new BasicConstraints(0));
    certGen.addExtension(
      X509Extensions.KeyUsage, true, new KeyUsage(
        KeyUsage.digitalSignature | KeyUsage.keyCertSign | KeyUsage.cRLSign));

    return certGen.generateX509Certificate(caKey, "BC");
}
```

Note that the number of parameters passed to the method has gone up. To create a certificate validated by another, details are required from the validation certificate in addition to the signing key and the public key that will be stored in the certificate. There are two other items of interest. The first is that the basic constraints extension indicates that this is a CA certificate and that the end entity certificate must follow it immediately. The second is that the key usage extension now identifies that the certificate can be used for validating other certificates and for validating certificate revocation lists (CRLs). You will see why these two items of interest are important when you look at path validation later.

Finally, you need an end entity certificate, and this is created by the `generateEndEntityCert()` method. This is also a version 3 certificate with a basic constraints extension that indicates as much, together with a key usage extension that makes it suitable for use with SSL/TLS. Also, as with the intermediate certificate, a subject key identifier extension is added to provide a linkage based on the public key, and an authority key identifier extension is added to provide a linkage back to the validating certificate.

Here is the code for the `generateEndEntityCert()` method, together with the final close brace for the class definition:

```
/**
 * Generate a sample V3 certificate to use as an end entity certificate
 */
public static X509Certificate generateEndEntityCert(
    PublicKey entityKey, PrivateKey caKey, X509Certificate caCert)
    throws Exception
{
    X509V3CertificateGenerator  certGen = new X509V3CertificateGenerator();

    certGen.setSerialNumber(BigInteger.valueOf(1));
    certGen.setIssuerDN(caCert.getSubjectX500Principal());
    certGen.setNotBefore(new Date(System.currentTimeMillis()));
    certGen.setNotAfter(
                new Date(System.currentTimeMillis() + VALIDITY_PERIOD));
    certGen.setSubjectDN(new X500Principal("CN=Test End Certificate"));
    certGen.setPublicKey(entityKey);
    certGen.setSignatureAlgorithm("SHA1WithRSAEncryption");

    certGen.addExtension(X509Extensions.AuthorityKeyIdentifier,
                    false, new AuthorityKeyIdentifierStructure(caCert));
    certGen.addExtension(X509Extensions.SubjectKeyIdentifier,
                    false, new SubjectKeyIdentifierStructure(entityKey));
    certGen.addExtension(X509Extensions.BasicConstraints,
                            true, new BasicConstraints(false));
    certGen.addExtension(X509Extensions.KeyUsage,
        true, new KeyUsage(KeyUsage.digitalSignature | KeyUsage.keyEncipherment));

    return certGen.generateX509Certificate(caKey, "BC");
}
}
```

Set up the `Utils` class for Chapter 7 and you are ready to proceed with the first topic — certificate revocation lists.

Certificate Revocation Lists

The original method for dealing with certificate revocation was to use certificate revocation lists, or CRLs. The concept is a fairly simple one to understand. In addition to the root certificate you are using to validate certificates that come your way, you have a CRL for the root certificate that contains a list of the certificates issued for that root certificate that have, for one reason or another, been revoked. Basically it is the same idea as the blacklists of bad credit card numbers given out to shopkeepers before it was possible to do these transactions online. As Figure 7-1 shows, CRLs are distributed by a server and held by the client that needs them to check certificates.

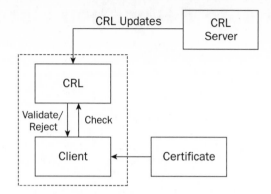

Certificate Check by Client Done on CRL It Holds,
Updates Distributed by Server

Figure 7-1

As well as providing a blacklist of certificates, a CRL is also said to have a particular *scope*, and it is the scope that defines what certificates can end up in a CRL. Generally the scope is defined by the identity of the issuer, which is to say the CRL will contain all certificates issued by some particular CA. The scope can be refined to suit, so you can also encounter CRLs where the scope is "all certificates issued by X and revoked for reasons of key compromise," and a CRL is regarded as complete if it lists all certificates that satisfy its scope that have not yet expired.

So, using CRLs to determine whether a given certificate is revoked involves finding a CRL of the correct scope and seeing if the certificate is present in it. The most general way of doing this in the JCA is provided by the CRL class in the `java.security.cert` package.

The CRL Class

The CRL class provides a high-level abstraction of a certificate revocation list. It is a very simple abstract class with only a few methods on it. Special cases of CRLs that conform to particular implementations, such as the CRLs defined in X.509, extend off the CRL class, and it provides the basic support for telling whether a particular certificate is revoked.

CRL.getType()

The `getType()` method returns a `String` representing the type of the CRL. The method is abstract, and in the case of the particular implementation of CRLs you are dealing with in this chapter, you would expect this method to return `"X.509"`.

CRL.isRevoked()

The `isRevoked()` method takes a single `Certificate` object as a parameter and returns `true` if the certificate is present in the CRL. If the `Certificate` object is not present in the CRL, the method returns `false`.

When I discuss the `X509CRL` class, you will see that the full answer to whether a certificate is revoked, and what it means can be a little bit more complicated than this method makes it sound. In practice you generally cast a CRL to the type that extends it in order to understand the full situation with the revocation. So, that being said, it is time to look at the specifics of CRLs as they apply to X.509.

231

X.509 Certificate Revocation Lists

As with certificates, X.509 also defines a set of structures to be used to represent CRLs. Not surprisingly, these structures are represented using ASN.1 and are also, for the most part, directly supported in the JCA. Before you look at the Java perspective on how to process a X.509 CRL, the first question I should probably answer is how, given an issuer X.509 certificate, you get a CRL for it in the first place.

Given a X.509 certificate, there are a couple of ways you might locate a valid CRL for it: It might be given to you, or the X.509 certificate may contain a CRL distribution points extension that gives you information on where to find the certificate. The extension is identified by the OID "2.5.29.31" (id-ce-cRLDistributionPoints), and its value is defined by the ASN.1 type CRLDistributionPoints.

There is a reasonably lengthy discussion of the type in RFC 3280 in section 4.2.1.14, but to give you a general idea about the extension, its ASN.1 definition is as follows:

```
CRLDistributionPoints ::= SEQUENCE SIZE (1..MAX) OF DistributionPoint
```

where DistributionPoint is defined as:

```
DistributionPoint ::= SEQUENCE {
        distributionPoint        [0]     DistributionPointName OPTIONAL,
        reasons                  [1]     ReasonFlags OPTIONAL,
        cRLIssuer                [2]     GeneralNames OPTIONAL }
```

Although the three fields are optional, a DistributionPoint should always contain a distributionPoint or a cRLIssuer.

The reasons field, if specified, gives a subset of reasons that a particular CRL will cover. ReasonFlags is a BIT STRING with the following definition:

```
ReasonFlags ::= BIT STRING {
        unused                   (0),
        keyCompromise            (1),
        cACompromise             (2),
        affiliationChanged       (3),
        superseded               (4),
        cessationOfOperation     (5),
        certificateHold          (6),
        privilegeWithdrawn       (7),
        aACompromise             (8) }
```

When the reasons field is used, you will often find there are several CRLs that can be downloaded, each representing certificates that are revoked for the particular reasons indicated by the bits that have been set in the reasons field.

The DistributionPointName type is defined as:

```
DistributionPointName ::= CHOICE {
        fullName                 [0]     GeneralNames,
        nameRelativeToCRLIssuer  [1]     RelativeDistinguishedName }
```

If it is the distributionPoint field that is set, you will generally find that the DistributionPointName will be a fullName and that the structure will contain a GeneralName representing a URL. The URL will give the location to get the CRL from. In the event that the fullName contains multiple names, they will all provide different ways of obtaining the same CRL. If the nameRelativeToCRLIssuer is present instead, it contains a fragment that should be appended to the issuer name and then used to look up an X.500 directory.

The cRLIssuer field identifies the entity that issued and signed the CRL. If the distributionPoint field is not set but the cRLIssuer field is, then the cRLIssuer should contain at least one X.500 name that can be used to look up the CRL using a directory service such as LDAP.

Having acquired a X.509 CRL, you then have to work out what to do with it. The first stop for doing this in Java is the X509CRL class.

The X509CRL Class

The java.security.cert.X509CRL class provides the basic support for X.509 CRLs in the JCA, and its design and how it interacts with other CRL-related classes could be seen as being related to the ASN.1 definition of its related ASN.1 structure — the CertificateList.

```
CertificateList  ::=  SEQUENCE  {
    tbsCertList          TBSCertList,
    signatureAlgorithm   AlgorithmIdentifier,
    signature            BIT STRING  }
```

Looking at the CertificateList structure, you can see that it is very similar to that given for a certificate or certification request. The CertificateList structure simply provides a wrapper that carries the content in the TBSCertList structure and the BIT STRING representation of a signature made using the algorithm and parameters specified by the signatureAlgorithm field.

I will start by looking at the methods applicable to the TBSCertList structure first and then look at the validation of the signature at the end.

X509CRL.getTBSCertList()

The getTBSCertList() method returns the bytes making up the ASN.1 encoding of the TBSCertList structure present in the tbsCertList field. These are the bytes used to provide the input for calculating the signature that is stored in the signature field in the CertificateList structure.

The TBSCertList has the following ASN.1 structure:

```
TBSCertList  ::=  SEQUENCE  {
    version                 Version OPTIONAL,
                            -- if present, must be v2
    signature               AlgorithmIdentifier,
    issuer                  Name,
    thisUpdate              Time,
    nextUpdate              Time OPTIONAL,
    revokedCertificates     SEQUENCE OF SEQUENCE  {
        userCertificate         CertificateSerialNumber,
```

```
          revocationDate          Time,
          crlEntryExtensions      Extensions OPTIONAL
                                  -- if present, must be v2 }  OPTIONAL,
    crlExtensions           [0]   EXPLICIT Extensions OPTIONAL
                                  -- if present, must be v2 }
```

As you will see, most of the `get()` methods associated with the X509CRL class are simply returning the values of the fields in the `TBSCertList` structure.

Looking at the definition, you can see there is one construct that you have not encountered before:

```
revokedCertificates     SEQUENCE OF SEQUENCE  {
        userCertificate         CertificateSerialNumber,
        revocationDate          Time,
        crlEntryExtensions      Extensions OPTIONAL
                                -- if present, must be v2 }
```

`SEQUENCE OF SEQUENCE` simply means that the `revokedCertificates` field is a `SEQUENCE` made of other `SEQUENCE` objects that are composed of two, possibly three, fields. An immediate parallel in Java would be an `ArrayList` of `ArrayList` objects, although this would not take full advantage of the type safety Java affords you. In this case a specific class is defined to represent each entry of three items in the `revokedCertificates` sequence — the `X509CRLEntry` class. You will take a closer look at this class a bit later.

X509CRL.getVersion()

The `getVersion()` method returns version number contained in the `TBSCertList` structure. In this case you would normally expect this to be the value 2.

X509CRL.getIssuerX500Principal()

The `getIssuerX500Principal()` method returns an `X500Principal` object representing the value contained in the `issuer` field of the `TBSCertList` structure.

You may also see the use of `getIssuerDN()` instead of `getIssuerX500Principal()`. Prior to JDK 1.4 the only option was to use the `getIssuerDN()` method. It returns a `java.security.Principal` object, the underlying implementation of which was provider-dependent. These days you should avoid using `getIssuerDN()` wherever possible.

X509CRL.getThisUpdate() and X509CRL.getNextUpdate()

The `getThisUpdate()` and `getNextUpdate()` return the values contained in the `thisUpdate` and `nextUpdate` fields as `Date` objects.

The value returned by `getThisUpdate()` represents the date and time the CRL was created by the issuer.

The value returned by `getNextUpdate()` represents the date and time at which the CRL should be treated as having expired, and a new one should be requested from the issuer. Although the `nextUpdate` field is optional, RFC 3280 mandates it and does not specify how to interpret the absence of the field.

X509CRL.getRevokedCertificates()

The getRevokedCertificates() method returns a Set of X509CRLEntry objects. The X509CRLEntry represents the three fields in the SEQUENCE OF SEQUENCE that defines the revokedCertificates field in the TBSCertList structure. If the revokedCertificates field is not present in the TBSCertList, then getRevokedCertificates() will return null.

X509CRL.getRevokedCertificate()

The getRevokedCertificate() method takes a single X509Certificate as a parameter and returns a X509CRLEntry representing the details of its revocation if one exists. If there is no CRL entry present for the certificate, then the method will return null.

X509CRL.getSignature()

The getSignature() method returns the bytes making up the signature stored in the BIT STRING contained in the signature field. These bytes are suitable for verification with a java.security.Signature class.

X509CRL.getSigAlgOID(), and X509CRL.getSigAlgParams()

The getSigAlgOID() method returns the value of the OBJECT IDENTIFIER in the algorithm field of the AlgorithmIdentifier structure in the signatureAlgorithm field in the CertificateList structure. The getSigAlgParams() returns a byte array that represents the DER encoding of the parameters field in the AlgorithmIdentifier structure in the signatureAlgorithm field.

You would have noticed there is a signature field in the TBSCertList structure, which is also of the type AlgorithmIdentifier. The purpose of this is to provide a cross check against the unsigned signatureAlgorithm field in the CertificateList structure. The contents of the signatureAlgorithm field and the signature field will always be equal in a valid CRL.

X509CRL.getSigAlgName()

The getSigAlgName() method will return a more (hopefully) human-friendly version of the name that is associated with the signature algorithm used — for example, SHA1withDSA rather than the 1.2.840.10040.4.3 that getSigAlgOID() would return.

X509CRL.verify()

The verify() method is used to check that the signature contained in the CRL can be verified using the public key of the entity that was supposed to have signed the CRL. There are two versions of the verify() method, one that just takes the public key to use for verification as a parameter and another that takes the public key to use and a provider name.

Unlike Signature.verify(), X509CRL.verify() is a void and can throw one of five exceptions when it is called. The most likely one, in the event the public key is of the wrong value, is a SignatureException, indicating the signature did not match what was expected. The other four exceptions that can be thrown are NoSuchProviderException if no provider can be found, NoSuchAlgorithmException if the signature algorithm used in the CRL is not recognized, InvalidKeyException if the public key passed in is for the wrong algorithm, and CRLException if there is a problem encoding the CRL in order to calculate any hash required as part of signature verification.

X509CRL.getEncoded()

The `getEncoded()` method returns a byte array containing the DER encoding of the CRL's ASN.1 structure.

The X509CRLEntry Class

The `X509CRLEntry` class provides a type-safe way of representing the three fields contained in the `SEQUENCE OF SEQUENCE` contained in the `revokedCertificates` field in the `TBSCertList`. If you remember, the ASN.1 definition of these fields was as follows:

```
userCertificate        CertificateSerialNumber,
revocationDate         Time,
crlEntryExtensions     Extensions OPTIONAL
```

The `crlEntryExtensions` field was added with version 2 of the X.509 CRL definition. You will see that some of the methods on the `X509CRLEntry` class actually use values from the `crlEntryExtensions` field if a particular extension is present. In the case of extensions that are locally defined or not handled by the base class, you can access the extension values using the methods defined on the `java.security` `.cert.X509Extension` interface in the same way you did with the `X509Certificate` class.

X509CRLEntry.getCertificateIssuer()

The `getCertificateIssuer()` method returns the issuer of the X.509 certificate described by the entry. By default this is the same as the issuer of the CRL; however, you should not assume this is the case, because a CRL entry with a `CertificateIssuer` extension will change the name of the issuer.

X509CRLEntry.getRevocationDate()

The `getRevocationDate()` method returns the date on which the revocation of the certificate came into effect.

As you will see a bit later when you look at the `InvalidityDate` extension, this is not necessarily the earliest time a certificate should be treated as being potentially invalid. You can think of it as representing when the paperwork for doing the revocation was finalized by the CA.

X509CRLEntry.getSerialNumber()

The `getSerialNumber()` method returns the serial number of the certificate that was revoked. This combined with the return value of the `getCertificateIssuer()` method will uniquely identify the certificate.

X509CRLEntry.hasExtensions()

The `hasExtensions()` method will return `true` if the optional `crlEntryExtensions` field is set in the entry. If the field is not set, the method will return `false`.

Now take a look at the possible values you can find inside the `crlEntryExtensions` field.

X.509 CRL Entry Extensions

As you can see from the ASN.1 definition, the `crlEntryExtensions` field can be absent altogether. RFC 3280 does recommend that two extensions in particular, the reason code extension and the invalidity date extension, be included if the information the extensions represent is available. As with certificates and CRLs themselves, it is also possible for people to define their own extensions for CRL entries. For these purposes, I will just concentrate on the common extensions you might encounter.

The ReasonCode Extension

The reason code extension is used to indicate the reason why the certificate has ended up in the CRL, if that information is available. It is indicated by the OID "2.5.29.21" (`id-ce-cRLReason`) and is defined in ASN.1 as follows:

```
reasonCode ::= { CRLReason }

CRLReason ::= ENUMERATED {
        unspecified             (0),
        keyCompromise           (1),
        cACompromise            (2),
        affiliationChanged      (3),
        superseded              (4),
        cessationOfOperation    (5),
        certificateHold         (6),
        removeFromCRL           (8),
        privilegeWithdrawn      (9),
        aACompromise            (10) }
```

If the reason code extension is not present, you should assume a reason code value of `unspecified`. The RFC 3280 profile actually goes so far as to say if the reason code value is `unspecified`, the reason code extension should be left out of the entry.

The HoldInstructionCode Extension

The hold instruction code allows a certificate to be temporarily suspended, rather than revoked. It is indicated by the OID "2.5.29.23" (`id-ce-holdInstructionCode`), and the extension value is an OBJECT IDENTIFIER, which can have one of three values:

```
holdInstruction     OBJECT IDENTIFIER ::=
                    { iso(1) member-body(2) us(840) x9-57(10040) 2 }

id-holdinstruction-none    OBJECT IDENTIFIER ::= {holdInstruction 1}
id-holdinstruction-callissuer
                           OBJECT IDENTIFIER ::= {holdInstruction 2}
id-holdinstruction-reject  OBJECT IDENTIFIER ::= {holdInstruction 3}
```

The OID value determines what action you should take if you are attempting to validate the certificate. The `id-holdinstruction-none` OID is equivalent to the extension being absent, so, although its use is not encouraged, seeing it means do nothing. If you find `id-holdinstruction-callissuer`, you must contact the issuer for further instructions or reject the certificate as invalid. Encountering an OID with the value `id-holdinstruction-reject` means that the certificate should be rejected out of hand.

The tricky bit with putting a certificate on hold is that going on to a CRL is a one-way trip; an entry should never be deleted until the actual certificate it represents expires. If you put a certificate on hold, the only way to make it valid again is to leave it on the CRL and change the reason code from certificateHold to removeFromCRL.

The InvalidityDate Extension

The invalidity date provides the date on which it is known, or suspected, that the certificate became invalid. It is indicated by the OID "2.5.29.24" (id-ce-invalidityDate) and has the following ASN.1 structure:

```
invalidityDate ::=  GeneralizedTime
```

The idea of introducing this extension was to take away the need to backdate the CRL entry if you wanted to indicate an earlier date for when the certificate had become invalid. The invalidityDate extension solves this problem, because the date it contains may be earlier than the revocation date in the CRL entry, which should represent the date on which the CA processed the revocation for the certificate, not when a particular certificate in the CRL became invalid.

The CertificateIssuer Extension

The certificate issuer extension is used to indicate who the real issuer of a certificate was. It is indicated by the OID "2.5.29.29" (id-ce-certificateIssuer) and has the following ASN.1 structure:

```
certificateIssuer ::= GeneralNames
```

Use of this extension requires a certain amount of housekeeping — for example, when it appears every CRL entry appearing after the CRL containing the extension can be considered to have the same value of the extension. The entry list should be treated like this until another certificate issuer extension is encountered. Until a certificate issuer extension is encountered in the entry list, the certificate issuer for a certificate indicated by an entry defaults to the CRL issuer.

X.509 CRL Extensions

The version 2 profile for CRLs introduced extensions. They provide extensions that take advantage of X.509 certificate extensions. They also attempted to deal with issues such as allowing partial updates and providing information to support cache renewal if it was necessary.

The Extensions type referred to in TBSCertList structure is defined as follows:

```
Extensions  ::=  SEQUENCE SIZE (1..MAX) OF Extension

Extension  ::=  SEQUENCE  {
    extnID      OBJECT IDENTIFIER,
    critical    BOOLEAN DEFAULT FALSE,
    extnValue   OCTET STRING  }
```

This is the exact same structure you saw in Chapter 6, and there is some overlap among the extensions that can be used.

The AuthorityKeyIdentifier Extension

The purpose of the authority key identifier extension is to identify the public key used to sign the CRL. Note that this does not have to be the same certificate whose certificates are being revoked, and both certificates can have the same issuer. The extension is otherwise the same as the one you looked at in Chapter 6, with the same OID and structure.

The IssuerAlternativeName Extension

The purpose of the issuer alternative name extension is to allow alternate identities to be associated with the issuer of the CRL. The extension has the same structure and identifying OID associated with it as the one with the same name that you looked at in Chapter 6.

The CRLNumber Extension

The CRL number extension is identified by the OID "2.5.29.20" (id-ce-cRLNumber). It contains a positive sequence number, which is defined as follows:

```
CRLNumber ::= INTEGER (0..MAX)
```

The purpose of the CRL number is to allow users of the CRL to be able to easily tell if a given CRL supersedes another one. A conforming CRL issuer will never produce two CRLs for the same scope at different times that have the same CRL number. RFC 3280 specifies that CRL numbers should not be longer than 20 octets, meaning they should be less than 2^{159} — don't forget you have to allow for that sign bit in the encoding of the INTEGER.

The DeltaCRLIndicator Extension

The delta CRL indicator extension is identified by the OID value "2.5.29.27" (id-ce-deltaCRLIndicator), and it has the following ASN.1 type as its value:

```
BaseCRLNumber ::= CRLNumber
```

If you find this extension in a CRL, it means that the CRL is *delta* relative to another CRL: the base CRL, the value of whose CRL number extension will be the same as the BaseCRLNumber the delta extension contains. The idea of a delta in the CRL context is that it contains only what has changed since the base CRL was issued, and it represents an attempt at limiting some of the overheads related to constantly distributing updates for CRLs.

How you merge a delta CRL with an existing one is a bit of an open question in some areas. Again, it is an issue that is only settled by the specific profile you are using. One example of how to do it can be seen in RFC 3280, section 5.2.4.

The IssuingDistributionPoint Extension

The issuing distribution point extension is identified by the OID value "2.5.29.28" (id-ce-issuingDistributionPoint), and it has the following ASN.1 structure:

```
issuingDistributionPoint ::= SEQUENCE {
    distributionPoint          [0] DistributionPointName OPTIONAL,
    onlyContainsUserCerts      [1] BOOLEAN DEFAULT FALSE,
```

```
        onlyContainsCACerts          [2] BOOLEAN DEFAULT FALSE,
        onlySomeReasons              [3] ReasonFlags OPTIONAL,
        indirectCRL                  [4] BOOLEAN DEFAULT FALSE,
        onlyContainsAttributeCerts [5] BOOLEAN DEFAULT FALSE }
```

The `issuingDistributionPoint` identifies the distribution point and scope for a particular CRL, and it indicates whether the CRL covers revocation for the following:

❏   *End entity certificates only* — `onlyContainsUserCerts` will be true.

❏   *CA certificates only* — `onlyContainsCACerts` will be true.

❏   *Attribute certificates only* — `onlyContainsAttributeCerts` will be true.

❏   *Some subset of the possible values of the `ReasonCode` extension in a CRL entry* — `onlySomeReasons` will have the relevant bits set in its `ReasonFlags` string.

❏   *Whether the CRL includes certificates issued by someone other than the CRL issuer* — `indirectCRL` will be true.

In addition, it may provide an actual location for obtaining the most current version of the CRL in the distribution point name.

The FreshestCRL Extension

The freshest CRL extension identifies how delta CRL information can be obtained for the CRL it is found in. It should only be seen in a complete CRL and never a CRL that has a delta CRL extension in it. It is identified by the OID value "2.5.29.46" (`id-ce-freshestCRL`) and has the following ASN.1 definition:

```
FreshestCRL ::= CRLDistributionPoints
```

As you can see, this is the same type that you looked at when you started discussing X.509 CRLs in the context of the CRL distribution points extension in a X.509 certificate, and as it happens, the information in the freshest CRL extension should be interpreted in the same way.

Try It Out   **Creating a CRL**

Have a look at the following example; it creates a basic CRL with one entry that is revoking a certificate issued by the CA certificate owner with the serial number 2. I have added two extensions to the CRL in line with the requirements for conformance in RFC 3280. Neither of the extensions are marked as critical, as the profile detailed in RFC 3280 does not require it.

```java
package chapter7;

import java.math.BigInteger;
import java.security.KeyPair;
import java.security.PrivateKey;
import java.security.cert.X509CRL;
import java.security.cert.X509CRLEntry;
import java.security.cert.X509Certificate;
import java.util.Date;

import org.bouncycastle.asn1.*;
import org.bouncycastle.asn1.x509.*;
```

```java
import org.bouncycastle.x509.X509V2CRLGenerator;
import org.bouncycastle.x509.extension.*;

/**
 * Basic Example of generating and using a CRL.
 */
public class X509CRLExample
{
    public static X509CRL createCRL(
        X509Certificate caCert,
        PrivateKey      caKey,
        BigInteger      revokedSerialNumber)
        throws Exception
    {
        X509V2CRLGenerator   crlGen = new X509V2CRLGenerator();
        Date                 now = new Date();

        crlGen.setIssuerDN(caCert.getSubjectX500Principal());

        crlGen.setThisUpdate(now);
        crlGen.setNextUpdate(new Date(now.getTime() + 100000));
        crlGen.setSignatureAlgorithm("SHA256WithRSAEncryption");

        crlGen.addCRLEntry(revokedSerialNumber, now, CRLReason.privilegeWithdrawn);

        crlGen.addExtension(X509Extensions.AuthorityKeyIdentifier,
                            false, new AuthorityKeyIdentifierStructure(caCert));
        crlGen.addExtension(X509Extensions.CRLNumber,
                                false, new CRLNumber(BigInteger.valueOf(1)));

        return crlGen.generateX509CRL(caKey, "BC");
    }

    public static void main(String[] args)
        throws Exception
    {
        // create CA keys and certificate
        KeyPair         caPair = Utils.generateRSAKeyPair();
        X509Certificate caCert = Utils.generateRootCert(caPair);
        BigInteger      revokedSerialNumber = BigInteger.valueOf(2);

        // create a CRL revoking certificate number 2
        X509CRL  crl = createCRL(caCert, caPair.getPrivate(), revokedSerialNumber);

        // verify the CRL
        crl.verify(caCert.getPublicKey(), "BC");

        // check if the CRL revokes certificate number 2
        X509CRLEntry entry = crl.getRevokedCertificate(revokedSerialNumber);
        System.out.println("Revocation Details:");
        System.out.println(" Certificate number: " + entry.getSerialNumber());
        System.out.println(" Issuer            : " +crl.getIssuerX500Principal());

        if (entry.hasExtensions())
        {
```

```
        byte[]      ext = entry.getExtensionValue(
                                X509Extensions.ReasonCode.getId());

        if (ext != null)
        {
            DEREnumerated      reasonCode =
                        (DEREnumerated)X509ExtensionUtil.fromExtensionValue(ext);

            System.out.println("  Reason Code       : "+reasonCode.getValue());
        }
    }
  }
}
```

Running the example produces the following output:

```
Revocation Details:
  Certificate number: 2
  Issuer            : CN=Test CA Certificate
  Reason Code       : 9
```

As you can see, the example has produced a CRL that contains a revocation for the certificate with the serial number 2, issued by the principal CN=Test CA Certificate. The reason code is given as number 9, which if you look at the back at the definition of CRLReason indicates that it is the value for privilegeWithdrawn.

How It Works

As you can see from the example, there are a number of steps to creating a CRL.

After creating the generator, you have to set the issuer DN for the certificate you want to revoke. In this case I have done this by using the subject of the issuer certificate, as in:

```
crlGen.setIssuerDN(caCert.getSubjectX500Principal());
```

Had I been doing this using the certificate that was being revoked, that is, the one that was issued, this line would have looked different, because I would have used the issuer of the issued certificate — something like:

```
crlGen.setIssuerDN(issuedCert.getIssuerX500Principal());
```

The next steps involve setting the time that this update was generated at using crlGen.setThisUpdate() and setting a time at which the CRL you are generating should no longer be considered reliable using crlGen.setNextUpdate(). After that you set the type of signature you want to sign the CRL with by calling crlGen.setSignatureAlgorithm().

After that you add the CRL entry by calling crlGen.addCRLEntry(). In this case, I'm adding only one, but as you can imagine, a lot of CRLs carry more than one entry. Looking at the call you can see there are three parameters:

```
crlGen.addCRLEntry(revokedSerialNumber, now, CRLReason.privilegeWithdrawn);
```

The first two are the serial number of the certificate being revoked, which fills in the userCertificate field of the CRL entry, and the next one fills in the revocationDate field, which represents the date on which the CRL issuer processed the revocation. The last parameter is the reason the certificate was revoked, and this is added as a ReasonCode extension in the crlEntryExtensions field of the CRL entry.

If you wanted to alert a user of the CRL that the certificate should have been revoked earlier than when you processed it, you would have written something like:

```
crlGen.addCRLEntry(
            revokedSerialNumber, now, CRLReason.privilegeWithdrawn, earlierDate);
```

and the value in *earlierDate* would have been added using an InvalidityDate extension on the CRL entry.

Finally, you add extensions providing a link back to the CA certificate using the AuthorityKeyIdentifier extension, assign a number to this CRL using the CRLNumber extension, and then generate the CRL, signing it with the issuer's private key.

Reading CRLs using the CertificateFactory Class

In addition to methods for reading certificates and certificate paths, the CertificateFactory class also supports the reading of CRLs from input streams. The methods are CertificateFactory. generateCRL() and CertificateFactory.generateCRLs().

CertificateFactory.generateCRL()

Other than the fact it returns a CRL, the generateCRL() method behaves in the same way as the generateCertificate() method does. It takes an InputStream as a parameter, which is meant to contain encoded CRLs. If the factory is of a specific type, such as X.509, the CRL object returned can be cast to whatever specific class is provided to support that type, such as, in the case of X.509, the X509CRL class. If an error is encountered the method will throw a CRLException.

Remember that, as with the generateCertificate() method, if you are trying to read multiple CRLs using this method the InputStream passed in must support InputStream.mark() and InputStream. reset(); otherwise, only the first CRL in the stream will be returned. In general if you are trying to read multiple CRLs from an InputStream, it is better to use the generateCRLs() method.

CertificateFactory.generateCRLs()

The generateCRLs() method returns a Collection containing all the CRLs that were found in the InputStream passed in. If a problem is encountered parsing the stream, a CRLException will be thrown.

Try It Out   Building a CRL Using the CertificateFactory

Have a look at the following example. It uses the CertificateFactory.generateCRL() method to recover an encoded CRL from an input stream. As you can see, generateCRL() method is used in the same way as the generateCertificate() method was.

```
package chapter7;

import java.io.ByteArrayInputStream;
```

```java
import java.math.BigInteger;
import java.security.KeyPair;
import java.security.cert.CertificateFactory;
import java.security.cert.X509CRL;
import java.security.cert.X509CRLEntry;
import java.security.cert.X509Certificate;

/**
 * Reading a CRL with a CertificateFactory
 */
public class CRLCertFactoryExample
{
    public static void main(String[] args) throws Exception
    {
        // create CA keys and certificate
        KeyPair         caPair = Utils.generateRSAKeyPair();
        X509Certificate caCert = Utils.generateRootCert(caPair);
        BigInteger      revokedSerialNumber = BigInteger.valueOf(2);

        // create a CRL revoking certificate number 2
        X509CRL            crl = X509CRLExample.createCRL(
                                caCert, caPair.getPrivate(), revokedSerialNumber);

        // encode it and reconstruct it
        ByteArrayInputStream bIn = new ByteArrayInputStream(crl.getEncoded());
        CertificateFactory   fact = CertificateFactory.getInstance("X.509", "BC");

        crl = (X509CRL)fact.generateCRL(bIn);

        // verify the CRL
        crl.verify(caCert.getPublicKey(), "BC");

        // check if the CRL revokes certificate number 2
        X509CRLEntry entry = crl.getRevokedCertificate(revokedSerialNumber);
        System.out.println("Revocation Details:");
        System.out.println("  Certificate number: " + entry.getSerialNumber());
        System.out.println("  Issuer            : " +crl.getIssuerX500Principal());
    }
}
```

Running the example, you will see the following output:

```
Revocation Details:
  Certificate number: 2
  Issuer            : CN=Test CA Certificate
```

indicating that the CRL was successfully recovered, verified, and had the details you expect.

How It Works

The `CertificateFactory.generateCRL()` method requires an `InputStream` as a parameter, and in this case you just used a `ByteArrayInputStream` derived from the output of the `getEncoded()` method on the CRL. As you can imagine, this was done more for the convenience of the example. In a normal situation you would probably be reading the information from a file or a stream derived from an HTTP response.

In the case of the example, because I know there is only one CRL present in the stream, I have just called generateCRL(), like this:

```
crl = (X509CRL)fact.generateCRL(bIn);
```

Had I been allowing for more than one CRL, and I was sure the stream supported mark() and reset(), I could have used

```
while ((crl = (X509CRL)fact.generateCRL(bIn)) != null)
{
      // processing code ...
}
```

Or, preferably, I could have used the method returning a Collection, generateCRLs(), as follows:

```
Collection crlCollection = fact.generateCRLs(bIn);
```

and then iterated through the contents of the Collection to do processing.

As it happens, objects of the CertStore class can also be used to store CRLs. So the other advantage of the generateCRLs() method is that, as it returns a Collection, its return value is ready-made for creating a CollectionCertStoreParameters object and creating a CertStore.

The X509CRLSelector Class

The java.security.cert.X509CRLSelector class provides an implementation of the CRLSelector interface that allows you to search a CertStore for CRLs that match on a variety of X.509 related fields. It has a variety of set() methods on it that allow you to specify criteria for matching a X.509 CRL that might be present in a CertStore object.

The CRLSelector interface carries two methods on it. One is Object.clone(), so any implementation of a CRLSelector should be clonable. The other is a match() method that takes a single certificate as a parameter and returns true or false depending on whether the code in the match() methods implementation decides the CRL passed in is one of those it is looking for.

The X509CRLSelector provides a range of set() methods, each of which can be used to provide values to be matched against in a X.509 CRL. If no set() methods are called, an X509CRLSelector will match every CRL in the store. If more than one set() method is called, the X509CRLSelector will only match CRLs for which every criteria specified via a set() method is matched.

You will just look at the more common ones here. For a fuller description of what is available, you should check the JavaDoc for the class.

X509CRLSelector.addIssuer() and X509CRLSelector.addIssuerName()

The addIssuer() method was introduced in JDK 1.5 and takes an X500Principal representing the issuer being looked for. It will cause the selector to match any issuer passed to it.

The addIssuerName() method predates 1.5. It has two versions, one of which takes a byte array representing an ASN.1 encoding of an X.500 Name, the other that takes a String version of the distinguished name. Use only the byte array version. The usual problems with converting X.500 Names into strings from their encoded forms and back into their encoded forms apply here also.

X509CRLSelector.setDateAndTime()

The `setDateAndTime()` method takes a `Date` object as a parameter and matches any CRLs whose `thisUpdate` and `nextUpdate` fields have values that bracket the value of the `Date` passed in.

X509CRLSelector.setMaxCRL() and X509CRLSelector.setMinCRL()

Both `setMaxCRL()` and `setMinCRL()` take a `BigInteger` as a parameter that represents either the maximum or minimum value the `CRLNumber` extension can have.

If only the `setMaxCRL()` method is called, or `setMinCRL()` is called with a `null` value as well, then any CRL with a `CRLNumber` extension whose value is less than or equal to the value of the parameter passed to `setMaxCRL()` will be matched.

If only the `setMinCRL()` method is called, or `setMaxCRL()` is called with a null value as well, then any CRL with a `CRLNumber` extension whose value is greater than or equal to the value of the parameter passed to `setMinCRL()` will be matched.

Try It Out   Retrieving a CRL from a CertStore

This example shows a simple use of an `X509CRLSelector`. It builds a `CertStore`, which contains just the CRL you have been using from previous examples and then retrieves it using the selector class. Try running it and have a look at what it does.

```java
package chapter7;

import java.math.BigInteger;
import java.security.KeyPair;
import java.security.cert.CertStore;
import java.security.cert.CollectionCertStoreParameters;
import java.security.cert.X509CRL;
import java.security.cert.X509CRLEntry;
import java.security.cert.X509CRLSelector;
import java.security.cert.X509Certificate;
import java.util.*;

/**
 * Using the X509CRLSelector and the CertStore classes.
 */
public class CRLCertStoreExample
{
    public static void main(String[] args)
        throws Exception
    {
        // create CA keys and certificate
        KeyPair         caPair = Utils.generateRSAKeyPair();
        X509Certificate caCert = Utils.generateRootCert(caPair);
        BigInteger      revokedSerialNumber = BigInteger.valueOf(2);

        // create a CRL revoking certificate number 2
        X509CRL         crl = X509CRLExample.createCRL(
                                caCert, caPair.getPrivate(), revokedSerialNumber);
```

```
        // place the CRL into a CertStore
        CollectionCertStoreParameters params = new CollectionCertStoreParameters(
                                            Collections.singleton(crl));
        CertStore               store = CertStore.getInstance(
                                            "Collection", params, "BC");
        X509CRLSelector         selector = new X509CRLSelector();

        selector.addIssuerName(caCert.getSubjectX500Principal().getEncoded());

        Iterator                it = store.getCRLs(selector).iterator();

        while (it.hasNext())
        {
            crl = (X509CRL)it.next();

            // verify the CRL
            crl.verify(caCert.getPublicKey(), "BC");

            // check if the CRL revokes certificate number 2
            X509CRLEntry entry = crl.getRevokedCertificate(revokedSerialNumber);
            System.out.println("Revocation Details:");
            System.out.println("   Certificate number: " + entry.getSerialNumber());
            System.out.println("   Issuer           : " +
                                    crl.getIssuerX500Principal());
        }
    }
}
```

Running the example, you will see the following output:

```
Revocation Details:
   Certificate number: 2
   Issuer           : CN=Test CA Certificate
```

indicating that the CRL was successfully located in the CertStore.

How It Works

You can see this example is very similar to the one discussed in the context of the X509CertSelector in Chapter 6. The CertStore is set up in exactly the same way as it would be if you were adding certificates to it. You then create a selector that will match any CRL with the issuer name set to the subject of the CA certificate using the following code:

```
selector.addIssuerName(caCert.getSubjectX500Principal().getEncoded());
```

which you can see essentially matches the manner in which the CRL is created. One note on this line of code: I have used X500Principal.getEncoded() to avoid the issue of having to convert the issuer DN into a String. Doing this is no longer necessary in JDK 1.5, because you can pass an X500Principal directly, but I have written the example so that it should work with JDK 1.4 as well.

Once you have set up the selector, it is simply a matter of calling store.getCRLs(), passing it the selector, and getting back a collection representing the matching CRLs. Too easy!

Online Certificate Status Protocol

There are a number of problems with CRLs that can make them unmanageable quite quickly if you have a rapid turnover in certificates. Issues with distributing updates, having all your clients connect to renew when the last CRL you sent them expires, and not being able to get a CRL out in time all add up. In the same manner that financial institutions found making online facilities available preferable to continually sending out black lists of credit cards, Online Certificate Status Protocol (OCSP), which is described in RFC 2560, is an answer to the online method for working out the revocation status of a certificate. As Figure 7-2 shows, an OCSP server, or *responder*, provides real-time responses to client queries about the status of certificates.

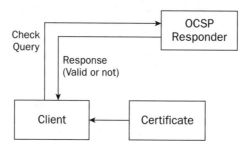

Certificate Check Done by Client Querying Responder

Figure 7-2

In addition to defining the basic protocol, RFC 2560 also defines a number of new extension types that use the same extensions structure that you have already seen in certificates and CRLs. The new extension types are all identified off the following OID:

```
id-pkix-ocsp            OBJECT IDENTIFIER ::= { 1 3 6 1 5 5 7 48 1 }
```

Take note of this value, because further on in this section, I refer to the identifiers associated with the various extensions in reference to it.

The JCA does not directly support OCSP at the moment. The Bouncy Castle APIs do, however, so you will look at how you would implement OCSP using the Bouncy Castle API. There are three main aspects to the OCSP protocol: how a request is formed, how a response is formed, and how a certificate is identified in a request or a response. You will have a look at how a certificate is identified first.

The CertificateID Class

The `org.bouncycastle.ocsp.CertificateID` class provides a high-level implementation of the `CertID` structure that appears in RFC 2560. The `CertID` structure is used to uniquely identify certificates that are the subject of an OCSP request or response and has the following ASN.1 definition:

```
CertID ::= SEQUENCE {
          hashAlgorithm          AlgorithmIdentifier,
          issuerNameHash         OCTET STRING,
          issuerKeyHash          OCTET STRING,
          serialNumber           CertificateSerialNumber }
```

As you can see, the last three fields of the `CertID` structure contain the information used to identify the certificate and the first field that identifies the algorithm that is used to create the second and third fields, both of which are based on message digests.

Objects of the type `CertificateID` are constructed directly using a `String` representing the hash algorithm, an issuer certificate, and the serial number of the certificate of interest. The necessary calculations are then done as part of construction, and the resulting values can be retrieved using a series of `get()` methods.

CertificateID.getHashAlgOID()

The `getHashAlgOID()` method returns a `String` representing the `OBJECT IDENTIFIER` value that identifies the hash algorithm used to create the values returned by `getIssuerNameHash()` and `getIssuerKeyHash()`.

CertificateID.getIssuerNameHash()

The `getIssuerNameHash()` method returns a byte array containing the octets contained in the `OCTET STRING` that represents the `issuerNameHash` field. The value of the octets is calculated by feeding the bytes representing the DER encoding of the issuer name field of the certificate being identified into the hash algorithm.

CertificateID.getIssuerKeyHash()

The `getIssuerKeyHash()` method returns a byte array containing the octets contained in the `OCTET STRING` that represents the `issuerKeyHash` field. The value of the octets is calculated by feeding the DER encoding (excluding the tag and length octets) of the `BIT STRING` present in the `subjectPublicKey` field in the `SubjectPublicKeyInfo` structure assigned to the `subjectPublicKeyInfo` field in the issuer's certificate structure.

CertificateID.getSerialNumber()

The `getSerialNumber()` method returns a `BigInteger` representing the serial number of the certificate the `CertificateID` represents.

The OCSPReq Class

The `org.bouncycastle.ocsp.OCSPReq` class is an implementation of the ASN.1 type `OCSPRequest` defined in RFC 2560. As its name implies, the `OCSPRequest` object provides the data structure that must be filled in to produce a valid OCSP request. It is defined with the following ASN.1 structure:

```
OCSPRequest ::= SEQUENCE {
        tbsRequest                  TBSRequest,
        optionalSignature   [0]     EXPLICIT Signature OPTIONAL }

Signature ::= SEQUENCE {
        signatureAlgorithm    AlgorithmIdentifier,
        signature             BIT STRING,
        certs                 [0] EXPLICIT SEQUENCE OF Certificate OPTIONAL}
```

Note that in this case the signature is optional — in general, most OCSP responders do not expect signed requests. The provision for the signature is to allow a server to be set up so that only authorized parties can talk to it. In such a situation, the signature becomes mandatory and allows the server to quickly reject requests it might be getting from unauthorized parties.

In addition to the AlgorithmIdentifier identifying the mechanism used to construct the signature and the BIT STRING representing the actual signature value, there is also provision in the Signature structure for including a sequence of certificates with the request using the certs field. If the certificate sequence is present, it should contain a valid certificate path leading from a certificate the server recognizes to the certificate that can be used to verify the signature on the request. The presence of this field allows the entity running the server to give its authorized users the right to extend their access rights to other parties unknown to the entity running the server. If the certs field is missing, then the server must be able to validate the signature directly.

The OCSPReq class is constructed using a byte array representing the DER encoding of an OCSPRequest structure or by using an object of the OCSPReqGenerator class, the use of which you will see in the next example.

As you will see next, the ASN.1 structure for TBSRequest includes an optional Extensions field, so the class also implements the java.security.cert.X509Extension interface.

OCSPReq.getTBSRequest()

The getTBSRequest() method returns a byte array representing the DER encoding of the value in the tbsRequest field in the OCSPRequest structure. In the case where the optional signature is used, it is the DER encoding of the tbsRequest field, which is used to calculate the signature.

The tbsRequest field is of type TBSRequest, which has the following structure:

```
TBSRequest ::= SEQUENCE {
        version             [0]      EXPLICIT Version DEFAULT v1,
        requestorName       [1]      EXPLICIT GeneralName OPTIONAL,
        requestList                  SEQUENCE OF Request,
        requestExtensions   [2]      EXPLICIT Extensions OPTIONAL }

Version  ::=   INTEGER  {  v1(0) }
```

and the get() methods on the OCSPReq class are a reflection of these.

OCSPReq.getVersion()

The getVersion() method simply returns the version number of the request. At the moment you would expect this to always be the value 1.

OCSPReq.getRequestorName()

The getRequestorName() method returns a GeneralName object representing the requestor. This field is optional, unless the requestor has chosen to sign the request, in which case the field must be set.

OCSPReq.getRequestList()

The getRequestList() method returns an array of org.bouncycastle.ocsp.Req objects. These represent the values found in the requestList field, which is a sequence of Request structures. The Request structure has the following ASN.1 definition:

```
Request ::= SEQUENCE {
                reqCert                      CertID,
                singleRequestExtensions      [0] EXPLICIT Extensions OPTIONAL }
```

and the `Req` class has a `getCertID()` method on it for retrieving the `reqCert` field as a `CertificateID`, as well as implementing the `java.security.cert.X509Extension` interface to allow retrieval of the values stored in the `singleRequestExtensions` field.

OCSPReq.isSigned()

The `isSigned()` method returns `true` if the OCSP request has been signed. Signing of an OCSP request is purely optional, unless it is mandated by the OCSP responder you want to talk to. If a request is signed, you should find that the `getRequestorName()` method returns the `GeneralName` identifying the requestor.

If `isSigned()` returns `true`, you will also get non-null return values from `OCSPReq.getSignature()` and `OCSPReq.getSignatureAlgOID()`. There may also be a certificate chain associated with the request that you can retrieve using `getCertificates()`.

OCSPReq.getSignature() and OCSPReq.getSignatureAlgOID()

The `getSignature()` and `getSignatureAlgOID()` return the bytes making up the signature and a `String` representing the OID identifying the algorithm that has been used to create the signature.

If `isSigned()` returns `false`, both the methods will return `null`.

OCSPReq.getCertificates()

If a request is signed the requestor may also include one or more certificates that can be used to verify the signature and its origins. The `getCertificates()` method returns a `CertStore` that contains the certificates, if any, that are contained in the request.

If `isSigned()` returns `false`, this method will return `null`.

OCSP Request Extensions

Request extensions can appear in both the `requestExtensions` field in the `TBSRequest` structure and the `singleRequestExtensions` field. The following standard extensions are currently defined for inclusion in OCSP requests.

The Nonce Extension

The `nonce` extension is used to bind a request to a response to prevent replay attacks. As the name implies, the `nonce` value is something that the client should only use once within a reasonably small period; the extension appears in the `requestExtensions` field in a request and should be echoed back as an extension in the response.

The `nonce` extension is identified by the following identifier as the extension type:

```
id-pkix-ocsp-nonce      OBJECT IDENTIFIER ::= { id-pkix-ocsp 2 }
```

What appears as the extension value is purely up to the client.

The Acceptable Response Types Extension

In situations where a server may be able to provide a variety of response messages, in addition to the basic one, an OCSP client may specify the response types it understands. It can do this by including the acceptable response types extension in the `requestExtensions` field of its request and an `AcceptableResponses` structure as the extension value. `AcceptableResponses` has the following ASN.1 definition:

```
AcceptableResponses ::= SEQUENCE OF OBJECT IDENTIFIER
```

where the `OBJECT IDENTIFIER` values represent the particular response type the client can handle.

The acceptable response types extension is identified by the following identifier as the extension type:

```
id-pkix-ocsp-response  OBJECT IDENTIFIER ::= { id-pkix-ocsp 4 }
```

The Service Locator Extension

In some cases an OCSP responder may be able reroute requests to another OCSP responder, which is known to be authoritative from information in the certificate being checked. If this is possible, the corresponding information in the certificate's authority information access extension should be copied into an extension in the `singleRequestExtensions` field associated with the certificate.

The extension is identified by the identifier

```
id-pkix-ocsp-service-locator OBJECT IDENTIFIER ::= { id-pkix-ocsp 7 }
```

and is defined as having the following value:

```
ServiceLocator ::= SEQUENCE {
    issuer    Name,
    locator   AuthorityInfoAccessSyntax OPTIONAL }
```

The `AuthorityInfoAcessSyntax` is defined as follows:

```
AuthorityInfoAccessSyntax ::= SEQUENCE SIZE (1..MAX) OF AccessDescription

AccessDescription ::=  SEQUENCE {
                            accessMethod        OBJECT IDENTIFIER,
                            accessLocation      GeneralName  }
```

and represents the same structure used in the authority information access structure in a X.509 certificate.

In a X.509 certificate the authority information access extension is identified by the `OBJECT IDENTIFIER` value `1.3.6.1.5.5.7.1.1` (`id-pe-authorityInfoAccess`) and, in the case of OCSP, the `accessMethod` will be set to the `OBJECT IDENTIFIER` `id-ad-ocsp`, which equates to `1.3.6.1.5.5.7.48.1` if the `accessLocation` in the `AccessDescription` structure is referring to an OCSP responder.

At this point you have covered the basics of OCSP request generation. Take a look at an example.

Try It Out   **OCSP Request Generation**

This example generates an unsigned OCSP request that incorporates a `nonce` extension into the request being generated. As you would expect, it also demonstrates use of the `OCSPReqGenerator` class to create the request. Have a look at the code and try running it.

```java
package chapter7;

import java.math.BigInteger;
import java.security.KeyPair;
import java.security.cert.X509Certificate;
import java.util.Vector;

import org.bouncycastle.asn1.DEROctetString;
import org.bouncycastle.asn1.ocsp.OCSPObjectIdentifiers;
import org.bouncycastle.asn1.x509.X509Extension;
import org.bouncycastle.asn1.x509.X509Extensions;
import org.bouncycastle.ocsp.CertificateID;
import org.bouncycastle.ocsp.OCSPException;
import org.bouncycastle.ocsp.OCSPReq;
import org.bouncycastle.ocsp.OCSPReqGenerator;
import org.bouncycastle.ocsp.Req;

/**
 * Example of unsigned OCSP request generation.
 */
public class OCSPClientExample
{
    public static OCSPReq generateOCSPRequest(
        X509Certificate issuerCert, BigInteger serialNumber) throws OCSPException
    {
        // Generate the id for the certificate we are looking for
        CertificateID   id = new CertificateID(
                            CertificateID.HASH_SHA1, issuerCert, serialNumber);

        // basic request generation with nonce
        OCSPReqGenerator    gen = new OCSPReqGenerator();

        gen.addRequest(id);

        // create details for nonce extension
        BigInteger nonce = BigInteger.valueOf(System.currentTimeMillis());
        Vector      oids = new Vector();
        Vector      values = new Vector();

        oids.add(OCSPObjectIdentifiers.id_pkix_ocsp_nonce);
        values.add(new X509Extension(
                            false, new DEROctetString(nonce.toByteArray())));

        gen.setRequestExtensions(new X509Extensions(oids, values));

        return gen.generate();
```

```
        }

    public static void main(String[] args) throws Exception
    {
        // create certificates and CRLs
        KeyPair         rootPair = Utils.generateRSAKeyPair();
        KeyPair         interPair = Utils.generateRSAKeyPair();

        X509Certificate rootCert = Utils.generateRootCert(rootPair);
        X509Certificate interCert = Utils.generateIntermediateCert(
                    interPair.getPublic(), rootPair.getPrivate(), rootCert);

        OCSPReq request = generateOCSPRequest(
                                    rootCert, interCert.getSerialNumber());

        Req[]   requests = request.getRequestList();

        for (int i = 0; i != requests.length; i++)
        {
            CertificateID certID = requests[i].getCertID();

            System.out.println("OCSP Request to check certificate number "
                                            + certID.getSerialNumber());
        }
    }
}
```

Running the example produces the following output:

```
OCSP Request to check certificate number 1
```

indicating that you have created an OCSP request containing a single request to verify certificate number 1 — the serial number of `interCert`.

How It Works

Generating a basic OCSP request is fairly simple. First, you collect the certificate IDs of the certificates you want to use. Then you bundle them up in a request, possibly adding some extensions, and send the request off.

The `generateOCSPRequest()` method of the example basically follows this process. The initial line

```
CertificateID   id = new CertificateID(
                        CertificateID.HASH_SHA1, issuerCert, serialNumber);
```

creates a certificate ID calculated using the SHA-1 algorithm.

After that, the ID generated is added to the sequence of `Request` structures in the `requestList` of the `TBSRequest` structure that forms the body of the OCSP request using `gen.addRequest()`. In this case there are no extensions required in the `Request` structure; if there were, I would have used the `addRequest()` method that takes a `X509Extensions` object as well, as in:

```
gen.addRequest(id, requestExtensions);
```

where *requestExtensions* would be appropriately set with the extensions I wanted to appear in the `singleRequestExtensions` field in the `Request` structure.

The last step before generation is to add the extensions I want present in the `TBSRequest` structure. In the example I have added a `nonce` extension, which as you probably recall should just contain some value for the responder to echo back to you. In my case I've just used the current time, but any value that will be unique over a particular period will do here. The idea of the `nonce` is to allow you to match requests to responses, as well as identify duplicate responses if you see them.

Finally, you generate the request by calling `gen.generate()`, which returns an unsigned OCSP request. If you were generating a signed request, you would have to use a `generate()` method that takes the details for the signature and, possibly, the optional certificate chain. If you were doing this, the `return` statement would look more like:

```
return gen.generate(
            "SHA256WithRSA", requestorPrivateKey, requestorX509Chain, "BC");
```

where *requestorPrivateKey* and *requestorX509Chain* represent the private key for the requestor and the certificates required to correctly verify the signature.

That's it for generating a request. Now you'll look at what comes back from an OCSP responder.

The OCSPResp Class

The `org.bouncycastle.ocsp.OCSPResp` class is an implementation of the ASN.1 type `OCSPResponse` defined in RFC 2560. As its name implies, the `OCSPResponse` object provides the data structure that defines a valid OCSP response. It has the following ASN.1 structure:

```
OCSPResponse ::= SEQUENCE {
    responseStatus          OCSPResponseStatus,
    responseBytes           [0] EXPLICIT ResponseBytes OPTIONAL }

OCSPResponseStatus ::= ENUMERATED {
    successful              (0),   --Response has valid confirmations
    malformedRequest        (1),   --Illegal confirmation request
    internalError           (2),   --Internal error in issuer
    tryLater                (3),   --Try again later
                                   --(4) is not used
    sigRequired             (5),   --Must sign the request
    unauthorized            (6)    --Request unauthorized }
```

In the event that the `responseStatus` field indicates `successful`, the answers to the OCSP requests that have being processed are in the `ResponseBytes` structure, which is defined as follows:

```
ResponseBytes ::= SEQUENCE {
                    responseType    OBJECT IDENTIFIER,
                    response        OCTET STRING }
```

where the `OCTET STRING` in the response field should contain the DER encoding of some detailed response object that has been created by the server.

The `OCSPResp` class is normally constructed using a byte array representing the DER encoding of the OCSP response or, if you are an OCSP responder, using an object of the type `OCSPRespGenerator`. Functionally it consists of two `get()` methods: `getStatus()` returns an object representing the `responseStatus` field, and `getResponseObject()` returns an object that should be cast to the appropriate object that represents the ASN.1 structure encoded in the response field of `ResponseBytes`.

Although the use of the `ResponseBytes` structure provides quite a bit of flexibility when it comes to responders deciding how best to provide information back to clients, RFC 2560 defines a basic response structure that everyone should be able to support. Basic OCSP responders return a DER encoding of a `BasicOCSPResponse` structure in the `response` field of the `ResponseBytes` structure. That this is the type of the response is indicated by the `responseType` in the `ResponseBytes` structure being set to `id-pkix-ocsp-basic`, which has the following value:

```
id-pkix-ocsp-basic      OBJECT IDENTIFIER ::= { id-pkix-ocsp 1 }
```

The BasicOCSPResponse structure itself is defined as:

```
BasicOCSPResponse ::= SEQUENCE {
        tbsResponseData         ResponseData,
        signatureAlgorithm      AlgorithmIdentifier,
        signature               BIT STRING,
        certs                   [0] EXPLICIT SEQUENCE OF Certificate OPTIONAL }
```

As you can see, this is very similar in layout to the `OCSPRequest` structure, but the signature is not optional. The `certs` field still is optional, but in this case it is more likely to be present, as an OCSP responder would be likely to renew its signing key frequently. The result is that the OCSP client would normally expect to have a "permanent" root certificate for the OCSP responder, which would then be used to verify the chain stored in the `certs` field — the target certificate of which would be used to verify the signature on the response.

API support for the `BasicOCSPResponse` structure is provided in the Bouncy Castle API by the `BasicOCSPResp` class, and in the normal case, it is a `BasicOCSPResp` object that will be returned by the `OCSPResp.getResponseObject()` method.

The BasicOCSPResp Class

Other than obtaining a `BasicOCSPResp` object using the `getResponseObject()` method on an `OCSPResp` object, if you are an OCSP responder, an object of the type `org.bouncycastle.ocsp.BasicOCSPResp` can also be created using a generator class — in this case the `BasicOCSPRespGenerator`.

You'll now look at the methods on the `BasicOCSPResp` class now.

BasicOCSPResp.getTBSResponseData()

The `getTBSResponseData()` method returns a byte array representing the DER-encoded `ResponseData` structure. The `ResponseData` structure is defined in RFC 2560 as follows:

```
ResponseData ::= SEQUENCE {
    version             [0] EXPLICIT Version DEFAULT v1,
    responderID             ResponderID,
```

```
        producedAt              GeneralizedTime,
        responses               SEQUENCE OF SingleResponse,
        responseExtensions   [1] EXPLICIT Extensions OPTIONAL }
```

As you can see, the responseExtensions field in the ResponseData structure is a tagged version of the Extensions type, so the BasicOCSPResp class also implements the java.security.cert .X509Extension interface to provide access to the extensions contained in the response.

BasicOCSPResponse.getVersion()

The getVersion() method returns an int representing the version number of the ResponseData structure that was contained in the BasicOCSPResponse. At the moment you would expect this method to return the value 1.

BasicOCSPResponse.getResponderID()

The getResponderID() returns a value object containing a ResponderID structure.

The ResponderID structure is defined as follows:

```
ResponderID ::= CHOICE {
    byName              [1] Name,
    byKey               [2] KeyHash }

KeyHash ::= OCTET STRING
```

In the event that the ResponderID is not an X.500 name, the key hash is calculated in the same way as the issuerKeyHash field in a CertID; only in this case, it is the public key of the entity signing the response that is used to calculate the hash, not the issuer of the original certificate.

BasicOCSPResponse.getProducedAt()

The getProducedAt() method returns a Date representing the time at which the response was signed by the OCSP responder.

BasicOCSPResponse.getResponses()

The getResponses() method returns an array of SingleResp objects that represent the responses to the requests about individual certificates that were contained in the OCSP request.

The SingleResponse structure has the following ASN.1 definition:

```
SingleResponse ::= SEQUENCE {
    certID                      CertID,
    certStatus                  CertStatus,
    thisUpdate                  GeneralizedTime,
    nextUpdate          [0]     EXPLICIT GeneralizedTime OPTIONAL,
    singleExtensions    [1]     EXPLICIT Extensions OPTIONAL }
```

and the SingleResp class provides the methods getCertID(), getCertStatus(), getThisUpdate(), and getNextUpdate() to return the values of the various fields as well implementing the java .security.cert.X509Extension interface to give access to the various extensions the singleExtensions field might contain. The getCertStatus() method returns a null if the certificate is okay; otherwise, it returns an object detailing the issues with the certificate. Both getThisUpdate() and getNextUpdate() return Date representations of the GeneralizedTime contained in the SingleReponse structure.

The getThisUpdate() method returns the time at which the status reported was known to be correct. If getNextUpdate() returns null, meaning the nextUpdate field is not present, then the responder is indicating that newer status information is always available for the certificate. Otherwise, if it is set and the local system time is outside the interval between the return values of getThisUpdate() and getNextUpdate(), then the response should be considered unreliable and another status request should be made.

OCSP Response Extensions

Response extensions can appear in both the responseExtensions field in the TBSResponse structure and the singleExtensions field. Apart from the nonce extension, which you have already seen and should be included in the responseExtensions field of any response to a request that contained a nonce extension, there are several other extensions that you can use in responses.

The CRL References Extension

In some cases, such as for auditing purposes, it can be useful for the OCSP responder to specify the CRL it found a revoked or "on hold" certificate on. This information will be included in the singleExtensions field of the SingleResponse the CRL is associated with, and the CRL may be specified using the URL at which the CRL is available, the CRL number, or the time at which the relevant CRL was created.

The extension is identified by the following identifier as the extension type:

```
id-pkix-ocsp-crl        OBJECT IDENTIFIER ::= { id-pkix-ocsp 3 }
```

and contains the following structure as the extension value:

```
CrlID ::= SEQUENCE {
    crlUrl              [0]     EXPLICIT IA5String OPTIONAL,
    crlNum              [1]     EXPLICIT INTEGER OPTIONAL,
    crlTime             [2]     EXPLICIT GeneralizedTime OPTIONAL }
```

The Archive Cutoff Extensions

In the case of a regular CRL, an expired certificate is normally removed from the certificate list it is contained in. In OCSP, a responder may choose to maintain a certificate's information past the expiry date of the certificate to enable its clients to help revalidate signatures verified by certificates well past their expiration date. The date obtained by subtracting the retention interval from the date of particular response is defined as the certificate's "archive cutoff" date.

OCSP responders that provide support for this should include the cutoff date in the singleExtensions for each SingleResponse they generate. The extension is identified by the object identifier:

```
id-pkix-ocsp-archive-cutoff  OBJECT IDENTIFIER ::= { id-pkix-ocsp 6 }
```

and has the value of the type `ArchiveCutoff`, which is defined as follows:

```
ArchiveCutoff ::= GeneralizedTime
```

X.509 CRL Entry Extensions

Any of the extensions you looked at in the section on X.509 CRL entry extensions can appear in the `singleExtensions` field in one of the `SingleResponse` structures making up the `ResponseData` in a basic OCSP response.

This brings you to the end of the response extensions; it is time for another example.

Try It Out   **Generating an OCSP Response**

This example is much larger than most of the previous ones you have looked at, so I've broken it up a bit so I can comment on some parts of it as I go. Before you start typing, don't forget you can find the source for the examples on the book's Web site.

This chunk represents the class header. There is not a great deal to say here other than you'll notice that I'm including `PrivateKey`, as a response must be signed.

```java
package chapter7;

import java.math.BigInteger;
import java.security.KeyPair;
import java.security.NoSuchProviderException;
import java.security.PrivateKey;
import java.security.PublicKey;
import java.security.cert.X509Certificate;
import java.util.Arrays;
import java.util.Date;
import java.util.Vector;

import org.bouncycastle.asn1.ocsp.OCSPObjectIdentifiers;
import org.bouncycastle.asn1.x509.*;
import org.bouncycastle.ocsp.*;

/**
 * Example of OCSP response generation.
 */
public class OCSPResponderExample
{
```

The next chunk provides a definition for the `generateOCSPResponse()` method:

```java
public static OCSPResp generateOCSPResponse(
    OCSPReq request, PrivateKey responderKey,
        PublicKey pubKey, CertificateID revokedID)
    throws NoSuchProviderException, OCSPException
{
    BasicOCSPRespGenerator basicRespGen = new BasicOCSPRespGenerator(pubKey);
```

```
X509Extensions          reqExtensions = request.getRequestExtensions();

if (reqExtensions != null)
{
    X509Extension       ext = reqExtensions.getExtension(
                                OCSPObjectIdentifiers.id_pkix_ocsp_nonce);

    if (ext != null)
    {
        Vector oids = new Vector();
        Vector values = new Vector();

        oids.add(OCSPObjectIdentifiers.id_pkix_ocsp_nonce);
        values.add(ext);

        basicRespGen.setResponseExtensions(
                                    new X509Extensions(oids, values));
    }
}

Req[] requests = request.getRequestList();

for (int i = 0; i != requests.length; i++)
{
    CertificateID certID = requests[i].getCertID();

    // this would normally be a lot more general!
    if (certID.equals(revokedID))
    {
        basicRespGen.addResponse(certID,
                new RevokedStatus(new Date(), CRLReason.privilegeWithdrawn));
    }
    else
    {
        basicRespGen.addResponse(certID, CertificateStatus.GOOD);
    }
}

BasicOCSPResp basicResp = basicRespGen.generate(
                    "SHA256WithRSA", responderKey, null, new Date(), "BC");

OCSPRespGenerator       respGen = new OCSPRespGenerator();

return respGen.generate(OCSPRespGenerator.SUCCESSFUL, basicResp);
}
```

As you can see, the method takes the request being processed, the responder's private and public key, and the certificate ID of the certificate that is regarded as revoked. The method body is a lot simpler than it would be in the real world, as you would normally be looking up a CRL or some other data structure to find out exactly what the story with a certificate contained in a particular request is about. However, it does give you enough to be able to play with the OCSP response generation, so it will serve the purposes here.

The next chunk you look at is just a method that returns a status message when passed a responder key pair, the CA certificate, a serial number for a certificate issued by the CA that has been revoked, and the

X.509 certificate you actually want to check. The method does this by generating the appropriate request for the certificate you want to check, generating a response based on the request, and then evaluating the response and returning the appropriate String.

Here's the code for the method. As you can see, the OCSP request is being generated using the generateOCSPRequest() method you defined in the Try It Out, "OCSP Request Generation."

```java
public static String getStatusMessage(
    KeyPair responderPair, X509Certificate caCert,
      BigInteger revokedSerialNumber, X509Certificate cert)
    throws Exception
{
    OCSPReq request = OCSPClientExample.generateOCSPRequest(
                                    caCert, cert.getSerialNumber());

    CertificateID revokedID = new CertificateID(
                    CertificateID.HASH_SHA1, caCert, revokedSerialNumber);
    OCSPResp response = generateOCSPResponse(
                        request, responderPair.getPrivate(),
                                responderPair.getPublic(), revokedID);

    BasicOCSPResp  basicResponse = (BasicOCSPResp)response.getResponseObject();

    // verify the response
    if (basicResponse.verify(responderPair.getPublic(), "BC"))
    {
        SingleResp[]       responses = basicResponse.getResponses();

        byte[] reqNonce = request.getExtensionValue(
                        OCSPObjectIdentifiers.id_pkix_ocsp_nonce.getId());
        byte[] respNonce = basicResponse.getExtensionValue(
                        OCSPObjectIdentifiers.id_pkix_ocsp_nonce.getId());

        // validate the nonce if it is present
        if (reqNonce == null || Arrays.equals(reqNonce, respNonce))
        {
            String message = "";
            for (int i = 0; i != responses.length; i++)
            {
                message += " certificate number "
                            + responses[i].getCertID().getSerialNumber();
                if (responses[i].getCertStatus() == CertificateStatus.GOOD)
                {
                    return message + " status: good";
                }
                else
                {
                    return message + " status: revoked";
                }
            }
        }

        return message;
    }
```

```
            else
            {
                return "response nonce failed to validate";
            }
        }
        else
        {
            return "response failed to verify";
        }
    }
```

Finally, you have the main driver and trailing brace to close off the class definition. The main driver generates some keys and then checks the status of the intermediate certificate, printing the resulting message:

```
    public static void main(
        String[] args)
        throws Exception
    {
        KeyPair         rootPair = Utils.generateRSAKeyPair();
        KeyPair         interPair = Utils.generateRSAKeyPair();

        X509Certificate rootCert = Utils.generateRootCert(rootPair);
        X509Certificate interCert = Utils.generateIntermediateCert(
                        interPair.getPublic(), rootPair.getPrivate(), rootCert);

        System.out.println(
                getStatusMessage(rootPair, rootCert,
                                        BigInteger.valueOf(1), interCert));
    }
}
```

Try running the example; you should see the following output:

```
    certificate number 1 status: revoked
```

showing that after the request generation and response processing, `interCert` has turned out to be revoked.

If you modify the main driver to use `BigInteger.valueOf(2)`, rather than `BigInteger.valueOf(1)`, you get the following output instead:

```
    certificate number 1 status: good
```

since `revokedID` would no longer match the `CertificateID` for `interCert`.

How It Works

As you can see, there are two new bodies of functionality in the example. The first is the generation of the response based on the inputs passed in. The second is the validation and processing of the response with the generation of the appropriate response message.

The first stage is carried out in the `generateOCSPResponse()` method and commences with the construction of the `BasicOCSPRespGenerator` object as follows:

```
BasicOCSPRespGenerator basicRespGen = new BasicOCSPRespGenerator(pubKey);
```

The generator is created to generate the `BasicOCSPResponse` structure that gets encoded in the `response` field of the `ResponseBytes` structure — the actual structure that appears in the `OCSPResponse` structure that forms the real OCSP response sent back to the client. As you can see, it takes the responder's public key as a parameter to its constructor. It does this because part of the construction process involves creating a `ResponderID` that will be included in the `ResponseData` structure in the basic response.

The next step of the example uses the `OCSPReq.getExtensions()` method to get the contents of the `requestExtensions` field if it is present in the request. If it turns out there are extensions, it checks the `X509Extensions` object that was returned to see whether it contains a `nonce` extension. If this is also the case, another `X509Extensions` object containing a copy of the `nonce` extension found in the request is created and then passed to the `basicRespGen.setResponseExtensions()` method so that it will be present in the `responseExtensions` field of the `ResponseData` structure contained in the basic response.

Having gotten this far, the method then iterates through the individual certificate requests that were contained in the request object, and if one of the certificate requests is for a `CertificateID` that matches the `revokedID` object, a response is added indicating the certificate has been revoked. Otherwise, a response is added indicating the certificate is "good," or not revoked. Individual certificate responses can also contain extensions. Had this been done, say, for a certificate response indicating "good," rather than seeing

```
basicRespGen.addResponse(certID, CertificateStatus.GOOD);
```

you would have seen

```
basicRespGen.addResponse(
                certID, CertificateStatus.GOOD, singleResponseExtensions);
```

where the *singleResponseExtensions* is an `X509Extensions` object containing the appropriate extension for the individual certificate response.

Finally, the signed basic response is generated using the call to `basicRespGen.generate()`, and this is, in turn, wrapped in an `OCSPResp` object that's generated using the `OCSPRespGenerator` object `respGen` by calling `respGen.generate()`. The `basicRespGen.generate()` method specifies the signature algorithm to use and provides the `Date` object that will be used to fill in the `producedAt` field in the `ResponseData` structure. In this case the certificate chain for validating the signature has been left out of the message, as it is optional and it is known that the "client" already has the necessary certificate in its possession.

The second and final stage of the example is carried out in the `getStatusMessage()` method. After the request is created and the response retrieved, the `BasicOCSPResponse` is retrieved from `response` by calling `response.getResponseObject()` and casting appropriately.

After retrieving the basic response into `basicResponse`, the signature on the object is verified using the public key of the responder. If the signature verifies and a `nonce` extension was present in the request, the `nonce` extension value inside the response is checked against it to see whether they are equal. If both these tests pass, the code then iterates through the individual certificate responses building a message string with the certificate's serial number and "good" or "revoked," depending on how the `SingleResp.getCertStatus()` method evaluates on the given response, and the message string is returned. In the event something goes wrong, an error message is returned instead.

The returned message is then printed out using the main driver, bringing you to the end of the example code.

One further point on this: The CA certificate is used both to validate the issued certificate and the OCSP response. Although this is acceptable, CAs will delegate the responsibility for validating a response to another certificate and use a different private key. If this is the case, then validating the OCSP response also means confirming that the certificate used for validating the OCSP response was issued by the CA and that it contains an extended key usage extension containing the following OID:

```
id-kp-OCSPSigning OBJECT IDENTIFIER ::= {id-kp 9}
```

indicating that the CA signing it signed it for the purpose of signing OCSP responses. If you do not find this OID or you do and the CA did not issue the certificate, the response you are getting is, at best, invalid, or, at worst, fraudulent, so it is important to include a check for this as well.

Certificate Path Validation

As I mentioned at the start of the chapter, the issue of knowing whether a particular certificate path is valid is more than just knowing that each certificate on the path has a signature you can validate. Knowing whether a path is valid is also about whether the certificates you have are being used in the manner intended. For example, a certificate authorized to be used to encrypt secret keys might not be appropriate for validating the signature on a piece of executable code.

Certificate path validation algorithms are provided to make sure the certificate is valid in all these senses. Generally, in addition to verifying the signature on the certificate, path validation algorithms also verify that the extensions are appropriate and that if any are critical, they have been correctly processed. An implementation of a path validation algorithm should fail if it finds an extension marked critical on a certificate in a path it is trying to validate.

As with most interpretation issues related to X.509 certificates, how path validation is done is dependent on what profile you use. In this case, the most relevant one is in Section 6 of RFC 3280, the PKIX profile, which covers a validation mechanism for working out whether a path starting with an end entity certificate you would like to trust leads you back to a certificate you are already prepared to trust.

The certificate you are prepared to trust is also often referred to as a *trust anchor*, and I will start the journey through the JCA classes for path validation by looking at the class that encapsulates this first.

The TrustAnchor Class

The `java.security.cert.TrustAnchor` class provides a container for a public key that you have to trust in order to be able to validate a certificate path.

There are three constructors for the `TrustAnchor` class. All of them can be supplied with optional name constraints via a byte array containing the DER-encoded value of a X.509 `NameConstraints` extension structure. After that, it is a question of whether you want to make use of a certificate containing the public key and use the constructor that takes an `X509Certificate`, or if you have to use the public key and an identifying X.500 Name to identify the trust anchor instead. As with most other classes that take X.500 Names, passing the identifying X.500 Name can be done by either passing an `X500Principal` or a `String` version of the DN.

The `NameConstraints` extension is talked about at length in RFC 3280 in section 4.2.1.11, so I will not go into full details here; however, if it is present in a certificate, it is identified by the OID `2.5.29.30` (`id-ce-nameConstraints`) and its value represents the following ASN.1 structure:

```
NameConstraints ::= SEQUENCE {
     permittedSubtrees        [0]      GeneralSubtrees OPTIONAL,
     excludedSubtrees         [1]      GeneralSubtrees OPTIONAL }

GeneralSubtrees ::= SEQUENCE SIZE (1..MAX) OF GeneralSubtree

GeneralSubtree ::= SEQUENCE {
     base                     GeneralName,
     minimum        [0]       BaseDistance DEFAULT 0,
     maximum        [1]       BaseDistance OPTIONAL }

BaseDistance ::= INTEGER (0..MAX)
```

RFC 3280 fixes the field `minimum` at zero, its default value, and specifies that the `maximum` should be absent, leaving you only with the `base` field, which is of the type `GeneralName`, to contend with in the `GeneralSubtrees` sequences. A certificate is only regarded as valid if its subject, and subject alternative name if present, does not match any of the values in the `excludedSubtrees` if present, and is in the `permittedSubtrees` if present. How matching gets done depends a little on the profile you are using, but by way of example from RFC 3280, if the base field in the `permittedSubtrees` sequence is a URI of the value `".bouncycastle.org"` it will match any subdomain of bouncycastle.org. Note this would not match the host bouncycastle.org that would have to be matched by having another URI present containing just `"bouncycastle.org"`. As you can imagine, the same applies for e-mail addresses, DNS names, IP addresses, and so on.

Note also that it is only the DER-encoded value of the `NameConstraints` structure that should be passed to the constructor of the `TrustAnchor` class — not `Extension` object, or the encoding of the `OCTET STRING` that carries the extension value.

The PKIXParameters Class

The `java.security.cert.PKIXParameters` class implements the `java.security.cert.CertPathParameters` interface, which is a marker interface that also adds the requirement that any class implementing it should be clonable.

There are two ways of constructing a `PKIXParameters` object. The first is by passing a `Set` containing one or more `TrustAnchor` objects; the other is to pass a `java.security.KeyStore` containing the certificates associated with entities you want to trust. I will be discussing the `KeyStore` class in Chapter 8. So for the examples in this chapter, I will concentrate on the constructor taking the `Set` parameter. As you will see, the principles are the same in any case.

Having created a `PKIXParameters` object, you can add a number of optional parameters to the object via set or add methods. If you look at the JavaDoc for this class, you will see there are quite a few options, many that revolve around certificate policy — which could almost be a book in itself. Although there is a good deal of information on this in RFC 3280, you don't need to deal with it right now, as it will distract from understanding how the path validation mechanisms in Java actually work. For now I will concentrate on the basic methods that you need to get up and running.

PKIXParameters.addCertStore() and PKIXParameters.setCertStores()

The `addCertStore()` method allows you to add a `CertStore` to be used for path validation. As an alternative to building up an internal list of `CertStore` objects in the `PKIXParameters` object, you can also pass a `List` of `CertStore` objects using `setCertStores()`, which will be used instead. Note that if you use the `setCertStores()` method, the `List` you pass in will be copied to prevent further modification.

PKIXParameters.setDate()

The `setDate()` method takes a single `Date` and is used to set the time for which the path validation is taking place. If the parameter passed to `setDate()` is a `null` value, or `setDate()` is not called, the validation is assumed to be taking place in the present.

PKIXParameters.setTargetCertConstraints()

The `setTargetCertConstraints()` method takes a single `CertSelector` as a parameter and is used to provide the constrains that the end entity, or target, certificate in the path being validated is supposed to satisfy.

In a simple case, where you already believe you have a valid ordered certificate path, it is generally unnecessary to call this method as the default will allow any certificate to match. In the context of path validation, you would use this method if you want to restrict the range of end entity certificates you regard as acceptable.

PKIXParameters.setRevocationEnabled()

The `setRevocationEnabled()` method takes a single boolean parameter and sets the return value for `isRevocationEnabled()` to `true` or `false` accordingly. The `isRevocationEnabled()` method is used by the underlying implementation of the path validation algorithm to determine whether you want it to apply the standard revocation checking when path validation is carried out.

By default, the `is()` method returns `true`, and if you are using an implementation that offers PKIX validation and you have the necessary CRLs, there is no need to call `setRevocationEnabled()`. If, on the other hand, you have your own mechanism for dealing with certificate revocation, such as an OCSP implementation, you can use `setRevocationEnabled()` to turn off the default revocation checking and enable your own using a `PKIXCertPathChecker` object.

The CertPathValidator Class

The `java.security.cert.CertPathValidator` class is another JCA class whose implementation is provider-based and is constructed using the `getInstance()` factory pattern, rather than a direct constructor. Like the other provider-based classes, it follows the precedence rules outlined by the configuration files being used by the JVM. The class has a very simple interface, with two informational methods, `getAlgorithm()` and `getDefaultType()`, and a `validate()` method that is where the actual validation is performed.

CertPathValidator.getDefaultType()

The `getDefaultType()` method is a static method that returns the value of the `certpathvalidator` `.type` property, or `PKIX` if the property is not set. Like other security properties, if you want to set the value of the `certpathvalidator.type` property for the JVM, you can do so by setting it in the `java.security` file.

Using the `getDefaultType()` method for selecting the algorithm name to use for path validation allows your code to be reconfigured to work with different path validation algorithms by changing a JVM property.

CertPathValidator.getAlgorithm()

The `getAlgorithm()` method returns the name of the profile the validation algorithm is using. For the Internet profile described in RFC 3280, this method will return `PKIX`.

CertPathValidator.validate()

The `validate()` method takes two parameters: The first is the `CertPath` object representing the certificate path being validated, and the second is a `PKIXParameters` object that provides the trust anchors and other details that might be required during the process of path validation.

The return type of the `validate()` method is a `java.security.cert.CertPathValidatorResult`. It is another marker interface that introduces the `clone()` method. A given path validation implementation will return an implementation of the interface that will provide the validation information that is appropriate to the profile being used. For our purposes, as you are using the "PKIX" profile, the `validate()` method will return a `PKIXCertPathValidatorResult`.

The PKIXCertPathValidatorResult Class

The `java.security.cert.PKIXCertPathValidatorResult` class contains methods that allow you to get all the possible outputs of the PKIX certificate path validation algorithm. The major ones are the trust anchor that was used to validate the path you can retrieve using `getTrustAnchor()` and the public key of the certificate validated by the path you can retrieve using `getPublicKey()`. If you are dealing with certificates that have policy extensions, as outlined in RFC 3280, you can also get back the policy tree that resulted from validating the path using `getPolicyTree()`.

Try It Out	Validating a Certificate Path

You have enough information now to try validating a certificate path. Have a look at the following class:

```
package chapter7;

import java.math.BigInteger;
import java.security.KeyPair;
import java.security.cert.CertPath;
import java.security.cert.CertPathValidator;
import java.security.cert.CertPathValidatorException;
import java.security.cert.CertPathValidatorResult;
import java.security.cert.CertStore;
import java.security.cert.CertificateFactory;
```

```
import java.security.cert.CollectionCertStoreParameters;
import java.security.cert.PKIXParameters;
import java.security.cert.TrustAnchor;
import java.security.cert.X509CRL;
import java.security.cert.X509Certificate;
import java.util.*;

/**
 * Basic example of certificate path validation
 */
public class CertPathValidatorExample
{
    public static void main(String[] args) throws Exception
    {
        // create certificates and CRLs
        KeyPair         rootPair = Utils.generateRSAKeyPair();
        KeyPair         interPair = Utils.generateRSAKeyPair();
        KeyPair         endPair = Utils.generateRSAKeyPair();

        X509Certificate rootCert = Utils.generateRootCert(rootPair);
        X509Certificate interCert = Utils.generateIntermediateCert(
                        interPair.getPublic(), rootPair.getPrivate(), rootCert);
        X509Certificate endCert = Utils.generateEndEntityCert(
                        endPair.getPublic(), interPair.getPrivate(), interCert);

        BigInteger      revokedSerialNumber = BigInteger.valueOf(2);
        X509CRL         rootCRL = X509CRLExample.createCRL(
                        rootCert, rootPair.getPrivate(), revokedSerialNumber);
        X509CRL         interCRL = X509CRLExample.createCRL(
                        interCert, interPair.getPrivate(), revokedSerialNumber);

        // create CertStore to support validation
        List list = new ArrayList();

        list.add(rootCert);
        list.add(interCert);
        list.add(endCert);
        list.add(rootCRL);
        list.add(interCRL);

        CollectionCertStoreParameters params = new CollectionCertStoreParameters(
                                                list);
        CertStore                   store = CertStore.getInstance(
                                                "Collection", params, "BC");

        // create certificate path
        CertificateFactory fact = CertificateFactory.getInstance("X.509", "BC");
        List               certChain = new ArrayList();

        certChain.add(endCert);
        certChain.add(interCert);

        CertPath certPath = fact.generateCertPath(certChain);
        Set     trust = Collections.singleton(new TrustAnchor(rootCert, null));

        // perform validation
```

```
                CertPathValidator validator = CertPathValidator.getInstance("PKIX", "BC");
                PKIXParameters      param = new PKIXParameters(trust);

                param.addCertStore(store);
                param.setDate(new Date());

                try
                {
                    CertPathValidatorResult result = validator.validate(certPath, param);

                    System.out.println("certificate path validated");
                }
                catch (CertPathValidatorException e)
                {
                    System.out.println("validation failed on certificate number "
                                    + e.getIndex() + ", details: " + e.getMessage());
                }
            }
        }
```

Run the example, and if nothing has been left out, you will get the following output:

```
certificate path validated
```

How It Works

As you can see, the CertPathValidator class pretty well encapsulates the whole process of evaluating a certificate path. Most of the code in the example is related to setting up. There are a few things worth discussing, though.

Have a look at the creation of the CertStore passed in using the PKIXParameters object. As you can see, it contains all the certificates as well as the CRLs for those certificates used to sign others. This is required, as the CertPathValidator implementation uses the CertStore to look up any CRLs or certificates it might need during the process of validating the certificates making up the path. The CRLs are required, because by default, PKIXParameters.isRevocationEnabled() returns true so, consequently, expects to find a valid CRL for any certificate used to sign another certificate in the path, including the trust anchor.

Next, you generate a CertPath to validate using the CertificateFactory.generateCertPath() method. Notice the path does not include the trust anchor. Because of their special role, trust anchors are handled using the TrustAnchor class, and you create a Set of TrustAnchor objects containing the self-signed root certificate that validates the intermediate certificate in the path.

After creating the CertPath and TrustAnchor objects, you then create a CertPathValidator and a PKIXParameters object based around the Set of TrustAnchor objects. Then it is just a matter of adding the CertStore to the PKIXParameters, assigning a validation date and calling validator.validate() to validate the path. If all goes well, you see the "certificate path validated" message and you are done.

It is interesting to try prodding the CertPathValidator object to see how it behaves when you change parameters. For example, try commenting out the line

```
list.add(rootCRL);
```

and see what happens. Likewise, you could introduce some target constraints on the path by introducing the following lines after the code setting up the `param` object:

```
X509CertSelector selector = new X509CertSelector();

selector.setSubject(new X500Principal("CN=No Match"));
param.setTargetCertConstraints(selector);
```

Both cases should cause exceptions to be raised. It's important to think about this, as not all certificate paths you will encounter will be valid, and the only way you'll learn how to deal with this fact is to start experiencing it first-hand. This is one place where a bit of experimentation is a good thing.

If you never add any private critical extensions of your own, or you are content with using CRLs rather than some other revocation mechanism, the standard PKIX `CertPathValidator` implementation will probably do you quite well. On the other hand, if you want to do any of these things, you need some way of customizing the `CertPathValidator`. Otherwise, none of your paths will validate correctly.

If you need to customize a `CertPathValidator` implementation, you can use the `PKIXCertPathChecker` class, which you look at next.

The PKIXCertPathChecker Class

The `java.security.cert.PKIXCertPathChecker` class provides you with the ability to introduce your own forms of validation, or other processing, into a `CertPathValidator` implementation provided by a JCA services provider. `PKIXCertPathChecker` objects are passed to `CertPathValidator` implementations using calls to the `addCertPathChecker()` method or a call to the `setCertPathCheckers()` method on the `PKIXParameters` object.

There are a few reasons why you might want to do this. The organization you are working for might have added some critical extensions of its own to X.509 certificates being used internally, so validating a `CertPath` will involve dealing with these new extensions as well. Otherwise, the provider-based validation will fail, as it cannot recognize the extensions. Alternatively, the `CertPathValidator` you are relying on might expect to use CRLs, as the standard PKIX one does, and you want to use OCSP instead. Whatever the reason, if you need to customize an existing `CertPathValidator`, `PKIXCertPathChecker` is the class you need to use.

The `PKIXCertPathChecker` class is abstract and has four methods on it that subclasses are expected to implement before they can be used with the `CertPathValidator`. The methods are `init()`, `isForwardCheckingSupported()`, `getSupportedExtensions()`, and `check()`, and all implementations of `PKIXCertPathChecker` are expected to be clonable as well.

PKIXCertPathChecker.init()

The `init()` method takes a single `boolean` as a parameter and is used to initialize the state of the checker. The value passed in will be `true` if the checker is being initialized for forward checking, `false` otherwise. Which direction the checking goes in is at the discretion of the writer of the path validation implementation being used, but for the purposes of path validation, forward means that the certificates will be presented in order from the end entity certificate and progress toward the trust anchor.

If the value passed to init is false, the certificates will be presented in reverse direction from the trust anchor to the target.

PKIXCertPathChecker.isForwardCheckingSupported()

The `isForwardCheckingSupported()` should return `true` if the checker supports forward direction processing. All checkers must support reverse processing.

PKIXCertPathChecker.getSupportedExtensions()

The `getSupportedExtensions()` method returns an immutable `Set` of `String` objects representing the OIDs of the X.509 extensions that the checker implementation can handle. If the checker does not handle any specific extensions, `getSupportedExtensions()` should return `null`.

PKIXCertPathChecker.check()

The `check()` method takes two parameters. The first is a `Certificate` object representing the certificate to be checked. The second is a mutable `Set` containing the `String` objects representing the OIDs of the critical X.509 extensions that the `CertPathValidator` has not been able to resolve.

The `check()` method is where all the processing gets done. If the purpose of your check method is to perform some validation on the certificate passed in, you should throw a `CertPathValidatorException` if the certificate fails to pass your tests. If the checking is applied to one or more X.509 extensions, then you should remove the `String` OIDs from the `Set` that was passed in as the second parameter. Removing the OIDs will signal to the `CertPathValidator` that the extensions have been dealt with — the idea being that once the `CertPathValidator` has done its own processing and called all the `PKIXCertPathChecker` implementations, it has been given its internal reference to the `Set` should indicate the `Set` is empty.

Try It Out   Using a PKIXCertPathChecker

This following example combines the simple OCSP classes you looked at earlier with a `PKIXCertPathChecker` to do revocation checking using the `PKIXCertPathChecker`. As it's rather large, I've broken it up into two parts: The first is a class providing an extension of the `PKIXCertPathChecker` class, `PathChecker`, which interacts with the OCSP classes, and the second is just the main driver for it.

As I'm still essentially using the `CertPathValidator` for driving the process, most of the new code is in the `PathChecker` class, which appears here:

```
package chapter7;

import java.math.BigInteger;
import java.security.KeyPair;
import java.security.cert.CertPathValidatorException;
import java.security.cert.Certificate;
import java.security.cert.PKIXCertPathChecker;
import java.security.cert.X509Certificate;
import java.util.*;

class PathChecker
    extends PKIXCertPathChecker
{
    private KeyPair          responderPair;
    private X509Certificate  caCert;
    private BigInteger       revokedSerialNumber;

    public PathChecker(
```

```
            KeyPair          responderPair,
        X509Certificate caCert,
        BigInteger       revokedSerialNumber)
    {
        this.responderPair = responderPair;
        this.caCert = caCert;
        this.revokedSerialNumber = revokedSerialNumber;
    }

    public void init(boolean forwardChecking)
        throws CertPathValidatorException
    {
        // ignore
    }

    public boolean isForwardCheckingSupported()
    {
        return true;
    }

    public Set getSupportedExtensions()
    {
        return null;
    }

    public void check(Certificate cert, Collection extensions)
        throws CertPathValidatorException
    {
        X509Certificate x509Cert = (X509Certificate)cert;

        try
        {
            String message = OCSPResponderExample.getStatusMessage(
                        responderPair, caCert, revokedSerialNumber, x509Cert);

            if (message.endsWith("good"))
            {
                System.out.println(message);
            }
            else
            {
                throw new CertPathValidatorException(message);
            }
        }
        catch (Exception e)
        {
            throw new CertPathValidatorException(
                                    "exception verifying certificate: " + e, e);
        }
    }
}
```

You can see that the first three methods in the class are just to provide implementations for the abstract methods required by the parent class. In this case, because of the simple nature of what you are doing, the only real work is being done in the `check()` method, which is just using the method you defined in the OCSP responder Try It Out ("Generating an OCSP Response").

The main driver, on the other hand, should look quite familiar to you and is listed here:

```java
package chapter7;

import java.math.BigInteger;
import java.security.KeyPair;
import java.security.cert.*;
import java.util.*;

/**
 * Basic example of certificate path validation using a PKIXCertPathChecker
 */
public class CertPathValidatorWithCheckerExample
{
    public static void main(String[] args) throws Exception
    {
        // create certificates and CRLs
        KeyPair         rootPair = Utils.generateRSAKeyPair();
        KeyPair         interPair = Utils.generateRSAKeyPair();
        KeyPair         endPair = Utils.generateRSAKeyPair();

        X509Certificate rootCert = Utils.generateRootCert(rootPair);
        X509Certificate interCert = Utils.generateIntermediateCert(
                        interPair.getPublic(), rootPair.getPrivate(), rootCert);
        X509Certificate endCert = Utils.generateEndEntityCert(
                        endPair.getPublic(), interPair.getPrivate(), interCert);

        BigInteger      revokedSerialNumber = BigInteger.valueOf(2);

        // create CertStore to support validation
        List list = new ArrayList();

        list.add(rootCert);
        list.add(interCert);
        list.add(endCert);

        CollectionCertStoreParameters params = new CollectionCertStoreParameters(
                                                                        list);
        CertStore                     store = CertStore.getInstance(
                                                "Collection", params, "BC");

        // create certificate path
        CertificateFactory fact = CertificateFactory.getInstance("X.509", "BC");
        List               certChain = new ArrayList();

        certChain.add(endCert);
        certChain.add(interCert);

        CertPath certPath = fact.generateCertPath(certChain);
        Set      trust = Collections.singleton(new TrustAnchor(rootCert, null));

        // perform validation
```

```
CertPathValidator validator = CertPathValidator.getInstance("PKIX", "BC");
PKIXParameters     param = new PKIXParameters(trust);

param.addCertPathChecker(new PathChecker(
                              rootPair, rootCert, revokedSerialNumber));
param.setRevocationEnabled(false);
param.addCertStore(store);
param.setDate(new Date());

try
{
    CertPathValidatorResult result = validator.validate(certPath, param);

    System.out.println("certificate path validated");
}
catch (CertPathValidatorException e)
{
    System.out.println("validation failed on certificate number "
                         + e.getIndex() + ", details: " + e.getMessage());
}
    }
}
```

As you can see there are a couple of differences from previous uses of the `CertPathValidator` in this case. First, because you are relying on the `PathChecker` to do the revocation checking for you, there are no CRLs. Second, you have to create the `PathChecker` and make it available to the `CertPathValidator` by calling the `PKIXParameters.addCertPathChecker()` method on the `param` object.

Run the example and you should see the following output:

```
certificate number 1 status: good
certificate number 1 status: good
certificate path validated
```

indicating that the two certificates forming the path back to the trust anchor are not on the OCSP revocation list. Again, you might want to change `revokedSerialNumber` to be `BigInteger.valueOf(1)` rather than `BigInteger.valueOf(2)` and see what happens when the certificates are revoked.

How It Works

The `PathChecker` object is able to do its job, as the `CertPathValidator` calls it for each certificate it has to validate in the path. Because the `check()` method on the `PKIXCertPathValidator` class is defined as throwing a `CertPathValidatorException`, the `PathChecker` object is able to interrupt the validation process as soon as it finds something wrong.

As you can see, the definition of the `PathChecker` object is fairly straightforward. Because all it is doing is revocation checking, it is able to override all the abstracts methods other than the `check()` method with methods that just return default values or do nothing. In the case of the `check()` method, the return value of the `OCSPResponderExample.getStatusMessage()` is examined and then, providing the status ends with the message "good," a trace message is printed. Otherwise, a `CertPathValidatorException` is thrown, indicating that a problem was discovered with the passed in certificate.

The only change required to introduce the use of the `PathChecker` object into the `CertPathValidator` is the calling of `param.addCertPathChecker()` to enable its use. The line

```
param.setRevocationEnabled(false);
```

is used to tell the `CertPathValidator` implementation not to expect to use CRLs, as some other revocation mechanism has been enabled — in this case the one performed by the `PathChecker` object.

Now you have one thing left to cover in this chapter: how to construct a valid certificate path from a random collection of X.509 certificates and CRLs.

Building a Valid Path from a CertStore

Being able to do validation is all very well, but as you will see in coming chapters, often certificate chains do not arrive well ordered and a collection of certificates and CRLs that arrive with a particular message may even include certificates and CRLs that are not relevant to the particular certificate you are trying to verify. Fortunately, the JCA includes a certificate path builder that works in conjunction with the `CertPathValidator` to allow you to easily create the certificate path that gets you from the root certificate you trust to the end entity certificate you are trying to validate. The class for doing this is the `CertPathBuilder` that returns an object implementing a `CertPathBuilderResult`, an interface that provides a single method, `getCertPath()`, which allows you to retrieve the constructed `CertPath` object.

The CertPathBuilder Class

Objects of the `java.security.cert.CertPathBuilder` class are created using the same `getInstance()` factory pattern that is followed with the other JCA classes that have underlying implementations implemented by providers. It has a single `build()` method that will construct a validated `CertPath` from the parameter information it is provided. The `build()` method takes a class implementing the `java.security.cert.CertPathParameters` interface and returns a `java.security.cert.CertPathBuilderResult`.

Like most of the parameter classes involved in certificate paths, the `CertPathParameters` interface just forces the introduction of the `clone()` method in implementations of it. The real functionality, and the methods that support it, are provided in classes that implement the interface. From the point of view of this chapter, the most important one of these is the one supplied with the JCA, the `PKIXBuilderParameters` class.

The PKIXBuilderParameters Class

The `java.security.cert.PKIXBuilderParameters` is an extension of the `PKIXParameters` class you looked at earlier. It adds one extra `set()` method, `setMaxPathLength()`, which takes a single `int` as a parameter and limits the number of non-self-issued certificates that can be put into a path. The main addition the `PKIXBuilderParameters` class makes to the `PKIXParameters` class it extends is in the manner of its construction. In addition to the trust anchors required to construct the `PKIXParameters`, the `PKIXBuilderParameters` also takes a `CertSelector` specifying the target constraints for the end entity certificate the path is to be built to.

Using the extra information the target constraints provide, the CertPathBuilder then tries to construct a valid path leading from the end entity certificate to one of the trust anchors that the PKIXBuilderParameters indicates the caller of the build() method is prepared to trust.

Try It Out   Building a Certificate Path Using CertPathBuilder

Here is an example of a simple path build done using the certificates that are provided by the Utils class as source material. Have a look at it and see what it does.

```java
package chapter7;

import java.math.BigInteger;
import java.security.KeyPair;
import java.security.cert.CertPath;
import java.security.cert.CertPathBuilder;
import java.security.cert.CertStore;
import java.security.cert.CollectionCertStoreParameters;
import java.security.cert.PKIXBuilderParameters;
import java.security.cert.PKIXCertPathBuilderResult;
import java.security.cert.TrustAnchor;
import java.security.cert.X509CRL;
import java.security.cert.X509CertSelector;
import java.security.cert.X509Certificate;
import java.util.*;

/**
 * Basic example of the use of CertPathBuilder.
 */
public class CertPathBuilderExample
{
    public static void main(String[] args) throws Exception
    {
        // create certificates and CRLs
        KeyPair         rootPair = Utils.generateRSAKeyPair();
        KeyPair         interPair = Utils.generateRSAKeyPair();
        KeyPair         endPair = Utils.generateRSAKeyPair();

        X509Certificate rootCert = Utils.generateRootCert(rootPair);
        X509Certificate interCert = Utils.generateIntermediateCert(
                        interPair.getPublic(), rootPair.getPrivate(), rootCert);
        X509Certificate endCert = Utils.generateEndEntityCert(
                        endPair.getPublic(), interPair.getPrivate(), interCert);

        BigInteger      revokedSerialNumber = BigInteger.valueOf(2);
        X509CRL         rootCRL = X509CRLExample.createCRL(
                            rootCert, rootPair.getPrivate(), revokedSerialNumber);
        X509CRL         interCRL = X509CRLExample.createCRL(
                            interCert, interPair.getPrivate(), revokedSerialNumber);

        // create CertStore to support path building
        List list = new ArrayList();

        list.add(rootCert);
        list.add(interCert);
```

```
                    list.add(endCert);
                    list.add(rootCRL);
                    list.add(interCRL);

                    CollectionCertStoreParameters params = new CollectionCertStoreParameters(
                                                                              list);
                    CertStore                   store = CertStore.getInstance(
                                                            "Collection", params, "BC");
```

```
            // build the path
            CertPathBuilder  builder = CertPathBuilder.getInstance("PKIX", "BC");
            X509CertSelector endConstraints = new X509CertSelector();

            endConstraints.setSerialNumber(endCert.getSerialNumber());
            endConstraints.setIssuer(endCert.getIssuerX500Principal().getEncoded());

            PKIXBuilderParameters buildParams = new PKIXBuilderParameters(
               Collections.singleton(new TrustAnchor(rootCert, null)), endConstraints);

            buildParams.addCertStore(store);
            buildParams.setDate(new Date());

            PKIXCertPathBuilderResult result =
                              (PKIXCertPathBuilderResult)builder.build(buildParams);
            CertPath                path = result.getCertPath();

            Iterator it = path.getCertificates().iterator();
            while (it.hasNext())
            {
                System.out.println(
                        ((X509Certificate)it.next()).getSubjectX500Principal());
            }

            System.out.println(
                    result.getTrustAnchor().getTrustedCert().getSubjectX500Principal());
        }
    }
```

Try running the example and you should see the following output:

```
CN=Test End Certificate
CN=Test Intermediate Certificate
CN=Test CA Certificate
```

showing that you have created a path from the certificate with the subject DN "CN=Test End Certificate" going back to the trust anchor with the subject DN "CN=Test CA Certificate".

How It Works

As you can see, the setup for this example is very similar to the previous ones; the real differences arise in the setting up of the PKIXBuilderParameters class and when you go to make use of the CertPathBuilder class.

Looking at the setup of the `PKIXBuilderParameters` class, you can see it goes through two stages. The first is where you specify the target constraints for the end entity certificate you are looking for. To do this, you uniquely specify the end entity certificate by using its serial number and issuer:

```
X509CertSelector endConstraints = new X509CertSelector();

endConstraints.setSerialNumber(endCert.getSerialNumber());
endConstraints.setIssuer(endCert.getIssuerX500Principal().getEncoded());
```

Having set up the constraints, you then use them and the `Set` of `TrustAnchor` objects to create a `PKIXBuilderParameters` object `buildParams`. After that it is a matter of adding the `CertStore` providing the source of certificates and CRLs to `buildParams` and letting the `CertPathBuilder` do its job.

Note that the path returned by `result.getCertPath()` does not contain the trust anchor. It is present in the `PKIXCertPathBuilderResult` object `result`, but because of its special role is only accessible using the `result.getTrustAnchor()` method.

This brings you to the end of the discussion of revocation and path validation as it applies to X.509 certificates.

Summary

In this chapter, you looked at the fundamentals of dealing with the validation and verification of X.509 certificates using the PKIX profile outlined in RFC 3280. You have seen two alternative mechanisms for checking whether the issuers have revoked their certificates, and you have also seen the JCA classes for supporting certificate path validation and certificate path building.

Over the course of this chapter, you have learned the following:

❑   What certificate revocation lists (CRLs) are and how they are represented in the JCA

❑   How to create, read, and process X.509 CRLs, as well as what underlying structures make them up

❑   How to use a `CertStore` to contain CRLs and use an `X509CRLSelector` to retrieve them

❑   What Online Certificate Status Protocol (OCSP) is and how it differs from regular CRLs

❑   How to implement OCSP clients and responders using the Bouncy Castle APIs

❑   What certificate path validation is and how it is done using the `CertPathValidator` class

❑   How to customize an existing PKIX path validation implementation using the `PKIXCertPathValidator` class

Finally, you also learned how to take a random collection of certificates and CRLs in a `CertStore` and create a certificate path that is valid for an end entity certificate that you need to use.

At this stage, you are able to build private keys and certificate chains for validating them. You have also seen in earlier chapters how to generate symmetric keys as well as how to encrypt private keys using them. As you might imagine, in some situations these all represent objects you might want to store somewhere safely for later retrieval or, possibly, import into another application. In the next chapter, you look at how this problem is solved using the `KeyStore` class, as well as learn which types of `KeyStore` implementations are suited to being used with particular applications and how they can be exported or imported as appropriate.

Exercises

1. In an application where you are expecting a large number of unexpired revoked certificates to be present at any one time, as well as a large number of clients, what is the most appropriate certificate checking mechanism to deploy on the application clients — regular CRLs or OCSP?

2. If you have to distribute CRLs in the case detailed in Exercise 1, what is one way you can reduce the cost of distributing updates? What is required to support this?

3. How can you introduce validation of locally defined critical extensions into a PKIX `CertPathValidator` without having to change the underlying `CertPathValidator` provider?

4. If you are using a PKIX `CertPathBuilder` to construct a certificate path for a given target certificate, what is the most straightforward way to construct the target constraints required for the path builder parameters?

Key and Certificate Management Using Keystores

At this point you should be fairly comfortable with what is required to create keys and certificates, but you are probably also wondering what you are supposed to do if you need them to be around for more than the duration of an example program. How can you store a private key safely and maintain the relationship it has with its associated certificates? What do you do if you need to pass a private key onto someone else? Is there a way of persisting a secret key for longer-term use?

This chapter looks at the keystore facilities offered in Java through the KeyStore class and some of the underlying variations in how KeyStore objects are implemented.

By the end of this chapter you should

❑   Understand what basic types of keystore are available and how they differ

❑   Have an understanding of PKCS #12 file structure for storing private credentials

❑   Know how to create PKCS #12 files using the KeyStore API and what variations there are between implementations

❑   Be familiar with the JVM's own ideas about trust anchors

Finally, you will also understand how to use the keytool command and integrate it with the work I covered in earlier chapters, as well as be aware of some of the other JVM features that make use of keystores.

Getting Started

Primarily, Java KeyStore objects are used to store private keys and their associated certificates. So, for the purposes of the examples of this chapter, you need some extra functionality in the Utils class to support this.

Fortunately, adding the extra functionality just means building on the certificate functionality you added in the last chapter and taking advantage of another Java class related to X500Principal — the X500PrivateCredential class.

The javax.security.auth.x500.X500PrivateCredential is a simple value object that can be used to contain a private key, its associated X.509 certificate, and an optional alias. It also has a destroy() method on it, which allows the credential to be destroyed when it is no longer required. For the purposes of giving you some instant key/certificate pairs, X500PrivateCredential will do nicely.

Here is the Utils class for the chapter8 package:

```java
package chapter8;

import java.security.KeyPair;
import java.security.PrivateKey;
import java.security.cert.X509Certificate;

import javax.security.auth.x500.X500PrivateCredential;

/**
 * Chapter 8 Utils
 */
public class Utils extends chapter7.Utils
{
    public static String ROOT_ALIAS = "root";
    public static String INTERMEDIATE_ALIAS = "intermediate";
    public static String END_ENTITY_ALIAS = "end";

    /**
     * Generate a X500PrivateCredential for the root entity.
     */
    public static X500PrivateCredential createRootCredential()
        throws Exception
    {
        KeyPair         rootPair = generateRSAKeyPair();
        X509Certificate rootCert = generateRootCert(rootPair);

        return new X500PrivateCredential(
                            rootCert, rootPair.getPrivate(), ROOT_ALIAS);
    }

    /**
     * Generate a X500PrivateCredential for the intermediate entity.
     */
    public static X500PrivateCredential createIntermediateCredential(
        PrivateKey      caKey,
        X509Certificate caCert)
        throws Exception
    {
        KeyPair         interPair = generateRSAKeyPair();
        X509Certificate interCert = generateIntermediateCert(
                                        interPair.getPublic(), caKey, caCert);

        return new X500PrivateCredential(
```

```
                                interCert, interPair.getPrivate(), INTERMEDIATE_ALIAS);
    }

    /**
     * Generate a X500PrivateCredential for the end entity.
     */
    public static X500PrivateCredential createEndEntityCredential(
        PrivateKey      caKey,
        X509Certificate caCert)
        throws Exception
    {

        KeyPair         endPair = generateRSAKeyPair();
        X509Certificate endCert = generateEndEntityCert(
                                        endPair.getPublic(), caKey, caCert);

        return new X500PrivateCredential(
                            endCert, endPair.getPrivate(), END_ENTITY_ALIAS);
    }
}
```

Type this in, compile it, and you are ready to proceed.

The KeyStore Class

The `java.security.KeyStore` class was introduced in JDK 1.2. Like other JCA classes, it follows the `getInstance()` factory pattern with the type of the `KeyStore` being given as the first argument and a provider being specified if appropriate. As usual, the `KeyStore.getInstance()` method obeys the precedence rules appropriate to the configuration of the Java runtime you are using. If the requested type is not available, the call to `getInstance()` will throw a `java.security.KeyStore` exception. JDK 1.5 has also seen some changes to the `KeyStore` class in that it is now more flexible than before in how it can be used, and some nested classes have been added to the class to make this possible.

The KeyStore API supports the persisting of three types of entries:

❑   **Private keys.** Private keys can be saved with their associated certificate chains. In most cases they can also be individually password protected.

❑   **Symmetric keys.** Although the API now supports this explicitly some `KeyStore` types do not. Where the saving of symmetric keys does work they can be individually password protected.

❑   **Trusted certificates.** These are the certificates used to create `TrustAnchor` objects when you need them. Ordinarily you will have obtained them from a third party and verified their authenticity through channels other than those you use for validating certificates that exist within certificate paths.

Entries are stored under a given *alias* in the `KeyStore` object, and the alias, together with a password if required, is used to retrieve the entry that was saved. The API also allows you to find out some of the characteristics of the individual entries, as well as supporting the retrieval of some basic properties about the `KeyStore` object itself, such as its size and creation date.

Before you look at the API presented by the KeyStore class, it is worth discussing what types of keystore are available first. As you will see, although they follow the same basic API, there are some less than subtle differences in what they do, even when the type has the same name.

Keystore Types

The range of the keystore types available is dependent on the providers you have installed. The Sun JCA and JCE both ship with some standard ones; other providers will contain variations on these and perhaps some extra. Variations do exist on the nonproprietary formats such as PKCS12, so some care needs to be exercised if you are provider swapping and you are using a more open format.

In addition to the list of available installed types, every JVM has a notion of the default type for a keystore, which is set by the "keystore.type" property in the java.security file. This can be retrieved using the static method KeyStore.getDefaultType() and by default, if the property is not set, the method will return "jks". With the Bouncy Castle provider installed, you have five basic keystore types to choose from, with some variations.

Let's have a look at the standard types that ship with the JDK first.

Standard JDK Keystore Types

There are three basic keystore types that ship with the JDK, which also have some minor variations:

❑   JCEKS — This is a Sun format type that was introduced with the JCE. In addition to being able to contain private keys and certificates, it can also contain symmetric keys. It differs from the JKS in that the encryption used to protect private keys is based on Triple-DES, which is much stronger than the algorithm used in the JKS. Aliases are case-insensitive.

❑   JKS — This is the original Sun format keystore type. It will only contain private keys and certificates, and aliases are case-insensitive. There is also a variation on it, CaseExactJKS, which recognizes the aliases with the same spelling but different case.

❑   PKCS12 — A version of the format defined in RSA Security's PKCS #12. Up till JDK 1.5 this type was read-only, but you can now write them as well. Aliases are case-insensitive. The store cannot be used to store trusted certificates.

As you can see from the list, one of these, PKCS12, is also an open format. I'll go through the Bouncy Castle keystore types now. Note that PKCS12 is also listed there — and it is not quite the same.

Bouncy Castle Keystore Types

The Bouncy Castle provider offers three types of keystore:

❑   BKS — This store encrypts keys using Triple-DES but otherwise creates the store with the same level of security as the JKS store. Aliases are case-sensitive and the store can handle symmetric keys as well as private keys and certificates.

❑   UBER — This store encrypts keys using Triple-DES and then encrypts the store using the Twofish algorithm. This offers a higher level of security than the BKS format, but it does mean it will not work with some tools, such as the keytool. Aliases are case-sensitive and the store can handle all the types the BKS store can handle.

❑ PKCS12 — Another version of the format defined in PKCS #12. The store is readable and writable, with case-sensitive naming. It can also be used to store trusted certificates. The type is also aliased, because BCPKCS12 and PKCS-12DEF. PKCS-12DEF uses the Sun certificate factory for creating X.509 certificates, rather than the Bouncy Castle one. Aliases are case-sensitive, and individual key passwords are ignored, but keys and certificates are encrypted using the password used to save the store.

As you can see, the PKCS #12 implementation is different. Several other providers also have implementations of PKCS #12, which again differ, and then there are still more issues about importing them into other applications. At the moment I want to discuss the KeyStore API, so I will do that next, but I will discuss PKCS #12 issues later on in the chapter. For now just remember they exist.

The Basic KeyStore API

As mentioned earlier, the KeyStore API changed with the introduction of JDK 1.5. First up I will start with the API as it stood pre–JDK 1.5 — the two APIs overlap and the JDK 1.5 changes can be considered to be an extension of the original KeyStore API. There are still a lot of organizations using earlier JVMs than 1.5, so breaking the discussion of the API into two parts makes sense as well. It is likely that you will come across code written for the earlier one, or even a JVM where the 1.5 extensions cannot be used. So the list that follows should work for any JVM from JDK 1.2.

KeyStore.aliases()

The `aliases()` method returns a `java.util.Enumeration` of `String` objects representing the alias names present in the `KeyStore`. The method will throw a `KeyStoreException` if the `KeyStore` object has not been initialized.

KeyStore.containsAlias()

The boolean `containsAlias()` method returns `true` if the passed-in `String` represents an alias name present in the store, `false` otherwise. Note there are also methods called `isKeyEntry()` and `isCertificateEntry()`. They allow you to tell if a given alias represents a key or a certificate. The method will throw a `KeyStoreException` if the `KeyStore` object has not been initialized.

KeyStore.deleteEntry()

The `deleteEntry()` method deletes the entry with the alias name represented by the passed-in `String` from the contents of the store. The method will throw a `KeyStoreException` if the `KeyStore` object has not been initialized, or if the entry cannot be removed.

KeyStore.getCertificate()

The `getCertificate()` method takes a `String` alias name as an argument and returns the certificate associated with that alias. The certificate can be either a trusted certificate, or if the alias is actually the alias for a private key, it will return the certificate containing the public key associated with that private key. If the entry does not exist, the method returns `null`. The method will throw a `KeyStoreException` if the `KeyStore` object has not been initialized.

KeyStore.getCertificateAlias()

The `getCertificateAlias()` method takes a `java.security.cert.Certificate` as an argument and returns a `String` representing the alias name of the first entry found in the store that contains the passed-in certificate. Note that the alias name may be for a key entry if the certificate is for a private key that is present in the store. Otherwise, it will be for a trusted certificate entry. If no suitable entry exists, the method returns `null`. The method will throw a `KeyStoreException` if the `KeyStore` object has not been initialized.

KeyStore.getCertificateChain()

The `getCertificateChain()` method returns an array of `java.security.cert.Certificate` objects representing the certificate chain of the private key entry associated with the passed-in `String` alias name. The chain is ordered with the private key associated certificate first and the root authority certificate last. The method will throw a `KeyStoreException` if the `KeyStore` object has not been initialized.

KeyStore.getCreationDate()

The `getCreationDate()` method takes a single `String` representing an alias name as an argument and returns the creation date of the alias if it is available. Some formats such as PKCS12 may not carry this information inside them. If that is the case, `getCreationDate()` will usually just return the current time. The method will throw a `KeyStoreException` if the `KeyStore` object has not been initialized.

KeyStore.getKey()

The `getKey()` method takes a `String` representing an alias name and a `char` array representing a password, returning the `java.security.Key` object that is associated with that alias name. If the alias does not exist, or does not represent a key, then the method returns `null`. The method can throw one of three exceptions found in the `java.security` package. If the key cannot be recovered, say, because the password is wrong, the method throws an `UnrecoverableKeyException`. If the store has not been initialized, the method throws a `KeyStoreException`, and if the algorithm required to recover the key is not available, the method throws a `NoSuchAlgorithm` exception.

KeyStore.getType()

The `getType()` method simply returns the string representing the format type of the `KeyStore` object.

KeyStore.isCertificateEntry()

The `isCertificateEntry()` method returns `true` if the passed-in `String` represents an alias name associated with a trusted certificate, `false` otherwise. The method will throw a `KeyStoreException` if the `KeyStore` object has not been initialized.

KeyStore.isKeyEntry()

The `isKeyEntry()` method returns `true` if the passed in `String` represents an alias name associated with a key, `false` otherwise. The method will throw a `KeyStoreException` if the `KeyStore` object has not been initialized.

KeyStore.load()

The early version of the `load()` method takes an `java.io.InputStream` and an array of `char` as parameters and reads in the keystore contained in the `InputStream` using the password to check the integrity of the store. If no password is given, then the integrity of the store is not checked.

You must do a `load()` to initialize a `KeyStore` object. If you are creating one afresh, you can pass `null` as both the `InputStream` and password parameters as follows:

```
keyStore.load(null, null);
```

Note that in some cases, such as the UBER keystore type and some versions of PKCS #12, the password is actually used as more than just a means of doing an integrity check. It is also used as an encryption key, and although this was not, strictly speaking, the intention of the KeyStore API designers, it was most definitely the intention of the people implementing the keystore types that do it. For the most part you will not notice this difference, but some tools are written on the basis that a keystore can always be loaded without giving a password, and it will be fairly obvious that keystore types that encrypt themselves fully on writing will not work with tools that make this assumption. So, this is something to watch out for, both when you are writing your own tools and when you are using other people's.

A second load() method was added in JDK 1.5. You will look at that a bit later when you look at the KeyStore.LoadStoreParameter class.

KeyStore.setCertificateEntry()

The setCertificateEntry() method takes a string and a java.security.cert.Certificate as arguments and adds a trusted certificate entry for the passed-in certificate using the alias name represented by the String. If the KeyStore object has not been initialized, or the given alias already exists but does not represent a trusted certificate, or something else fails, the method will throw a KeyStoreException.

KeyStore.setKeyEntry()

There are two versions of the setKeyEntry() method. The first argument in both cases is a String representing an alias name, and if the alias name already exists, it will be overwritten by the new key entry. Both methods will throw a KeyStoreException if the KeyStore has not been initialized or in the event of some other failure.

The first version takes an additional three arguments to the alias name: a java.security.Key, a char array, and a java.security.cert.Certificate array, representing the key object to be saved; the password to be used for protecting the key; and the certificate chain for the key if there is one.

The second version allows you to pass in an already encrypted key. It takes the alias name and an extra two arguments: a byte array representing the encrypted key and an array of Certificate representing the certificate chain if there is one available. You might find yourself using this version if you are using a machine that has a hardware cryptography adapter in it for storing private keys, or you have just received a key from someone who is using one. What the byte array should contain is largely up to the provider you are working with, but in the case of private keys, it will normally be the DER encoding of an EncryptedPrivateKeyInfo object.

KeyStore.size()

The size() method returns the number of entries in the KeyStore object. The method will throw a KeyStoreException if the KeyStore object has not been initialized.

KeyStore.store()

As with the load() method there are now two versions of the store() method — the second one being added in JDK 1.5. You will have a look at the second one later when you read about the KeyStore.LoadStoreParameter class, but the original version takes two parameters, an OutputStream, which is the stream the KeyStore is to write to, and an array of char representing a password to protect the encoded store.

The same footnote applies to `store()` as concerns `load()`. Although the word "protect" in this context implies that the password is used to generate an integrity check, in some cases, the password is also used as the source of an encryption key. You shouldn't ever notice the difference in this case. It is really only loading where this becomes an issue. However, it is important to keep this issue in mind and be aware of it.

This covers all the APIs you need to get up and running with a `KeyStore`. It is time to look at another example.

Try It Out   Using a JKS Keystore

This example shows the basic use of a keystore of the JKS type. Because it is the JKS type, it can store only private keys and trusted certificates. Therefore, the example demonstrates storing one of each. Have a look at what it does and try running it.

```
package chapter8;

import java.io.ByteArrayInputStream;
import java.io.ByteArrayOutputStream;
import java.security.KeyStore;
import java.security.cert.Certificate;
import java.util.Enumeration;

import javax.security.auth.x500.X500PrivateCredential;

/**
 * Example of basic use of KeyStore.
 */
public class JKSStoreExample
{
    public static char[] keyPassword = "keyPassword".toCharArray();

    public static KeyStore createKeyStore() throws Exception
    {
        KeyStore store = KeyStore.getInstance("JKS");

        // initialize
        store.load(null, null);

        X500PrivateCredential rootCredential = Utils.createRootCredential();
        X500PrivateCredential interCredential = Utils.createIntermediateCredential(
                rootCredential.getPrivateKey(), rootCredential.getCertificate());
        X500PrivateCredential endCredential = Utils.createEndEntityCredential(
                interCredential.getPrivateKey(), interCredential.getCertificate());

        Certificate[]        chain = new Certificate[3];

        chain[0] = endCredential.getCertificate();
        chain[1] = interCredential.getCertificate();
        chain[2] = rootCredential.getCertificate();

        // set the entries
        store.setCertificateEntry(
```

```
                                rootCredential.getAlias(), rootCredential.getCertificate());
            store.setKeyEntry(
                            endCredential.getAlias(), endCredential.getPrivateKey(),
                            keyPassword, chain);

            return store;
    }

    public static void main(String[] args) throws Exception
    {
        KeyStore store = createKeyStore();
        char[]    password = "storePassword".toCharArray();

        ByteArrayOutputStream bOut = new ByteArrayOutputStream();

        // save the store
        store.store(bOut, password);

        // reload from scratch
        store = KeyStore.getInstance("JKS");

        store.load(new ByteArrayInputStream(bOut.toByteArray()), password);

        Enumeration en = store.aliases();
        while (en.hasMoreElements())
        {
            String alias = (String)en.nextElement();
            System.out.println("found " + alias
                        + ", isCertificate? " + store.isCertificateEntry(alias));
        }
    }
}
```

Running the example should produce the following output:

```
found root, isCertificate? true
found end, isCertificate? false
```

listing the two entries that have been added to the `KeyStore` object and printing `"isCertificate? true"` if the entry represents a trusted certificate.

How It Works

The example is divided up into two steps. The first is the keystore creation in the `createKeyStore()` method; the second is in the main driver where the keystore is reloaded and its contents listed.

Looking at the `createKeyStore()` method, note that `KeyStore.getInstance()` is called to create an uninitialized `KeyStore` object, and then the line

```
        store.load(null, null);
```

is invoked to initialized the object. This line is important; if it is missing, you will get a `KeyStoreException` when the entries are added further down.

After the creation of the credentials for the two parties required to validate the end entity certificate and the creation of the end entity credentials, a certificate chain is built up in an array with the end entity first. The root certificate is then saved as a trusted certificate entry, and the private key for the end entity and its associated certificate chain are saved as well.

The `KeyStore` object is then returned to the main driver, where it is written out to an `OutputStream` and then reloaded from an `InputStream`, and `KeyStore.aliases()` is invoked so the example can list the aliases present in the `KeyStore` object.

An interesting point to note about the reloading: You can replace the line where the keystore is reloaded:

```
store.load(new ByteArrayInputStream(bOut.toByteArray()), password);
```

with this instead:

```
store.load(new ByteArrayInputStream(bOut.toByteArray()), null);
```

and the program will still work. The reason, as mentioned earlier, is that for most keystore types, not specifying the password is equivalent to saying you do not want to do an integrity check, and the JKS keystore type is one of those. Consequently, the call to `store.load()` with a null is just saying "load up the keystore but don't bother verifying the data has not been tampered with." This isn't something I'm trying to encourage, but it is an aspect of keystore behavior that you need to be aware of; otherwise, sometimes weird things will appear to happen.

This more or less describes the world as it was prior to JDK 1.5. Now it is time for you to look at some of the recent changes.

KeyStore Nested Classes and Interfaces

JDK 1.5 saw the introduction of a number of nested classes and interfaces to the `KeyStore` class. They can be divided into four groups. The first group is represented by the classes implementing the interface `KeyStore.Entry`, the second the classes implementing the interface `KeyStore.ProtectionParameter`, and the last two are groups with only one member made up of the `KeyStore.Builder` class and the `KeyStore.LoadStoreParameter` interface, respectively.

The most immediately useful of these is the classes implementing the `KeyStore.Entry`. They are also used in conjunction with the classes that implement `KeyStore.ProtectionParameter`, so let's look at these two interfaces and their implementing objects first.

The KeyStore.ProtectionParameter Interface

The `KeyStore.ProtectionParameter` interface is a marker interface for parameters that are used to provide information used to protect keystore entries. Objects implementing the class can carry passwords or other authorizing information that can be used as source material for integrity checks and encryption. The `KeyStore` class includes two nested classes that implement the `KeyStore.ProtectionParameter` interface: `KeyStore.CallbackHandlerProtection` and `KeyStore.PasswordProtection`.

KeyStore.CallbackHandlerProtection

The `KeyStore.CallbackHandlerProtection` class is a value object that's constructed with a `javax.security.auth.callback.CallbackHandler` object. It has a single method on it — `getCallbackHandler()`. You can use this method to retrieve the instance of `CallbackHandler` the object was constructed with.

`CallbackHandler` is actually an interface with a single method on it — `handle()`, which takes an array of `Callback` objects. `Callback` is also an interface defined in `javax.security.auth.callback`, and if you have a look at the JavaDoc for it, you will see there are a large number of security-related classes that implement `Callback` in the same package for helping deal with identity, passwords, and the like. This protection mode is relatively new, though, so at this writing, few keystore types appear to support it, but you can probably expect that to change.

KeyStore.PasswordProtection

The `KeyStore.PasswordProtection` class is a value object with a single constructor that takes an array of `char` representing the password. It has a `getPassword()` method on it that returns a reference to the password `char` array the object contains and a `destroy()` method on it to erase the password.

Note the password passed to the constructor of the object may be `null`. If the password has been destroyed through a call to the `destroy()` method, a call to `getPassword()` will throw an `IllegalStateException`. Because this protection mode is just a replacement for the original use of the password in the older methods on the KeyStore API, it is well supported. You will look at its use in the example later.

The KeyStore.Entry Interface

The `KeyStore.Entry` interface is a marker interface for keystore entry objects that can be utilized using three methods that were added to the KeyStore API in JDK 1.5: `KeyStore.getEntry()`, `KeyStore.setEntry()`, and `KeyStore.entryInstanceOf()`. Three nested classes were also added to the `KeyStore` class that implement `KeyStore.Entry`. The class names are `KeyStore.PrivateKeyEntry`, `KeyStore.SecretKeyEntry`, and `KeyStore.TrustedCertificateEntry`. The chapter covers these after covering the new methods.

KeyStore.getEntry()

The `getEntry()` method takes two arguments: a `String` representing the alias name for the entry and an optional protection parameter object implementing `KeyStore.ProtectionParameter`. It returns an object implementing `KeyStore.Entry` if the given alias exists and the protection parameter is valid. The method will throw a `NullPointerException` if the alias name is `null`, an `UnrecoverableEntryException` if the passed in `KeyStore.ProtectionParameter` object is invalid, a `NoSuchAlgorithmException` if the algorithm required to recover the entry cannot be found, and a `KeyStoreException` if the `KeyStore` object is not initialized.

KeyStore.setEntry()

The `setEntry()` method takes three arguments: a `String` representing the alias name for the entry, an entry object implementing `KeyStore.Entry`, and an optional object implementing `KeyStore.ProtectionParameter`. The method will throw a `NullPointerException` if either the alias name or the entry object is `null` and a `KeyStoreException` if the `KeyStore` object is not initialized.

KeyStore.entryInstanceOf( )

The boolean `entryInstanceOf()` method takes a `String` representing an alias name and a `Class` object representing a class or interface that is an extension of `KeyStore.Entry`. If the alias exists and its entry can be cast to the specified type, the method returns `true`; otherwise, it returns `false`. The method will throw a `NullPointerException` if either the alias name or the type object is `null`, and a `KeyStoreException` if the `KeyStore` object is not initialized.

KeyStore.PrivateKeyEntry

The `KeyStore.PrivateKeyEntry` class enables the creation of value objects that take a `java.security.PrivateKey` object and an array of `java.security.cert.Certificate` objects representing the private key and the associated certificate chain of the entry you want to create. It has three methods: `getPrivateKey()` returns the private key the entry was constructed with, `getCertificateChain()` returns a copy of the certificate chain, and `getCertificate()` returns the certificate at position zero in the chain, which should be the certificate containing the public key for the private key in the entry. An interesting feature of the `getCertificateChain()` method is that it will return the array to suit the subclass of `Certificate` it contains, so, in the case of a chain made up of `X509Certificate` objects, `getCertificateChain()` will return a `X509Certificate` array.

KeyStore.SecretKeyEntry

The `KeyStore.SecretKeyEntry` class allows creation of value objects for carrying a `javax.crypto.SecretKey`. It has a single constructor that takes a `SecretKey` and a method, `getSecretKey()`, that retrieves it. Only some keystore types can handle storage of `KeyStore.SecretKeyEntry` objects; `JKS` and `PKCS12` types cannot.

KeyStore.TrustedCertificateEntry

The `KeyStore.TrustedCertificateEntry` class allows creation of value objects that carry trusted certificate entries. It has a single constructor that takes a `java.security.cert.Certificate` object and a method, `getTrustedCertificate()`, which allows the retrieval of the `Certificate` object the entry contains.

Having looked at the `KeyStore.ProtectionParameter` and `KeyStore.Entry` classes, you are now at the stage where you can look at an example of the new way of doing things.

Try It Out	Using KeyStore.setEntry()

This example is using both the "new look" and a different keystore type. I've done this so that I can demonstrate the storage of secret keys using one of the Sun-based keystores. The JKS does not support this, but the JCEKS does. Have a look at it and see what it is doing.

```
package chapter8;

import java.io.ByteArrayInputStream;
import java.io.ByteArrayOutputStream;
import java.security.KeyStore;
import java.security.SecureRandom;
import java.security.cert.Certificate;
import java.util.Enumeration;
```

```java
import javax.crypto.SecretKey;
import javax.security.auth.x500.X500PrivateCredential;

/**
 * Example of using a JCEKS keystore with KeyStore.Entry and
 * KeyStore.ProtectionParameter objects.
 */
public class JCEKSStoreEntryExample
{
    public static char[]    keyPassword = "endPassword".toCharArray();
    public static char[]    secretKeyPassword = "secretPassword".toCharArray();

    public static KeyStore createKeyStore()
        throws Exception
    {
        KeyStore store = KeyStore.getInstance("JCEKS");

        // initialize
        store.load(null, null);

        X500PrivateCredential rootCredential = Utils.createRootCredential();
        X500PrivateCredential interCredential = Utils.createIntermediateCredential(
                rootCredential.getPrivateKey(), rootCredential.getCertificate());
        X500PrivateCredential endCredential = Utils.createEndEntityCredential(
                interCredential.getPrivateKey(), interCredential.getCertificate());
        Certificate[]         chain = new Certificate[3];

        chain[0] = endCredential.getCertificate();
        chain[1] = interCredential.getCertificate();
        chain[2] = rootCredential.getCertificate();

        SecretKey           secret = Utils.createKeyForAES(256, new SecureRandom());

        // set the entries
        store.setEntry(rootCredential.getAlias(),
                new KeyStore.TrustedCertificateEntry(
                                rootCredential.getCertificate()), null);
        store.setEntry(endCredential.getAlias(),
                new KeyStore.PrivateKeyEntry(
                                endCredential.getPrivateKey(), chain),
                                new KeyStore.PasswordProtection(
                                                keyPassword)));
        store.setEntry("secret",
                new KeyStore.SecretKeyEntry(secret),
                new KeyStore.PasswordProtection(secretKeyPassword));

        return store;
    }

    public static void main(String[] args) throws Exception
    {
        KeyStore store = createKeyStore();
```

```
      char[]   password = "storePassword".toCharArray();

      ByteArrayOutputStream bOut = new ByteArrayOutputStream();

      // save the store
      store.store(bOut, password);

      // reload from scratch
      store = KeyStore.getInstance("JCEKS");

      store.load(new ByteArrayInputStream(bOut.toByteArray()), password);

      Enumeration en = store.aliases();
      while (en.hasMoreElements())
      {
          String alias = (String)en.nextElement();
          System.out.println("found " + alias
                          + ", isCertificate? " + store.isCertificateEntry(alias)
                          + ", secret key entry? " + store.entryInstanceOf(
                                      alias, KeyStore.SecretKeyEntry.class));
      }
    }
  }
```

Running the example produces the following output:

```
found root, isCertificate? true, secret key entry? false
found end, isCertificate? false, secret key entry? false
found secret, isCertificate? false, secret key entry? true
```

As you can see, you have managed to save the secret key as well, and it has been correctly identified as such when you rebuilt the store.

How It Works

This example is a similar structure to the previous one. The keystore is created in the `createKeyStore()` method, and then the alias names present are listed after the keystore has been written out and reloaded. Both the `createKeyStore()` method and the main driver show differences because of the new API that is being used, so I will go through those in order of execution.

The first difference is in the `createKeyStore()` method where not only is the example now generating a secret key, but it is using the `KeyStore.setEntry()` method to save each entry in the keystore. As you can see, this is all done using nested `KeyStore` classes that implement `KeyStore.Entry` to package the keys and certificates and using the `KeyStore.PasswordProtection` class to carry the password protecting the entry. I have given the certificate a `null` protection parameter, as the default behavior for a keystore implementation is to throw an exception if an attempt is made to password-protect a certificate. Other than that, it is fairly obvious what is going on.

The second difference is in the manner the entries get checked in the main driver. As well as using the older `KeyStore.isCertificate()` method, the example is also using the `KeyStore.entryInstanceOf()` method, and in a similar fashion to the `instanceof` keyword in Java, it simply checks the entry for the passed-in alias against the passed-in type, returning `true` if there is a match.

You can use both the BKS and UBER keystore types in the same fashion as the JCEKS. With flexibility that the KeyStore.Entry and KeyStore.ProtectionParameter changes lend the API, you can probably expect to see a much broader range of keystore implementations in the future.

The KeyStore.Builder Class

The idea of the KeyStore.Builder class is that you can bundle the information required to create a keystore into a KeyStore.Builder but delay creation of the actual keystore until it is really required. This can be useful if you want to set up the keystore but delay actual construction until some later time, such as when a user can type in a password. The class also allows you to take an already created KeyStore object and pass it off to another object together with a protection parameter that might be required to access the entry.

The KeyStore.Builder class is also constructed using a factory pattern that behaves similar to the standard getInstance() method but, in this case, is called newInstance(). It also has two methods on it, getKeyStore() and getProtectionParameter().

KeyStore.Builder.getKeyStore()

This returns the KeyStore object that the builder is encapsulating. It may return the same object every time or it might create a new keystore on each invocation — it depends on which version of newInstance() was called. If the KeyStore.Builder object is unable to return a keystore, the method will throw a KeyStoreException. The getKeyStore() method needs to be invoked before it is possible to call the getProtectionParameter() method.

KeyStore.Builder.getProtectionParameter()

The getProtectionParameter() class takes a single String as an argument representing the alias name for the entry the protection parameter is being requested for and returns the protection parameter if one exists. If the alias is null, the method will throw a NullPointerException; if the getKeyStore() method has not yet been invoked, the method will throw an IllegalStateException; and if some other problem occurs, the method will throw a KeyStoreException.

KeyStore.Builder.newInstance()

There are three variations on the static newInstance() method available on the class, two of which include a JCA provider name in their argument list. In cases where a provider name is required but is passed in as null, the usual precedence rules for finding a suitable KeyStore.Builder will apply.

The first one is for the purpose of encapsulating a KeyStore object and a protection parameter, and it takes a KeyStore object and a KeyStore.ProtectionParameter as arguments. The idea is that the protection parameter can be retrieved later and used to access one or more entries in the keystore that the builder was created with. Both calls to getKeyStore(), and getProtectionParameter() will return the objects the builder was created with. In this case, the method will throw a NullPointerException if either of its arguments is null and an IllegalArgumentException if the keystore passed in has not been initialized.

The second newInstance() method takes three arguments: a String indicating the type of the keystore to be built, a String giving the provider name to use, and a KeyStore.ProtectionParameter. In this case, each call to getKeyStore() will create a new KeyStore object that will be initialized using the new load() method that takes a KeyStore.LoadStoreParameter. The getProtectionParameter()

method will return the parameter passed in when `newInstance()` is invoked. The method will throw a `NullPointerException` if either the type or protection parameter arguments are `null`.

The third `newInstance()` method takes a `File` parameter in addition to the three parameters the second `newInstance()` method does. A call to `getKeyStore()` on a builder created using this `newInstance()` method will return the same `KeyStore` object, with the object being constructed on the first call using the given type and provider and then the `InputStream`-based load method being invoked with a password being recovered from the protection parameter either directly or via a callback. Calls to `getProtection Parameter()` will return a `KeyStore.PasswordProtection` object that contains the password that was recovered during the `KeyStore` object construction. The method will throw a `NullPointerException` if any of the type, file, or protection parameter arguments are `null`. It will also throw an `Illegal ArgumentException` if the file argument does not exist, does not refer to a regular file, or the protection parameter argument is not an instance of `KeyStore.CallbackHandlerProtection` or `KeyStore.PasswordProtection`.

A simple example would probably help here!

Try It Out   Using KeyStore.Builder

This example shows the use of the first `newInstance()` method on the `KeyStore.Builder` class. In this case, I am just using it to encapsulate a keystore with a password for a particular entry, although you could imagine if I was dealing with a personal credential file such as PKCS #12, which you will look at next, the password could be for the keystore as well as the entries. It's quite short — have a look at it and try running it.

```java
package chapter8;

import java.security.KeyStore;

/**
 * Basic example of use of KeyStore.Builder to create an object that
 * can be used recover a private key.
 */
public class JCEKSStoreBuilderExample
{
    public static void main(String[] args) throws Exception
    {
        KeyStore store = JCEKSStoreEntryExample.createKeyStore();

        char[]   password = "storePassword".toCharArray();

        // create the builder
        KeyStore.Builder builder = KeyStore.Builder.newInstance(
                                store, new KeyStore.PasswordProtection(
                                        JCEKSStoreEntryExample.keyPassword));

        // use the builder to recover the KeyStore and obtain the key
        store = builder.getKeyStore();

        KeyStore.ProtectionParameter param = builder.getProtectionParameter(
```

```
                                                        Utils.END_ENTITY_ALIAS);

        KeyStore.Entry entry = store.getEntry(Utils.END_ENTITY_ALIAS, param);

        System.out.println("recovered " + entry.getClass());
    }
}
```

Running the example produces the following message:

```
recovered class java.security.KeyStore$PrivateKeyEntry
```

indicating that the main driver has been able to recover the private key entry using the `KeyStore.Builder` object.

How It Works

In this case, all the work is being done in the main driver; the sample keystore being used is generated using the previous Try It Out ("Using KeyStore.setEntry()"), and then a `KeyStore.Builder` object is constructed using the keystore and the password for one of the entries. After that, the entry is recovered by first recovering the keystore using `builder.getKeyStore()`, and the protection parameter is recovered using `builder.getProtectionParameter()`. This then allows the example to recover the entry from the keystore.

A couple of minor notes: In this case, it doesn't matter what you pass to the builder to recover the protection parameter; you'll always get the same thing back — even the string `"fred"` will work quite well. It would be a mistake to rely on this, though. There should be nothing to stop the code being invoked with a builder that might be more fully featured. The nice thing about this particular use of the builder is that rather than having to rely on a system property, or something similar, to get the password for a given entry to the method that needs to use it, the builder allows you to encapsulate both pieces of information in a manner that is also abstract enough that even if the underlying keystore changes quite radically, the code will continue to work.

The KeyStore.LoadStoreParameter Interface

With JDK 1.5 new versions of `KeyStore.load()` and `KeyStore.store()` were added to the KeyStore API. They differ from the older versions in two respects: They take only a single parameter, and they will throw an `IllegalArgumentException` if the parameter is not recognized.

The single parameter is of the type `KeyStore.LoadStoreParameter`, which is a marker interface with a single method on it: `getProtectionParameter()`. As you might expect by now, the `getProtection Parameter()` method returns an object of the type `KeyStore.ProtectionParameter`. As you can see, this allows `KeyStore` objects to be built on things other than streams but still forces them to fit the standard convention for how they are accessed. At this writing this is still quite a new idea, and it will be interesting to see what `KeyStore` provider writers do with it in the future.

The PKCS #12 Format

The PKCS #12 format is defined in RSA Security's PKCS #12 standard and was primarily designed as a means of encoding personal credentials that consisted of private keys and certificates. It can be used in several ways that are based around the combination of two privacy modes and two integrity modes. The privacy mode can be one of password-based encryption (PBE), or through public key encryption. Likewise the integrity mode can be one of an HMAC based on a password and PBE or a digital signature. The format is important, as it is the most common way of dealing with private keys when you need to import them into another application such as a Web browser to introduce personal credentials or some other application that allows you to receive encrypted data or send signed information.

The encoding specified for the format is ASN.1 using the BER rules and the file structure is built around the PFX structure, which is defined as follows:

```
PFX ::= SEQUENCE {
          version INTEGER {v3(3)}(v3,...),
          authSafe ContentInfo,
          macData MacData OPTIONAL }

MacData ::= SEQUENCE {
            mac DigestInfo,
            macSalt OCTET STRING,
            iterations INTEGER DEFAULT 1 }
```

The MacData structure is present only if PBE is used for the integrity mode of the PFX. It is very rare to see iterations set to its default value; normally it will be over 1,000.

The ContentInfo structure is defined in PKCS #7 as follows:

```
ContentInfo ::= SEQUENCE {
    contentType  ContentType,
    content      [0] EXPLICIT CONTENTS.&Type({Contents}{@contentType}) OPTIONAL }
```

which, in case you've forgotten, translates into English as: What you will find in the content field depends on what the value is in the contentType field. The type of the contentType field, ContentType, is derived from a set of OIDs and reduces to a restricted version of the following:

```
ContentType ::= OBJECT IDENTIFIER
```

You will have a closer look at ContentInfo in the next chapter when you read about Cryptographic Message Syntax (CMS), but for the sake of PKCS #12, two object identifiers are recognized in the contentType field of the ContentInfo structure contained in the PFX structure: data and signedData. These two object identifiers have the following definition:

```
pkcs-7      OBJECT IDENTIFIER ::=
                        { iso(1) member-body(2) us(840) rsadsi(113549) pkcs(1) 7 }
data        OBJECT IDENTIFIER ::= { pkcs-7 1 }
signedData  OBJECT IDENTIFIER ::= { pkcs-7 2 }
```

and which one you will find in the contentType field depends on whether the content of the PFX is integrity-protected using a password — in which case it will be data, or integrity-protected using a digital signature — in which case it will be signedData.

I will leave the `signedData` content type alone for the moment because you'll be looking at it in the next chapter and in practice you will only see PFX objects using both password-based integrity mode and passwo̓d-based privacy mode. In any case, whether you encounter `signedData`, or just the `data` type the actual structure that contains the key and certificate information present in the file is an `AuthenticatedSafe`, which is defined as follows:

```
AuthenticatedSafe ::= SEQUENCE OF ContentInfo
```

And it is the encoding of the `AuthenticatedSafe` that is present in the `content` field of the relevant `ContentInfo` structure as an ASN.1 `OCTET STRING`. In the case of the password-based files, the relevant `ContentInfo` structure is the one contained in the `PFX` structure. The `content` field of each `ContentInfo` structure can contain either plaintext, password-encrypted data, or public key–encrypted data as `OCTET STRING` values based on the BER encoding of another structure — the `SafeContents`.

The `SafeContents` structure and its associated structures are defined as follows:

```
SafeContents ::= SEQUENCE OF SafeBag

SafeBag ::= SEQUENCE {
            bagId BAG-TYPE.&id ({PKCS12BagSet})
            bagValue [0] EXPLICIT BAG-TYPE.&Type({PKCS12BagSet}{@bagId}),
            bagAttributes SET OF PKCS12Attribute OPTIONAL }

PKCS12Attribute ::= SEQUENCE {
            attrId ATTRIBUTE.&id ({PKCS12AttrSet}),
            attrValues SET OF ATTRIBUTE.&Type ({PKCS12AttrSet}{@attrId}) }
```

And as you might imagine, there is a range of `bagId` values that indicate the `bagValue` is an object containing a certificate, key, a PKCS #8 encrypted private key, or a CRL. As you can see, the `PKCS12Attribute` structure is pretty much the same as the `Attribute` structure you saw in Chapter 5, the only difference being a name change and a syntax update to reflect the removal of the `ANY` type from ASN.1 in 1994. There are two common attributes that appear in relation to `SafeBag` attributes, both of which are defined in PKCS #9: the "friendly name," which is a `BMPString` identifier associated with the object in the `SafeBag`, and the local key ID, which is an `OCTET STRING` associated with the key or certificate in the `SafeBag` the attribute is attached to.

You can recognize the friendly name and the local key ID by the following OIDs in the `attrId` field of the `PKCS12Attribute` structure:

```
pkcs-9-at-friendlyName OBJECT IDENTIFIER ::= {pkcs-9 20}
pkcs-9-at-localKeyId   OBJECT IDENTIFIER ::= {pkcs-9 21}
```

where `pkcs-9` is defined as:

```
pkcs-9 OBJECT IDENTIFIER ::= {
                       iso(1) member-body(2) us(840) rsadsi(113549) pkcs(1) 9 }
```

In the context of PKCS #12 the local key ID is the most important of these, because it is generally used to tell the program reading the file which end entity certificate is related to which private key.

So, a complete PFX is a loosely defined nested structure, commonly with the kind of layout you see in Figure 8-1. The definition affords a great deal of flexibility in implementation and this is where you start to run into difficulties — if you think about it for a while, there are only some ways of constructing one of these files that will work with the Java KeyStore API, and many variations on the way.

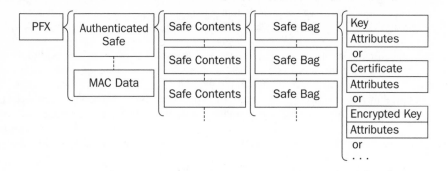

Basic structure of a password integrity-protected PKCS 12 file, note that the safe contents may be stored encrypted

Figure 8-1

As I hope you can see, to deal with the import and export issues you might run into with these files, it is a good idea to keep in mind some idea of how they function internally. The myriad of implementations out there often means the treating of PKCS #12 files as a "black box" does not always work.

Using PKCS #12 with the KeyStore API

So if you are using a keystore implementation of PKCS #12, where are the dragons lurking?

If you are using another tool to create them and then importing them into Java, the first point to be careful of is that, ideally, any keys in the imported file will have the friendly name attribute set, because some implementations rely on that to use as an alias name. It's certainly a lot easier to use one if it has a "friendly name" set; otherwise, the first thing you have to do is dump the aliases for the KeyStore object to find out what name the provider has assigned to it if it has been able to.

Usually PKCS #12 files you import, and ones you are planning to export, employ the same password for integrity checking as they do for encryption of individual entries in the AuthenticatedSafe. This is largely because PKCS #12 is meant for storing private credentials. In the case of the Bouncy Castle implementation, you dealt with this by ignoring individual entry passwords. Doing otherwise would have meant people would have unwittingly generated files they could not export. On the other hand, the JDK 1.5 implementation from Sun allows you to do this. This does not mean that either implementation is wrong — but whether you want to take advantage of the features of either depends a lot on whether you are planning to export the files to other applications and what those applications will cope with.

You'll also find that storing multiple private keys or just trusted certificates in a PKCS #12 keystore might be problematic depending on the provider. Although the PKCS #9 friendly name attribute allows aliases to be added to certificates, not everyone supports this, with the result that alias information on lone certificates may well be lost, and they simply won't show up in the alias list for the keystore. The implementation might also refuse to store trusted certificates altogether. In any case, some of the non-Java applications you will need to import PKCS #12 files into may cope properly only with files that have a single private key and certificate chain.

Another issue you might find is how certificate chains get picked up from the PKCS #12 file. Some applications will happily reconstruct a certificate chain using the subject and issuer DNs in the certificates and whether the public key of one certificate validates another. Others insist on the presence of the AuthorityKeyIdentifier and SubjectKeyIdentifier extensions to correctly recover the chain. The safest bet when you are creating your own chains is to make sure both extensions are present in any certificates that aren't trust anchors as well — they don't do any harm by being there.

A common problem you might encounter with a PKCS12 keystore is that not all software that claims to be able to read PKCS #12 files can read BER-encoded data. If you are using the Bouncy Castle PKCS12 implementation that does use BER, it may be necessary to transform the keystore file from BER to DER to get it to import. Fortunately, this is fairly easy to do, as the following code fragment shows:

```
ByteArrayOutputStream bOut = new ByteArrayOutputStream();

pkcs12Store.store(bOut, password);

ASN1InputStream        aIn = new ASN1InputStream(bOut.toByteArray());

bOut.reset();

DEROutputStream        dOut = new DEROutputStream(bOut);

dOut.writeObject(aIn.readObject());

byte[] derPKCS12 = bOut.toByteArray();
```

where derPKCS12 will end up being the DER encoding of the PKCS #12 PFX structure. If this is happening, it is unlikely the application will tell you that this is what the problem is — if you start having "bizarre" password issues, the BER/DER issue is the most common cause.

Finally, you might find it simply impossible to read a PKCS #12 store that has been generated by another application. This is fairly unlikely now because the BC implementation is four years old and the Sun one is about the same, but if it does, I guess the best advice I can give is that it's time to start working with your favorite dump utility and asking around. The org.bouncycastle.asn1.util.ASN1Dump class is a good place to start, and it would be worth getting your hands on the source of a PKCS #12 implementation, such as that found in JDKPKCS12KeyStore.java in the org.bouncycastle.jce.provider package of the Bouncy Castle distribution.

Still, after all, for the most part the PKCS #12 implementations that are available under Java do the job. So that being said, let's have a look at an example.

Try It Out   Using a PKCS #12 Keystore

This example is very similar to the first one in this chapter ("Try It Out: Using a JKS Keystore"), only this time it is using a PKCS12 keystore type to store a trusted certificate entry and a private key and its associated certificate chain.

```java
package chapter8;

import java.io.ByteArrayInputStream;
import java.io.ByteArrayOutputStream;
import java.security.KeyStore;
import java.security.cert.Certificate;
import java.util.Enumeration;

import javax.security.auth.x500.X500PrivateCredential;

/**
 * Example of the creation of a PKCS #12 store
 */
public class PKCS12StoreExample
{
    public static KeyStore createKeyStore()
        throws Exception
    {
        KeyStore store = KeyStore.getInstance("PKCS12", "BC");

        // initialize
        store.load(null, null);

        X500PrivateCredential rootCredential = Utils.createRootCredential();
        X500PrivateCredential interCredential = Utils.createIntermediateCredential(
                rootCredential.getPrivateKey(), rootCredential.getCertificate());
        X500PrivateCredential endCredential = Utils.createEndEntityCredential(
                interCredential.getPrivateKey(), interCredential.getCertificate());

        Certificate[]          chain = new Certificate[3];

        chain[0] = endCredential.getCertificate();
        chain[1] = interCredential.getCertificate();
        chain[2] = rootCredential.getCertificate();

        // set the entries
        store.setCertificateEntry(
                    rootCredential.getAlias(), rootCredential.getCertificate());
        store.setKeyEntry(
            endCredential.getAlias(), endCredential.getPrivateKey(), null, chain);

        return store;
    }

    public static void main(
        String[]    args)
        throws Exception
    {
        KeyStore store = createKeyStore();
        char[]    password = "storePassword".toCharArray();

        ByteArrayOutputStream bOut = new ByteArrayOutputStream();

        store.store(bOut, password);
```

```
store = KeyStore.getInstance("PKCS12", "BC");

store.load(new ByteArrayInputStream(bOut.toByteArray()), password);

Enumeration en = store.aliases();
while (en.hasMoreElements())
{
    String alias = (String)en.nextElement();
    System.out.println("found " + alias
                + ", isCertificate? " + store.isCertificateEntry(alias));
}
    }
}
```

Running the example produces the following output:

```
found end, isCertificate? false
found root, isCertificate? true
```

How It Works

There is not a lot to say about how this example works, but there are a few items of note.

The first is you will notice that the private key password is null. The reason is that with the Bouncy Castle implementation the password given when the keystore is saved is used both to generate the integrity check and to encrypt the data contained in the keystore.

The second issue to think about is what will happen if you are using JDK 1.5 and remove the specification of the BC provider. If you change the line in the main driver to just be

```
store = KeyStore.getInstance("PKCS12");
```

you will find the output changes to

```
found end, isCertificate? false
```

Because the parser in the JDK-provided implementation doesn't pick up the fact there is a certificate with the friendly name attribute set on it.

If you go one step further and change the use of KeyStore.getInstance() in the createKeyStore() method in the same fashion, you will find the example will throw an exception when it tries to add the certificate to the keystore. Comment that line out and you will find it throws an exception when it tries adding the key because the password is null. Change the lines adding the key entry to read

```
store.setKeyEntry(
        endCredential.getAlias(), endCredential.getPrivateKey(),
                            "storePassword".toCharArray(), chain);
```

and you will find the example then works. Notice that I have used the same password as is used to save the KeyStore object. The Sun implementation will let you use different passwords for saving the key and saving the password. However, if you are creating the file for import into another application, you will normally find it will be unable to load the PKCS #12 file, because it will assume the password for protecting the keys is the same one used to create the HMAC integrity check.

As you will realize from the outline I gave of the PKCS #12 PFX format earlier, there is nothing in PKCS #12 that says the Sun implementation is not compliant compared to the Bouncy Castle implementation — in some ways it is more so; it just happens to be different. As previously mentioned, you will find this is fairly common, especially when you introduce PKCS #12 files generated by other applications. Consequently, if you are using PKCS #12 files to pass credentials between applications, the first step is to make sure that the Java mechanisms you are using to load and save the files are compatible with the other applications you are using and that your use of the features of a particular Java implementation of PKCS #12 is restricted so that your users can reliably produce PKCS #12 files that will work across applications.

The JDK/JRE also comes with an application that can be very useful for examining keystores for the purposes of exporting keys, debugging, or just having a look at their contents. You will look at that now.

The Keytool

The keytool is a basic command-line tool for manipulating keystores. It provides a range of basic facilities for generation of keys with version 1 certificates, export and import of X.509 certificates, as well as the ability to produce certification requests.

You can find the `keytool` command in the `bin` directory of your Java distribution — the same place as the `java` command.

Keytool Commands

The `keytool` command syntax follows the pattern of

```
keytool command options
```

where *command* is the command you are trying to get the keytool to perform and *options* is one or more options appropriate to the *command*. The `keytool` command can also pass options directly to the underlying JVM it is running in. If you need to do this, the option to use is -J, which has the syntax *Jjava_option*, where *java_option* is one of the interpreter options you can pass to the java command when you are executing a class file.

General Command Options

The following options apply to all keytool commands, other than -printcert, which can be used independently of a keystore:

❑   keystore *store_name* — This option tells the keytool to use the location *store_name* as the source of the InputStream to pass to the KeyStore.load() method. If the word "NONE" is passed instead, then a null will be passed to KeyStore.load(). You might use "NONE" if the keystore you are using is provided by some hardware and specifying the provider is all that is required to locate the keystore — an example of this is the Sun PKCS #11 provider. If -keystore is not specified, the keytool uses the default .keystore file.

❑   -provider *provider_class_name* — This option tells the keytool to use the provider that is implemented by the specified class name as the provider to instantiate the keystore with.

❑   -storepass *password* — This option provides the keytool with the *password* that was used to integrity-protect the keystore. If this option is not specified, the keytool will attempt to open the keystore without performing the integrity check. As you can imagine, specifying the password means it is visible as a command-line argument. Given the security implications, this may not always be something you want.

❑   storetype *type* — This option tells the keytool what type of keystore is to be instantiated. If the option is not provided, the keytool will default to the type specified by the return value of the KeyStore.getDefaultType() method.

In addition, the -v option can also be passed to most commands to print extra information.

Commands and Their Options

Most of the important options that can be used with commands have default values. If -alias is not provided, its value is considered to be "mykey"; if -keyalg is not provided, its value is considered to be "DSA"; if -keysize is not given it defaults to 1,024; and the default validity for certificate generation when -validity is not given is 90 days.

The keytool will also derive signature algorithms from the private key being used if no signature algorithm is provided using the -sigalg option. In the case of a DSA private key, the algorithm will always be "SHA1withDSA," and in the case of an RSA key, the algorithm will default to "MD5withRSA."

Keeping the default option values in mind, the commands available with the keytool and their individual options are as follows:

❑   -certreq [-alias *alias*] [-sigalg *sigalg*] [-file *file*] [-keypass *keypass*] — This command generates a PKCS #10 certification request. The tool generates the request from the certificate and the private key associated with *alias* and signs it with the algorithm specified by the *sigalg*. If *sigalg* is not provided, an algorithm will be derived from the type of the private key. By default the certification request will be written to stdout; otherwise, it will be to the file indicated by the *file*. If *keypass* is not specified and it is different from the default password for the keystore, the keytool will prompt for it. As always bear in mind that if -keypass is used, it means the key password will be visible in your system as a command-line argument.

❑   -delete [-alias *alias*] — Deletes the entry with the alias name *alias* from the keystore being operated on. If alias is not specified, the keytool will prompt for it.

❑   -export [-alias *alias*] [-file *file*] [-rfc] — Exports the certificate specified by alias name *alias*. By default the certificate will be written to stdout, or if specified, it will be written to the location indicated by *file*. If the -rfc option is specified, the output will be in PEM format; otherwise, the certificate will be dumped using its binary ASN.1 encoding. If *alias* does not refer to a trusted certificate but to a private key, then the end entity certificate associated with the private key will be dumped out instead.

❑   -genkey [-alias *alias*] [-keyalg *keyalg*] [-keysize *keysize*] [-sigalg *sigalg*] [-dname *dname*] [-keypass *keypass*] [-validity *valDays*] — Creates a new entry named alias with password given by keypass, if it is provided. The new entry contains a private key and a X.509 version 1 self-signed certificate that are generated from the other arguments.

If the -keyalg option is not provided, a DSA private key will be generated. If the -keysize option is not provided, the key will be 1,024 bits in size. If *sigalg* is not provided, an algorithm will be derived from the type of the private key. The *dname* value is meant to be an X.500 name and is used to define both the issuer and the subject of the certificate. If the *dname* value is not provided, the keytool will prompt for one. If *keypass* is not present, the keytool will prompt for one; if the user simply presses <RETURN>, then the key will have the same password as the key-store. The certificate will be valid for the number of days indicated by the -validity option; otherwise, the certificate will be valid for 90 days.

❑ -help — Lists all commands and their options.

❑ -identitydb [-file *file*] — Reads a JDK 1.1 identity database from the location *file*, extract-ing the trusted entries from it and adding them to the keystore as entries. If file is not provided, the command reads from stdin.

❑ -import [-alias *alias*] [-file *file*] [-keypass *keypass*] [-noprompt] [*-trustcacerts*] — Reads an X.509 certificate, or PKCS #7 formatted certificate chain, from the location given by the file, or stdin if the file is not specified. The certificate, or certificate chain, is stored in the entry referred to by the alias name alias. The -import command will also recognize PEM-encoded files.

If a certificate chain, or a single certificate, representing a certification reply is provided, the key-tool will attempt to validate the chain before using it, and if the -trustcacerts option is given, the JVM's collection of CA certificates will be included in the set of possible trust anchors. If the certificate chain validates, it will replace the old one associated with the private key associated with the alias name *alias*. If validating the chain requires accepting a new trust anchor, the key tool will prompt the user to see whether this is really what is wanted. In the event the -noprompt option has been provided, the user will not be prompted and the new certificate representing the trust anchor for the imported certification reply will be accepted as trusted.

If the input to the import is a single certificate and the alias specified does not exist as an entry in the keystore, the keytool will assume you are trying to import a trusted certificate. If the certificate is not self-signed, the keytool will first try to validate the certificate using a self-signed certificate it knows about, including the JVM's collection of CA certificates if the *-trustcacerts* option is specified. If the certificate is self-signed, or otherwise unrecognized, the user will be prompted as to how to proceed — unless *-noprompt* has been specified, in which case the new certificate will be accepted.

As you might imagine, you should not do these without a lot of thought. The consequences of accepting a bogus trust anchor could be quite far-reaching. Doing so may put you in the position where you accept a certificate path as valid when you should, in fact, reject it.

❑ -keyclone [-alias *alias*] [-dest *dest_alias*] [-keypass *keypass*] [-new *new_keypass*] — Creates a new key entry in the keystore with the alias name *dest_alias*, which is a copy of the entry with the alias name *alias*. If the *-keypass* option is not provided and the password for the entry represented by *alias* is not the same as for the keystore, the key password will be prompted for. If the *-new* option is not provided, the password for the new entry will be prompted for, and if the user responds with nothing more than a <RETURN>, the new entry will be given the same password as the original one.

❑ -keypasswd [-alias *alias*] [-keypass *old_keypass*] [-new *new_keypass*] — Changes the password on the key entry associated with the alias name *alias* from *old_keypass* to *new_keypass*. The keytool will prompt for the passwords if they are not provided on the command line.

❑ -list [-alias *alias*] [-v | -rfc] — Prints to stdout the keystore entry with the alias name alias. If alias is not provided, then the contents of the entire keystore are printed.

By default, this command just prints the MD5 fingerprints for the certificates present in each entry. If -v is specified, then more details are printed about each entry; otherwise, if -rfc is specified instead, each certificate found is printed in PEM format.

❑ -printcert [-file *file*] — Reads the ASN.1 binary-encoded or PEM-encoded certificate from the file *file* and prints it in a human-readable manner. If the -file option is not provided, the command will read from stdin.

❑ -selfcert [-alias *alias*] [-sigalg *sigalg*] [-dname *dname*] [-validity *valDays*] [-keypass *keypass*] — Generates an X.509 version 1 self-signed certificate using the private key and the associated public key in the entry with the alias name *alias* with a signature of the type *sigalg*. If *sigalg* is not provided, it will be derived from the type of the private key. If *dname* is provided, it will be used to generate the X.500 name to be used as the issuer and subject DNs of the resulting certificate. If *dname* is not provided, the subject of the certificate containing the public key for the private key will be used to provide the issuer and subject DNs instead. The -validity option specifies the number of days the certificate will be valid for, with the usual default of 90 days applying if it is not provided. If *keypass* is not provided and it is different from the keystore password, the keytool will prompt for it.

❑ -storepasswd [-new *new_storepass*] — Changes the password for the keystore being operated on to the new password given by *new_storepass*. If the -storepass option, or -new option, is not provided, the keytool will prompt for the relevant password.

You probably noticed in the discussion of the -import command that the JVM has its own idea of what CAs it will trust. Take a look at that file now as a way of starting to make some use of the keytool.

> **Note the examples that follow assume you have correctly set up your command path so that you can simply enter keytool as a command without having to specify the full directory path in front of it. Make sure your environment is properly set up before you go further.**

The JVM's CA Keystore

In addition to the java.security file that lives in *JDK_HOME*/jre/lib/security, or *JRE_HOME*/lib/security depending on which type of distribution you are looking at, there is a also file called cacerts.

Change the directory so you are in the same directory as the java.security file. Providing you haven't changed the password on the cacerts file, you can have a look it by running the command:

```
keytool -list -keystore cacerts -storepass changeit
```

What you will see represents all the certificates your JVM is prepared to use as a trust anchor when you include -trustcacerts in the -import command. As you will see in Chapter 10, the cacerts file is also used by the SSL API, among others.

As it is just a regular JKS file, you can also use the keytool command to import your own trusted certificates into cacerts — something you might want to do to add your own trust anchors, by running the command:

```
keytool -import -alias trust -file trust.cer -keystore cacerts -storepass changeit
```

where `trust` is the alias you want to assign to your new trust anchor and `trust.cer` is a file containing either the ASN.1 binary or PEM encoding of your trust anchor.

As you can see, the default password is `changeit` — in this case, if you are going to be relying on the contents of the `cacerts` file for path validation, a good piece of advice. If you are shipping a Java application that derives its security from the path validation that happens due to the `cacerts` file, be it using the default contents or through trust anchors you have added yourself, leaving the `cacerts` file with its default password may provide an opening for making mischief that someone may find impossible to resist. Don't forget you can use the `-storepasswd` command to do this. I'll say it once again.

> **If you rely on the integrity of the JVM's `cacerts` file to help secure your application, change the file's password to something other than the default.**

At this point it would be worth getting some experience with some of the more in-depth uses of the `keytool` command, but the `cacerts` file is hardly a good thing to be experimenting on. You will have a look at how you can to set yourself up and do so now.

Some Keytool Experiments

By default the `keytool` works on a file with the name `.keystore`, which the command options that are used for generating keys and importing data will create for you if it does not already exist. The `.keystore` file normally resides in whatever your system considers to be your home directory. In this case, you will avoid using the default file by specifying a filename on the command line. Apart from the fact it means you will not overwrite anything you should not by mistake, which could be as bad, if not worse, than damaging your `cacerts` file, it will also allow you to have a look at some of the example `KeyStore` objects you have generated by saving them to disk and using the `keytool` command.

Generating Some Sample Keystore Files

This utility class uses the KeyStore generations methods you used in two previous Try It Outs: "Using a JKS Keystore" and "Using a PKCS #12 Keystore" to create two files using the `keytool` command.

```
package chapter8;

import java.io.FileOutputStream;
import java.security.KeyStore;

/**
 * Create some keystore files in the current directory.
 */
public class KeyStoreFileUtility
{
    public static void main(
        String[]    args)
        throws Exception
    {
        char[]    password = "storePassword".toCharArray();

        // create and save a JKS store
```

```
        KeyStore store = JKSStoreExample.createKeyStore();

        store.store(new FileOutputStream("keystore.jks"), password);

        // create and save a PKCS #12 store
        store = PKCS12StoreExample.createKeyStore();

        store.store(new FileOutputStream("keystore.p12"), password);
    }
}
```

Create a temporary directory to experiment in, change your directory to it, and run the class. Use your favorite directory list command and you will find the utility class has created two files — one called `keystore.jks` that contains a JKS keystore and one called `keystore.p12` that contains a PKCS12 keystore.

Try It Out   Using Some Keytool Commands

Having created the files, first try to list the contents of both keystores using the command

```
keytool -list -keystore keystore.jks -storepass storePassword
```

and

```
keytool -list -keystore keystore.p12 -storetype PKCS12 -storepass storePassword
```

The output for the `keystore.jks` will start something like the following:

```
Keystore type: jks
Keystore provider: SUN

Your keystore contains 2 entries
```

and the output for the `keystore.p12` will start something like this instead:

```
Keystore type: PKCS12
Keystore provider: SunJSSE

Your keystore contains 1 entry
```

If you remember from the PKCS12StoreExample program, the keystore actually has a certificate in it as well that the SunJSSE PKCS12 implementation does not pick up. You'll have a look at what to do about this when I describe what is going on.

Now try adding a key to the JKS keystore using -genkey using the following:

```
keytool -genkey -alias eric -keystore keystore.jks -storepass storePassword
```

As you have not provided the -dname option, the command will prompt you for input leading to an exchange that might look like the following, where what you might type is in bold:

```
What is your first and last name?
  [Unknown]: Eric Echidna
```

```
What is the name of your organizational unit?
  [Unknown]:  Monotremes
What is the name of your organization?
  [Unknown]:  The Legion of the Bouncy Castle
What is the name of your City or Locality?
  [Unknown]:  Melbourne
What is the name of your State or Province?
  [Unknown]:  Victoria
What is the two-letter country code for this unit?
  [Unknown]:  AU
Is CN=Eric Echidna, OU=Monotremes, O=The Legion of the Bouncy Castle,
L=Melbourne, ST=Victoria, C=AU correct?
  [no]:  yes

Enter key password for <eric>
        (RETURN if same as keystore password):  newKey
```

If you execute the list command again on keystore.jks, you will now see the following header on the output:

```
Keystore type: jks
Keystore provider: SUN

Your keystore contains 3 entries
```

And the rest of the output lists the fingerprints for eric, end, and root. If you add a -v to the command, you will also see that the new certificate for the key entry eric is self-signed with the subject and issuer DNs being set to what you entered previously.

One last thing to try: exporting a certificate from the PKCS12 store and importing it into the JKS one. First you need to export a certificate — in this case, the one associated with key entry end:

```
keytool -export -alias end -rfc -file end.pem -keystore keystore.p12 -storetype
PKCS12 -storepass storePassword
```

which should produce the following output:

```
Certificate stored in file <end.pem>
```

Then you import the file into keystore.jks with

```
keytool -import -alias new -file end.pem -keystore keystore.jks -storepass
storePassword
```

In this case, because the certificate won't be recognized as trusted, you'll get prompted with the certificate details and asked whether you are willing to trust the certificate. The resulting interaction will look something like the following:

```
Owner: CN=Test End Certificate
Issuer: CN=Test Intermediate Certificate
Serial number: 1
Valid from: startTime until: expiryTime
```

```
Certificate fingerprints:
        MD5:   16 bytes of hex...
        SHA1:  20 bytes of hex...
Trust this certificate? [no]:  yes
Certificate was added to keystore
```

indicating the certificate was added successfully. Note that this means that if you now do a list on `keystore.jks`, you will see that the entry now has been added as a trusted certificate entry — in some circumstances not something to be taken lightly.

How It Works

In some respects, things work here because they pretty well follow the manual. However, there are some interesting things going on that aren't in the manual and might not be immediately obvious, and there are also a few other details that should be kept in mind, so you will look at those.

The initial attempt at listing the PKCS12 keystore showed you that you were using the JDK-provided PKCS12 implementation, so it did not pick up the certificate entry. In theory all you should have to do is add a `-provider` option giving you something like:

```
keytool -list -keystore keystore.p12 -storetype PKCS12 -storepass storePassword
-provider org.bouncycastle.jce.provider.BouncyCastleProvider
```

telling the keytool to use the Bouncy Castle provider instead of the SunJSSE one. Try it; you will see it does not work. For some reason the keytool will use the SunJSSE only if you specify PKCS12 — especially inconvenient if you are using JDK 1.4, where the SunJSSE implementation is read-only. I'm not sure why this particular quirk exists. It would be a great relief if it didn't, but it has been a problem long enough for us at Bouncy Castle to create two workarounds: PKCS12-DEF, which uses the Sun X.509 certificate factory, and BCPKCS12, which uses the Bouncy Castle one. I recommend using PKCS12-DEF, as it gets around some compatibility issues that some of the Java tools have when it comes to dealing with non-Sun provider X.509 certificates. In any case, if you try instead

```
keytool -list -keystore keystore.p12 -storetype PKCS12-DEF -storepass storePassword
```

you will see the following:

```
Keystore type: PKCS12-DEF
Keystore provider: BC

Your keystore contains 2 entries
```

showing that the Bouncy Castle provider is now being used instead and the certificate entry is now being recognized. If you're using another provider that offers the PKCS12 type, you will probably find they have similar workarounds.

The next point is in your `-genkey` example. In this case, you have not specified a key algorithm, key size, or a length of time for the self-signed certificate to be valid. The result is that you have produced a DSA key of 1,024 bits with a certificate signed using "SHA1withDSA" and an expiry date of 90 days. You could have changed this by including options like `-keyalg`, `-keysize`, `-sigalg`, and `-validity`, to change the key algorithm, key size, signature algorithm used, or the lifetime of the certificate.

Naturally, the certificate is self-signed. If you wanted to get it validated by one of your trust anchors, or perhaps someone else's, you would need to use -certreq to generate a PKCS #10 certification request for you. After that, you could process the certification request using the methods you saw in Chapter 6 producing a CertPath, write it out in "PKCS7" format, and then use the -import command to replace the self-signed certificate with the certificate chain you just constructed.

Finally, have a look at the contents of the end.pem. You will see it looks like just it should — a PEM-encoded certificate. You can probably see that if you needed to import trust anchors from other applications, or generators of your own, it is fairly easy to do.

Jarsigning and Java Policy

There are some other tools and features of JDK/JRE that also make use of keystore files: the jarsigner tool and the Java policy mechanisms. I won't go into detailed discussion about them here, as they are well documented in the Java tools document set and they are not immediately relevant to the topic of this book, but it is worth being aware of their existence, so I will give a brief outline so you have a place to start if you decide to do further reading.

The Jarsigner

The jarsigner is used to sign Java archive files (JAR) and to verify the signatures, if any, that are attached to them. The basic command syntax for the two modes is as follows:

```
jarsigner options jar-file key_entry_alias
```

to sign a JAR file and

```
jarsigner -verify options jar-file
```

to verify the signatures attached to one. You can find the jarsigner in the same bin directory you found the keytool command.

I'll leave it as an exercise to look at the provided documentation for the full list of options, but in terms of its keystore usage, the jarsigner also defaults to using the .keystore file in your home directory and supports the options -keypass, -keystore, -storepass, and -storetype, which have exactly the same meaning as they do with the keytool command.

You can see how this command could be useful. In the case of a cryptographic provider such as Bouncy Castle, it is the signature on the JAR file that is used to tell the JDK that the service provider it is being presented with is one of those authorized for use with the JCE. You can use it for shipping signature protected data as well as class files, and the ability to sign JAR files also forms the basis of some of the security features that the Java policy mechanisms make possible.

Java Policy Files

The JVM has a system policy file as well as a notion of a user policy file. The system policy file, called java.policy, can be found in the lib/security directory along with the cacerts file and the `java.security` file. The user policy file is called `.java.policy` and can be found in the system's idea of what the user's home directory is.

Policy files can be manipulated using the `policytool`, which is also in the same bin directory as the `jarsigner`, or by using a regular text editor. Policy files are used by the JVM's policy provider, a class that's responsible for seeing that the conditions laid out by the policy files are followed. There is extensive documentation on policy files and the `policytool` in the JDK documentation set, but briefly, a policy configuration file is simply a `keystore` entry followed by one or more `grant` entries.

In respect to signed code, the `keystore` entry tells the policy provider where to find the keystore that will be used for verifying the signatures on the JAR files. It has the following syntax:

```
keystore "keystore_url", "keystore_type", "keystore_provider";
keystorePasswordURL "password_url";
```

where `keystore_type` and `keystore_provider` are optional — although the `keystore_type` is required if the `keystore_provider` is specified. If `keystore_type` is left out, the policy provider will default to the return value of `KeyStore.getDefaultType()`.

The `grant` entry can then start with an optional `signedBy` clause as in:

```
grant signedBy "eric" {
    permission_list...
}
```

granting the permissions detailed in `permission_list` to the class files that come from a source signed by the key entry with the name `"eric"` from the keystore file described by the `keystore` entry.

A lot more than this can go in a grant entry; however, you get the idea. You can do more to lock down a Java application than just change the password on the `cacerts` file. Properly used the Java policy mechanisms can go a long way in helping secure a Java application.

Summary

In this chapter, you looked at the use of the `KeyStore` class as well as its associated tool, the `keytool`. In addition to that, you also looked at the PKCS #12 format, which is often used for transferring private keys between applications, as well as some of the implementation issues that surround it.

Over the course of this chapter you have learned the following:

- ❑ The basic types of keystores that are commonly available and how they differ
- ❑ How a PKCS #12 PFX structure is put together for storing private credentials
- ❑ How to create PKCS #12 files using the KeyStore API and what some of the underlying provider issues are, as well as what issues can arise with non-Java applications
- ❑ Where the JVM gets its own ideas about trust anchors and how to add your own
- ❑ How to use the `keytool` command for analyzing and manipulating keystore files

Finally, you should also have some idea how work you've done in previous chapters can be used in conjunction with the `keytool`, as well as be aware of some of the other JVM features and tools that make use of keystore files.

You're now at the point where you can make use of symmetric cryptography, asymmetric cryptography, MACs, digests, and digital signatures, as well as create and validate certificates in addition to being able to store credentials securely and export them if required. As it happens, just as there are standard mechanisms for transferring credentials, there are also standard protocols for defining messages containing encrypted and signed data. One of the most common of these is Cryptographic Message Syntax, or CMS, which is also used as the basis for securing other forms of messaging, such as e-mail, through S/MIME. In the next chapter, you look at example of how CMS and S/MIME can be used in Java and how processing of the CMS protocol ties in with the topics already covered.

Exercises

1. What available keystore types support the storing of symmetric keys?

2. What is one important thing to do if you are relying on the integrity of the JVM's `cacerts` file to help secure your application?

3. You have imported a PKCS #12 file into a Java application but there doesn't appear to be an alias for the key entry you are looking for, or it is just appearing as some random string of hex. What is most likely to be the issue with the PKCS #12 file?

4. You have generated a PKCS #12 file using a Java application you have written, but you are unable to import it into another third-party application. What are the three most likely problems with the PKCS #12 file you have generated?

5. Using the `keytool` command, the `org.bouncycastle.openssl.PEMReader` class, the `Utils` class, and the Chapter 6 examples "Try It Out: Creating a Certificate from a Certification Request" and "Try It Out: Writing a CertPath" as helpers, show how to create a certificate request using the `keytool` for a keystore key entry, create a `PKCS7`-encoded certificate chain in response to the request, and update the key entry with the chain.

CMS and S/MIME

Although you're probably getting comfortable with using the cryptography facilities in Java and working with the both the Sun providers and the Bouncy Castle providers, you probably don't want to rush out and develop your own messaging protocol if you don't need to. Even if you do want to, it is worth spending some time on what some of the existing practices are. A lot of work has already been done in the area and there is a great deal of benefit to be gained from it.

This chapter looks at the secure messaging standards known as Cryptographic Message Syntax (CMS) and a related standard built on top of CMS for processing MIME messages securely — S/MIME. As well as providing some background into how these two standards work, the chapter also provides details on how to make use of the Bouncy Castle APIs that implement them.

By the end of this chapter you should

- ❑ Understand the basic building blocks of a CMS message
- ❑ Know how to create signed, encrypted, and compressed CMS messages
- ❑ Know how to process signed CMS messages using the CertPath API
- ❑ Understand the basic message types in S/MIME
- ❑ Know how to create and process signed, encrypted, and compressed S/MIME messages

Finally, you should also know how to combine S/MIME messaging types and be able to deal with MIME multipart data when doing so.

Getting Started

The first thing you'll notice looking at the utilities class is that it is making use of the JavaMail API. So before you try entering it, you will need to download the JavaMail distribution, follow the installation instructions, and install it into your Java environment, if you have not already. Note the JavaMail API also requires you to install the JavaBeans Activation Framework (JAF)—you'll find details on this on the JavaMail Web page as well.

As it happens, the Bouncy Castle APIs for CMS and S/MIME I'll be using in this chapter are also distributed in a different JAR file from the provider, so you will need to install that as well. You can find it at the same place you got the provider, on http://www.bouncycastle.org/latest_releases.html. Similar to the provider jar file, the Bouncy Castle mail API JAR files follow the naming convention bcmail-JdkVersion-Version.jar. So if you are looking at version 1.28 for JDK 1.4, the filename would be bcmail-jdk14-128.jar. As with the provider JAR in Chapter 1, all you need to do to install the Bouncy Castle mail JAR file is copy the JAR file into the lib/ext (or lib\ext) directory of the JRE you are using.

After you have installed the JavaMail and Bouncy Castle mail JARs, you can proceed with compiling the following Utils class to begin the chapter9 package:

```java
package chapter9;

import java.security.KeyStore;
import java.security.cert.*;
import java.util.*;

import javax.mail.Address;
import javax.mail.Message;
import javax.mail.MessagingException;
import javax.mail.Session;
import javax.mail.internet.InternetAddress;
import javax.mail.internet.MimeMessage;
import javax.security.auth.x500.X500PrivateCredential;

/**
 * Chapter 9 Utils
 */
public class Utils extends chapter8.Utils
{
    public static char[] KEY_PASSWD = "keyPassword".toCharArray();

    /**
     * Create a KeyStore containing the a private credential with
     * certificate chain and a trust anchor.
     */
    public static KeyStore createCredentials() throws Exception
    {
        KeyStore store = KeyStore.getInstance("JKS");

        store.load(null, null);

        X500PrivateCredential rootCredential = Utils.createRootCredential();
        X500PrivateCredential interCredential = Utils.createIntermediateCredential(
                rootCredential.getPrivateKey(), rootCredential.getCertificate());
        X500PrivateCredential endCredential = Utils.createEndEntityCredential(
                interCredential.getPrivateKey(), interCredential.getCertificate());

        store.setCertificateEntry(
                    rootCredential.getAlias(), rootCredential.getCertificate());
        store.setKeyEntry(
            endCredential.getAlias(), endCredential.getPrivateKey(), KEY_PASSWD,
```

```
                    new Certificate[] {
                            endCredential.getCertificate(),
                            interCredential.getCertificate(),
                            rootCredential.getCertificate() });

        return store;
    }

    /**
     * Build a path using the given root as the trust anchor, and the passed
     * in end constraints and certificate store.
     *
     * Note: the path is built with revocation checking turned off.
     */
    public static PKIXCertPathBuilderResult buildPath(
        X509Certificate  rootCert, X509CertSelector endConstraints,
        CertStore certsAndCRLs) throws Exception
    {
        CertPathBuilder      builder = CertPathBuilder.getInstance("PKIX", "BC");
        PKIXBuilderParameters buildParams = new PKIXBuilderParameters(
                            Collections.singleton(
                                new TrustAnchor(rootCert, null)), endConstraints);

        buildParams.addCertStore(certsAndCRLs);
        buildParams.setRevocationEnabled(false);

        return (PKIXCertPathBuilderResult)builder.build(buildParams);
    }

    /**
     * Create a MIME message from using the passed-in content.
     */
    public static MimeMessage createMimeMessage(
        String subject, Object content, String contentType)
        throws MessagingException
    {
        Properties props = System.getProperties();
        Session session = Session.getDefaultInstance(props, null);

        Address fromUser = new InternetAddress(
                                    "\"Eric H. Echidna\"<eric@bouncycastle.org>");
        Address toUser = new InternetAddress("example@bouncycastle.org");

        MimeMessage message = new MimeMessage(session);

        message.setFrom(fromUser);
        message.setRecipient(Message.RecipientType.TO, toUser);
        message.setSubject(subject);
        message.setContent(content, contentType);
        message.saveChanges();

        return message;
    }
}
```

The new `Utils` class adds three items of functionality. The `createCredentials()` method creates a `KeyStore` containing a private key, a validating certificate chain, and the trust anchor for the chain. The `buildPath()` method allows you to create certificate paths given a trust anchor, some end constraints, and a collection of certificates. Finally, the `createMimeMessage()` method creates a `MimeMessage` with sufficient headers so it will work as a mail message .

I'm not going to be giving an in-depth discussion of the JavaMail API in this chapter, except as is relevant to its use with the Bouncy Castle S/MIME API. However, if you have a look at the documentation that accompanies the JavaMail API, you will realize that not much more work is required to take a `MimeMessage` object such as the one created by `Utils.createMimeMessage()` and feed it into a mailer.

At this point, if the `Utils` class has compiled successfully and you have installed the JavaMail and the Bouncy Castle mail JAR files, you are ready to proceed with the first topic — Cryptographic Message Syntax.

Cryptographic Message Syntax

Cryptographic Message Syntax, or CMS, provides an encapsulation syntax for data that is encrypted or signed. A feature of it is that it allows different types of protection mechanisms to be nested(a signed message can then be used as the plaintext for an encrypted one, or an encrypted one can be signed. Signed messages can also have attributes attached to them that can be included in the final signature. It's an important protocol because not only is it used by itself, but it also forms the basis of other protocols such as those used by S/MIME and its variants, such as AS2 (Applicability Statement 2) and RosettaNet. If you are interested, you can find some references on these in Appendix D. It also works very well with the other PKIX standards you have looked at, so you can take full advantage of things like certificate path validation and the like.

CMS was originally defined in RSA Security's PKCS #7. Along the way it was picked up as an RFC and is now represented by RFC 3852, which is the definition I will be working from here. In the Bouncy Castle APIs, there are two packages devoted to CMS: `org.bouncycastle.cms` contains the high-level classes that handle the creation of messages involving encryption, signing, and compression, as well as their processing; and `org.bouncycastle.asn1.cms` is a collection of low-level classes that provide Java object equivalents for the ASN.1 structures defined in the CMS ASN.1 module. The packages actually represent a subset of what is detailed in the RFC, but it is the subset that is most commonly used and the same subset that is required to implement S/MIME.

For the most part the high-level package is all you need to use. However, because the classes in it are related to the ASN.1 structures that make up the protocol, I'll work through them both in tandem so you have a feel for the API as well as a feel for what is going on under the covers.

Basic CMS

The basic structure in CMS is the `ContentInfo` object. You saw this structure in Chapter 8, where it provided a general construct for building a PKCS #12 keystore. PKCS #7 is where the `ContentInfo` structure is originally derived from. You probably remember the definition of it given in Chapter 8, but I'll give it again here. You'll note that this definition is different in that it shows use of the older style of ASN.1, because I am using the definition from the RFC. Although the encoded structure of the two `ContentInfo` objects will look the same, the definition you are now working from is as follows:

```
ContentInfo ::= SEQUENCE {
                contentType ContentType,
                content [0] EXPLICIT ANY DEFINED BY contentType }
```

where the `ContentType` type is defined as:

```
ContentType ::= OBJECT IDENTIFIER
```

As you saw in Chapter 8, the idea of the `ContentInfo` structure is to carry other objects tagged with an object identifier. As it turns out, `ContentInfo` can even contain other `ContentInfo` objects — in which case the OID that you will find in the `contentType` field is

```
id-ct-contentInfo OBJECT IDENTIFIER ::= { iso(1) member-body(2) us(840)
                          rsadsi(113549) pkcs(1) pkcs9(9) smime(16) ct(1) 6 }
```

In the discussion here, you will be looking closely at four types that can be contained in a `ContentInfo` object: `Data`, `SignedData`, `EnvelopedData`, and `CompressedData`.

The last three of these message structures are versioned; the versioning is indicated by a number found at the start of the structure. Because this standard has been evolving for a while, there is a range of different version numbers for CMS structures defined in the type `CMSVersion` as follows:

```
CMSVersion ::= INTEGER  { v0(0), v1(1), v2(2), v3(3), v4(4) v5(5) }
```

A number of other structures are also versioned in CMS. Usually the CMS version number associated with a particular structure depends on the presence, or not, of optional fields or `CHOICE` types in the structure being looked at, or it depends on the value of the CMS version numbers in fields of the structure that represent other CMS structures. If this is the case, I will generally discuss the version number value last when reviewing a structure, even though, when present, it is normally the first field.

The Data Content Type

The fundamental content type in CMS is the `Data` content type. Its presence in a `ContentInfo` structure is indicated by the `contentType` field being set to the following value:

```
id-data OBJECT IDENTIFIER ::= {
            iso(1) member-body(2) us(840) rsadsi(113549) pkcs(1) pkcs7(7) 1 }
```

You will probably recognize this as being the same value given for the `data` OID in Chapter 8 but with a different name. This will happen a few times in this chapter, so I won't bring it up again, but if anything, it will tell you something about what tends to happen as ASN.1 modules are developed for related standards.

The `Data` content type indicates that the content field in the `ContentInfo` is simply an OCTET STRING. The octets referred to might well have some other structure hidden in them, but from the point of view of CMS, they will be treated simply as a string of octets with any further interpretation being done later by the application. Likewise, in the Bouncy Castle API, a generic interface is provided to represent the data objects for processing by the API.

The CMSProcessable Interface

The `org.bouncycastle.CMSProcessable` interface provides the means for introducing a stream of data into the CMS classes, in some ways providing a Java equivalent to the `Data` content type.

Because the interface is both quite small and very important, I've reproduced it here.

```
package org.bouncycastle.cms;

import java.io.IOException;
import java.io.OutputStream;

public interface CMSProcessable
{
    public void write(OutputStream out)
        throws IOException, CMSException;

    public Object getContent();
}
```

As you can see, it has two methods. The first one, `write()`, takes an `OutputStream` as a parameter and is invoked by the CMS API when it needs the data being signed, encrypted, or compressed to be made available. The `write()` method may be invoked multiple times, and each time it is, all the bytes representing the object being processed should be written to the stream passed in. The second method, `getContent()`, is provided as a means of retrieving the data in some other form and is provided as a convenience method that can be used to recover the data if it was encapsulated in the CMS message.

The CMS package also includes a class called `CMSProcessableByteArray` that can act as a carrier for an array of bytes to be processed by the API. If you need to process other data objects, such as files, you can use the source of `CMSProcessableByteArray` as a guide to implementing the appropriate object. You learn how to use `CMSProcessableByteArray` in the next section when you look a CMS signed-data.

CMS Signed-Data

CMS signed-data consists of a content holder, zero or more signature structures, and optionally a collection of certificates and CRLs that may be associated with the signatures. The content holder can contain the data the signature structures were generated for, but it can also be empty, indicating that the signed-data message is actually detached and represents signatures created for an external data source, giving you the two processes you see in Figure 9-1. If there are no signature structures attached to the message, the message exists purely to carry the certificates and CRLs it contains — messages of this type are created when a certificate path is encoded in PKCS #7 format.

Verifying a signature for a given signer is a matter of finding the signature structure that matches the signer you are trying to verify for. Once you have a match, the process is one of using the source data for the signature to verify the signature value using the public key of the signer you have matched.

External Signed-Data Generation

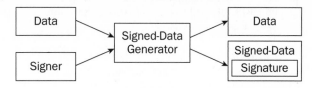

Encapsulated Signed-Data Generation

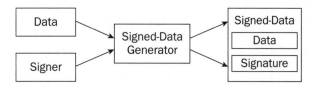

The Two Types of Signed-Data Structure Generation

Figure 9-1

As usual, signature values are constructed using a combination of hashing and encryption. The recommend hash algorithms for signed-data are defined in RFC 3370. Although I use different algorithms in the examples in the chapter, it is worth noting that SHA-1 is still mandated as the algorithm of choice. For your own purposes, although it is safe to use the better hash algorithms, you will probably find you will need to use SHA-1 to produce signed messages that a variety of other applications understand. It is likely that work on a revision of RFC 3370 will begin soon, but keep this warning in mind as you look at the ASN.1 structure and move on to the Java examples.

ASN.1 Structure

CMS signed-data is created by wrapping a `SignedData` structure in a `ContentInfo` structure with the `contentType` field set to the OID `id-signedData`, which is defined as:

```
id-signedData OBJECT IDENTIFIER ::= {
        iso(1) member-body(2) us(840) rsadsi(113549) pkcs(1) pkcs7(7) 2 }
```

When the value `id-signedData` is found in the `contentType` field of a `ContentInfo` structure, the value present in the `content` field will be

```
SignedData ::= SEQUENCE {
            version CMSVersion,
            digestAlgorithms DigestAlgorithmIdentifiers,
            encapContentInfo EncapsulatedContentInfo,
            certificates [0] IMPLICIT CertificateSet OPTIONAL,
            crls [1] IMPLICIT RevocationInfoChoices OPTIONAL,
            signerInfos SignerInfos }
```

As each signature for the data being signed is generated for each signer, the signature and attribute information are used to create a signer information structure that is accumulated in the `signerInfos` field, and the certificates and CRLs relevant to the signature are accumulated directly in the `SignedData` structure in the `certificates` and `crls` fields.

The Java equivalent for the structure is represented by the `CMSSignedData` class in the `org` `.bouncycastle.cms` package. As the `CMSSignedData` class abstracts some of the internals of the `SignedData` structure, I'll go through the details of how the ASN.1 structure is put together first and then look at the related Java classes.

The DigestAlgorithms Field

The `digestAlgorithms` field has the type `DigestAlgorithmIdentifiers`, which is defined as:

```
DigestAlgorithmIdentifiers ::= SET OF DigestAlgorithmIdentifier

DigestAlgorithmIdentifier ::= AlgorithmIdentifier
```

which is the same structure you saw in Chapter 5.

The EncapContentInfo Field

The `encapContentInfo` field has the type `EncapsulatedContentInfo`, which is defined as:

```
EncapsulatedContentInfo ::= SEQUENCE {
                               eContentType ContentType,
                               eContent [0] EXPLICIT OCTET STRING OPTIONAL }
```

Most signatures you deal with will be what are commonly referred to as *detached* or *external* signatures, where the signature and the data the signature is for are separate. When the data is contained in the signature, the data plus signature is referred to as *encapsulated signed data*. In the case of a signature where the data is encapsulated, the `eContent` field in the `EncapsulatedContentInfo` will contain an `OCTET STRING` that represents the BER or DER encoding of the data that was signed. In the case where the signature is external, the `eContent` field will be missing and the `eContentType` will be set with a value that is appropriate to the data that was signed — normally `id-data`.

If you have a look at the ASN.1 module for PKCS #7, you'll realize that the field in the `SignedData` structure that would represent `encapContentInfo` is defined as being of the type `ContentInfo`, meaning that the `content` field is of type `ANY` rather than having an `eContent` field of the type `OCTET STRING`. In practice this does not generally matter, but it does mean that, technically, it is possible to produce a message with an orthodox PKCS #7 implementation that you cannot process simply using CMS as defined by RFC 3852. If you need to process messages like this, some working around is required, as described in section 5.2.1 of the RFC.

The Certificates and Crls Fields

The `certificates` and `crls` fields have the types `CertificateRevocationLists` and `CertificateSet` respectively. These two types are defined as:

```
RevocationInfoChoices ::= SET OF RevocationInfoChoice

RevocationInfoChoice ::= CHOICE {
```

```
                                 crl CertificateList,
                                 other [1] IMPLICIT OtherRevocationInfoFormat }

OtherRevocationInfoFormat ::= SEQUENCE {
                             otherRevInfoFormat OBJECT IDENTIFIER,
                             otherRevInfo ANY DEFINED BY otherRevInfoFormat }

CertificateSet ::= SET OF CertificateChoices

CertificateChoices ::= CHOICE {
                             certificate Certificate,
                             v2AttrCert [2] IMPLICIT AttributeCertificateV2,
                             other [3] IMPLICIT OtherCertificateFormat }

AttributeCertificateV2 ::= AttributeCertificate

OtherCertificateFormat ::= SEQUENCE {
                             otherCertFormat OBJECT IDENTIFIER,
                             otherCert ANY DEFINED BY otherCertFormat }
```

If you look at the RFC you'll see I've deleted two obsolete fields from the `CertificateChoices` structure in order to simplify things. However, the `CertificateList` type is just the same one you saw for a CRL in Chapter 7, and the definition of `Certificate` is the same as the one given in Chapter 6. The `AttributeCertificate` type is defined in RFC 3281 and represents a version 2 attribute certificate. `OtherCertificateFormat` you can leave to your imagination!

For the purposes of this chapter I'll be ignoring certificates of type `OtherCertificateFormat` and crls of the type `OtherRevocationInfoFormat`, as the types are provided to allow later expansion to CMS. I will also ignore attribute certificates, as they are not used for validating signatures — they don't contain a public key. Instead they contain role information and are used to represent a digitally signed identity with certain privileges rather than a digitally signed key.

The SignerInfos Field

The `signerInfos` field has the type `SignerInfos`, which, together with its associated structure, `SignerInfo`, is defined as follows:

```
SignerInfos ::= SET OF SignerInfo

SignerInfo ::= SEQUENCE {
                 version CMSVersion,
                 sid SignerIdentifier,
                 digestAlgorithm DigestAlgorithmIdentifier,
                 signedAttrs [0] IMPLICIT SignedAttributes OPTIONAL,
                 signatureAlgorithm SignatureAlgorithmIdentifier,
                 signature SignatureValue,
                 unsignedAttrs [1] IMPLICIT UnsignedAttributes OPTIONAL }
```

The version number of the `SignerInfo` structure is determined by the type of the value that the `SignerIdentifier` contains. The `SignerIdentifier` is of type `CHOICE` and is defined as follows:

```
SignerIdentifier ::= CHOICE {
                       issuerAndSerialNumber IssuerAndSerialNumber,
                       subjectKeyIdentifier [0] SubjectKeyIdentifier }
```

Where `IssuerAndSerialNumber` is defined as:

```
IssuerAndSerialNumber ::= SEQUENCE {
                          issuer Name,
                          serialNumber CertificateSerialNumber }
```

and `SubjectKeyIdentifier` is the same value as you would find in the `SubjectKeyIdentifier` extension on the certificate associated with the signer's private key. You should be able to recognize the `IssuerAndSerialNumber` structure as being made up of the two values that you were using with the `X509CertSelector` class in Chapter 6 to specify search criteria that will match only one certificate by using the issuer `X500Principal` and the certificate serial number.

Now getting back to the version number, if the `SignerIdentifier` contains an item of the type `IssuerAndSerialNumber`, the version number of the `SignerInfo` structure will be 1. If the `SignerIdentifier` contains a `SubjectKeyIdentifier` instead, the version number will be 3.

You have already seen that the type of the `digestAlgorithm` field, `DigestAlgorithmIdentifier` reduces to an `AlgorithmIdentifier`, and it will probably be no surprise to find that the type of the `signatureAlgorithm` field, `SignatureAlgorithmIdentifier` does too. The actual `signature` field's type `SignatureValue` is simply an OCTET STRING.

This leaves you with the `signedAttrs` and `unsignedAttrs` fields left. The definitions of the types associated with these two implicitly tagged fields are

```
SignedAttributes ::= SET SIZE (1..MAX) OF Attribute

UnsignedAttributes ::= SET SIZE (1..MAX) OF Attribute
```

with `Attribute` being essentially the same structure you saw in Chapter 5.

The signed attributes are worth a bit of further discussion, as, if they are present, it means that the signature contained in the `SignerInfo` structure is really calculated on the hash of the DER encoding of the signed attribute set, not the data that is the subject of the `SignedData` structure. In this case the actual hash of the data will be present in a signed attribute called the *message-digest attribute*, and there will also be a content-type attribute that must match the value stored in the `eContentType` field in the `EncapsulatedContentInfo` structure contained in the `SignedData` structure.

The message-digest attribute is identified by the OID:

```
id-messageDigest OBJECT IDENTIFIER ::= { iso(1) member-body(2)
                             us(840) rsadsi(113549) pkcs(1) pkcs9(9) 4 }
```

and it will contain an OCTET STRING in its value set representing the bytes making up the hash.

The content-type attribute can be identified by the OID:

```
id-contentType OBJECT IDENTIFIER ::= { iso(1) member-body(2)
                           us(840) rsadsi(113549) pkcs(1) pkcs9(9) 3 }
```

and it will contain an OBJECT IDENTIFIER in its value set that must match the one in the `eContentType` field.

Although you can find a complete list of possible attributes in section 11 of RFC 3852, I'll mention one other signed attribute here as you will encounter it a lot — the signing-time attribute. It is identified by the OID:

```
id-signingTime OBJECT IDENTIFIER ::= { iso(1) member-body(2)
                          us(840) rsadsi(113549) pkcs(1) pkcs9(9) 5 }
```

and it contains a value of the type `Time` in its value set. The `Time` type is defined as:

```
Time ::= CHOICE {
   utcTime          UTCTime,
   generalizedTime  GeneralizedTime }
```

which is the same structure that you saw used in X.509 certificates in Chapter 6. As the name suggests, the signing-time attribute allows the signer to include the time at which the signing process was performed in the `SignerInfo` structure.

The Version Field

The value of `version` field in a `SignedData` structure depends on which optional fields are present, as well as what some of them contain. If the `certificates` or the `crls` field is present and either of them contain structures representing the choice item `other`, then the version `field` will have the value 5. If the `certificates` field contains version 2 attribute certificates, the `version` field will have the value 4. Otherwise, ignoring obsolete values, if any `SignerInfo` structure is version 3, or the `eContentType` field of the structure contained in `encapContentInfo` is not `id-data`, then the `version` field of the `SignedData` structure will be 3. If none of the previous conditions apply, the `version` field will have the value 1.

This concludes how the internal structure of a CMS signed-data message is put together. Next you'll look at the Java classes available to support it.

The SignerInformation Class

The `org.bouncycastle.cms.SignerInformation` class provides the Java equivalent to the `SignerInfo` objects. You will never construct one of these classes directly; instead, they are created as a result of creating `CMSSignedData` objects or from editing other `SignerInformation` objects.

As I go through the methods, you will see that the structure of the class largely reflects the `SignerInfo` structure, with the addition of some `verify()` methods for checking the signature and a static convenience method to allow the creation of a new `SignerInformation` object from another one that has different unsigned attributes.

SignerInformation.getDigestAlgOID()

The `getDigestAlgOID()` method returns a `String` representing the OID of the algorithm used as to create the message digest used in the signature calculation.

SignerInformation.getDigestAlgParams()

The `getDigestAlgParams()` method returns a byte array containing the DER-encoded parameters for the message digest used or `null` if they are absent.

SignerInformation.getEncryptionAlgOID()

The `getEncryptionAlgOID()` method returns a `String` representing the OID of the algorithm used to encrypt the message digest to create the signature in the `SignerInfo` structure.

SignerInformation.getEncryptionAlgParams()

The `getEncryptionAlgParams()` method returns a byte array containing the DER-encoded parameters for the algorithm used to encrypt the digest or `null` if they are absent.

SignerInformation.getSID()

The `getSID()` method returns an object representing the `sid` field in the `SignerInfo` structure. The object is of the type `SignerId` and can be used to identify the signer — it overrides both `Object.equals()` and `Object.hashCode()`. The `SignerId` class is also an extension of the `X509CertSelector` class, so the object returned by `getSID()` can be used to index a `CertStore` to find the `X509Certificate` object the `SignerInfo` structure's `sid` value refers to.

SignerInformation.getSignature()

The `getSignature()` method returns the actual bytes that make up the signature stored in the `signatureValue` field in the `SignerInfo` structure. If you are planning to do any processing with these bytes, remember: If the signed attributes are present, the signature returned by this method represents a signature calculated from the signed attributes, not from the actual data that is the subject of the `SignerInfo` structure.

SignerInformation.getSignedAttributes()

The `getSignedAttributes()` method returns an `org.bouncycastle.asn1.cms.AttributeTable` object containing `org.bouncycastle.asn1.cms.Attribute` objects representing the signed attributes contained in the `SingerInfo` structure.

SignerInformation.getUnsignedAttributes()

The `getUnsignedAttributes()` method returns an `AttributeTable` object containing Attribute objects representing the unsigned attributes contained in the `SingerInfo` structure.

SignerInformation.verify()

The `verify()` method is used to verify the signature contained in the `SignerInfo` structure the `SignerInformation` object represents. There are two versions of the method. The first takes a `PublicKey` and a `String` representing the provider name to use for creating any necessary message digest and signature objects. The other takes an `X509Certificate` and a `String` representing the provider name to use for creating any cryptographic services required. In either case, if the provider is null, the JVM's default provider is used.

Both versions of the method return `true` if the signature validates, `false` otherwise. If the method taking the `X509Certificate` is used and there is a `signingTime` attribute present in the `SignerInfo` object, the certificate will be checked for validity at the time indicated by the `signingTime` attribute.

Both methods' versions can throw `NoSuchAlgorithmException` if it is not possible to create objects implementing the necessary algorithms to verify the signature, `NoSuchProviderException` if a provider was requested and could not be found, and `CMSException` if some other failure takes place. If the method taking the `X509Certificate` is used, it may also throw a `CertificateExpiredException`, or a `CertificateNotYetValidException` if the `signingTime` attribute is present and the certificate was not valid at the time indicated by the attribute.

SignerInformation.replaceUnsignedAttributes()

The `replaceUnsignedAttributes()` method is a static method that takes a `SignerInformation` object and an `AttributeTable` object and returns a new `SignerInformation` object. The return value is a copy of the one passed to the method, but with its unsigned attributes now being the attributes contained in the `AttributeTable` that the method was called with.

The SignerInformationStore Class

The `org.bouncycastle.cms.SignerInformatiomStore` class is a simple collection class for containing `SignerInformation` objects. It has a single constructor that takes a collection of `SignerInformation` objects as its parameters and three methods: `get()`, `getSigners()`, and `size()`.

SignerInformationStore.get()

The `get()` method takes a `SignerId` object as its parameter and returns the `SignerInformation` object that matches it. If there is no matching object, the method returns `null`.

SignerInformationStore.getSigners()

The `getSigners()` method returns a collection containing all the `SignerInformation` objects contained in the store.

SignerInformationStore.size()

The `size()` method returns the number of `SignerInformation` objects contained in the store.

The CMSSignedData Class

The `org.bouncycastle.cms.CMSSignedData` class has four public constructors for general use. Objects and objects of the class can also be made using objects of the `CMSSignedDataGenerator` class, which is in the same package. Two are for dealing with CMS signed-data where the data is encapsulated in the signed-data message and take either an `InputStream` or a byte array that provides the bytes making up a `ContentInfo` structure and the `SignedData` structure it contains. The second two are for detached, or external, signatures and take a `CMSProcessable` in addition to an `InputStream` or a byte array. In the case of these last two constructors, the only thing expected in the `InputStream` or byte array is the encoded signed-data message with signatures. The verification calculations will be done using the data gained from the `CMSProcessable`. The constructors will throw a `CMSException` if there is a problem parsing the `ContentInfo` or `SignedData` structure from the source provided.

The `CMSSignedData` class is also designed to work in conjunction with the `java.security.cert.CertStore` class and to work with the `SignerInformationStore` class. As this is the case, it doesn't provide an immediate parallel to the ASN.1 structure, as some simplifications have been possible. With this in mind, you'll look at the methods on `CMSSignedData` now.

CMSSignedData.getCertificatesAndCRLs()

The `getCertificatesAndCRLs()` method returns a `CertStore` containing any regular X.509 certificates and certificate revocation lists found in the `SignedData` structure. Note that both the `certificates` and `crls` fields are optional. Therefore, although a `CertStore` will always be returned, it might be empty.

CMSSignedData.getEncoded()

The `getEncoded()` method returns the ASN.1 binary encoding of the `SignedData` structure contained in the object, together with its encapsulating `ContentInfo` object. This will normally be encoded using the BER rules rather than the DER ones. The method will throw an `IOException` if a problem occurs generating the encoding.

CMSSignedData.getSignedContent()

The `getSignedContent()` method returns the `CMSProcessable` that contains the source data for the signatures contained in the `SignerInfo` structures making up the message. You can either recover the data by passing an `OutputStream` to the `write()` method or by calling `getContent()`. If the data that the signatures in the message were calculated on is encapsulated in the `SignedData` structure, this is the method you need to call to recover the encapsulated data.

CMSSignedData.getSignedContentOID()

The `getSignedContentOID()` returns a `String` representing the object identifier found in the `eContentType` field of the `EncapsulatedContentInfo` structure found in the `SignedData` structure. Generally this will just be the value `id-data`, but some applications that use CMS as the transport mechanisms do demand specific values, so you should not assume it always will be.

CMSSignedData.getSignerInfos()

The `getSignerInfos()` method returns a `SignerInformationStore` that contains a collection of `SignerInformation` objects representing the `SignerInfo` structures contained in the `SignedData` structure.

CMSSignedData.replaceSigners()

The static `replaceSigners()` method takes a `CMSSignedData` object and a `SignerInformation` store as parameters and returns a new `CMSSignedData` object that is a copy of the one passed in, except its `SignerInfo` objects have been replaced with the ones contained in the `SignerInformation` store. This may seem like a strange thing to do, but if you have created some new `SignerInformation` objects by adding unsigned attributes to already existing ones and you want to replace the originals on the `CMSSignedData` object, they came from the replaceSigners() method is the one you want to use.

That covers all the classes and methods you need to create an example. Let's try doing it.

Try It Out   Creating and Validating a Detached Signature

Before showing the example, I will define a parent class, which I'll be using for the other signed-data examples appearing in the chapter as well. The object of the parent class is to provide a method for validating the first signature contained in a `SignedData` structure against a given trust anchor and a store of certificates. Here is the parent class:

```
package chapter9;

import java.security.cert.*;
import java.util.Iterator;

import org.bouncycastle.cms.CMSSignedData;
import org.bouncycastle.cms.SignerInformation;
import org.bouncycastle.cms.SignerInformationStore;

/**
 * Base class for signed examples.
 */
public class SignedDataProcessor
{
    /**
     * Return a boolean array representing keyUsage with digitalSignature set.
     */
    static boolean[] getKeyUsageForSignature()
    {
        boolean[] val = new boolean[9];

        val[0] = true;

        return val;
    }

    /**
     * Take a CMS SignedData message and a trust anchor and determine if
     * the message is signed with a valid signature from a end entity
     * entity certificate recognized by the trust anchor rootCert.
     */
    public static boolean isValid(
        CMSSignedData signedData, X509Certificate rootCert) throws Exception
    {
        CertStore certsAndCRLs = signedData.getCertificatesAndCRLs(
                                                "Collection", "BC");
        SignerInformationStore  signers = signedData.getSignerInfos();
        Iterator                it = signers.getSigners().iterator();

        if (it.hasNext())
        {
            SignerInformation           signer = (SignerInformation)it.next();
            X509CertSelector            signerConstraints = signer.getSID();

            signerConstraints.setKeyUsage(getKeyUsageForSignature());

            PKIXCertPathBuilderResult result = Utils.buildPath(
                                    rootCert, signer.getSID(), certsAndCRLs);

            return signer.verify(result.getPublicKey(), "BC");
        }

        return false;
    }
}
```

Next, you have the actual example class. It uses the `CMSSignedDataGenerator` to create a `CMSSignedData` object representing a detached signature for some byte data. The `CMSSignedData` object then gets encoded and reconstructed. You then use the `isValid()` method from the parent class to verify the signature. Here is the example class:

```java
package chapter9;

import java.security.KeyStore;
import java.security.PrivateKey;
import java.security.cert.*;
import java.util.Arrays;

import org.bouncycastle.cms.CMSProcessable;
import org.bouncycastle.cms.CMSProcessableByteArray;
import org.bouncycastle.cms.CMSSignedData;
import org.bouncycastle.cms.CMSSignedDataGenerator;

/**
 * Example of generating a detached signature.
 */
public class SignedDataExample
    extends SignedDataProcessor
{
    public static void main(String[] args) throws Exception
    {
        KeyStore        credentials = Utils.createCredentials();
        PrivateKey      key = (PrivateKey)credentials.getKey(
                                    Utils.END_ENTITY_ALIAS, Utils.KEY_PASSWD);
        Certificate[]   chain = credentials.getCertificateChain(
                                                Utils.END_ENTITY_ALIAS);
        CertStore       certsAndCRLs = CertStore.getInstance(
                            "Collection", new CollectionCertStoreParameters(
                                            Arrays.asList(chain)), "BC");
        X509Certificate cert = (X509Certificate)chain[0];

        // set up the generator
        CMSSignedDataGenerator gen = new CMSSignedDataGenerator();

        gen.addSigner(key, cert, CMSSignedDataGenerator.DIGEST_SHA224);
        gen.addCertificatesAndCRLs(certsAndCRLs);

        // create the signed-data object
        CMSProcessable  data = new CMSProcessableByteArray(
                                                "Hello World!".getBytes());

        CMSSignedData signed = gen.generate(data, "BC");

        // re-create
        signed = new CMSSignedData(data, signed.getEncoded());

        // verification step
        X509Certificate rootCert = (X509Certificate)credentials.getCertificate(
                                                Utils.ROOT_ALIAS);

        if (isValid(signed, rootCert))
```

```
            {
                System.out.println("verification succeeded");
            }
            else
            {
                System.out.println("verification failed");
            }
        }
    }
```

Running the example, you should see the following output:

```
verification succeeded
```

This indicates that the data was signed successfully and the signature in the signed-data message was verified.

How It Works

Because this example is in two parts, I'll start by describing the `SignedDataProcessor` class and then review how the `SignedDataExample` class interacts with it.

Looking at `SignedDataProcessor`, you can see the `isValid()` method uses the `buildPath()` method you added to `Utils` for creating a validated `CertPath` and builds on the work you did in Chapter 7 on path validation using the CertPath API. The return value of the `signer.getSID()` provides the target constraints for the path building. Once the path is built, the public key for the end entity certificate is obtained from the `PKIXCertPathBuilderResult` object and the signature carried in the signer object is verified using a call to `signer.verify()`. The one extra twist is the use of the `getKeyUsageForSignature()` method, which returns a boolean array that will match a `KeyUsage` extension if the `digitalSignature` bit is set. Adding this to the `signerConstraints` object means that, if the `KeyUsage` extension is present in the signer's certificate, the certificate will only match if it can be used for validating digital signatures.

This brings you to the main driver in the `SignedDataExample` class. After the initialization code, a `CMSSignedDataGenerator` object is created to allow you to create the `CMSSignedData` object you want. A signer is added to the generator using the following code:

```
gen.addSigner(key, cert, CMSSignedDataGenerator.DIGEST_SHA224);
```

where `key` represents the signer's private key, `cert` represents the end entity certificate associated with the signer's private key, and the constant parameter at the end tells the generator that this signer wants to use the algorithm SHA-224.

Next, the certificates associated with the signer are added to the generator using

```
gen.addCertificatesAndCRLs(certsAndCRLs);
```

After a sample data object using `CMSProcessableByteArray` is created, the `CMSSignedData` object is created with the following line:

```
CMSSignedData signed = gen.generate(data, "BC");
```

Then `signed` is re-created using its ASN.1 binary encoding and the data object:

```
signed = new CMSSignedData(data, signed.getEncoded());
```

You have to pass the data object to the constructor because, in this case, the signature generated has been a detached one that does not encapsulate the data. If the `CMSSignedData` object was created with encapsulated data, the lines of code involving generation and re-creation would have read

```
CMSSignedData signed = gen.generate(data, true, "BC");

// re-create
signed = new CMSSignedData(signed.getEncoded());
```

As you can see, the constructor no longer requires the data to be passed to the constructor, because the binary encoding of the message produced by `signed.getEncoded()` contains the data as well.

After generation and re-creation, the example tries to verify the signature included in the `CMSSignedData` object. This just involves passing `signed` and the trust anchor `rootCert` to the `isValid()` method and letting the CertPath API go to work.

One last note before you go on to enveloped-data. RFC 3852 does not require either the certificates or CRLs related to the signers to be present in the `SignedData` structure. Therefore, depending on where your messages are coming from, the path validation associated with signature verification might be a bit more complicated or even a lot easier. You might be using a hard-coded certificate. In any case, you should get the general idea, just keep the things that are not specifically required by the RFC in mind. It will help avoid surprises.

CMS Enveloped-Data

Enveloped-data is constructed by first encrypting the data to be enveloped with a symmetric key and then encrypting the symmetric key with the algorithms appropriate for the intended recipients of the message using the process described in Figure 9-2.

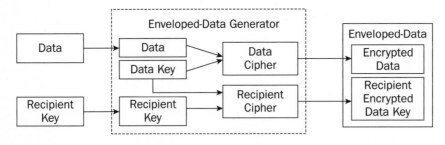

Enveloped-Data Structure Generation

Figure 9-2

The enveloped-data message is then the result of encapsulating the encrypted data in the message along with the information required for each recipient. When a recipient receives an enveloped-data message, the recipient extracts the pertinent recipient information and use it to recover the key used to encrypt the data. The recipient can then recover the encrypted data.

The recommended encryption algorithms that can be used for enveloping data were initially defined in RFC 3370 as DES-EDE and RC2. There is a wider choice than that, with mechanisms based on the ciphers CAST (RFC 2984), IDEA (RFC 3058), SKIPJACK (RFC 2876), and AES (RFC 3565) also available, to name but a few. As you'll see, there are also a variety of mechanisms available for transporting the symmetric keys used to encrypt the data.

ASN.1 Structure

CMS enveloped-data is created by wrapping an `EnvelopedData` structure in a `ContentInfo` structure with the `contentType` field set to the OID `id-envelopedData`, which is defined as:

```
id-envelopedData OBJECT IDENTIFIER ::= { iso(1) member-body(2)
                            us(840) rsadsi(113549) pkcs(1) pkcs7(7) 3 }
```

When the value `id-envelopedData` is found in the `contentType` field of a `ContentInfo` structure, the value present in the `content` field will be

```
EnvelopedData ::= SEQUENCE {
    version CMSVersion,
    originatorInfo [0] IMPLICIT OriginatorInfo OPTIONAL,
    recipientInfos RecipientInfos,
    encryptedContentInfo EncryptedContentInfo,
    unprotectedAttrs [1] IMPLICIT UnprotectedAttributes OPTIONAL }
```

The Java class for representing enveloped-data is the `CMSEnvelopedData` class.

The OriginatorInfo Field

The `originatorInfo` field, if present, provides information about the originator of the enveloped-data. The ASN.1 definition of `OriginatorInfo` type is given in RFC 3852 as follows:

```
OriginatorInfo ::= SEQUENCE {
    certs [0] IMPLICIT CertificateSet OPTIONAL,
    crls [1] IMPLICIT RevocationInfoChoices OPTIONAL }
```

How the contents of the `certs` and the `crls` fields are interpreted is largely up to the application reading it. Ideally there will be enough information to validate any end entity and attribute certificates present in the `CertificateSet` representing the `certs` field. However, RFC 3852 does allow for both unnecessary certificates and CRLs to be present, as well as insufficient certificates and CRLs to be present.

The RecipientInfos Field

The `recipientInfos` field is a collection representing the recipients the enveloped-data has been created for its ASN.1 definition and that of its member structure. `RecipientInfo` is as follows:

```
        RecipientInfos ::= SET SIZE (1..MAX) OF RecipientInfo

        RecipientInfo ::= CHOICE {
            ktri KeyTransRecipientInfo,
            kari [1] KeyAgreeRecipientInfo,
            kekri [2] KEKRecipientInfo,
            pwri [3] PasswordRecipientinfo,
            ori [4] OtherRecipientInfo }
```

As you can see, the definition requires that there must be at least one recipient for an enveloped-data message to be valid.

RFC 3852 mandates that conforming CMS implementations should be able to support the first three recipient choices: `KeyTransRecipientInfo`, `KeyAgreeRecipientInfo`, and `KEKRecipientInfo`. In practice, the first and third are the two common ones, although `PasswordRecipientInfo`, originally detailed in RFC 3211, is starting to generate a lot of interest these days. For the purposes of this chapter, I am just going to discuss the two most common ones — the `KeyTransRecipientInfo` type and the `KEKRecipientInfo` type.

A message can have more than one recipient type, but if you are doing this, you should always remember that the message can only be regarded as secure as the weakest recipient you have included, since compromising the weakest recipient will allow an attacker to recover the key used to encrypt the message.

The reason, as already mentioned, is that the recipients stored in an `EnvelopedData` structure are created as key wrappers for a symmetric key. Another aspect is that, as it is a common property, you will find the ASN.1 structure of the different recipient types reflects this. If you look at the ASN.1 module at the end of RFC 3852, you will find that the structures defining the first four choices all define two fields of the following ASN.1 types at some level:

```
        EncryptedKey ::= OCTET STRING

        KeyEncryptionAlgorithmIdentifier ::= AlgorithmIdentifier
```

with a field of the type `EncryptedKey` representing the bytes making up the wrapped symmetric key used to encrypt the data enveloped in the message and the `KeyEncryptionAlgorithmIdentifier` representing the algorithm that was used to do the wrapping. Keep these types in mind, as you will encounter them again when you look at the Java classes that are used to represent the various recipients and how they relate to the lower-level `RecipientInfo` choice items they represent.

The EncryptedContentInfo Field

The `encryptedContentInfo` field holds the data that was enveloped and the algorithm details for the encryption algorithm used to encrypt the data as part of enveloping it. The definition of its ASN.1 type is given as follows:

```
        EncryptedContentInfo ::= SEQUENCE {
            contentType ContentType,
            contentEncryptionAlgorithm ContentEncryptionAlgorithmIdentifier,
            encryptedContent [0] IMPLICIT EncryptedContent OPTIONAL }
```

As you can see, the structure is fairly straightforward. There is an OID hinting at what the plaintext of the encrypted content looks like — usually this is just `id-data`. The `ContentEncryptionAlgorithmIdentifier` type is defined as `AlgorithmIdentifier` and provides the details of the encryption algorithm used to create the encrypted content. Finally, there is the encrypted content itself, with the `EncryptedContent` type, which is defined as OCTET STRING.

If you look at RFC 3370 to see some of the encryption algorithms that can be used with CMS, you will see that they are block ciphers. As this is the case, RFC 3852 also defines the padding mechanism to be applied to the data before encryption if the data is not block aligned. It is the same scheme as that specified in PKCS #7, and if you are trying to decrypt the bytes stored in the `encryptedContent` field by hand, and the cipher used is a block cipher, you will need to remove the pad bytes to correctly recover the data if your cipher implementation does not do so.

The UnprotectedAttrs Field

The `unprotectedAttrs` field provides a mechanism for carrying attributes along with the `EnvelopedData` structure. Like the signed and unsigned attributes associated with a `SignerInfo`, it is just a SET of Attribute objects. RFC 3852 does not define any specific attributes for use here, but you could use the unprotected attributes to carry things like a digital timestamp of the encrypted data or other associated information that does not need to be encrypted.

The Version Field

The value of the `version` field in an `EnvelopedData` structure depends on which optional fields are present, as well as what some of them contain. If the `CertificateSet` contained in the `originatorInfo` field contains version 2 attribute certificates or the `recipientInfos` field contains recipients of the types `PasswordRecipientInfo` or `OtherRecipientInfo`, the `version` field will have the value 3. Otherwise, if `orginatorInfo` field is present or the `unprotectedAttrs` field is present or any `RecipientInfo` structure is other than version 0, then the `version` field will be 2. If none of the previous conditions apply, the `version` field will have the value 0.

This brings your look at the ASN.1 structures directly involved in the construction of an `EnvelopedData` structure to an end. I'll now start going through the Java classes, starting with the recipient-related ones and building up to the class representing the `EnvelopedData` structure.

The RecipientInformation Class

As you saw earlier, `RecipientInfo` is actually a CHOICE type with a range of possible types under it. The `org.bouncycastle.cms.RecipientInfomation` class is the parent class for the classes that implement the functionality required to recover keys that have been encrypted using the techniques represented by the possible choice items for `RecipientInfo`.

Objects of the type `RecipientInformation` and its extensions do not get created directly but are instead created as a result of constructing `CMSEnvelopedData` objects. As you will see when the extension classes are looked at, the methods on the `RecipientInformation` class capture what is common in the ASN.1 structures that are valid choice items for `RecipientInfo`.

RecipientInformation.getContent()

The getContent() method is an abstract method that takes a Key and a String representing the name of a provider to use and attempts to decrypt the data contained in the EnvelopedData structure, returning it in a byte array if successful.

The method will throw a NoSuchProviderException if it is unable to locate the provider with the passed-in name or a CMSException if any other problems occur.

RecipientInformation.getKeyEncryptionAlgOID()

The getKeyEncryptionAlgOID() returns a String representing the OID identifying the encryption algorithm used to encrypt this RecipientInformation objects version of the data encryption key.

RecipientInformation.getKeyEncryptionAlgorithmParameters()

The getKeyEncryptionAlgorithmParameters() method takes a String representing a provider to use and attempts to generate an AlgorithmParameters object that holds the encryption parameters used to encrypt the version of the data encryption key the RecipientInformation object holds.

It will throw a NoSuchProviderException if it is unable to locate the provider with the passed-in name or a CMSException if any other problems occur.

RecipientInformation.getKeyEncryptionAlgParams()

The getKeyEncryptionAlgParams() method returns a byte array containing the DER-encoded parameters that the key encryption algorithm for this RecipientIdentifier object used. The method returns null if the parameters are absent.

RecipientInformation.getRID()

Every recipient type also has some notion of a recipient identifier attached to it. The getRID() method returns an object representing a general identifier type for recipients — the RecipientId. A RecipientId object can be used to identify recipients, as it overrides both Object.equals() and Object.hashCode().

Like the SignerId class, it is also an extension of the X509CertSelector class, so if the recipient type indicates a public key was used to the encrypt the data encryption key, the object returned by getRID() can be used to index a CertStore to find the X509Certificate object carrying the public key that was used.

The KeyTransRecipientInformation Class

The org.bouncycastle.cms.KeyTransRecipientInformation class is an extension of the RecipientInfomation class and provides the necessary functionality to deal with enveloped-data where the data encryption key has been encrypted with a public key using an algorithm like RSA.

Recipients where the data encryption key has been handled in this fashion are indicated by the presence of a KeyTransRecipientInfo structure in the RecipientInfo CHOICE type. The KeyTransRecipientInfo structure has the following definition:

```
KeyTransRecipientInfo ::= SEQUENCE {
    version CMSVersion,
    rid RecipientIdentifier,
    keyEncryptionAlgorithm KeyEncryptionAlgorithmIdentifier,
    encryptedKey EncryptedKey }
```

where `RecipientIdentifier` is defined as:

```
RecipientIdentifier ::= CHOICE {
    issuerAndSerialNumber IssuerAndSerialNumber,
    subjectKeyIdentifier [0] SubjectKeyIdentifier }
```

which is identical to the `SignerIdentifier` type you saw earlier in the `SignedData` structure.

The class provides the implementation for the `getContent()` method required by the `RecipientInformation` class. The `rid` field becomes a `RecipientId`, with the fields of the type `RecipientIdentifier` being absorbed by that class, and the values in the `keyEncryptionAlgorithm` field are made available through the parent class. The version number is not exposed by the API but will either be 0 if the `RecipientId.getSubjectKeyIdentifier()` method returns a null, indicating the `RecipientId` object has been set with the details in a `IssuerAndSerialNumber` structure, or 2 otherwise.

The RecipientInformationStore Class

The `org.bouncycastle.cms.RecipientInformationStore` class is a simple collection class for containing `RecipientInformation` objects. It has one constructor that takes a collection of `RecipientInformation` objects as its parameter and three methods: `get()`, `getRecipients()`, and `size()`.

RecipientInformationStore.get()

The `get()` method takes a `RecipientId` object as its parameter and returns the `RecipientInformation` object that matches it. If there is no matching object, the method returns `null`.

RecipientInformationStore.getRecipients()

The `getRecipients()` method returns a collection containing all the `RecipientInformation` objects contained in the store.

RecipientInformationStore.size()

The `size()` method returns the number of `RecipientInformation` objects contained in the store.

The CMSEnvelopedData Class

The `org.bouncycastle.cms.CMSEnvelopedData` class has two constructors of for general use. Objects of the class can also be constructed using objects of the `CMSEnvelopedDataGenerator` class that can be found in the same package. The two constructors take a byte array and an input stream, respectively, where the parameter passed to the constructor is assumed to be a source for an ASN.1 binary-encoded `ContentInfo` structure containing an `EnvelopedData` object. The constructors will throw a `CMSException` if there is a problem parsing the `ContentInfo` or `EnvelopedData` structure from the source provided.

CMSEnvelopedData.getEncoded()

The getEncoded() method returns the ASN.1 binary encoding of the EnvelopedData structure contained in the CMSEnvelopedData object together with its encapsulating ContentInfo object. This will normally be encoded using the BER rules rather than the DER ones. The method will throw an IOException if a problem occurs generating the encoding.

CMSEnvelopedData.getEncryptionAlgOID()

The getEncryptionAlgOID() method returns a String representing the OID that identifies the algorithm used to encrypt the data contained in the object's EnvelopedData structure.

CMSEnvelopedData.getEncryptionAlgorithmParameters()

The getEncryptionAlgorithmParameters() method takes a single String representing the name of a provider to use and attempts to create an AlgorithmParameters object representing the algorithm parameters used to encrypt the data contained in the EnvelopedData structure the CMSEnvelopedData object represents.

The method will throw a NoSuchProviderException if it is unable to locate the provider with the passed-in name or a CMSException if any other problems occur.

CMSEnvelopedData.getEncryptionAlgParams()

The getEncryptionAlgParams() method returns a byte array representing the DER encoding of the algorithm parameters that were used to generate the encrypted data contained in the CMSEnvelopedData object's EnvelopedData structure.

CMSEnvelopedData.getRecipientInfos()

The getRecipientInfos() method returns a RecipientInformationStore containing all the RecipientInformation objects representing the contents of the recipientInfos field in the EnvelopedData structure represented by the CMSEnvelopedData object.

CMSEnvelopedData.getUnprotectedAttributes()

The getUnprotectedAttributes() method returns an AttributeTable of the unprotected attributes attached to the EnvelopedData structure. If the unprotectedAttrs field is missing, the method will return null.

At this point you have covered one recipient type and the support classes. Let's have a look at applying them.

Try It Out   Creating and Decoding CMS Enveloped-Data

This example shows how to create an enveloped-data message with a public key–based recipient in it. Have a look at it and try running it.

```
package chapter9;

import java.security.KeyStore;
import java.security.PrivateKey;
```

```java
import java.security.cert.Certificate;
import java.security.cert.X509Certificate;
import java.util.Arrays;

import org.bouncycastle.cms.CMSEnvelopedData;
import org.bouncycastle.cms.CMSEnvelopedDataGenerator;
import org.bouncycastle.cms.CMSProcessable;
import org.bouncycastle.cms.CMSProcessableByteArray;
import org.bouncycastle.cms.RecipientId;
import org.bouncycastle.cms.RecipientInformation;
import org.bouncycastle.cms.RecipientInformationStore;

/**
 * Demonstrate creation and processing a public key recipient enveloped-message.
 */
public class KeyTransEnvelopedDataExample
{
    public static void main(String[] args) throws Exception
    {
        KeyStore        credentials = Utils.createCredentials();
        PrivateKey      key = (PrivateKey)credentials.getKey(
                                        Utils.END_ENTITY_ALIAS, Utils.KEY_PASSWD);
        Certificate[]   chain = credentials.getCertificateChain(
                                                    Utils.END_ENTITY_ALIAS);
        X509Certificate cert = (X509Certificate)chain[0];

        // set up the generator
        CMSEnvelopedDataGenerator gen = new CMSEnvelopedDataGenerator();

        gen.addKeyTransRecipient(cert);

        // create the enveloped-data object
        CMSProcessable    data = new CMSProcessableByteArray(
                                                "Hello World!".getBytes());

        CMSEnvelopedData enveloped = gen.generate(
                            data,
                            CMSEnvelopedDataGenerator.AES128_CBC, "BC");

        // re-create
        enveloped = new CMSEnvelopedData(enveloped.getEncoded());

        // look for our recipient identifier
        RecipientId     recId = new RecipientId();

        recId.setSerialNumber(cert.getSerialNumber());
        recId.setIssuer(cert.getIssuerX500Principal().getEncoded());

        RecipientInformationStore   recipients = enveloped.getRecipientInfos();
        RecipientInformation        recipient = recipients.get(recId);

        if (recipient != null)
        {
            // decrypt the data
```

```
            byte[] recData = recipient.getContent(key, "BC");

            // compare recovered data to the original data
            if (Arrays.equals((byte[])data.getContent(), recData))
            {
                System.out.println("data recovery succeeded");
            }
            else
            {
                System.out.println("data recovery failed");
            }
        }
        else
        {
            System.out.println("could not find a matching recipient");
        }
    }
}
```

Running the example should produce the following output:

```
data recovery succeeded
```

indicating that the encrypted data stored in the enveloped-message was successfully recovered.

How It Works

After the basic initialization code, a CMSEnvelopedGenerator object is created and the recipient's public key information is added using the following line:

```
gen.addKeyTransRecipient(cert);
```

Adding the recipient extracts the serial number and the issuer from the certificate to store in the rid field of a KeyTransRecipientInfo structure that is created when the CMSEnvelopedData object is finally produced by the generator. It also extracts the public key so that it can be used for wrapping the symmetric key that is generated to encrypt the data when gen.generate() is finally called. For this recipient, the algorithm used for encrypting the symmetric key is derived from the type of the public key present in the certificate.

In the next step, the data is wrapped in a class that implements CMSProcessable. An EnvelopedData structure is generated and returned, wrapped in a CMSEnvelopedData object.

```
CMSEnvelopedData enveloped = gen.generate(
                        data,
                        CMSEnvelopedDataGenerator.AES128_CBC, "BC");
```

After that, the CMSEnvelopedData object is reconstructed from its encoded form and a RecipientId is created from the certificate to find the corresponding recipient in the enveloped message. The message is recovered, and after the decrypted data is verified, the output is printed.

Of course, there are a variety of ways you can use the RecipientId; it depends on your circumstances. In some situations, you might have a couple of private keys that you use for decrypting messages you receive. If this is the case, you are probably better off using the information contained in the `RecipientId` object attached to the `RecipientInformation` object to determine whether you have a match against a particular private key first. Once you find a match against a `RecipientId`, you should be confident that the `RecipientInformation` object you have is one that should be used with your private key.

The following code shows one way of doing this. You add the necessary imports and replace everything following the line

```
// look for our recipient identifier
```

with

```
    // set up to iterate through the recipients
    RecipientInformationStore    recipients = enveloped.getRecipientInfos();
    CertStore                    certStore = CertStore.getInstance(
                       "Collection", new CollectionCertStoreParameters(
                                        Collections.singleton(cert)), "BC");
    Iterator                     it = recipients.getRecipients().iterator();
    RecipientInformation         recipient = null;

    while (it.hasNext())
    {
        recipient = (RecipientInformation)it.next();
        if (recipient instanceof KeyTransRecipientInformation)
        {
            // match the recipient ID
            Collection matches = certStore.getCertificates(recipient.getRID());

            if (!matches.isEmpty())
            {
                // decrypt the data
                byte[] recData = recipient.getContent(key, "BC");

                // compare recovered data to the original data
                if (Arrays.equals((byte[])data.getContent(), recData))
                {
                    System.out.println("data recovery succeeded");
                    break;
                }
                else
                {
                    System.out.println("data recovery failed");
                    break;
                }
            }
        }
    }

    if (recipient == null)
    {
        System.out.println("could not find a matching recipient");
    }
```

You should also see the `data recovery succeeded` message, indicating that the enveloped message was successfully decrypted and the plaintext recovered.

Still another approach when you're using a keystore is to match the certificate and then use `KeyStore .getCertificateAlias()` to find out the alias name of the key entry associated with the certificate. You then retrieve the key using the alias name returned. It depends a lot on how you manage your private keys and certificates, so you can think of solving this problem as being left as an exercise in imagination, rather than just as an exercise.

The KEKRecipientInformation Class

The `org.bouncycastle.cms.KEKRecipientInformation` is the processing class for the second kind of recipient(those protected with key-encryption keys. It is also an extension of the `RecipientInfomation` class, and the class provides the necessary functionality to deal with enveloped-data where the data encryption key has been encrypted with a key-encryption key (KEK) using a symmetric algorithm such Triple-DES or AES, rather than a public key as you saw with the `KeyTransRecipientInformation` class.

Recipients using key-encryption keys are indicated by the presence of an implicit tag of value 2 containing a structure of the `KEKRecipientInfo` type in the `RecipientInfo` CHOICE type. The `KEKRecipientInfo` type has the following ASN.1 definition:

```
KEKRecipientInfo ::= SEQUENCE {
    version CMSVersion,
    kekid KEKIdentifier,
    keyEncryptionAlgorithm KeyEncryptionAlgorithmIdentifier,
    encryptedKey EncryptedKey }
```

with the `KEKIdentifier` type defined as:

```
KEKIdentifier ::= SEQUENCE {
    keyIdentifier OCTET STRING,
    date GeneralizedTime OPTIONAL,
    other OtherKeyAttribute OPTIONAL }
```

The class provides the implementation for the `getContent()` method required by the `RecipientInformation` class. In a similar fashion to the `KeyTransRecipientInformation` class, the `kekid` field becomes a `RecipientId` with the fields of the type `KeyIdentifier` being absorbed by that class and the values in the `keyEncryptionAlgorithm` field made available through the parent class. The version number is not exposed by the API but will always have the value 4.

A recipient of this type is also indicated by the `getKeyIdentifier()` method of its `RecipientId` object returning a byte array, representing the value of the `keyIdentifier` field, rather than `null`. It is the values in the returned byte array that the `RecipientInformation` store will use to match a `KEKRecipient`.

Other than the difference in the `RecipientId` identifier information, you'll see that using this recipient type is very similar to using the public-key-based recipient.

Try It Out   **Using Key-Encrypted Keys with Enveloped-Data**

This example shows the processing required for creating and using a key-encrypted key recipient in an enveloped-data message. Have a look at the code and try running it.

```java
package chapter9;

import java.util.Arrays;

import javax.crypto.*;

import org.bouncycastle.cms.*;

/**
 * Demonstrate creation and processing a key-encrypted key enveloped-message.
 */
public class KEKEnvelopedDataExample
{
    public static void main(String[] args) throws Exception
    {
        KeyGenerator    keyGen = KeyGenerator.getInstance("DESEDE", "BC");
        SecretKey       key = keyGen.generateKey();

        // set up the generator
        CMSEnvelopedDataGenerator edGen = new CMSEnvelopedDataGenerator();

        byte[]  kekID = new byte[] { 1, 2, 3, 4, 5 };

        edGen.addKEKRecipient(key, kekID);

        // create the enveloped-data object
        CMSProcessable  data = new CMSProcessableByteArray(
                                            "Hello World!".getBytes());

        CMSEnvelopedData enveloped = edGen.generate(
                        data,
                        CMSEnvelopedDataGenerator.AES128_CBC, "BC");
        // re-create
        enveloped = new CMSEnvelopedData(enveloped.getEncoded());

        // look for our recipient
        RecipientId     recId = new RecipientId();

        recId.setKeyIdentifier(kekID);

        RecipientInformationStore   recipients = enveloped.getRecipientInfos();
        RecipientInformation        recipient = recipients.get(recId);

        if (recipient != null)
        {
            // decrypt the data
            byte[] recData = recipient.getContent(key, "BC");

            // compare recovered data to the original data
            if (Arrays.equals((byte[])data.getContent(), recData))
```

```
        {
            System.out.println("data recovery succeeded");
        }
        else
        {
            System.out.println("data recovery failed");
        }
    }
    else
    {
        System.out.println("could not find a matching recipient");
    }
}
}
```

Running the example should produce the following output:

```
data recovery succeeded
```

indicating that the symmetric key was successfully matched against the recipients and the data recovered.

How It Works

As you can see, this example is very similar to the one for the public key–based recipient, with only a few differences.

The first difference is, because you are using a symmetric key rather than an asymmetric one, the key has no certificates associated with it. To make things easy, you use the KeyGenerator class to create the key, but ordinarily you might instead fetch the key from some type of keystore. As far as the choice of algorithm goes, in this case you are using a Triple-DES key, but there are also wrapping algorithms defined for RC2 and AES, so either of those two would work as well. It is largely up to the recipient, but remember, if you are mixing key-wrapping methods, the weakest recipient is also the weakest link in security. Likewise, when you are dealing with a group of recipients, the minimum level of security any of the recipients is willing to accept is the minimum level required for the keys of all recipients.

The next difference is in the manner the entry is added to the generator:

```
        edGen.addKEKRecipient(key, kekID);
```

In this case, rather than using identifying information gained from a certificate, the key is identified using the byte array referenced by keyID. As you can imagine, in a real-life situation, this would also be information that would need to be known to the recipient.

You can see that by taking advantage of the RecipientInformationStore class, the code for looking up a recipient is identical to the public key–based recipient. Likewise, if you wanted to, you could iterate through the recipients instead to find the one you want. It all depends on how you want to do it.

The last content type you will look at in CMS is the one used for creating compressed-data content. Although it is not directly related to cryptography, it can be quite useful and is included as a content type in S/MIME.

Data Compression in CMS

The compressed-data content type for CMS is defined separately from RFC 3852 — it is defined in RFC 3274. As it does not involve encryption or authentication, it has a simpler ASN.1 structure than the others, and as you will see by the code in the example, it is also a lot more straightforward to use.

ASN.1 Structure

CMS compressed-data is created by wrapping a `CompressedData` structure in a `ContentInfo` structure with the `contentType` field set to the OID `id-ct-compressedData`, which is defined as:

```
id-ct-compressedData OBJECT IDENTIFIER ::= { iso(1) member-body(2)
                us(840) rsadsi(113549) pkcs(1) pkcs-9(9) smime(16) ct(1) 9 }
```

and the `CompressedData` structure is defined as:

```
CompressedData ::= SEQUENCE {
                version CMSVersion,
                compressionAlgorithm CompressionAlgorithmIdentifier,
                encapContentInfo EncapsulatedContentInfo }
```

As you can probably guess, `CompressionAlgorithmIdentifier` is further defined as being of the type `AlgorithmIdentifier`, and `EncapsulatedContentInfo` is the same type you encountered when you looked at CMS signed-data. The version number is always 0.

Currently the only compression algorithm specified is ZLIB, which is identified using the following OID:

```
id-alg-zlibCompress OBJECT IDENTIFIER ::= { iso(1) member-body(2)
                us(840) rsadsi(113549) pkcs(1) pkcs-9(9) smime(16) alg(3) 8 }
```

Compared to the other CMS structures you have looked at, this one is quite simple. Fortunately, the Java classes related to compressed-data reflect this.

The CMSCompressedData Class

The `org.bouncycastle.cms.CMSCompressedData` class has two general use constructors that can take either a byte array or an `InputStream` representing a binary encoding of a `ContentInfo` structure and the `CompressedData` structure it contains. As you will see in the next example, `CMSCompressedData` objects can also be created using objects of the `CMSCompressedDataGenerator` class.

CMSCompressedData.getContent()

The `getContent()` method returns a byte array representing the contents of the `encapContentInfo` field after uncompressing.

The method will throw a `CMSException` if a problem occurs uncompressing the data.

CMSCompressedData.getEncoded()

The `getEncoded()` method returns the binary ASN.1 encoding of the object. The encoding may follow the BER or DER encoding rules.

The method will throw an IOException if a problem occurs generating the encoding.

Try It Out   Using Compression with CMS

Here is a simple example showing how to use the compressed-content type. As you can see, it is much easier to deal with than the previous content types discussed.

```java
package chapter9;

import java.util.Arrays;

import org.bouncycastle.cms.CMSCompressedData;
import org.bouncycastle.cms.CMSCompressedDataGenerator;
import org.bouncycastle.cms.CMSProcessableByteArray;

/**
 * Basic use of CMS compressed-data.
 */
public class CompressedDataExample
{
    public static void main(String args[]) throws Exception
    {
        // set up the generator
        CMSCompressedDataGenerator gen = new CMSCompressedDataGenerator();

        //compress the data
        CMSProcessableByteArray  data = new CMSProcessableByteArray(
                                            "Hello world!".getBytes());

        CMSCompressedData compressed = gen.generate(data,
                                        CMSCompressedDataGenerator.ZLIB);

        // re-create and uncompress the data
        compressed = new CMSCompressedData(compressed.getEncoded());

        byte[] recData = compressed.getContent();

        // compare uncompressed data to the original data
        if (Arrays.equals((byte[])data.getContent(), recData))
        {
            System.out.println("data recovery succeeded");
        }
        else
        {
            System.out.println("data recovery failed");
        }
    }
}
```

Running the example produces the following message:

```
data recovery succeeded
```

indicating the data compressed without problems.

How It Works

This example follows a similar pattern to the earlier ones in that a generator is created and used to create a `CMSCompressedData` object from an implementation of `CMSProcessable` using the following line:

```
CMSCompressedData compressed = gen.generate(data,
                               CMSCompressedDataGenerator.ZLIB);
```

where `CMSCompressedDataGenerator.ZLIB` is a string representing the OID for the ZLIB algorithm.

After this, the `CMSCompressedData` object is reconstructed from its binary encoding, and the original data is recovered from it.

One thing to note here is that, although ZLIB is a lossless compression algorithm, not all compression algorithms are — especially those that can be used with images and sound. If you ever get to the point of using other compression algorithms and combining the compressed-content type with the signed-data type, compress the data before creating the signed-data; otherwise, the use of a "lossy" compression algorithm will mean your signatures are invalid.

CMS is not just an end in itself, but is used as the basis for a number of other protocols. Chief amongst these is S/MIME.

Secure/Multipurpose Internet Mail Extensions (S/MIME)

S/MIME, or the Secure/Multipurpose Internet Mail Extensions, defines a method of sending MIME data securely. If you have ever received an e-mail that indicated it was signed or encrypted, chances are it was an S/MIME message you were looking at.

Like other Internet standards, S/MIME is defined using an RFC, in this case RFC 3851, that describes S/MIME version 3.1. There are additional standards based on S/MIME, which define variants such as AS2, which are used for business-to-business electronic commerce.

In the Bouncy Castle APIs there are two packages devoted to S/MIME: `org.bouncycastle.smime`, which contains the high-level classes that handle creation and processing of MIME messages involving encryption, signing, and compression, and `org.bouncycastle.asn1.smime`, which is a collection of low-level classes that provide Java object equivalents for the ASN.1 structures defined in the S/MIME ASN.1 module. As S/MIME is a combination of MIME objects and the structures used in CMS, using S/MIME also involves using the JavaMail API, and you will also find some of the classes in the Bouncy Castle CMS API talked about earlier in this chapter will be useful from time to time.

I've written this section of the chapter in a manner that does not assume you are already familiar with the JavaMail API — the examples will tell you the minimum you need to know. I would recommend, however, that you take some time to read the documentation accompanying the JavaMail API if you want to take full advantage of S/MIME.

Before I start on the particulars of the API for the three content types, I'll just start with two of the general classes that make up the API so I can refer to them later. They are `CMSProcessableBodyPart` and `SMIMEUtil`.

The CMSProcessableBodyPart Class

The `org.bouncycastle.mail.smime.CMSProcessableBodyPart` class is a general implementation of `CMSProcessable` that just uses the `Part.writeTo()` method to output the data to the stream passed in to the `CMSProcessable.write()` method. It is used by the classes involved with processing enveloped and compressed mime messages to feed the bytes making up the MIME message into the appropriate classes in the CMS API. Usually you will not need to use this class directly, but it is worth being aware of its existence.

The SMIMEUtil Class

The `org.bouncycastle.mail.smime.SMIMEUtil` class provides a couple of utility methods that are of general use when working with S/MIME messages. The two methods are `toMimeBodyPart()` and `createIssuerAndSerialNumberFor()`.

SMIMEUtil.toMimeBodyPart()

The `toMimeBodyPart()` method takes a byte array and returns a `MimeBodyPart` created from the byte array. You can use this method for recovering a `MimeBodyPart` from the bytes you extract from the two classes representing compressed and enveloped S/MIME message — `SMIMECompressed` and `SMIMEEnveloped`.

SMIMEUtil.createIssuerAndSerialNumberFor()

The `createIssuerAndSerialNumberFor()` method returns an `IssuerAndSerialNumber` object for the `X509Certificate` object passed to it as a parameter. The `IssuerAndSerialNumber` class is in the `org.bouncycastle.asn1.cms` package and represents the Java equivalent to the `IssuerAndSerialNumber` structure in the CMS ASN.1 definitions you saw earlier in the chapter. You will mainly find this useful for creating the encryption key preference attribute, which is one of the attributes you can attach to a S/MIME signed message. You'll look at how to do this in the next section.

S/MIME Signed Messages

Signed messages in S/MIME can be represented using either single MIME body part messages or MIME multipart messages. You'll encounter the MIME multipart message when the data signed has not being encapsulated in the signature. In this case the message will be in two body parts, the first part containing the contents that was signed and the second part containing the signature. When the data is encapsulated or the message is a certificate management message and only created to carry certificates, you will receive the message in a single MIME body part. In general, for signing data, you should use the multipart format whenever possible. As it is what is known as a *clear signing* technique, it has the advantage that the body part containing the data that was signed is readable by anyone, even if they use a MIME processor that is unable to deal with the body part containing the CMS signed-data message in the second part.

The "Content-Type" header in the MIME message will reflect the kind of signed message you are looking at. If the MIME type indicated by the header is `application/pkcs7-mime`, then the body part contains either a signature with encapsulated data or a certificate management message. If it is an encapsulated data message, the header will also include a `smime-type` parameter that will be set to `"signed-data"`. If it is a certificate management message, the `smime-type` parameter will be `"certs-only"`. In the case of a multipart message, the MIME type of the body part containing the signature will be `application/pkcs7-signature` with the `smime-type` parameter set to `"signed-data"` and the MIME type of the actual multipart will be `multipart/signed` with a `protocol` parameter that is set to the string `"application/pkcs7-signature"`.

The only real complication with creating S/MIME signed messages has to do with what happens to text when it passes through various mail agents. The main issue is that some platforms terminate lines with a line-feed character (LF), and others terminate them with a carriage-return character followed by a line-feed character (CRLF), and as a mail message moves around the line, endings may change from what it was created with. As a result of this decision made in S/MIME, all text is considered to end with CRLF for the purposes of signature calculation. The process of treating a text file like this is referred to as *CRLF canonicalization*. The Bouncy Castle API will now do this for you by default on nonbinary data, which is fine for applications built to follow RFC 3851, but not so good if you are using something like AS2 where the default transfer encoding is binary, not 7 bit as it is in RFC 3851. I'll explain how to vary the default transfer encoding a bit later, but as you can probably guess, it is simply a matter of knowing how to set your own defaults.

It doesn't stop there either. Depending on your environment, other weird and not-so-wonderful things can happen to MIME messages as they wander around the network. For example, some gateways will remove trailing whitespace between the last non-whitespace character and the end of line marker. These things tend to be the exception rather than the rule now, but if you are "lucky" enough to run into one of these gateways, the important thing to remember when signatures fail to validate for MIME text data is to check to see what's changed. If something has changed and you cannot explain it as result of CRLF canonicalization, then you may need to introduce some extra canonicalization processing of your own.

With this in mind, I'll introduce the two `CMSProcessable` implementations that look after canonicalization. Ordinarily you will never need to use them directly, but it is worth knowing they are there. After that I will move on to the Java class used to represent an S/MIME signed message.

The CMSProcessableBodyPartInbound Class

The `org.bouncycastle.mail.smime.CMSProcessableBodyPartInbound` class is an implementation of `CMSProcessable`, which applies CRLF canonicalization to the `BodyPart` object it is constructed with if the "Content-Transfer-Encoding" header does not indicate the data being processed is binary. The class is used exclusively by the signed MIME message class `SMIMESigned` to correctly canonicalize data during the process of signature verification.

The CMSProcessableBodyPartOutbound Class

The `org.bouncycastle.mail.smime.CMSProcessableBodyPartOutbound` class is also an implementation of `CMSProcessable`, which applies CRLF canonicalization to a nonbinary data `BodyPart`. In this case the class is used exclusively by the signed MIME message generator class `SMIMESignedGenerator` to correctly canonicalize data during the process of signature creation.

The SMIMESigned Class

The `org.bouncycastle.mail.smime.SMIMESigned` class is an extension of the `CMSSignedData` class you saw earlier and adds a few methods peculiar to the requirement of dealing with S/MIME signed messages in Java — the need to be able to extract MIME data in the form of the `MimeBodyPart` and `MimeMessage` classes.

It has three constructors. Two take a `MimeMultipart` that is assumed to contain two mime body parts, one containing the data that was signed and one containing a detached CMS signed-data object, and one takes a single `Part` object that is assumed to contain a CMS signed-data object with encapsulated data. The first two constructors can throw `MessagingException` and `CMSException` if there is a problem processing the `MimeMultipart`, and the third one will also throw a `SMIMEException` if the MIME message encapsulated in the CMS signed-data object cannot be extracted.

The second of the `MimeMultipart` constructors also takes a default value for the "Content-Transfer-Encoding" header. This indicates how the message should be treated if the header is not specified in the MIME object's header. This is important to remember. Although RFC 3851 does define the default content-transfer-encoding as "7 bit," not all S/MIME related standards use "7 bit" as the default. AS2, for example, defaults to "binary," and you can imagine how successfully signatures are created or verified if binary data they are based on gets CRLF canonicalized during the process.

The methods follow. As you can see, they just deal with MIME objects — the real functionality required for validation of signatures is the same as you have already looked at in the `CMSSignedData` class.

SMIMESigned.getContent()

The `getContent()` method returns the `MimeBodyPart` representing the data that the signatures contained in the `SMIMESigned` object were created against.

SMIMESigned.getContentAsMimeMessage()

The `getContentAsMimeMessage()` method is a convenient method that returns the data that the messages signatures were created for as a `MimeMessage` object.

SMIMESigned.getContentWithSignature()

The `getContentWithSignature()` method returns the object that was used to create the `SMIMESigned` object. The object returned will be either a `MimeBodyPart` or a `MimeMultipart` depending on whether the signed message was created with encapsulated data or not.

Try It Out   Creating and Validating a S/MIME Signed Message

This example shows how to create and process a multipart S/MIME signed message. It's rather long, so I'll break it up so I can give you some commentary before getting to the full explanation in the How It Works that follows.

The first part is represented by the class header. As you'll notice, there is a CMS API class being used and several classes from the S/MIME API. The example also makes use of the JavaMail API, and the example class extends the `SignedProccessor` class that you created earlier in "Try It Out: Creating and Validating a Detached Signature."

```
package chapter9;

import java.security.KeyStore;
import java.security.PrivateKey;
import java.security.cert.*;
import java.util.Arrays;

import javax.mail.internet.MimeBodyPart;
```

```
import javax.mail.internet.MimeMessage;
import javax.mail.internet.MimeMultipart;

import org.bouncycastle.asn1.ASN1EncodableVector;
import org.bouncycastle.asn1.cms.AttributeTable;
import org.bouncycastle.asn1.smime.SMIMECapabilitiesAttribute;
import org.bouncycastle.asn1.smime.SMIMECapability;
import org.bouncycastle.asn1.smime.SMIMECapabilityVector;
import org.bouncycastle.asn1.smime.SMIMEEncryptionKeyPreferenceAttribute;
import org.bouncycastle.mail.smime.SMIMESigned;
import org.bouncycastle.mail.smime.SMIMESignedGenerator;
import org.bouncycastle.mail.smime.SMIMEUtil;

/**
 * a simple example that creates and processes a signed mail message.
 */
public class SignedMailExample
    extends SignedDataProcessor
{
```

The second part provides the functionality that creates the multipart signed message. It defines a method called `createMultipartWithSignature()`, which just takes the required credentials to do the signing and the `MimeBodyPart` holding the data to be signed as parameters. Upon its completion, the method returns the `MimeMultipart` containing the `MimeBodyPart` passed in and its signature.

```
    public static MimeMultipart createMultipartWithSignature(
        PrivateKey key, X509Certificate cert, CertStore certsAndCRLs,
                                     MimeBodyPart dataPart) throws Exception
    {
        // create some smime capabilities in case someone wants to respond
        ASN1EncodableVector      signedAttrs = new ASN1EncodableVector();
        SMIMECapabilityVector    caps = new SMIMECapabilityVector();

        caps.addCapability(SMIMECapability.aES256_CBC);
        caps.addCapability(SMIMECapability.dES_EDE3_CBC);
        caps.addCapability(SMIMECapability.rC2_CBC, 128);

        signedAttrs.add(new SMIMECapabilitiesAttribute(caps));
        signedAttrs.add(new SMIMEEncryptionKeyPreferenceAttribute(
                           SMIMEUtil.createIssuerAndSerialNumberFor(cert)));

        // set up the generator
        SMIMESignedGenerator gen = new SMIMESignedGenerator();

        gen.addSigner(key, cert, SMIMESignedGenerator.DIGEST_SHA256,
                                    new AttributeTable(signedAttrs), null);

        gen.addCertificatesAndCRLs(certsAndCRLs);

        // create the signed message
        return gen.generate(dataPart, "BC");
    }
```

The third, and last part, is the main driver. It uses the `createMultipartWithSignature()` method to create a signed multipart. It then uses the `Utils` method you added at the start of the chapter to produce a template for a mail message from the signed multipart you have created, recovers the multipart from the mail template, and checks the signature for validity.

```java
public static void main(String args[]) throws Exception
{
    KeyStore        credentials = Utils.createCredentials();
    PrivateKey      key = (PrivateKey)credentials.getKey(
                                Utils.END_ENTITY_ALIAS, Utils.KEY_PASSWD);
    Certificate[]   chain = credentials.getCertificateChain(
                                            Utils.END_ENTITY_ALIAS);
    CertStore       certsAndCRLs = CertStore.getInstance(
                            "Collection",
                            new CollectionCertStoreParameters(
                                        Arrays.asList(chain)),
                            "BC");
    X509Certificate cert = (X509Certificate)chain[0];

    // create the message we want signed
    MimeBodyPart    dataPart = new MimeBodyPart();

    dataPart.setText("Hello world!");

    // create the signed message
    MimeMultipart multiPart = createMultipartWithSignature(
                                    key, cert, certsAndCRLs, dataPart);

    // create the mail message
    MimeMessage mail = Utils.createMimeMessage(
            "example signed message", multiPart, multiPart.getContentType());

    // extract the message from the mail message
    if (mail.isMimeType("multipart/signed"))
    {
        SMIMESigned         signed = new SMIMESigned(
                                    (MimeMultipart)mail.getContent());

        // verification step
        X509Certificate rootCert = (X509Certificate)credentials.getCertificate(
                                                Utils.ROOT_ALIAS);

        if (isValid(signed, rootCert))
        {
            System.out.println("verification succeeded");
        }
        else
        {
            System.out.println("verification failed");
        }

        // content display step
```

```
        MimeBodyPart                content = signed.getContent();

        System.out.print("Content: ");
        System.out.println(content.getContent());
    }
    else
    {
        System.out.println("wrong content found");
    }
  }
}
```

Running the example should produce the following output:

```
verification succeeded
Content: Hello world!
```

indicating that both the signature verification succeeded and the content that was signed was successfully recovered.

How It Works

You are probably already familiar with the initialization code in the main driver by now; the only change in this case is that you are creating a MimeBodyPart to sign rather than a CMSProcessable. You can do this because, as mentioned earlier, the S/MIME API has three implementations of CMSProcessable for processing MIME objects that it makes use of internally.

After initialization, the code enters the createMultipartWithSignature() method, where it starts by creating some attributes to be included in the CMS signed-data message that will end up containing a signature for the content of dataPart. Just as there are attributes available in CMS, there are also additional attributes that can be used with signed-data if it is being used in conjunction with S/MIME. In this case, the method is creating the two most typical ones — the S/MIME capabilities attribute and the encryption key preference attribute.

The capabilities attribute tells the receivers of the message something about what you can process if they want to respond to you. This example indicates that you are willing to accept messages encrypted using the algorithms AES (256-bit key), Triple-DES, and RC2 (128-bit key). As you can see, the capabilities are mainly indicated by OIDs with the odd parameter thrown in where needed. The order in which these appear is significant, because the receiver will assume that the first encryption algorithm identified is your preferred choice if they are going to send you an enveloped message. You can find more information about some of the others by consulting RFC 3851, but other capabilities that can be specified include which signing algorithms you can read and whether you can handle compressed data.

The encryption key preference attribute indicates which public key you would prefer people to use if they are including you in their list of recipients in an enveloped message. The encryption key preference attribute contains a SMIMEEncryptionKeyPreference structure, which is defined as follows:

```
        SMIMEEncryptionKeyPreference ::= CHOICE {
                        issuerAndSerialNumber   [0] IssuerAndSerialNumber,
                        recipientKeyId          [1] RecipientKeyIdentifier,
                        subjectAltKeyIdentifier [2] SubjectKeyIdentifier }
```

In the case of the example, you are just using the `issuerAndSerialNumber` choice item and you are using the certificate you are providing to validate the message with as the one you want people to use as your encryption key. The main reason I've done this is to reduce the complexity of the example. In general, it is a good idea to make sure that the certificate you give people to validate your signatures and the certificate you give people to use when they want to encrypt something with your public key are two distinct certificates with two distinct keys. Keeping a certificate single purpose reduces the possible avenues by which people can attempt to compromise the private key associated with it.

After creating the attributes, the method creates a generator for `SMIMESigned` objects and adds a signer to it using the following line:

```
gen.addSigner(key, cert, SMIMESignedGenerator.DIGEST_SHA256,
                             new AttributeTable(signedAttrs), null);
```

You'll notice this method is really the same as that on the `CMSSignedDataGenerator` class — not really surprising because it is to one of those that the information is being passed. The parameters mean the same as they did before. `Key` is the private key the signature will be created with. `Cert` is passed in to provide identifying information to help the entity who will eventually verify the signature locate the right public key certificate to use. The next parameter specifies the message digest to be used for signature calculation, and it is followed by the signed attributes and the unsigned attributes.

Once the generator is properly set up, `gen.generate()` is called with the `BodyPart` you want signed and the generator returns a containing a multipart signed S/MIME object.

The mulitpart signed MIME object is then wrapped in a `MimeMessage`, which could serve as a mail message. Then, a `SMIMESigned` object is created using the `MimeMessage` content and the example proceeds with the verification step. As `SMIMESigned` is an extension of `CMSSignedData`, this is just a matter of calling the `isValid()` method that is defined on the parent class and then printing the appropriate message.

That brings you to the end of S/MIME signed messages. By way of further information, the `SMIMESignedGenerator` also has methods for creating MIME objects representing signatures with encapsulated data and certificate management messages. You can generate these by using the `generateEncapsulated()` and `generateCertificateManagement()` methods, respectively.

Now you will take a look at S/MIME enveloped messages. These carry CMS enveloped-data in order to achieve their purpose.

S/MIME Enveloped Messages

Unlike S/MIME signed messages, S/MIME enveloped messages are only represented as a single MIME body part. The reason is that, as they contain CMS enveloped-data messages, the encrypted data that they hold the details for is also carried inside them. You can identify S/MIME enveloped messages as their MIME type will be `application/pkcs7-mime` with a `smime-type` parameter of `"enveloped-data"`.

As they contain the data within them, and it is encrypted in any case, none of the canonicalization issues that you saw with S/MIME signed messages apply. For this reason, the Java classes for creating and processing them use the `CMSProcessableBodyPart` class for both the encryption and the decryption steps when dealing with MIME body parts that are being used in relation to S/MIME enveloped messages. The class that represents these messages in the Bouncy Castle S/MIME API is the `SMIMEEnveloped` class.

The SMIMEEnveloped Class

The org.bouncycastle.cms.SMIMEEnveloped class is an extension of the CMSEnvelopedData class you saw earlier in the chapter. It can be constructed with either a MimeMessage or a MimeBodyPart, which is assumed to contain a CMS enveloped-data message. The constructors can throw either a MessagingException if there is a problem using the passed-in MIME object or a CMSException if there is a problem with the processing the CMS message contained in the passed-in MIME object.

The class adds only one method getEncryptedContent(), which simply returns the MimePart it was constructed with. Like the SMIMESigned class, the methods on the parent class, CMSEnvelopedData, provide all the functionality required to process the enveloped message.

As you can see, it is a lot simpler to deal with than creating an S/MIME signed message. Fortunately, the code is simpler as well.

Try It Out   **Using S/MIME Enveloped Messages**

This example creates an S/MIME enveloped message from some data and then recovers the data in the second step. If you compare it to "Try It Out: Creating and Decoding CMS Enveloped-Data," you will see that, other than the use of the MIME and S/MIME objects, the two examples are quite similar.

```java
package chapter9;

import java.security.KeyStore;
import java.security.PrivateKey;
import java.security.cert.Certificate;
import java.security.cert.X509Certificate;

import javax.mail.internet.MimeBodyPart;
import javax.mail.internet.MimeMessage;

import org.bouncycastle.cms.RecipientId;
import org.bouncycastle.cms.RecipientInformation;
import org.bouncycastle.cms.RecipientInformationStore;
import org.bouncycastle.mail.smime.SMIMEEnveloped;
import org.bouncycastle.mail.smime.SMIMEEnvelopedGenerator;
import org.bouncycastle.mail.smime.SMIMEUtil;

/**
 * a simple example that creates and processes an enveloped mail message.
 */
public class EnvelopedMailExample
{
    public static void main(String args[]) throws Exception
    {
        KeyStore        credentials = Utils.createCredentials();
        PrivateKey      key = (PrivateKey)credentials.getKey(
                                    Utils.END_ENTITY_ALIAS, Utils.KEY_PASSWD);
        Certificate[]   chain = credentials.getCertificateChain(
                                    Utils.END_ENTITY_ALIAS);
        X509Certificate cert = (X509Certificate)chain[0];

        // create the message we want encrypted
```

```
MimeBodyPart      dataPart = new MimeBodyPart();

dataPart.setText("Hello world!");

// set up the generator
SMIMEEnvelopedGenerator  gen = new SMIMEEnvelopedGenerator();

gen.addKeyTransRecipient(cert);

// generate the enveloped message
MimeBodyPart envPart = gen.generate(
                  dataPart, SMIMEEnvelopedGenerator.AES256_CBC, "BC");

// create the mail message
MimeMessage mail = Utils.createMimeMessage(
                     "example enveloped message",
                     envPart.getContent(), envPart.getContentType());

// create the enveloped object from the mail message
SMIMEEnveloped  enveloped = new SMIMEEnveloped(mail);

// look for our recipient identifier
RecipientId     recId = new RecipientId();

recId.setSerialNumber(cert.getSerialNumber());
recId.setIssuer(cert.getIssuerX500Principal().getEncoded());

RecipientInformationStore   recipients = enveloped.getRecipientInfos();
RecipientInformation        recipient = recipients.get(recId);

if (recipient != null)
{
    // decryption step
    MimeBodyPart      recoveredPart = SMIMEUtil.toMimeBodyPart(
                                 recipient.getContent(key, "BC"));

    // content display step
    System.out.print("Content: ");
    System.out.println(recoveredPart.getContent());
}
else
{
    System.out.println("could not find a matching recipient");
}
    }
}
```

Running the example will print the original content that was used to create the message, giving the following output:

```
Content: Hello world!
```

which shows that the recipient was matched correctly and the original MIME content was successfully recovered.

How It Works

As already mentioned, the example has a strong relationship to its CMS relative — the real difference being more that you are dealing with `MimeBodyPart` and `MimeMessage` objects than anything else. In a similar fashion to the CMS example, after the basic initialization is complete, a `SMIMEEnvelopedGenerator` object is created and a public key-based recipient is added to it using the `gen.addKeyTransRecipient()` method.

The generator object is then invoked with the following line:

```
MimeBodyPart envPart = gen.generate(
                          dataPart, SMIMEEnvelopedGenerator.AES256_CBC, "BC");
```

which takes the object `dataPart`, encrypts its content, and returns a `MimeBodyPart` object containing an S/MIME enveloped message. After this, a `MimeMessage` is created from the body part, and then a `SMIMEEnveloped` message is created from the `MimeMessage`, so beginning the process of recovering the encrypted data.

You've already seen the recipient matching process in the CMS enveloped-data example. As before, a `RecipientId` is being created for the certificate used in the encryption and that is being used to recover a `RecipientInformation` object that can be processed with the private key corresponding to the public key in the certificate. The difference in the recovery step is that this time you are expecting the enveloped-data structure to contain the encoding of a MIME body part, not just a text message. You still get a byte array back from the `RecipientInformation` object, but as it happens, the `SMIMEUtil` class has a method, `toMimeBodyPart()`, which allows you to take a raw byte stream that represents a MIME body part and create a `MimeBodyPart` object that represents it. You use the method to re-create the MIME body part and then you are able to display its content, which ends the example.

One last issue you might be pondering: The example shows that as far as the generation of S/MIME enveloped messages goes, it is a case of a single body part in, a single body part out. As you've already seen, signed messages can be multipart messages. Therefore, an interesting question is how to take a multipart message and create an enveloped message from it. As you'll see in the next section, fortunately, it is quite straightforward.

Combining Signing with Encryption

Often you want to sign and encrypt data to produce a single message. In some respects how you do this depends a lot on what you are trying to do. If you encrypt then sign, it makes it possible for the signatures to be checked without decrypting the data — you can reject data without having to decrypt it. On the other hand, perhaps you want the signatures to be protected as well.

The general philosophy, if you have no reason for bias, is to "sign what you mean." In respect of most enveloped messages, what this means is normally the data that has been enveloped. Consequently, the normal practice is to sign first and then encrypt. This is the approach taken in the next example.

Try It Out   Enveloping a Signed Message

This example first signs a message, envelopes it, and then reverses the process — recovering the data and verifying the signature. It uses the `SignedMailExample.createMultipartWithSignature()` method that you created earlier in "Try It Out: Creating and Validating a S/MIME Signed Message" to perform the signing step and, also, extends the `SignedProcessor` class. However, it is still rather large — mainly because there is a lot going on. As this is the case, I will split it up a bit to make sure what is happening at each step is a bit clearer.

The first stage, as always, is the initialization phase, where you collect the necessary certificates and keys. Including the class header, here is how the code looks for that:

```
package chapter9;

import java.security.KeyStore;
import java.security.PrivateKey;
import java.security.cert.*;
import java.util.Arrays;

import javax.mail.internet.*;

import org.bouncycastle.cms.*;
import org.bouncycastle.mail.smime.*;

/**
 * a simple example that creates and processes an enveloped signed mail message.
 */
public class EnvelopedSignedMailExample extends SignedDataProcessor
{
    public static void main(String[] args) throws Exception
    {
        KeyStore        credentials = Utils.createCredentials();
        PrivateKey      key = (PrivateKey)credentials.getKey(
                                        Utils.END_ENTITY_ALIAS, Utils.KEY_PASSWD);
        Certificate[]   chain = credentials.getCertificateChain(
                                                    Utils.END_ENTITY_ALIAS);
        CertStore       certsAndCRLs = CertStore.getInstance(
                                    "Collection",
                                    new CollectionCertStoreParameters(
                                                    Arrays.asList(chain)),
                                    "BC");
        X509Certificate cert = (X509Certificate)chain[0];
```

In the next stage, the `MimeBodyPart` you want to process gets created, and then you create a multipart signed S/MIME object using the `SignedMailExample.createMultipartWithSignature()` method:

```
        // create the message we want signed
        MimeBodyPart    dataPart = new MimeBodyPart();

        dataPart.setText("Hello world!");

        // create the signed message
        MimeMultipart signedMulti = SignedMailExample.createMultipartWithSignature(
                                            key, cert, certsAndCRLs, dataPart);
```

The multipart signed message is represented by the `MimeMultipart` object. The first step to enveloping is to wrap it in another body part so that you reduce the problem to that of having a single `MimeBodyPart` to envelope. This is done in the following code:

```
// create the body part containing the signed message
MimeBodyPart signedPart = new MimeBodyPart();


signedPart.setContent(signedMulti);
```

After that, all you need to do is envelope it like you did earlier and create a `MimeMessage` that you can then feed into a mailer:

```
// set up the enveloped message generator
SMIMEEnvelopedGenerator  gen = new SMIMEEnvelopedGenerator();

gen.addKeyTransRecipient(cert);

// generate the enveloped message
MimeBodyPart envPart = gen.generate(
                signedPart, SMIMEEnvelopedGenerator.AES256_CBC, "BC");

// create the mail message
MimeMessage mail = Utils.createMimeMessage(
                        "example signed and enveloped message",
                        envPart.getContent(), envPart.getContentType());
```

Having come as far as creating the `MimeMessage`, you then reverse the process, first using the message to create a `SMIMEEnveloped` you can process and then finding a `RecipientInformation` object that matches your public key so you can recover the `MimeBodyPart` that was enveloped using your private key.

```
// create the enveloped object from the mail message
SMIMEEnveloped      enveloped = new SMIMEEnveloped(mail);

// look for our recipient identifier
RecipientId        recId = new RecipientId();

recId.setSerialNumber(cert.getSerialNumber());
recId.setIssuer(cert.getIssuerX500Principal().getEncoded());

RecipientInformationStore   recipients = enveloped.getRecipientInfos();
RecipientInformation        recipient = recipients.get(recId);

// decryption step
MimeBodyPart        res = SMIMEUtil.toMimeBodyPart(
                                    recipient.getContent(key, "BC"));
```

After that, it is a matter of taking the content of the `MimeBodyPart` and, if it is what you expect, creating a `SMIMESigned` object and using the `isValid()` method to verify the signature:

```
                   // extract the multipart from the body part.
                   if (res.getContent() instanceof MimeMultipart)
                   {
                       SMIMESigned      signed = new SMIMESigned(
                                                  (MimeMultipart)res.getContent());

                       // verification step
                       X509Certificate rootCert = (X509Certificate)credentials.getCertificate(
                                                            Utils.ROOT_ALIAS);

                       if (isValid(signed, rootCert))
                       {
                           System.out.println("verification succeeded");
                       }
                       else
                       {
                           System.out.println("verification failed");
                       }

                       // content display step
                       MimeBodyPart            content = signed.getContent();

                       System.out.print("Content: ");
                       System.out.println(content.getContent());
                   }
                   else
                   {
                       System.out.println("wrong content found");
                   }
               }
           }
```

When you run the example, you should see that all the things that have been mentioned take place and you see the following output:

```
verification succeeded
Content: Hello world!
```

showing that after everything was said and done, the signatures validated correctly and you recovered the original content.

How It Works

This example also contains a lot of code that you have seen before, even if it has not been organized in quite the same fashion. The signing, encryption, decryption, and verification processes are ones you are already familiar with. In many respects, the real "magic" in this example has little to do with the cryptography being used. It is more about the following lines of code using the JavaMail API:

```
MimeBodyPart signedPart = new MimeBodyPart();

signedPart.setContent(signedMulti);
```

As you've seen so far, and as will be confirmed again when you read about compression and S/MIME in the next section, S/MIME message creation involves the processing of single MIME body parts to produce various kinds of secure MIME messages. However, if you start applying this technology, you will rapidly discover that multipart messages are quite common and the previous two lines of code are the key to dealing with them. You take the multipart and wrap it in a single body part.

This explains how you are able to carry out the task in the example. From initialization, you go to generation of a signed message that returns a `MimeMultipart` object; you then wrap that in a `MimeBodyPart` object representing a single MIME body part and can pass that into the `generate()` method on a `SMIMEEnvelopedGenerator` object to get back an S/MIME enveloped message contained in another `MimeBodyPart` object. Likewise, because `MimeBodyPart` objects know something about the content they contain, when the content of the S/MIME enveloped message is decrypted, you can tell that the `MimeBodyPart` object created contains a `MimeMultipart` object and the signature verification can then proceed from that.

> One thing to watch out for with creating signed messages containing other MIME objects: Some S/MIME clients will ignore certain headers in the contained MIME object when doing the signature calculation. Typically, this applies to the signature on a message containing a forwarded mail message — some clients will ignore the standard mail headers in the MIME object representing the forwarded e-mail. If you find yourself in the situation where signatures validate successfully on one client but not on another, it could be this problem you are dealing with.

There are other uses for wrapping a `MimeMultipart` in a `MimeBodyPart`: signing a multipart MIME object, for example, or even encrypting a regular multipart MIME object — it doesn't have to be a signed one. Another area where you could use the technique is for taking a multipart MIME object and using it to create an S/MIME compressed message using the classes you will look at in the next section.

S/MIME Compressed Messages

Like S/MIME enveloped messages, compressed messages do not have to deal with canonicalization issues, as the data they carry is obscured by the compression. You can identify S/MIME enveloped messages as their MIME type will be `application/pkcs7-mime` with a `smime-type` parameter of `"compressed-data"`.

As this is the case, the Java classes for creating and processing them use the `CMSProcessableBodyPart` class when dealing with MIME body parts that are being compressed or decoded. The class that represents these messages in the Bouncy Castle S/MIME API is the `SMIMECompressed` class.

The SMIMECompressed Class

The `org.bouncycastle.cms.SMIMECompressed` class is an extension of the `CMSCompressedData` class you saw earlier in the chapter. It can be constructed with either a `MimeMessage` or a `MimeBodyPart`, which is assumed to contain a CMS compressed-data message. The constructors can throw either a `MessagingException` if there is a problem using the passed-in MIME object or a `CMSException` if there is a problem with processing the CMS message contained in the passed-in MIME object.

The class adds only one method `getCompressedContent()`, which simply returns the `MimePart` it was constructed with. As you will see in the following example, like the other S/MIME message classes, the methods on the parent class, `CMSCompressedData`, provide all the functionality required to process the compressed message.

Using S/MIME Compression

This is the last example and it is probably also the simplest. It creates a compressed message carrying a MIME body part, which is then used to create a `MimeMessage`. The data is then extracted from the compressed message and printed to `stdout`.

```
package chapter9;

import javax.mail.internet.MimeBodyPart;
import javax.mail.internet.MimeMessage;

import org.bouncycastle.mail.smime.SMIMECompressed;
import org.bouncycastle.mail.smime.SMIMECompressedGenerator;
import org.bouncycastle.mail.smime.SMIMEUtil;

/**
 * a simple example that creates and processes an compressed mail message.
 */
public class CompressedMailExample
{
    public static void main(String args[]) throws Exception
    {
        // create the message we want compressed
        MimeBodyPart    dataPart = new MimeBodyPart();

        dataPart.setText("Hello world!");

        // set up the generator
        SMIMECompressedGenerator  gen = new SMIMECompressedGenerator();

        // generate the compressed message
        MimeBodyPart comPart = gen.generate(
                                    dataPart, SMIMECompressedGenerator.ZLIB);

        // create the mail message
        MimeMessage mail = Utils.createMimeMessage(
                                "example compressed message",
                                comPart.getContent(), comPart.getContentType());

        // create the enveloped object from the mail message
        SMIMECompressed  compressed = new SMIMECompressed(mail);

        // uncompression step
        MimeBodyPart     recoveredPart = SMIMEUtil.toMimeBodyPart(
                                            compressed.getContent());
        // content display step
        System.out.print("Content: ");
        System.out.println(recoveredPart.getContent());
    }
}
```

Try running the example; you should see the following output:

```
Content: Hello world!
```

showing that the compressed body part was successfully extracted.

How It Works

Not surprisingly, this example is almost identical to the CMS example you looked at for building compressed-data messages. The only difference is that, in this case, you are dealing with MIME objects.

A generator is created to produce `MimeBodyPart` objects carrying compressed data, a `MimeBodyPart` object is created, and the `gen.generate()` method is used to create a `MimeBodyPart` object that contains a CMS compressed-data message with the original `MimeBodyPart` object's contents compressed using ZLIB. This is then used to create a `MimeMessage` and the process is reversed. The `MimeMessage` is used to create an `SMIMECompressed` object that enables the recovery of the raw bytes making up the MIME body part that was compressed. These raw bytes are then used by `SMIMEUtil.toMimeBodyPart()` to re-create a `MimeBodyPart` object containing the original data.

Simple enough with one other point to remember. If you are signing data and then compressing it, make sure the choice of compression algorithm is such that it does not result in the data being changed, as it will be with some image, or sound, compression algorithms. If this can be the case, you need to compress first and then sign — not the other way around.

Summary

In this chapter, you looked at two secure messaging standards: CMS, or Cryptographic Message Syntax, and a related standard for processing MIME messages securely, S/MIME. You should now have a good understanding of how messages are constructed in both standards, as well as understand what some of the variations are and what being a variant might mean to your message processing.

Over the course of this chapter, you have learned the following:

❑   What the basic building blocks of a CMS message are

❑   How to use the Bouncy Castle CMS API to create signed, encrypted, and compressed CMS messages

❑   How to combine signed CMS messages with the CertPath API for the purposes of validation

❑   What the basic message types in S/MIME are

❑   How to use the Bouncy Castle S/MIME API to create and process signed, encrypted, and compressed S/MIME messages

Finally, you have also seen the differences between mulitpart and single-part data in S/MIME and how these data types can be combined to create S/MIME messages that are combinations of some, or all of, the signed, encrypted, or compressed message types.

CMS and S/MIME give you ways of sending discrete messages that are either signed, encrypted, or both. The next question to ask is how would you do this for a possible unlimited amount of data? Of course, one answer is to break the data down into fix-sized packets and use CMS. A better solution is to set up a secure channel between the two points you want to send the data between and just start sending it. You will see how you can achieve this in the next chapter when you read about the Secure Sockets Layer (SSL) protocol and its successor, the Transport Layer Security protocol (TLS).

Exercises

1. The `CMSProcessable` interface is for the purpose of allowing the implementation of objects that write byte data to a CMS object for processing. How would you implement one that takes `java.io.File` objects?

2. What is the best policy to adopt with the creation of certificates for encryption and signature validation?

3. Under what circumstances will a CMS signed-data message not contain any signers?

4. How would you modify the `SignedMailExample.createMultipartWithSignature()` method so that it takes a `MimeMultipart` and signs it rather than a `MimeBodyPart`?

5. If you wrap a mail message in another MIME body part, sign the result, and then find another application that will not validate the signature, what is most likely to be the problem?

6. When you are mixing signing and compression, under what circumstances is it mandatory that the signatures are calculated for the data after it has been compressed rather than before compression?

SSL and TLS

Having created discrete secured messages using CMS and S/MIME, it is now time to turn your attention to the issue of creating secure links over which you can transfer data and exchange messages.

This chapter looks at SSL and its offspring, TLS. This family of protocols is very different from protocols like CMS. The main reason is that they are socket-based and designed to allow the creation of secured links between two end points for data transmission and exchange. You are probably already familiar with SSL at some level; you probably encountered URLs that begin with "https" while buying items over the Internet. HTTPS connections are created using SSL, but as you will see, the possible uses for the protocol go much further than that.

The SSL API for Java is referred to as the JSSE (Java Secure Socket Extension). By the end of this chapter, using the JSSE, you should

❑   Understand the basics of the SSL protocol

❑   Know how to create a basic SSL client and server to secure communications

❑   Know how to use client-side authentication

❑   Know how to access SSL session information

Finally, you will be able to write client-side programs that can use and configure URL connections based on HTTPS.

The SSL and TLS Protocols

SSL (Secure Sockets Layer) was originally developed by Netscape as a means of securing communications across the Internet, primarily for electronic commerce. A total of three versions of the protocol were developed, with the last one, SSL version 3.0, being released in 1996. Since then, the development of the original idea has continued with TLS (Transport Layer Security), with the first version being published in RFC 2246 in January 1999. At this point, virtually all financial institutions have endorsed the use of SSL for electronic commerce.

The protocol is an interesting one, as it designed to be extensible. The initial handshake done between two end points when they are setting up an SSL channel includes negotiation for both the algorithms to be used and the key size. The algorithm set used for an SSL channel normally includes at least one public key mechanism, a symmetric cipher, a MAC algorithm, as well as their associated key sizes. This collection of algorithms is normally referred to as a *cipher suite*, and as you may well imagine, some cipher suites are better than others from a security point of view. The presence of weak cipher suites is largely for historical reasons, but you do need to be aware that they exist, as when you are using SSL, you should to take care to configure the link creation with specific cipher suites. You should do this so that a possibly malicious server or client cannot dumb down the cryptography being used on the link by using the negotiation phase to its advantage and subsequently fool your end of the link into transmitting the data across a link with much lower security than you wanted.

Normally you would have seen SSL being used where only one end point is actually authenticated(the server end. This is the common practice for Internet shopping; however, the protocol does allow for both ends of the link to authenticate to the other one. This type of link is usually described as one with client-side authentication, because it is assumed the server side is always authenticated.

Since RFC 2246 came out, other RFCs have also been published that add the use of Kerberos cipher suites (RFC 2712), extensions (RFC 3546), the AES algorithm (RFC 3268), and compression methods (RFC 3749). The RFCs read quite differently than the normal ones you run into in security, as, unlike the PKIX RFCs on the use of public key certificates, the TLS-related RFCs have their message formats documented in a C-like language rather than ASN.1. Currently, TLS is still at version 1.0, but at this writing, there is a TLS version 1.1 RFC under development, which will probably be released at the end of 2005. You can find out more about the development of TLS by looking at the Web site for the TLS Working Group, which is listed in Appendix D.

Having said all that, as SSL and TLS are both low-level protocols that operate just above the socket layer, you do not really need to be familiar with the RFCs to be able to use it in Java. The Java API that deals with SSL and TLS is the Java Secure Socket Extension, or JSSE for short. At its simplest, it can be summed up as providing two additional socket factory types and two additional socket types that can be used in the same way as regular socket factories and sockets defined in the `java.net` package. The JSSE goes a lot further than that, but that should give you an idea.

Like SSL itself, the JSSE has now gone through several versions. It was previously a standard extension to the JDK, versions 1.2 and 1.3. As of JDK 1.4, the JSSE was integrated into the JDK. This did result in some changes to the API, as prior to its integration with the JDK, some of the classes now found in the `javax.net.ssl` package were originally found in `com.sun.net.ssl`. So, if you are trying to use the examples with older versions of the JSSE, you might need to change the imports used in the examples accordingly and make a few other minor adjustments.

As of JDK 1.5, the JSSE can also support the Kerberos cipher suites outlined in RFC 2712. I won't discuss Kerberos support here in any detail, because I want to concentrate on using SSL with X.509, but it is a fact worth being aware of.

Getting Started

The `Utils` class for this chapter is quite simple; all it does is define some constants that will be used by the examples. You also need some keystores to use for the server and client sides of the links you'll be creating in the examples. By way of further reading, although it won't stop you from running the examples, or probably even understanding them, being familiar with some of the classes in the java.net package will not hurt.

I'll start with the Utils class and then move onto the keystore creation utility. Here is the new Utils class:

```java
package chapter10;

/**
 * Chapter 10 Utils
 */
public class Utils extends chapter9.Utils
{
    /**
     * Host name for our examples to use.
     */
    static final String HOST = "localhost";

    /**
     * Port number for our examples to use.
     */
    static final int PORT_NO = 9020;

    /**
     * Names and passwords for the keystore entries we need.
     */
    public static final String SERVER_NAME = "server";
    public static final char[] SERVER_PASSWORD = "serverPassword".toCharArray();

    public static final String CLIENT_NAME = "client";
    public static final char[] CLIENT_PASSWORD = "clientPassword".toCharArray();

    public static final String TRUST_STORE_NAME = "trustStore";
    public static final char[] TRUST_STORE_PASSWORD =
                                        "trustPassword".toCharArray();
}
```

and here is the keystore creation utility:

```java
package chapter10;

import java.io.FileOutputStream;
import java.security.KeyStore;
import java.security.cert.Certificate;

import javax.security.auth.x500.X500PrivateCredential;

/**
 * Create the various credentials for an SSL session
 */
public class CreateKeyStores
{
    public static void main(String[] args)
```

```
                    throws Exception
        {
            X500PrivateCredential rootCredential = Utils.createRootCredential();
            X500PrivateCredential interCredential = Utils.createIntermediateCredential(
                    rootCredential.getPrivateKey(), rootCredential.getCertificate());
            X500PrivateCredential endCredential = Utils.createEndEntityCredential(
                    interCredential.getPrivateKey(), interCredential.getCertificate());

            // client credentials
            KeyStore keyStore = KeyStore.getInstance("PKCS12", "BC");

            keyStore.load(null, null);

            keyStore.setKeyEntry(
                Utils.CLIENT_NAME, endCredential.getPrivateKey(), Utils.CLIENT_PASSWORD,
                new Certificate[] { endCredential.getCertificate(),
                                    interCredential.getCertificate(),
                                    rootCredential.getCertificate() });

            keyStore.store(
              new FileOutputStream(Utils.CLIENT_NAME + ".p12"), Utils.CLIENT_PASSWORD);

            // trust store for both ends
            keyStore = KeyStore.getInstance("JKS");

            keyStore.load(null, null);

            keyStore.setCertificateEntry(
                            Utils.SERVER_NAME, rootCredential.getCertificate());

            keyStore.store(
                    new FileOutputStream(Utils.TRUST_STORE_NAME + ".jks"),
                    Utils.TRUST_STORE_PASSWORD);

            // server credentials
            keyStore = KeyStore.getInstance("JKS");

            keyStore.load(null, null);

            keyStore.setKeyEntry(
                Utils.SERVER_NAME, rootCredential.getPrivateKey(), Utils.SERVER_PASSWORD,
                    new Certificate[] { rootCredential.getCertificate() });

            keyStore.store(
              new FileOutputStream(Utils.SERVER_NAME + ".jks"), Utils.SERVER_PASSWORD);
        }
    }
```

As you can see, the keystore creation utility, `CreateKeyStores`, creates three keystores, using methods on the `Utils` class that were defined in previous chapters. The first file is for client credentials, the second file contains a single trusted certificate that will be used as the trust anchor for (eventually) both ends to validate the X.509 credentials passed to them, and the third keystore contains the server credentials.

For the rest of chapter, I refer to SSL to cover both SSL and TLS. This convention is used in the Java API, and my explanations will become rather labored if I'm constantly writing "SSL and TLS." When a distinction needs to be drawn between the two protocols, I mention the protocol explicitly; otherwise, wherever you see "SSL" think "SSL and TLS."

A Basic SSL Client and Server

In its most common form, SSL is used between an authenticated server and a client. What takes place is described in Figure 10-1.

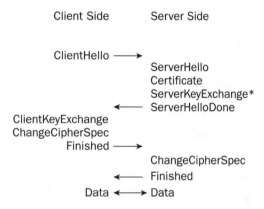

Message Flow for Authenticated Server, Unauthenticated Client Handshake
* Means Message Not Always Sent

Figure 10-1

In the case of an X.509-based cipher suite, this is done by the server presenting the client with a certificate chain (the Certificate message) after the client initially connects. If the protocol is using RSA, the client then uses the end entity certificate to encrypt an appropriate pre-master secret, which it sends back to the server(the `ClientKeyExchange` message. The pre-master secret is then converted by both ends into a master secret, which provides the bits required for a symmetric key required for doing encryption on the data and the MACs used for verifying the integrity of the data. Both ends start encrypting and communication on the link then proceeds.

You might be wondering what the optional `ServerKeyExchange` message is for. It's there because SSL includes key agreement in the mechanisms that can be used for the client and the server to arrive at an agreed secret. If the server is using key agreement, this message will be used to pass the server's parameters to the client so the necessary calculations can be done on the client side.

Raised up to the level of the JSSE API, you need to be able to use only four JSSE classes to get this to work. Two of them are factory classes, and the other two are socket classes used to represent the end points of the SSL connection.

Let's look at the factory classes first.

The SSLSocketFactory Class

The `javax.net.ssl.SSLSocketFactory` is used to create `SSLSocket` socket objects.

The class is an extension of the `java.net.SocketFactory` class and, in the same way as its parent class, is not created directly but normally by the `getDefault()` method. Like the `SSLServerSocketFactory` class, it is also possible to create `SSLSocketFactory` objects using an `SSLContext` object. I will cover this further on. Other than that, this class is quite straightforward, as you can see from the method descriptions that follow.

SSLSocketFactory.createSocket()

The `createSocket()` method returns a `Socket` object, which can be cast to `SSLSocket` if required.

Most of the `createSocket()` methods on the `SSLSocketFactory` class are inherited from the `SocketFactory` class and take the equivalent parameters.

The `SSLSocketFactory` also provides one additional `createSocket()` method, which takes an existing `Socket`, the host and port it refers to as a `String` and an `int`, respectively, and a `boolean`, which determines whether the `Socket` parameter passed to the method should close automatically when the `SSLSocket` returned by the method does. You can use this method if you want to create an SSL "tunnel" over the top of an existing connection.

SSLSocketFactory.getDefault()

The static `getDefault()` method returns an object providing a default implementation of the `SSLSocketFactory` class.

The default implementation can be changed by setting the value of the `ssl.SocketFactory.provider` security property to the desired class. The property should be set in the `java.security` file if you want to change it. This is the same file you configured the Bouncy Castle provider in.

SSLSocketFactory.getDefaultCipherSuites()

The `getDefaultCipherSuites()` method on both classes returns an array of `String` objects representing the cipher suites that are enabled by default. The default list excludes null ciphers.

SSLSocketFactory.getSupportedCipherSuites()

The `getSupportedCipherSuites()` method on both classes returns an array of `String` objects representing the cipher suites that are available to be used for SSL.

The SSLServerSocketFactory Class

The `javax.net.ssl.SSLServerSocketFactory` is used to create `SSLServerSocket` socket objects.

It is an extension of the `java.net.ServerSocketFactory` class and, like its parent, is not created directly but is created instead by other factory methods. Generally, this is from `SSLServerSocketFactory.getDefault()`, but you will also see later that it is possible to create them using `SSLContext` objects.

As you can see from the method descriptions that follow, this class is also quite straightforward and only adds two extra methods to the class signature inherited from `ServerSocketFactory`.

SSLServerSocketFactory.createServerSocket()

The `createServerSocket()` methods on `SSLServerSocketFactory` are all inherited from its parent class and are the same, other than the fact the `ServerSocket` objects they return can be safely cast to `SSLServerSocket`.

SSLServerSocketFactory.getDefault()

The static `getDefault()` method returns an object providing a default implementation of the `SSLServerSocketFactory` class.

The default implementation can be changed by setting the value of the security property `ssl .ServerSocketFactory.provider` to the desired class. The property should be set in the `java .security` file if you want to change it. This is the same file you configured the Bouncy Castle provider in.

SSLServerSocketFactory.getDefaultCipherSuites() and SSLServerSocketFactory.getSupportedCipherSuites()

Both the `getDefaultCipherSuites()` method and the `getSupportedCipherSuites()` method provide the same information as the methods of the same name on the `SSLSocketFactory` class.

The SSLSocket Class

Like the class it is an extension of, `java.net.Socket`, objects of the type `javax.net.ssl.SSLSocket` are not created directly but are created using a factory methods on `SSLSocketFactory` objects or as a result of an `SSLServerSocket.accept()` returning.

The extra methods added by the `SSLSocket` class can be divided into three categories: methods for basic configuration, adding listeners, and configuring client-side authentication. Initially I will just discuss the basic configuration messages and discuss the other two categories as appropriate later in the chapter.

The following methods are for basic configuration.

SSLSocket.setEnabledCipherSuites()

The `setEnabledCipherSuites()` method takes an array of `String` objects representing the cipher suites that can be used with sockets that result from this server socket doing an accept. The method has a corresponding `get()` method, `getEnabledCipherSuites()`, which returns a `String` array representing what cipher suites are currently enabled.

The method throws an `IllegalArgumentException` when one or more of the ciphers named in its parameter do not appear in the array returned by `getSupportedCipherSuites()`, or when the parameter is `null`.

In general you should always call this method, or its equivalent on `SSLServerSocket`, at least once. If you look at the list of supported cipher suites, you will realize that the security offered by them varies, and by explicitly setting the enabled cipher suites, using `setEnabledCipherSuites()`, you can ensure that any SSL connections that take place are done with the security level you expected.

SSLSocket.setEnabledProtocols()

The setEnabledProtocols() method takes an array of String objects representing the variations on the SSL protocol that can be used with this socket. The method has a corresponding get() method, getEnabledProtocols(), which returns a String array representing what protocols are currently enabled.

The method throws an IllegalArgumentException when one or more of the ciphers named in its parameter do not appear in the array returned by getSupportedProtocols(), or when the parameter is null.

As with setEnabledCipherSuites(), in many situations it is also a good idea to explicitly specify which version of the protocol you want to use rather than leaving it to chance.

SSLSocket.setEnableSessionCreation()

The setEnableSessionCreation() method takes a single boolean parameter, which if true, allows the SSLSocket object to create new SSL sessions. If the parameter value is false, then the socket can only be used to resume existing sessions.

The method has a corresponding get() method, getEnableSessionCreation(), that returns true if new SSL sessions may be established by this socket. A return value of false indicates the socket can only be used to resume an existing session.

SSLSocket.setUseClientMode()

In general, you will never need to use this; however, the setUseClientMode() method takes a single boolean as a parameter, which if true, specifies that when a handshake is done on this socket this end of the link will process in client mode. The method needs to be called before any initial handshaking has been done on the socket and will throw an IllegalArgumentException if this is not the case.

The method has a corresponding get() method, getUseClientMode(), that returns true if connections on the socket will be in SSL client mode, false otherwise.

SSLSocket.startHandshake()

The startHandshake() method starts an SSL handshake on the socket on which it is called.

The method will throw an IOException if there is a problem performing the handshake. If a handshake fails, the SSLSocket is closed and no further communication can be done.

Strictly speaking, a handshake will be done for you the moment you try writing to the socket, but you may want to use this method so that any exceptions thrown due to handshake failure are explicit. You may want do this so you can handle the exception yourself or to make sure you get the original exception rather than one that may have been wrapped and thrown again by another object that is wrapping one of the socket's streams. Other reasons for using the method include the need to use new encryption keys or to initiate a new session. If the current session has been invalidated, a call to startHandshake() will cause a complete reauthentication to take place.

The SSLServerSocket Class

The `javax.net.ssl.SSLServerSocket` class is an extension of `java.net.ServerSocket`, and objects of the `SSLServerSocket` type are created using factory objects of the type `SSLServerSocketFactory`. They are used to accept incoming connection requests using the `accept()` method, which returns `Socket` objects that can be cast to `SSLSocket`.

The extra methods added by the `SSLServerSocket` class can be divided into two categories: methods for basic configuration and for the configuration of client-side authentication.

The following methods are for basic configuration.

SSLServerSocket.setEnabledCipherSuites()

Other than the fact the method applies the setting to any sockets produced as a result of an `accept()` on this `SSLServerSocket` object, the `setEnabledcipherSuites()` method has the same meaning and definition as its equivalent on the `SSLSocket` class. As with `SSLSocket`, there is also a `getEnabledCipherSuites()` method.

Remember that this is a method you should probably be calling if it is important to you to guarantee a certain level of security. As mentioned earlier, the strength of an SSL connection is based on negotiation and there is no guarantee a connecting client will always be interested in making sure the connection is running at its maximum level of security.

SSLServerSocket.setEnabledProtocols()

The `setEnabledProtocols()` method has the same meaning and definition as its equivalent on the `SSLSocket` class, but applies the settings passed in to any sockets produced as a result of an `accept()` method returning. As with `SSLSocket`, there is also a `getEnabledProtocols()` method.

SSLServerSocket.setEnableSessionCreation()

The `setEnableSessionCreation()` method has the same meaning and definition as its equivalent on the `SSLSocket` class, but applies the settings passed in to any sockets produced as a result of an `accept()` method returning. As with `SSLSocket`, there is also a `getEnableSessionCreation()` method.

SSLServerSocket.setUseClientMode()

The `setUseClientMode()` method has the same meaning and definition as its equivalent on the `SSLSocket` class, but applies the settings passed in to any sockets produced as a result of an `accept()` method returning. As with `SSLSocket`, there is also a `getUseClientMode()` method.

This concludes basic configuration. Now take a look at an example.

Try It Out   A Basic SSL Client and Server

This example is written to use a simple protocol that just terminates its messages with a "!" character, and, unlike most examples you have done before, this one is in two parts. (You need different programs to run on the server and client ends.) Both programs also require the use of some command-line arguments. You will also need to use the `CreateKeyStores` utility that was listed in the section called "Getting Started," so make sure you have that class compiled before you go any further.

First up, here is the source for the client end of the SSL link you will create. As you can see, the SSL-related work is done in the main driver.

```
package chapter10;

import java.io.IOException;
import java.io.InputStream;
import java.io.OutputStream;
import java.net.Socket;

import javax.net.ssl.SSLSocket;
import javax.net.ssl.SSLSocketFactory;

/**
 * Basic SSL Client - using the '!' protocol.
 */
public class SSLClientExample
{
    /**
     * Carry out the '!' protocol - client side.
     */
    static void doProtocol(Socket cSock) throws IOException
    {
        OutputStream    out = cSock.getOutputStream();
        InputStream     in = cSock.getInputStream();

        out.write(Utils.toByteArray("World"));
        out.write('!');

        int ch = 0;
        while ((ch = in.read()) != '!')
        {
            System.out.print((char)ch);
        }

        System.out.println((char)ch);
    }

    public static void main(String[] args) throws Exception
    {
        SSLSocketFactory fact = (SSLSocketFactory)SSLSocketFactory.getDefault();
        SSLSocket       cSock = (SSLSocket)fact.createSocket(
                                            Utils.HOST, Utils.PORT_NO);

        doProtocol(cSock);
    }
}
```

This program will run on the server side of the SSL link. Once again, notice that all the SSL-related work is done in the main driver.

```
package chapter10;

import java.io.IOException;
import java.io.InputStream;
```

```java
import java.io.OutputStream;
import java.net.Socket;

import javax.net.ssl.SSLServerSocket;
import javax.net.ssl.SSLServerSocketFactory;
import javax.net.ssl.SSLSocket;

/**
 * Basic SSL Server - using the '!' protocol.
 */
public class SSLServerExample
{
    /**
     * Carry out the '!' protocol - server side.
     */
    static void doProtocol(Socket sSock) throws IOException
    {
        System.out.println("session started.");

        InputStream in = sSock.getInputStream();
        OutputStream out = sSock.getOutputStream();

        out.write(Utils.toByteArray("Hello "));

        int ch = 0;
        while ((ch = in.read()) != '!')
        {
            out.write(ch);
        }

        out.write('!');

        sSock.close();

        System.out.println("session closed.");
    }

    public static void main(String[] args) throws Exception
    {
        SSLServerSocketFactory fact =
                    (SSLServerSocketFactory)SSLServerSocketFactory.getDefault();
        SSLServerSocket      sSock =
                    (SSLServerSocket)fact.createServerSocket(Utils.PORT_NO);

        SSLSocket sslSock = (SSLSocket)sSock.accept();

        doProtocol(sslSock);
    }
}
```

The first step to running the example is to create a temporary directory you can work in. Once you have done that, you should change directory to it and run the following command:

```
java chapter10.CreateKeyStores
```

If this doesn't work, make sure you have your copy of the chapter10 package in your Java class path and then try again. If it does work, you should find you have three files in your directory: client.p12, server.jks, and trustStore.jks. You won't use the client.p12 file just yet, but you will need the other two.

Now you can start the server using the following command that should be entered on one line:

```
java -Djavax.net.ssl.keyStore=server.jks
 -Djavax.net.ssl.keyStorePassword=serverPassword chapter10.SSLServerExample
```

If you're running under Windows, your firewall might prompt you for authorization to continue. You'll need to grant this so the example can run.

The next step is to create another window, change its directory to the temporary working directory you have set up, and run the client using the following command:

```
java -Djavax.net.ssl.trustStore=trustStore.jks chapter10.SSLClientExample
```

You will then see this in the server window:

```
session started.
session closed.
```

and the server will exit.

In the client window, you will see

```
Hello World!
```

and the client will exit.

How It Works

There's obviously a bit of "magic" going on here. In this case, it is possible because the defaults for the JSSE are set up so that the common use of SSL is also the default one. This example takes full advantage of that fact.

Looking at the server code first, you can see that only the following lines were required to create the SSL server end:

```
SSLServerSocketFactory fact =
                (SSLServerSocketFactory)SSLServerSocketFactory.getDefault();
SSLServerSocket         sSock =
                (SSLServerSocket)fact.createServerSocket(Utils.PORT_NO);

SSLSocket sslSock = (SSLSocket)sSock.accept();

doProtocol(sslSock);
```

The code creates a default server socket factory, creates a server socket on the port you want, does an accept(), and then performs the protocol. The "magic" is the default factory that picks up the values of the system properties you have passed to the command line configuring a keystore and the password to be used with it. The keystore is used by the default factory implementation to provide the necessary credentials to be used to identify the server to the other end of the link.

The client is even simpler, with only the following lines of code required to handle the setting up of an SSL connection:

```
SSLSocketFactory fact = (SSLSocketFactory)SSLSocketFactory.getDefault();
SSLSocket        cSock = (SSLSocket)fact.createSocket(
                                        Utils.HOST, Utils.PORT_NO);

doProtocol(cSock);
```

Here, you create a default socket factory, create the socket, and perform the protocol. Once again, the "magic is performed by the default factory. It uses the value of the system property you passed to the JVM to find a keystore that contains trusted certificates. These trusted certificates allow the default factory to validate any credentials, in this case a certificate chain from the server, presented to it.

The default factories also have a default place to look for the trust store if the command-line setting of the `javax.net.ssl.trustStore` property is not specified. I have already mentioned in Chapter 8 that the JVM's security directory contains a file called `cacerts` that contains a keystore. It is also possible to create a keystore in the same directory called `jssecacerts`, and if the `javax.net.ssl.trustStore` property is not set, the JVM will first look for the `jssecacerts` file. If the `jssecacerts` file does not exist, it will use the `cacerts` file.

Other properties that can be set for the trust store are `javax.net.ssl.trustStorePassword`, which represents the password to be used with the trust store keystore; `javax.net.ssl.trustStoreProvider`, which is the provider used to create it; and `javax.net.ssl.trustStoreType`, which is the type of keystore being used as a trust store if it isn't the JVM's default one. In production, you should use the `javax.net.ssl.trustStorePassword` property, because it will force an integrity check on the file. If the trust store you are using is actually a hardware device rather than a file, the keystore type you use for the trust store is NONE.

The properties `javax.net.ssl.keyStoreProvider` and `javax.net.ssl.keyStoreType` can also be used in a similar fashion for specifying a source of identifying credentials for a server or a client.

The HandshakeCompletedListener Interface

It is also possible to attach a listener to an SSLSocket so that you can be informed as to when the handshake calculation has finally been done between the two ends of the link.

This is done by `SSLSocket.addHandshakeCompletedListener()`, which takes a single object implementing the `javax.net.ssl.HandshakeCompletedListener` interface as a parameter and registers it to receive notifications that an SSL handshake has completed on this socket. There is also a corresponding `SSLSocket.removeHandshakeCompletedListener()` method that can be used to remove the listener once it is no longer required.

The `HandshakeCompletedListener` interface has a single method, `handshakeCompleted()`, which is invoked by the `SSLSocket` that the listener is attached to when an SSL handshake completes. The `handshakeCompleted()` method is passed a `javax.net.ssl.HandshakeCompletedEvent` object. If you look at the JavaDoc for this class, you will see that it contains the full details of the session that has just been established. You can use this information for doing connection logging and other processing.

Both the addHandshakeCompletedListener() and the removeHandshakeCompletedListener() methods will throw an IllegalArgumentException if the parameter passed to them is null. The remove() method will also throw an IllegalArgumentException if the parameter passed to it does not represent a current listener on the SSLSocket concerned.

Client-Side Authentication

So far, the connection you have created is authenticated only on the server side. Although this is fine for most applications related to, say, Internet shopping, a lot of business-to-business and corporate applications require that both sides of the link are authenticated. Additional messages are used in the handshake leading to a process like the one described in Figure 10-2.

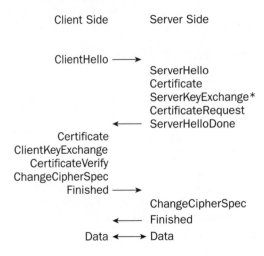

Message Flow for Authenticated Server, Authenticated Client Handshake
* Means Message Not Always Sent

Figure 10-2

As you can see, the SSL protocol enables this by allowing the client to also send back a certificate chain in the Certificate message along with the pre-master secret and then sending a signature, the CertificateVerify message, which can be validated using the end entity certificate in the client's certificate chain. The signature is calculated on the data stream that represents all the messages that have been exchanged starting from the initial client message. Doing it this way is quite useful, as it does not require the client to have a public key that can be used for encryption. Instead, the client can also use a range of digital signature specific algorithms as well to authenticate itself.

As client-side authentication is an option with SSL, introducing it requires you to make use of some additional configuration methods. Normally you will just use the ones on the SSLServerSocket class; however, it is also possible to customize an SSLSocket object in server mode to use client-side authentication. The next section starts with the configuration methods on the SSLServerSocket class.

SSLServerSocket Configuration

Configuring an `SSLServerSocket` to request client configuration is very straightforward, with two methods now being provided for the purpose; the older `setNeedClientAuth()` method and a newer method added in JDK 1.4, `setWantClientAuth()`.

SSLServerSocket.setNeedClientAuth()

The `setNeedClientAuth()` method takes a single `boolean` parameter. If the parameter has the value `true`, a server-mode socket created as a result of an `accept()` will enforce client-side authentication. If the client is unable to provide authentication, the connection will be dropped. Calling this method overrides any previous use of `setWantClientAuth()`. The method has a corresponding `get()` method called `getNeedClientAuth()`, which returns a `boolean` indicating whether optional client-side authentication will be requested.

SSLServerSocket.setWantClientAuth()

The `setWantClientAuth()` method takes a single `boolean` parameter. If the parameter has the value `true`, a server-mode socket created as a result of an `accept()` will initially request client-side authentication. If the client is unable to provide authentication, the connection will proceed regardless. Calling this method overrides any previous use of `setNeedClientAuth()`. The method has a corresponding `get()` method called `getWantClientAuth()`, which returns a `boolean` indicating whether optional client-side authentication will be requested.

The methods `setWantClientAuth()` and `getWantClientAuth()` are only available in JDK 1.4 and later.

Server-Mode SSLSocket Configuration

There are also some methods on `SSLSocket` that allow you to customize the settings for client-side authentication for an individual socket being used in server mode. As you would expect, they are the same as the ones available on the `SSLServerSocket` class and need to be invoked before the `SSLSocket.startHandshake()` method has been called.

The setNeedClientAuth() Method

The `setNeedClientAuth()` method takes a single boolean value. Its meaning is the same as the method with the same name on the `SSLServerSocket` class, except it only applies to the `SSLSocket` object it is called on. Likewise, a corresponding `get()` method, `getNeedClientAuth()`, is also available.

The setWantClientAuth() Method

The `setWantClientAuth()` method takes a single boolean value. Its meaning is the same as the method with the same name on the `SSLServerSocket` class, except it only applies to the `SSLSocket` object it is called on. Likewise, a corresponding `get()` method, `getWantClientAuth()`, is also available, and the `get()` and `set()` methods are only available in JDK 1.4 and later.

The SSLContext Class

The `javax.net.ssl.SSLContext` class is used as a carrier for the credentials and other information associated with particular SSL links. You have already used this class indirectly, because the default factory objects are created using an SSLContext object, which uses the system properties you were setting to locate the credentials that were used to identity the server and the trust store that was used by the client to validate them.

You can also create your own SSLContext objects using the getInstance() factory pattern that you saw in the JCE and the JCA. All the getInstance() methods take a String as a parameter that represents the protocol being requested. In addition to the method that just takes a single String parameter and uses a default implementation, there are two additional versions of the method that take the name of the provider required or a class representing the provider required if you want to specify which provider should be used to provide the underlying implementation of the SSLContext object.

Legitimate values for the protocol String parameter are "SSL" or "TLS", where "SSL" is an alias for "SSLv3" and "TLS" is an alias for "TLSv1". If the protocol you are requesting is not available, the getInstance() method will throw a NoSuchAlgorithmException. If you use the alternate methods that allow you to specify a provider, the getInstance() method may throw an IllegalArgumentException if the parameter representing the provider is null, and if you use the getInstance() method that accepts a String representing the provider name and the provider cannot be found, a NoSuchProviderException will be thrown.

I'll only cover the commonly used methods on the class here. If you look at the JavaDoc for JDK 1.5, you'll find that a few extra methods have been added, such as those allowing you to create your own javax.net.ssl.SSLEngine objects if you require. These can be useful if you want to work with the non-blocking I/O library. I won't go into details on non-blocking I/O here, but you can find details on using it with SSL in the "JSSE Reference Guide" that forms part of the Java documentation set.

SSLContext.init()

The init() method is used to initialize the context. It takes three parameters: an array of KeyManager objects, an array of TrustManager objects, and a SecureRandom. If any of the parameter values are null, a default implementation of the required parameter value will be used. You will look at how you create KeyManager and TrustManager objects over the next two examples, but as you have probably guessed, the KeyManager objects are used to provide credentials needed to identify the local end of the SSL connection to the peer at the other end, and the TrustManager objects are used to provide the resources required to validate the identity the peer is presenting.

The method will throw a KeyManagementException if the operation fails.

SSLContext.getClientSessionContext()

The getClientSessionContext() method returns a javax.net.ssl.SSLSessionContext object associated with the handshake phase of client-side connections. In the case where the session context is not available, the method returns null.

If an SSLSessionContext object is returned, you can use it for finding out and setting the session timeout, finding out and setting the number of sessions that can be cached in the context, and finding out the IDs of all the sessions associated with the context.

SSLContext.getProtocol()

The getProtocol() method returns a String representing the name of the protocol associated with this context. It will be the same name that was specified in the getInstance() call that created this SSLContext object.

SSLContext.getServerSessionContext()

The `getServerSessionContext()` method returns an `SSLSessionContext` object associated with the handshake phase of server-side connections. In the case where the session context is not available, the method returns `null`.

SSLContext.getServerSocketFactory()

The `getServerSocketFactory()` returns an `SSLServerSocketFactory` that will create `SSLSocket` objects on accepted connections that will use the protocol, key managers, and trust managers associated with this context.

SSLContext.getSocketFactory()

The `getSocketFactory()` returns an `SSLSocketFactory` that will create `SSLSocket` objects that will use the protocol, key managers, and trust managers associated with this context.

The KeyManagerFactory Class

The `javax.net.ssl.KeyManagerFactory` class is used to create objects that implement the `javax.net.ssl.KeyManager` interface. Like other security-related classes, it is created using the `getInstance()` pattern and follows the usual rules in regards to provider precedence when `getInstance()` is called and the provider is not explicitly specified along with the algorithm requested. The standard algorithm to use with the `getInstance()` method is `"SunX509"`.

A provider can be specified to `getInstance()` explicitly as either a `String` representing the provider's name or as an object representing the provider's implementation. If the algorithm requested is not available, the method throws a `NoSuchAlgorithmException`. In the event the provider is specified explicitly, the method throws an `IllegalArgumentException` if the provider parameter is `null` or if the `getInstance()` method that takes a provider name is used and the provider cannot be found, the method throws a `NoSuchProviderException`.

The class has only a few methods on it, and its use as a factory is straightforward. As you will see in the example following the method descriptions, use of the factory is a simple two-step process.

KeyManagerFactory.init()

There are two `init()` methods on the `KeyManagerFactory` class. Both methods serve the purpose of providing the `KeyManagerFactory` with a source for the private keys required for allowing the `SSLContext` holding `KeyManager` objects produced by this factory to create an authenticated connection.

The first `init()` method takes a `KeyStore` object and a `char` array representing a key password. If there is more than one private key in the keystore, the `KeyManagerFactory` object will assume that all keys in the keystore passed in have the same password. The method can throw any of `KeyStoreException`, `NoSuchAlgorithmException`, or `UnrecoverableKeyException`, depending on which problems occur when processing the passed in keystore.

The second `init()` method takes an object implementing the `javax.net.ssl.ManagerFactory` `Parameters` interface. The method will throw an `InvalidAlgorithmParameterException` if a problem occurs.

`ManagerFactoryParameters` is a simple marker interface with no methods on it, and how the parameter object that implements it is interpreted is up to the underlying provider implementing the `KeyManagerFactory` object you are using. One use of this interface worth looking at is the `KeyStoreBuilderParameters` class, which is also in the `javax.net.ssl` package. The class is an interesting one because it will show you an application of the `KeyStore.Builder` class that was mentioned in Chapter 8.

KeyManagerFactory.getAlgorithm( )

The `getAlgorithm()` method returns a `String` representing the algorithm name for this `KeyManagerFactory` object. This will be the same as the algorithm parameter passed to `KeyManagerFactory.getInstance()`.

KeyManagerFactory.getDefaultAlgorithm( )

The static `getDefaultAlgorithm()` returns a `String` representing the default algorithm name for `KeyManagerFactory` objects created using the JVM.

The default algorithm can be changed setting the value of the `ssl.KeyManagerFactory.algorithm` security property in the `java.security` file. Alternately, it can be changed at runtime by calling the `Security.setProperty()` method with the property name and the desired algorithm.

KeyManagerFactory.getKeyManagers( )

The `getKeyManagers()` method returns an array of objects implementing the `KeyManager` interface, one for each type of key material the `KeyManagerFactory` object was initialized with.

The `KeyManager` interface is a marker interface with no methods on it, and what actual implementations are returned in the array generated by `getKeyManagers()` depends on the underlying provider. In the case of SSL based on X.509, the standard JSSE `KeyManagerFactory` will return objects implementing the `javax.net.ssl.X509KeyManager` interface or `javax.net.ssl.X509ExtendedKeyManager`.

Fortunately, you don't have to worry so much about what is returned by the `KeyManagerFactory` as long as the array contains objects that are compatible with the `SSLContext` object you are initializing. Having a basic understanding of the return value of the `getKeyManagers()` method is enough to allow you to create a client that has client-side authentication, without the need to make use of Java system properties as you did with the server in the last example. You will look at how that is done now.

Try It Out   **Introducing Client-Side Authentication**

This example introduces client-side authentication and the use of the `KeyManagerFactory` class. As before, it is in two parts. Both parts extend from the classes you created for the last example, so that it isn't necessary to reproduce the code that supports the "!" protocol that is used to test the connections.

The first thing you will notice is that most of the changes are on the client class and that they relate to the creation of an `SSLContext` object, which can be used to create the `SSLSocket` object that the client uses to connect to the server process.

Here is the source for the new client:

```java
package chapter10;

import java.io.FileInputStream;
import java.security.KeyStore;

import javax.net.ssl.KeyManagerFactory;
import javax.net.ssl.SSLContext;
import javax.net.ssl.SSLSocket;
import javax.net.ssl.SSLSocketFactory;

/**
 * SSL Client with client-side authentication.
 */
public class SSLClientWithClientAuthExample extends SSLClientExample
{
    /**
     * Create an SSL context with a KeyManager providing our identity
     */
    static SSLContext createSSLContext() throws Exception
    {
        // set up a key manager for our local credentials
        KeyManagerFactory mgrFact = KeyManagerFactory.getInstance("SunX509");
        KeyStore clientStore = KeyStore.getInstance("PKCS12");

        clientStore.load(new FileInputStream("client.p12"), Utils.CLIENT_PASSWORD);

        mgrFact.init(clientStore, Utils.CLIENT_PASSWORD);

        // create a context and set up a socket factory
        SSLContext sslContext = SSLContext.getInstance("TLS");

        sslContext.init(mgrFact.getKeyManagers(), null, null);

        return sslContext;
    }

    public static void main(String[] args) throws Exception
    {
        SSLContext        sslContext = createSSLContext();
        SSLSocketFactory  fact = sslContext.getSocketFactory();
        SSLSocket         cSock = (SSLSocket)fact.createSocket(
                                            Utils.HOST, Utils.PORT_NO);

        doProtocol(cSock);
    }
}
```

The new server class is very similar to the one in the previous example. All you need to do is call the configuration method that specifies that you only want to accept authenticated clients.

Here is the source for the new server:

```
package chapter10;

import javax.net.ssl.SSLServerSocket;
import javax.net.ssl.SSLServerSocketFactory;
import javax.net.ssl.SSLSocket;

/**
 * Basic SSL Server with client authentication.
 */
public class SSLServerWithClientAuthExample extends SSLServerExample
{
    public static void main(
        String[] args)
        throws Exception
    {
        SSLServerSocketFactory fact =
                    (SSLServerSocketFactory)SSLServerSocketFactory.getDefault();
        SSLServerSocket        sSock =
                    (SSLServerSocket)fact.createServerSocket(Utils.PORT_NO);

        sSock.setNeedClientAuth(true);

        SSLSocket sslSock = (SSLSocket)sSock.accept();

        doProtocol(sslSock);
    }
}
```

As with the last example, you should run this example using two windows in the same temporary directory you set up before. You'll need to do this because this example requires all the keystores that you created previously. Note that each command should be entered on one line as before. (Any line breaks you see here are due to the formatting requirements of this book.)

The first thing to do is to start the new server using the following command:

```
java -Djavax.net.ssl.keyStore=server.jks
 -Djavax.net.ssl.keyStorePassword=serverPassword
 -Djavax.net.ssl.trustStore=trustStore.jks chapter10.SSLServerWithClientAuthExample
```

As you can see, the client is now authenticating itself. You need to provide the server with a trust store.

Now that the server is running, you can run the new client as well:

```
java -Djavax.net.ssl.trustStore=trustStore.jks
 chapter10.SSLClientWithClientAuthExample
```

In this case, you haven't had to set the `javax.net.ssl.keyStore` properties as you did for the server, because the client is providing its own `KeyManager` objects.

You will then see this in the server window:

```
session started.
session closed.
```

and the server will exit.

In the client window, you will see

```
Hello World!
```

and the client will exit.

How It Works

In this example, the server end of the link is still largely taking advantage of the default `SSLServerSocketFactory` that the JSSE makes available. There are only two changes you had to make to create a server that expects authenticated clients.

The first change is the addition of the line

```
sSock.setNeedClientAuth(true);
```

which forces the creation of `SSLSocket` objects that will work only for authenticated clients each time an `accept()` occurs.

The second change is the setting of the `javax.net.ssl.trustStore` parameter on the command line. This needed to be done because, otherwise, the server would have tried using one of the default trust store locations and would have been unable to validate the client's certificate chain.

On the client side, because you are now creating your own `SSLContext`, there is considerably more code than before, but in some ways it works nearly the same way. Most of the changes are restricted to the addition of the `createSSLContext()` method. The use of the `SSLSocketFactory` is still the same; it's just the underlying context that it is created with that is different.

Initially, the `createSSLContext()` method creates a `KeyManagerFactory` of the `"SunX509"` type using the default provider and initializes it using a keystore created from the `client.p12` file. Next, an `SSLContext` object, `sslContext`, is created for the TLS version 1 protocol using the default provider, and the `init()` method is called on `sslContext`, passing it a `KeyManager` array generated by the `KeyManagerFactory` object `mgrFact` and two `null` parameters.

As the other two parameters passed to `sslContext.init()` are null, you have created an `SSLContext` object that uses your provided `KeyManager` objects and uses the system default `TrustManager` objects and a system default `SecureRandom` object. This is the reason why the `javax.net.ssl.trustStore` system property still needs to be set on the command line(the `SSLContext` object that is being created still needs to use the default `TrustManager` object and the default `TrustManager` object requires the property to be set. Otherwise, it will be retrieving the trust anchor used to validate the certificate path from the wrong keystore.

The answer to avoiding use of the system property is to create your own `TrustManager` objects. To do this, you need to use the `TrustManagerFactory` class.

The TrustManagerFactory Class

The `javax.net.ssl.TrustManagerFactory` class is used to create objects that implement the `javax.net.ssl.TrustManager` interface. Like other security-related classes, it is created using the `getInstance()` pattern and follows the usual rules with regard to provider precedence when `getInstance()` is called, and the provider is not explicitly specified along with the algorithm requested. The standard algorithms to use with the `getInstance()` method are `"SunX509"` or `"SunPKIX"`.

A provider can be specified to `getInstance()` explicitly as either a `String` representing the provider's name or an object representing the provider's implementation. If the algorithm requested is not available, the method will throw a `NoSuchAlgorithmException`. In the event the provider is specified explicitly, the method will throw an `IllegalArgumentException`. If the provider parameter is `null` or if the `getInstance()` method that takes a provider name is used and the provider cannot be found, the method will throw a `NoSuchProviderException`.

The class has only a few methods on it, and as you will see in the example following the method descriptions, the use of the factory object is the same as for the `KeyManagerFactory`.

TrustManagerFactory.init()

There are two `init()` methods on the `TrustManagerFactory` class. Both methods serve the purpose of providing the `TrustManagerFactory` with a source for the trust anchors required for allowing the `SSLContext` holding `TrustManager` objects produced by this factory to create and authenticate the entity at the other end of the connection it is attached to.

The first `init()` method simply takes a `KeyStore` object and uses any trusted certificates stored in it as trust anchors that it will recognize when the other party in the connection presents their credentials. The method will throw a `KeyStoreException` if there is a problem extracting the certificates from the passed-in keystore.

The second `init()` method takes an object implementing the `ManagerFactoryParameters` interface. As mentioned earlier, this is a simple marker interface, but in the case of the `TrustManagerFactory` class, there is a parameters object defined called `CertPathTrustManagerParameters` that is also in the `javax.net.ssl` package. The `CertPathTrustManagerParameters` class allows you to pass `CertPathParameters` for use by the `TrustManager` that will be created by the `TrustManagerFactory` object. This can be quite useful if you want to rely on something other then the default certificate path validation performed by the `TrustManager` either because you want to use OCSP or your certificates are carrying locally defined extensions, which are marked as critical.

TrustManagerFactory.getAlgorithm()

The `getAlgorithm()` method returns a `String` representing the algorithm name for this `TrustManagerFactory` object. This will be the same as the algorithm parameter passed to `TrustManagerFactory.getInstance()`.

TrustManagerFactory.getDefaultAlgorithm()

The static `getDefaultAlgorithm()` returns a `String` representing the default algorithm name for `TrustManagerFactory` objects created using the JVM.

The default algorithm can be changed by setting the value of the `ssl.TrustManagerFactory.algorithm` security property in the `java.security` file. Alternately, it can be changed at runtime by calling the `Security.setProperty()` method with the property name and the desired algorithm.

TrustManagerFactory.getTrustManagers()

The `getTrustManagers()` method returns an array of objects implementing the `TrustManager` interface, one for each type of trust information the `TrustManagerFactory` object was initialized with.

The `TrustManager` interface is a marker interface with no methods on it, and what actual implementations are returned in the array generated by `getTrustManagers()` depends on the underlying provider. In the case of SSL based on X.509, the standard JSSE `TrustManagerFactory` will return objects implementing the `javax.net.ssl.X509TrustManager` interface. As you will see in the example that follows, the situation with `TrustManager` objects is the same as with `KeyManager` objects — the important thing about the return value from the `getTrustManagers()` method is that it is compatible with the `SSLContext` object being used.

Try It Out   Using the TrustManagerFactory

This example includes the use of a `TrustManagerFactory` object in the initialization of the `SSLContext` object. As you can see from the code, all the functional changes are in the `createSSLContext()` method.

```
package chapter10;

import java.io.FileInputStream;
import java.security.KeyStore;

import javax.net.ssl.KeyManagerFactory;
import javax.net.ssl.SSLContext;
import javax.net.ssl.SSLSocket;
import javax.net.ssl.SSLSocketFactory;
import javax.net.ssl.TrustManagerFactory;

/**
 * SSL Client with client-side authentication.
 */
public class SSLClientWithClientAuthTrustExample
    extends SSLClientExample
{
    /**
     * Create an SSL context with both identity and trust store
     */
    static SSLContext createSSLContext()
        throws Exception
    {
        // set up a key manager for our local credentials
      KeyManagerFactory mgrFact = KeyManagerFactory.getInstance("SunX509");
      KeyStore clientStore = KeyStore.getInstance("PKCS12");

      clientStore.load(
              new FileInputStream("client.p12"), Utils.CLIENT_PASSWORD);

      mgrFact.init(clientStore, Utils.CLIENT_PASSWORD);
```

```
            // set up a trust manager so we can recognize the server
            TrustManagerFactory trustFact = TrustManagerFactory.getInstance("SunX509");
            KeyStore            trustStore = KeyStore.getInstance("JKS");

            trustStore.load(
                    new FileInputStream("trustStore.jks"), Utils.TRUST_STORE_PASSWORD);

            trustFact.init(trustStore);

            // create a context and set up a socket factory
            SSLContext sslContext = SSLContext.getInstance("TLS");

            sslContext.init(
                        mgrFact.getKeyManagers(), trustFact.getTrustManagers(), null);

        return sslContext;
    }

    public static void main(String[] args) throws Exception
    {
        SSLContext        sslContext = createSSLContext();
        SSLSocketFactory fact = sslContext.getSocketFactory();
        SSLSocket        cSock = (SSLSocket)fact.createSocket(
                                                    Utils.HOST, Utils.PORT_NO);

        doProtocol(cSock);
    }
}
```

As with the last example, you should run this example using two windows in the same temporary directory you set up before. Once again, each command should be entered on one line; any line breaks are due to the formatting requirements of this book.

The first thing to do is to start the server as before, using the following command:

```
java -Djavax.net.ssl.keyStore=server.jks
 -Djavax.net.ssl.keyStorePassword=serverPassword
 -Djavax.net.ssl.trustStore=trustStore.jks chapter10.SSLServerWithClientAuthExample
```

This is the same as before, which should not be any surprise, because you have only needed to change the client.

Next, you should run the client in the other window using

```
java chapter10.SSLClientWithClientAuthTrustExample
```

Because the SSLContext is now initialized with a TrustManager object as well as a KeyManager object, you no longer have to set the JVM properties on the command line.

You will then see this in the server window:

```
session started.
session closed.
```

and the server will exit.

In the client window, you will see

```
Hello World!
```

and the client will exit.

This indicates that the client has successfully connected, identified itself, and validated the server.

How It Works

As you can see from the highlighted code in createSSLContext(), creating and using the TrustManagerFactory object is virtually the same as for the KeyManager. The main difference is that there is no need to provide a password to the init() method, because only trusted certificate entries are extracted from the KeyStore parameter passed in.

The introduction of the TrustManagerFactory object on the client side now means that the only system default the SSLContext is relying on is the SecureRandom implementation it is using. This frees you from having to set any system properties on the client side to get the client to run, because the SSLContext now has all the information it needs to provide identification information for its end of the link and to identify other entities connecting to it.

The SSLContext provides an environment in which an SSL connection can be established, but when a connection is in use, it doesn't provide any information as to who connected or what cipher suite is being used. This information is associated with the SSL session.

Managing SSL Session Information

In addition to connections having a context associated with them, the JSSE also makes it possible to get access to and manage session information that is related to the connection taking place. This is done via objects that implement the SSLSession interface.

The SSLSession Interface

Objects implementing the javax.net.ssl.SSLSession interface are not created directly, but are returned by the getSession() method on SSLSocket. As you can see from the method descriptions that follow, an object implementing SSLSession acts not only as a carrier of connection information but also allows for the session to be invalidated and for other objects to be associated with the session if need be.

SSLSession.getCipherSuite()

The getCipherSuite() method returns a String representing the name of the SSL cipher suite, which is in use with all connections in the session.

SSLSession.getCreationTime()

The getCreationTime() method returns a long representing the time at when this SSLSession object was created. The time value is in milliseconds since midnight, January 1, 1970 UTC.

SSLSession.getId()

The getId() method returns a byte array representing the identifier that has been assigned to the session this SSLSession object represents.

SSLSession.getLastAccessedTime()

The getLastAccessedTime() method returns a long representing the last time this SSLSession object was accessed by the session-level infrastructure. As with getCreationTime(), the value is in milliseconds since midnight, January 1, 1970 UTC.

SSLSession.getLocalCertificates()

The getLocalCertificates() method returns an array of Certificate objects representing the certificate chain sent to the peer during handshaking. If no certificate chain was sent the method returns null.

SSLSession.getLocalPrincipal()

The getLocalPrincipal() method returns a Principal representing the principal that was used to identify this end of the connection to the peer. If no principal was provided, this method returns null. If the cipher suite in use is X.509-certificate based, the return value can be cast to X500Principal.

SSLSession.getPeerCertificates()

The getPeerCertificates() method returns an array of Certificate objects representing the certificate chain that you received from the peer during handshaking.

The method will throw an SSLPeerUnverifiedException if the peer did not authenticate itself during handshaking or if the cipher suite being used is not based on X.509 certificates but is instead based on another mechanism, such as that used by Kerberos.

SSLSession.getPeerHost()

The getPeerHost() method returns a String representing the hostname or the Internet address of the peer. The method will return null if the information is not available.

The return value of this method is not authenticated, so it should be considered to be a hint as to the identity of the peer's host.

SSLSession.getPeerPort()

The getPeerPort() method returns the port number being used on the peer. The method will return -1 if the information is not available. The method is only available in JDK 1.5 or later.

Like getPeerHost(), the return value of this method is not authenticated, so it should be considered to be a hint.

SSLSession.getPeerPrincipal()

The getPeerPrincipal() method returns a Principal object representing the principal that was used to identify the peer during handshaking. If the cipher suite used is based on the use of X.509 certificates, the object returned can be cast to X500Principal. The method is only available in JDK 1.5 and later.

The method will throw an `SSLPeerUnverifiedException` if the peer did not authenticate itself during handshaking.

SSLSession.getProtocol()

The `getProtocol()` method returns a `String` representing the standard name of the protocol that will be used for all connections associated with this `SSLSession` object.

SSLSession.getSessionContext()

The `getSessionContext()` method returns a `javax.net.ssl.SSLSessionContext` object that provides additional context information specific to this session. In the case where the environment does not have the session context available, the method will return `null`.

If an `SSLSessionContext` object is returned, you can use it for finding out and setting the session timeout, finding out and setting the number of sessions that can be cached in the context, and finding out the IDs of all the sessions associated with the context.

SSLSession.invalidate()

The `invalidate()` method invalidates the session. In this case that means that future connections will not be able to resume or join the session; however, any existing connection using the session will be able to continue until the connection is closed.

SSLSession.isValid()

The `isValid()` method returns a boolean value that will be `true` if it is possible to resume or join a connection to the session, `false` otherwise. The method is only available in JDK 1.5 or later.

SSLSession.putValue()

The `putValue()` method takes two parameters, a `String` and an `Object`, with the `String` representing a name that the `Object` parameter is to be stored under. The object that has been stored can be retrieved later using the `getValue()` method. The `getValue()` method takes a single `String` as a parameter representing an object name previously stored by `putValue()` and returns an `Object` that is associated with that name, or `null` if there isn't one. Objects can be removed using the `removeValue()` method.

A `String` array representing the names of all the objects that have been stored in the session can be retrieved from the `SSLSession` object using the `getValueNames()` method. If no `Objects` are stored in the session, the method will return a zero length array.

The `putValue()`, `getValue()`, and `removeValue()` methods will all throw an `IllegalArgumentException` if any of the parameters passed to them are `null`.

As you can see, an object implementing `SSLSession` can carry any information that you want to associate with a session, as well as the basic information about the parties involved in the SSL connection the session object represents. The next example shows how a session object can be used to further check the identity of a client that has connected to a server.

Try It Out   **Using SSLSession**

This example uses the information about a client's principal in an `SSLSession` object to restrict connections that can be made to the server to only those where the principal the client is using is the one belonging to the example end entity certificate. The example also incorporates the use of the `TrustManagerFactory` and `KeyManagerFactory` classes, which you have seen in the client-side programs.

```java
package chapter10;

import java.io.FileInputStream;
import java.security.KeyStore;
import java.security.Principal;

import javax.net.ssl.KeyManagerFactory;
import javax.net.ssl.SSLContext;
import javax.net.ssl.SSLPeerUnverifiedException;
import javax.net.ssl.SSLServerSocket;
import javax.net.ssl.SSLServerSocketFactory;
import javax.net.ssl.SSLSession;
import javax.net.ssl.SSLSocket;
import javax.net.ssl.TrustManagerFactory;
import javax.security.auth.x500.X500Principal;

/**
 * Basic SSL Server with client authentication and id checking.
 */
public class SSLServerWithClientAuthIdExample extends SSLServerExample
{
    /**
     * Check that the principal we have been given is for the end entity.
     */
    static boolean isEndEntity(SSLSession session)
        throws SSLPeerUnverifiedException
    {
        Principal id = session.getPeerPrincipal();
        if (id instanceof X500Principal)
        {
            X500Principal x500 = (X500Principal)id;

            return x500.getName().equals("CN=Test End Certificate");
        }

        return false;
    }

    /**
     * Create an SSL context with the identity and trust stores in place
     */
    static SSLContext createSSLContext() throws Exception
    {
        // set up a key manager for our local credentials
        KeyManagerFactory mgrFact = KeyManagerFactory.getInstance("SunX509");
        KeyStore serverStore = KeyStore.getInstance("JKS");

        serverStore.load(
```

```
                                new FileInputStream("server.jks"), Utils.SERVER_PASSWORD);

                mgrFact.init(serverStore, Utils.SERVER_PASSWORD);

                // set up a trust manager so we can recognize the server
                TrustManagerFactory trustFact =
        TrustManagerFactory.getInstance("SunX509");
                KeyStore            trustStore = KeyStore.getInstance("JKS");

                trustStore.load(
                    new FileInputStream("trustStore.jks"), Utils.TRUST_STORE_PASSWORD);

                trustFact.init(trustStore);

                // create a context and set up a socket factory
                SSLContext sslContext = SSLContext.getInstance("TLS");

                sslContext.init(
                    mgrFact.getKeyManagers(), trustFact.getTrustManagers(), null);

                return sslContext;
        }

        public static void main(String[] args) throws Exception
        {
            // create a context and set up a socket factory
            SSLContext              sslContext = createSSLContext();
            SSLServerSocketFactory fact = sslContext.getServerSocketFactory();
            SSLServerSocket         sSock =
                            (SSLServerSocket)fact.createServerSocket(Utils.PORT_NO);

            sSock.setNeedClientAuth(true);

            SSLSocket sslSock = (SSLSocket)sSock.accept();

            sslSock.startHandshake();

            // process if principal checks out
            if (isEndEntity(sslSock.getSession()))
            {
                doProtocol(sslSock);
            }
        }
    }
```

Now that both ends of the link are setting up their own SSLContext objects, you no longer need to use system properties. You will still need to run the example in the same directory as you have with the previous ones, preferably using two windows, but in this case you can start the server with just

java chapter10.SSLServerWithClientAuthIdExample

and run the last client you used with

java chapter10.SSLClientWithClientAuthTrustExample

You will then see this in the server window:

```
session started.
session closed.
```

and the server will exit.

In the client window, you will see

```
Hello World!
```

and the client will exit.

Both of these indicate that everything has worked successfully.

How It Works

You are already familiar with the contents `createSSLContext()` method from the client examples. The only change from its design on the server side is that it is now using `server.jks` rather than the `client.p12` file, because you now need the server's credentials, not the client's. As with the client, creating your own `SSLContext` in the server frees you from having to use command-line property setting to provide local identity information and a trust store.

Ordinarily, the SSL handshaking is done when an attempt is made to use a stream off an `SSLSocket`. In this case, you want to establish the session before anything is sent to the other end so that you can check the principal being used to identify the client. The call to the `startHandshake()` method forces this to take place.

When `startHandshake()` returns, you are able to get a session object for the connection. This is obtained using `SSLSocket.getSession()`, and the `SSLSession` object is passed to the `isEndEntity()` method. This checks the principal of the peer to see that it is the principal for the certificate you expected(the example end entity certificate. If the principal is correct, the method returns `true` and the protocol proceeds; if the method returns `false`, the server quietly exits. If you've run the correct client, the method will return `true` and the client will receive the "Hello World!" message. It is also worth running the client from the first example ("Try It Out: A Basic SSL Client and Server") to see how the server reacts.

Dealing with HTTPS

The most common experience most users of the Internet have with SSL is via HTTPS. HTTPS stands for Hypertext Transport Protocol (Secure) and is simply HTTP done over an SSL connection.

Just as Java provides the `HttpURLConnection` class in `java.net` for dealing with regular HTTP connections, the JSSE provides a class for dealing with HTTPS connections — `HttpsURLConnection`.

The HttpsURLConnection Class

The `javax.net.ssl.HttpsURLConnection` class is an extension of `HttpURLConnection` and has some extra methods to make retrieving some of the SSL-related information about the connection more accessible, as well as providing for the use of a specific socket factory and doing hostname verification against the host the URL points to. Like its parent class, HttpsURLConnection objects are not created directly but are created using the openConnection() method on java.net.URL.

I'll describe the SSL specific methods here; however, it would also be worth having a look at the JavaDoc for the parent class HttpURLConnection if you are not already familiar with it. You will see in the next example that, as it was with the SSLSocket class compared to the Socket class, the actual mechanics of doing the connection are the same as for the parent class.

HttpsURLConnection.getCipherSuite()

The getCipherSuite() method returns a String representing the name of the cipher suite that is in use for this connection.

This method will throw an IllegalStateException if the method is called before a connection has been established.

HttpsURLConnection.getHostnameVerifier()

The getHostnameVerifier() method is used to return the HostnameVerifier that will be used to verify the hostname of the server against the credentials it provides when the connect() method on the object is invoked. You'll look at HostnameVerifier in more detail in the next section.

The method has a corresponding set() method, setHostnameVerifier(), which can be used to pass your own HostnameVerifier. After the set() method is called, any calls to connect() will verify the hostname of the server using the new HostnameVerifier object.

HttpsURLConnection.getLocalCertificates()

The getLocalCertificates() method returns an array of Certificate objects representing the certificate chain, if there was one, that was sent to the server when the connection was established. In the event no certificate chain was sent, a null is returned. As you have already seen from the discussion of SSLContext, it is possible to have more than one possible certificate chain that can be used when connections are established. This method will return the chain that was actually used.

This method will throw an IllegalStateException if the method is called before a connection has been established.

HttpsURLConnection.getLocalPrincipal()

The getLocalPrincipal() method returns the principal that was sent to the server when the connection was set up. In the case of JDK 1.4 and later, you can normally cast this value to an X500Principal for an X.509-based cipher suite.

This method will throw an IllegalStateException if the method is called before a connection has been established.

HttpsURLConnection.getPeerPrincipal()

The getPeerPrincipal() method returns the principal that the server sent back to you when the connection was set up. In the case of JDK 1.4 and later, you can normally cast this value to an X500Principal for an X.509-based cipher suite.

The method will throw an SSLPeerUnverifiedException if no principal for the server has been correctly established and an IllegalStateException if the method is called before a connection has been established.

HttpsURLConnection.getServerCertificates()

The getServerCertificates() method returns an array of Certificate objects representing the certificate chain for the server taking part in this session.

The method will throw an SSLPeerUnverifiedException if no principal for the server has been correctly established and an IllegalStateException if the method is called before a connection has been established.

HttpsURLConnection.getSSLSocketFactory()

The getSSLSocketFactory() method is used to return the SSLSocketFactory that will be used to create a connection when the connect() method on the object is invoked.

The method has a corresponding set() method, setSSLSocketFactory(), which can be used to pass your own SSLSocketFactory for the SSLContext you want to use. After the set() method is called, any calls to connect() will use the new SSLSocketFactory object.

HttpsURLConnection.setDefaultSSLSocketFactory()

Initially an HttpsURLConnection is created with a default SSLSocketFactory. The setDefaultSSLSocketFactory() method is a static method on the HttpsURLConnection class that allows you to provide your own SSLSocketFactory that will be used to create connections rather than the default one. After this method is called, new instances of HttpsURLConnection will be created using the SSLSocketFactory object that was passed in. There is also a static method, getDefaultSSLSocketFactory(), which returns the current SSLSocketFactory being used.

HttpsURLConnection.setDefaultHostnameVerifier()

The setDefaultHostnameVerifier() method is a static method on the HttpsURLConnection class that allows you to specify your own HostnameVerifier implementation that overrides the default one. After this method is called, new instances of HttpsURLConnection objects will be created using the passed-in HostnameVerifier. There is also a static method, getDefaultHostnameVerifier(), which returns the current verifier object.

The HostnameVerifier Interface

The first thing you need to be aware of if you are dealing with the HttpsURLConnection class and using your own certificates is the javax.net.ssl.HostnameVerifier interface.

The javax.net.ssl.HostnameVerifier interface has a single boolean method on it called verify(), which is passed a String representing the hostname the URL connection handler found and an SSLSession object representing the session that is being created. If the method returns true, the URL connection handler will assume everything is okay; if the method returns false, an exception will be thrown warning that the HTTPS hostname is wrong.

When a connection is established, the default `HostnameVerifier` implementation verifies the name of the host against the common name field (CN) in the subject DN for the end entity certificate the host presented. If the common name value and the hostname differ, the connection is terminated and an exception is thrown. In some cases, especially in intranet environments, this behavior is too restrictive, so the answer is to provide your own implementation of `HostnameVerifier` and pass it to the `setHostnameVerifier()` method on the `HttpsURLConnection` class. You will see an example of this next.

Try It Out   Using HttpsURLConnection and HostnameVerifier

Because you are now using HTTP as the protocol, you need different client and server programs. These can still take advantage of the methods you have already developed for creating `SSLContext` objects, but you need to provide extra code to support the different protocol.

The first step is to provide a client program that will also deal with the fact the common name in the certificate is not what is expected. As mentioned earlier, in a real situation, it would be the name of the host the server process is running on. Here is the code for the client, including its `HostnameVerifier` implementation:

```
package chapter10;

import java.io.InputStream;
import java.net.URL;

import javax.net.ssl.HostnameVerifier;
import javax.net.ssl.HttpsURLConnection;
import javax.net.ssl.SSLContext;
import javax.net.ssl.SSLSession;
import javax.net.ssl.SSLSocketFactory;
import javax.security.auth.x500.X500Principal;

/**
 * SSL Client with client-side authentication.
 */
public class HTTPSClientExample extends SSLClientWithClientAuthTrustExample
{
    /**
     * Verifier to check host has identified itself using "Test CA Certificate".
     */
    private static class Validator implements HostnameVerifier
    {
        public boolean verify(String hostName, SSLSession session)
        {
            try
            {
                X500Principal hostID = (X500Principal)session.getPeerPrincipal();

                return hostID.getName().equals("CN=Test CA Certificate");
            }
            catch (Exception e)
            {
                return false;
            }
        }
    }
```

```
        }

        public static void main(String[] args) throws Exception
        {
            SSLContext          sslContext = createSSLContext();
            SSLSocketFactory fact = sslContext.getSocketFactory();

            // specify the URL and connection attributes
            URL url = new URL("https://"+ Utils.HOST + ":" + Utils.PORT_NO);

            HttpsURLConnection connection = (HttpsURLConnection)url.openConnection();

            connection.setSSLSocketFactory(fact);
            connection.setHostnameVerifier(new Validator());

            connection.connect();

            // read the response
            InputStream  in = connection.getInputStream();

        int ch = 0;
        while ((ch = in.read()) >= 0)
        {
            System.out.print((char)ch);
        }
    }
}
```

Next, you need to provide a simple HTTPS server. Here's a simple one that accepts any request it gets and always responds with a "Hello World!" page:

```
package chapter10;

import java.io.IOException;
import java.io.InputStream;
import java.io.OutputStream;
import java.io.OutputStreamWriter;
import java.io.PrintWriter;
import java.security.Principal;

import javax.net.ssl.SSLContext;
import javax.net.ssl.SSLPeerUnverifiedException;
import javax.net.ssl.SSLServerSocket;
import javax.net.ssl.SSLServerSocketFactory;
import javax.net.ssl.SSLSession;
import javax.net.ssl.SSLSocket;

/**
 * Basic SSL Server with optional client authentication.
 */
public class HTTPSServerExample extends SSLServerWithClientAuthIdExample
{
    /**
     * Read a HTTP request
```

```
    */
    private static void readRequest(InputStream in) throws IOException
    {
        System.out.print("Request: ");
        int ch = 0;
        int lastCh = 0;
        while ((ch = in.read()) >= 0 && (ch != '\n' && lastCh != '\n'))
        {
            System.out.print((char)ch);
            if (ch != '\r')
                lastCh = ch;
        }

        System.out.println();
    }

    /**
     * Send a response
     */
    private static void sendResponse(OutputStream out)
    {
        PrintWriter pWrt = new PrintWriter(new OutputStreamWriter(out));
        pWrt.print("HTTP/1.1 200 OK\r\n");
        pWrt.print("Content-Type: text/html\r\n");
        pWrt.print("\r\n");
        pWrt.print("<html>\r\n");
        pWrt.print("<body>\r\n");
        pWrt.print("Hello World!\r\n");
        pWrt.print("</body>\r\n");
        pWrt.print("</html>\r\n");
        pWrt.flush();
    }

    public static void main(String[] args) throws Exception
    {
        SSLContext              sslContext = createSSLContext();
        SSLServerSocketFactory fact = sslContext.getServerSocketFactory();
        SSLServerSocket        sSock =
                        (SSLServerSocket)fact.createServerSocket(Utils.PORT_NO);

        // client authenticate where possible
        sSock.setWantClientAuth(true);

        for (;;)
        {
            SSLSocket sslSock = (SSLSocket)sSock.accept();

            try
            {
                sslSock.startHandshake();
            }
            catch (IOException e)
            {
                continue;
```

```
            }

            readRequest(sslSock.getInputStream());

            SSLSession session = sslSock.getSession();

            try
            {
                Principal clientID = session.getPeerPrincipal();

                System.out.println("client identified as: " + clientID);
            }
            catch (SSLPeerUnverifiedException e)
            {
                System.out.println("client not authenticated");
            }

            sendResponse(sslSock.getOutputStream());

            sslSock.close();
        }
    }
}
```

Starting the server is a simple matter of running:

java chapter10.HTTPSServerExample

Once the server is running, you can try running the client program as follows:

java chapter10.HTTPSClientExample

and you will see the following output in the server window:

```
Request: GET / HTTP/1.1
client identified as: CN=Test End Certificate
```

and the following in the client window:

```
<html>
<body>
Hello World!
</body>
</html>
```

showing that the "Hello World!" page has been served correctly to an authenticated client.

Next, try using your favorite browser, pointing it at the URL https://localhost:9020. If the browser supports SSL, it will prompt you to see whether you accept the certificate being offered by the server program. Respond in the affirmative and your browser should respond by displaying "Hello World!" in a page, showing that the server program is also accepting connections from clients that are not offering client-side authentication.

How It Works

There is quite a bit of new code here; in the case of the server, most of it is related to the mechanics of dealing with HTTP, so I'll start by looking at how the SSL-related code in the server works first.

The main driver in the server commences by creating an SSLContext object as you have done previously and using it to create an SSLServerSocketFactory, which is then used to create an SSLServerSocket. The server socket is then configured to produce sockets that will authenticate the client by calling SSLServerSocket.setWantClientAuth() with the value true. After that the program loops, accepting connections, attempting a handshake, reading the incoming request, printing whether the client is validated, and then sending back the "Hello World!" page.

On the client side, the main driver also begins by creating an appropriate SSLContext object and then a socket factory from it. A URL object is then created with the URL pointing at the server process and specifying HTTPS as the protocol. Next, a HttpsURLConnection object is created by calling URL.openConnection(), and it is set up to use the locally created socket factory and a custom object implementing the HostnameVerifier interface. Finally, the connect() method is called on the HttpsURLConnection object and the response is read in from the server and printed along the way.

The SSLSocketFactory you pass in and the HostnameVerifier implementation are both used when the connect() method is called. As you can probably guess, the SSLSocketFactory is simply used to provide a socket to use for the connection. The verifier is called once the name of the host has been resolved and, providing the method returns true, the call to connect() will finish without an exception being thrown. In the same way you checked the client identity in the last example, the Validator class simply checks the peer principal to see whether it is the one you expect using the SSLSession object that is made available to it.

A useful exercise would be to comment-out the use of the Validator class and see how the client reacts. You should see that it rejects the server, because the common name in the certificate and the name of the server host do not match.

Summary

In this chapter, you looked at how to use the JSSE to create SSL and TLS clients and servers in Java. You should now have a good understanding of the API and how to use it, as well as some idea of what is actually taking place when the SSL/TLS protocol handshake is taking place.

Over the course of this chapter, you learned

- ❑   How the basics of the SSL protocol work
- ❑   How to create a basic SSL client and server to secure communications
- ❑   How to use client-side authentication with SSL
- ❑   How to use an SSL session information

Finally, you can make use of HTTPS, configuring your own SSL contexts using the KeyManagerFactory and TrustManagerFactory classes, as well as using the HostnameVerifier interface if you need to.

This brings the book to an end. At this point you should have a good grounding in many of the Java APIs related to cryptography and secure communications, as well as some ideas as to how to use them. Cryptography and security are constantly evolving areas, however, so always remember the title of this book started with the word "beginning," and good luck and best wishes with the rest of your journey.

Exercises

1. What system properties are available to configure the key and trust managers for default SSL socket and server socket factories? Which of these properties has default values and what are they?

2. Most Java keystore types allow access to trusted certificate entries without the need to specify a password for loading the keystore file. Why is it important to use a password when loading a keystore with trusted certificate entries?

3. What class do you use to provide your own `KeyManager` and `TrustManager` objects and create your own `SSLServerSocketFactory` and `SSLSocketFactory` objects that will be configured using them?

4. Usually, an SSL handshake is done when one of the streams involved in an SSL link is written to. This might mean that exceptions thrown during handshaking are hidden beneath other exceptions. What method do you need to use to see explicit handshake exceptions when an SSL connection is initiated?

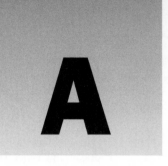

Solutions to Exercises

Chapter 1 Solutions

1. Some colleagues come to you with a problem they are having using a JCE provider they have downloaded. They have installed the provider correctly in the `jre/lib/ext` area and added it to the configuration file in `java.security`, but they are getting a `java.lang` `.SecurityException` with the message `Unsupported keysize or algorithm parameters`. What have they forgotten?

They have forgotten to install the unrestricted policy files for the JCE. This happens rather a lot.

2. You are running in a Windows environment. You have downloaded and installed everything into your JDK that is required to support the provider you want to use, but you still find that some Java applications you are using fail to find the provider, even though you are sure you have installed it. Why might this be happening?

The problem is most likely that the application is running out of the JRE installed on the Windows machine, not the JDK. You need to make sure that the JRE is configured the same way as the JDK with the right JAR files installed.

3. You are attempting to use an algorithm that is available in a provider you have installed, but you are finding that when you create an object to use it via the `getInstance()` method, the object does not have all the capabilities that the documentation that comes with the provider indicates. Why might this be the case?

Chances are this is happening because the provider name has not been specified and, because of the precedence rules, some other provider is being used to create the object. Verify that `getInstance()` has been called with the provider name specified.

Chapter 2 Solutions

1. A colleague has written a program for decrypting a padded byte stream that was created by encrypting with a block cipher. For some reason the program the colleague has written is appending one or more zero bytes to the data created by decrypting the stream. What is the most likely reason for the extra bytes? How would you fix the program?

The key words here are "padded byte stream." This tells you that the extra zero bytes are most likely an artifact from the padding mechanism that was used to create the encrypted data. A look at the program will probably show that the program was written using the value returned from `Cipher.getOutputSize()` *but does not take into account the fact that the number of bytes returned by* `Cipher.doFinal()` *can be less than that.*

2.   You have written a program that is decrypting a block cipher encrypted stream created using CBC mode. For the most part, the data appears to be encrypting correctly, but the first block of the decrypted data is always wrong. What is the most likely cause of this?

The initialization vector, or IV, is probably incorrect. Remember, CBC mode is performed by XORing the previous block of cipher-text produced with the current block of input. In the case of the first block of input, the (nonexistent) block of cipher text is provided by the IV.

3.   If you have a `Cipher` object initialized in encryption mode that uses an IV, what are the two ways you can retrieve the IV's value?

You can use either `Cipher.getIV()`*, which returns a simple byte array, or* `Cipher` `.getParameters()`*, which returns an* `AlgorithmParameters` *object.*

4.   If you have a `Cipher` object that is using PBE-based encryption, how would you retrieve the parameters passed to the key generation function, other than the password?

You need to use `Cipher.getParameters()` *and pass a* `PBEParameterSpec` *class to the* `AlgorithmParameters.getParameterSpec()` *method of the object returned by* `getParameters()`*.*

5.   What is the most likely problem if data written through a `CipherOutputStream` appears to be truncated?

In the case of truncated data, the most likely problem is that `CipherOutputStream.close()` *has not been called.*

Chapter 3 Solutions

1.   Why are message digests and MACs a necessary part of sending a message using encryption?

Encryption does not necessarily prevent an attacker from tampering with a message.

2.   You have been asked to implement a protocol that does not require encryption of the messages used in it, but it does require that the messages be tamperproof. How can you solve this problem while still allowing messages to be sent without encryption? What extra piece of information is now required when two parties want to communicate?

Use a MAC based on either a message digest or a cipher, whichever is most convenient while being appropriate to the security needs of the data. The use of a MAC now means that two parties who want to communicate must be aware of the key material used to initialize the MAC.

3.   What is the primary limitation of the use of a MAC or message digest?

The primary limitation of a MAC or message digest is the amount of data that it is safe to feed into it. The data limitation exists because, beyond a certain size, the likelihood of different data computing to the same digest or MAC value becomes too high.

4. What is wrong with the following code?

```
cipher.init(Cipher.ENCRYPT_MODE, key);

String encrypted = new String(cipher.doFinal(input));

cipher.init(Cipher.DECRYPT_MODE, key);

byte[] decrypted = cipher.doFinal(encrypted.getBytes());
```

What kind of `String` is created from `new String(cipher.doFinal(input))` and what bytes are returned by `encrypted.getBytes()` is dependent on the default charset used by your Java runtime and will almost always mean that `encrypted.getBytes()` will not produce the same byte array that came out of `cipher.doFinal(input)`.

Chapter 4 Solutions

1. A colleague is attempting to use RSA for key exchange and the implementation is failing whenever the leading byte of the key happens to be zero. What will be causing this problem? How do you fix it?

Leading zeros will go missing because the input data has to be converted to a big integer before it can be used with RSA. The solution is to use a padding mechanism like OAEP or PKCS #1.

2. The maximum amount of data that can be encrypted with RSA or El Gamal is normally limited by the size of the key, less any padding overhead that might exist. If you wanted to use either of these algorithms to help encrypt an arbitrarily large amount of data, how would you do it?

The answer is to combine the asymmetric algorithm with a symmetric one. Generate a random key for the symmetric algorithm and encrypt the data using it. Then encrypt the symmetric key using the public key for the person you want to send data to. The person can then use the private key to recover the symmetric key and then recover the data using the symmetric key.

3. Key agreement is different from key exchange in that it makes it possible for two or more people to arrive at the same key independently. What is the important thing to combine with a key agreement scheme if you are going to use one safely?

Key agreement schemes need to be combined with an authentication scheme to authenticate the keys being used; otherwise, the agreement scheme is open to a "man-in-the-middle" attack.

4. You saw previously that it was possible to use a MAC to authenticate data but that it had the disadvantage that it required a shared secret between all the parties wishing to check the same MAC. What asymmetric technique can you use instead that avoids this problem? What is it about it that makes it easier?

Digital signatures based on asymmetric algorithms are the best way of dealing with this. The feature of a digital signature is it has to be created using a person's private key, which should be known only to that person and it can be verified using the person's public key, which can be made freely available.

Chapter 5 Solutions

1. What happens to fields set to their default values when the ASN.1 structure that contains them is encoded using DER?

They are left out of the encoding.

2. How would you implement the following ASN.1 type using the Bouncy Castle ASN.1 API?

```
MyChoice ::= CHOICE {
               message UTF8String,
               id      INTEGER }
```

Here is one way of doing it. As you can see, the implementation reads a lot like a Java version of a C, or Pascal, union. Note the use of the ASN1Choice interface. Use of this will reduce the likelihood that this object is mistakenly tagged implicitly.

```java
public class MyChoice
    extends ASN1Encodable
    implements ASN1Choice
{
    ASN1Encodable value;

    public MyChoice(DERInteger value)
    {
        this.value = value;
    }

    public MyChoice(DERUTF8String value)
    {
        this.value = value;
    }

    public boolean isInteger()
    {
        return (value instanceof DERInteger);
    }

    public DERUTF8String getMessage()
    {
        if (isInteger())
        {
            throw new IllegalStateException("not a message!");
        }

        return (DERUTF8String)value;
    }

    public DERInteger getId()
    {
        if (isInteger())
        {
            return (DERInteger)value;
        }

        throw new IllegalStateException("not an id!");
```

```
    }

    public DERObject toASN1Object()
    {
        return value.toASN1Object();
    }
}
```

3. What is meant by the word IMPLICIT in respect to a style of tagging? Think of a simple example of how it would be done using one of the classes representing an ASN.1 primitive in the Bouncy Castle API. What implication does the implicit style have for items that are derived from the CHOICE type?

Objects that are assigned a tag value using the implicit style have their own tag value overridden by the tag value assigned. In the Bouncy Castle API, this is done by setting the explicit *parameter in the tagged object constructor to* false. *For example, the ASN.1 declaration*

```
    value [0] IMPLICIT INTEGER
```

would be created as a DER tagged value using the following:

```
    DERTaggedObject t = new DERTaggedObject(false, derIntegerValue);
```

and then recovered using the following:

```
    derIntegerValue = DERInteger.getInstance(t, false);
```

Remember too that if an object is already tagged, implicitly tagging it will remove the tag value. For this reason, as they commonly contain tagged values, any tag applied to an item of type CHOICE is applied explicitly.

4. What are the two classes used to hold the DER encodings of public and private keys, respectively? What class is used to convert the encodings back into actual keys?

The X509EncodedKeySpec *is used to contain public keys. The* PKCS8EncodedKeySpec *is used for carrying the encodings of private keys. The* KeyFactory *class is used to take the information in the encoded key specification objects and produce actual keys.*

5. What does an EncryptedPrivateKeyInfo object contain?

An EncryptedPrivateKeyInfo *contains an encrypted encoding of a PKCS #8* PrivateKeyInfo *object and the parameter and algorithm details that were used to do the encryption. On decryption, the recovered information is used to create a* PKCS8EncodedKeySpec, *which is then used to create a private key.*

Chapter 6 Solutions

1. What is the biggest danger of trying to manipulate X.500 names as String objects in Java?

Some application software expects the X.500 name to have a specific encoding when it processes it, and converting from an encoded DN to String *and back can lose this information. The reason this happens is that while several ASN.1 string types can be transformed into a Java* String *trivially, there is no way to determine which of those ASN.1 string types were used originally if you want to transform back the other way.*

2. How do you add an e-mail address for a certificate subject to a version 3 X.509 certificate?

You should add the e-mail address to a SubjectAltName *extension attached to the certificate. Use the* GeneralName *choice item for the* rfc822Name.

3. How do you request the CA to add a certificate extension when you issue a certification request?

Create an extensionRequest *attribute and add an* Extensions *structure containing the extensions you want as the contents of the attribute value set. This attribute is then added to the attribute set that is carried with the certification request and processed by the CA.*

4. What is a certificate path, or chain? What roles do the root certificate and the end entity certificates play, respectively?

A certificate path, or chain, represents a linkage from an end entity certificate back to a root certificate where each certificate in the chain is signed by the next one after it. The root certificate is generally self-signed and has to be accepted on trust. It is the certificate the others derive their validity from. The end entity certificate cannot be used to validate any other members of the chain and is the certificate you are trying to validate when the chain is examined.

5. What is the easiest way to generate a particular type of encoding for a certificate path?

Convert the path, or chain, into a CertPath *object and then use the* CertPath.getEncoded() *method requesting the format desired. You can find out which formats the* CertPath *objects of a particular provider can generate by calling* CertPath.getEncodings().

Chapter 7 Solutions

1. In an application where you are expecting a large number of unexpired revoked certificates to be present at any one time, as well as a large number of clients, what is the most appropriate certificate checking mechanism to deploy on the application clients: regular CRLs or OCSP?

OCSP. You are most likely to encounter problems with regular CRLs, as the size of the lists being distributed may easily become prohibitive, and having a large number of clients all trying to update their CRLs at the same time may result in severe performance degradation on the CRL server, with the usual unpleasant consequences.

2. If you have to distribute CRLs in the case detailed in Exercise 1, what is one way you can reduce the cost of distributing updates? What is required to support this?

You can distribute deltas as updates, rather than sending out a new CRL. If you do this, the complete CRLs you send out need to have the CRLNumber *extension present in them and the delta CRLs you send out need to use the* DeltaCRLIndicator *extension. Bear in mind that you need to have an algorithm, such as the one given in RFC 3280, for adding the deltas to the earlier complete CRL that was sent.*

3. How can you introduce validation of locally defined critical extensions into a PKIX CertPathValidator without having to change the underlying CertPathValidator provider?

Validation of private critical certificate extensions can be introduced to a PKIX CertPathValidator *by using the* PKIXCertPathChecker *class. Remember that the checker you write must remove the extensions you are processing from the unresolved critical extensions* Set *that is passed to the* check() *method for the validation to succeed.*

4. If you are using a PKIX `CertPathBuilder` to construct a certificate path for a given target certificate, what is the most straightforward way to construct the target constraints required for the path builder parameters?

Use the issuer and serial number of the target certificate, because these should always uniquely identify the certificate. For example, given the `X509Certificate targetCert` *that is the target of the path build, the target constraints would be defined as*

```
X509CertSelector targetConstraints = new X509CertSelector();

targetConstraints.setSerialNumber(targetCert.getSerialNumber());
targetConstraints.setIssuer(
            targetCert.getIssuerX500Principal().getEncoded());
```

Of course, if you are fortunate enough to be using JDK 1.5 or later, you can leave off the `getEncoded()`.

Chapter 8 Solutions

1. What available keystore types support the storing of symmetric keys?

Of the standard Java keystore types, the `JCEKS` *supports storing symmetric keys. The Bouncy Castle provider also supports symmetric key storage with the* `BKS` *and* `UBER KeyStore` *type.*

2. What is one important thing to do if you are relying on the integrity of the JVM's `cacerts` file to help secure your application?

Change the default password!

3. You have imported a PKCS #12 file into a Java application, but there doesn't appear to be an alias for the key entry you are looking for, or it is just appearing as some random string of hex. What is most likely to be the issue with the PKCS #12 file?

There is no "friendly name" attribute attached to the `SafeBag` *containing the private key. If the file does import and you see a hex string, chances are it will be the value of the local key ID. Some applications still insist and having the "friendly name" attribute provided in order to successfully import a PKCS #12 file, so this can sometimes be a cause of failure as well.*

4. You have generated a PKCS #12 file using a Java application you have written, but you are unable to import it into another third-party application. What are the three most likely problems with the PKCS #12 file you have generated?

The first one is that the PKCS #12 store you are using may have been saved as a BER file, but the application can only import DER files — you'll need to convert the file. The second one is the PKCS #12 store you are using may allow you to have an integrity password that is different from the privacy password, and the application can deal only with files that have the same password for both integrity and privacy. The third, and last, one is that the application may expect the certificates, other than the trust anchor, making up the validation path for the key's certificate to have the `AuthorityKeyIdentifier` *and* `SubjectKeyIdentifier` *extensions present, and if it cannot find them, it is unable to build the validation path and accept the key as usable.*

5. Using the `keytool`, the `org.bouncycastle.openssl.PEMReader` class, the `Utils` class, and the Chapter 6 examples "Try It Out: Creating a Certificate from a Certification Request" and "Try It Out: Writing a CertPath" as helpers, show how to create a certificate request using the `keytool` for a keystore key entry, create a `PKCS7` encoded certificate chain in response to the request, and update the key entry with the chain.

Most of the code for this you can cut and paste, but I'll reproduce one solution here. The first thing I'll do is provide the Java code and then just go through the command sequence.

Here's the Java code for parsing the request and creating the certificate response. It reads the request from a file called `pkcs10.req` and generates the certificate path making up the response in `PKCS7` format in a file called `pkcs7.pth`.

```
package chapter8;

import java.io.*;
import java.math.BigInteger;
import java.security.cert.*;
import java.util.*;
import javax.security.auth.x500.X500PrivateCredential;

import org.bouncycastle.asn1.x509.*;
import org.bouncycastle.jce.PKCS10CertificationRequest;
import org.bouncycastle.openssl.PEMReader;
import org.bouncycastle.x509.X509V3CertificateGenerator;
import org.bouncycastle.x509.extension.*;

/**
 * Example showing the processing of a PEM encoded PKCS #10 encoded request
 * in a file called "pkcs10.req". A PKCS7 certificate path is generated as a
 * response in the file "pkcs7.pth".
 * <p>
 * The certificate and its chain will be valid for 50 seconds.
 */
public class CertReqSolution
{
    public static void main(String[] args) throws Exception
    {
        // create the CA certificates
        X500PrivateCredential rootCredential = Utils.createRootCredential();
        X500PrivateCredential interCredential = Utils.createIntermediateCredential(
                rootCredential.getPrivateKey(), rootCredential.getCertificate());

        // parse the request
        PEMReader   pRd = new PEMReader(
                            new InputStreamReader(
                                    new FileInputStream("pkcs10.req")));

        PKCS10CertificationRequest request =
                                (PKCS10CertificationRequest)pRd.readObject();

        // get our validation certificate
        X509Certificate caCert = interCredential.getCertificate();

        X509V3CertificateGenerator  certGen = new X509V3CertificateGenerator();

        certGen.setSerialNumber(BigInteger.valueOf(System.currentTimeMillis()));
        certGen.setIssuerDN(caCert.getSubjectX500Principal());
        certGen.setNotBefore(new Date(System.currentTimeMillis()));
        certGen.setNotAfter(new Date(System.currentTimeMillis() + 50000));
        certGen.setSubjectDN(request.getCertificationRequestInfo().getSubject());
```

```
            certGen.setPublicKey(request.getPublicKey("BC"));
            certGen.setSignatureAlgorithm("SHA256WithRSAEncryption");

            // provide some basic extensions and mark the certificate
            // as appropriate for signing and encipherment
            certGen.addExtension(
                            X509Extensions.AuthorityKeyIdentifier,
                            false, new AuthorityKeyIdentifierStructure(caCert));

            certGen.addExtension(
                            X509Extensions.SubjectKeyIdentifier,
                            false, new SubjectKeyIdentifierStructure(
                                                request.getPublicKey("BC")));

            certGen.addExtension(
                    X509Extensions.BasicConstraints, true, new BasicConstraints(false));

            certGen.addExtension(
                    X509Extensions.KeyUsage, true, new KeyUsage(
                            KeyUsage.digitalSignature | KeyUsage.keyEncipherment));

            // create the chain
            List chain = Arrays.asList(
                    new Certificate[] {
                            certGen.generateX509Certificate(
                                            interCredential.getPrivateKey(), "BC"),
                            interCredential.getCertificate(),
                            rootCredential.getCertificate() });

            // create the CertPath
            CertificateFactory fact = CertificateFactory.getInstance("X.509", "BC");

            CertPath path = fact.generateCertPath(chain);

            // write it out
            FileOutputStream fOut = new FileOutputStream("pkcs7.pth");

            fOut.write(path.getEncoded("PKCS7"));

            fOut.close();
    }
}
```

There's nothing new in this code, although if you do find some of it confusing, it would be worth having another look at the examples and descriptions in Chapter 6 before going any further. Compile up the code into your class hierarchy and you're ready to proceed.

Now to use it with the keytool *— I've used* test.jks *as the keystore file here so that the commands avoid touching your* .keystore *file. Remember, both the java code you are using and the* keytool *will be operating on the current directory.*

First, generate a key to use, responding appropriately to the questions the keytool *prompts you with:*

```
keytool -genkey -alias testKey -keystore test.jks -storepass testStore -keypass
  testKey
```

Next, generate the certification request into the file `pkcs10.req`:

```
keytool -certreq -alias testKey -keystore test.jks -storepass testStore
 -keypass testKey -file pkcs10.req
```

Next, run the Java program to read the request and generate the response:

```
java -cp your_class_hierarchy chapter8.CertReqSolution
```

where `your_class_hierarchy` *is wherever you compiled the class file to.*

Finally, import the certificate response:

```
keytool -import -alias testKey -keystore test.jks -storepass testStore -keypass
 testKey -file pkcs7.pth
```

You will be prompted to determine whether you want to trust the root certificate. Respond with a `yes` *and you're done. Do a*

```
keytool -list -v -keystore test.jks -storepass testStore
```

and you should see the certificate path has now been added to the entry.

Chapter 9 Solutions

1. The `CMSProcessable` interface is for the purpose of allowing the implementation of objects that write byte data to a CMS object for processing. How would you implement one that takes `java.io.File` objects?

   Here's one way of doing it:

```
package chapter9;

import java.io.*;

import org.bouncycastle.cms.*;

/**
 * CMSProcessable that handles File objects.
 */
public class CMSProcessableFile implements CMSProcessable
{
    private File file;
    private static final int BUF_SIZE = 4096;

    /**
     * Base constructor.
     *
     * @param file a File object representing the file we want processed.
     */
    public CMSProcessableFile(File file)
    {
        this.file = file;
    }
```

```
/**
 * Write the contents of the file to the passed in OutputStream
 *
 * @param out the OutputStream passed in by the CMS API.
 */
public void write(OutputStream out) throws IOException, CMSException
{
    FileInputStream fIn = new FileInputStream(file);
    byte[]          buf = new byte[BUF_SIZE];

    int count = 0;
    while ((count = fIn.read(buf)) > 0)
    {
        out.write(buf, 0, count);
    }

    fIn.close();
}

/**
 * Return the File object we were created with.
 */
public Object getContent()
{
    return file;
}
}
```

One thing to note: Be sure to close the `InputStream` you are using in the `write()` method, as I've done here. The `write()` method can be called multiple times.

2. What is the best policy to adopt with the creation of certificates for encryption and signature validation?

   Make them purpose-built. That means a certificate is for one purpose only and the public key will be used either for encryption or signature validation. There is an interesting slant on this in Chapter 13 of Practical Cryptography, where the authors point out that for a key to be different, just the public exponent needs to change; the modulus can be reused.

3. Under what circumstances will a CMS signed-data message not contain any signers?

   A CMS signed-data message will not contain any signers if it is being used only to carry certificates and/or CRLs. Messages of this type are called certificate management messages and are also created when you encode a `CertPath` by passing the `String` to "PKCS7" to the `CertPath` object's `getEncoded()` method.

4. How would you modify the `SignedMailExample.createMultipartWithSignature()` method so that it takes a `MimeMultipart` and signs it rather than a `MimeBodyPart`?

   Strictly speaking, you don't have to! Here is the modified method with the changes highlighted:

```
public static MimeMultipart createMultipartWithSignature(
    PrivateKey key, X509Certificate cert, CertStore certsAndCRLs,
                            MimeMultipart multiPart) throws Exception
{
    // create some smime capabilities in case someone wants to respond
```

```
ASN1EncodableVector          signedAttrs = new ASN1EncodableVector();
SMIMECapabilityVector        caps = new SMIMECapabilityVector();

caps.addCapability(SMIMECapability.aES256_CBC);
caps.addCapability(SMIMECapability.dES_EDE3_CBC);
caps.addCapability(SMIMECapability.rC2_CBC, 128);

signedAttrs.add(new SMIMECapabilitiesAttribute(caps));
signedAttrs.add(new SMIMEEncryptionKeyPreferenceAttribute(
                        SMIMEUtil.createIssuerAndSerialNumberFor(cert)));

// set up the generator
SMIMESignedGenerator gen = new SMIMESignedGenerator();

gen.addSigner(key, cert, SMIMESignedGenerator.DIGEST_SHA256,
                           new AttributeTable(signedAttrs), null);

gen.addCertificatesAndCRLs(certsAndCRLs);

MimeBodyPart dataPart = new MimeBodyPart();

dataPart.setContent(multiPart);

// create the signed message
return gen.generate(dataPart, "BC");
}
```

As you can see, this could have been more easily achieved by wrapping multiPart *before passing it to the method and leaving the method's parameter list alone.*

5. If you wrap a mail message in another MIME body part, sign the result, and then find another application that will not validate the signature, what is most likely to be the problem?

    The other application is probably ignoring some of the headers in the mail message when it is doing the signature calculation. Typical headers that are ignored (when it happens) are "Reply-To," "From," and "To."

6. When you are mixing signing and compression, under what circumstances is it mandatory that the signatures are calculated for the data after it has been compressed rather than before compression?

    If you are using a "lossy" compression technique, you have to sign the compressed data rather than the original data. Because this compression technique involves some loss of information, signatures calculated on the original data will not match the results of the verification process at the other end on the reduced data.

Chapter 10 Solutions

1. What system properties are available to configure the key and trust managers for default SSL socket and server socket factories? Which of these properties has default values and what are they?

The key manager properties are javax.net.ssl.keyStore, javax.net.ssl.keyStorePassword, *javax.net.ssl.keyStoreProvider, and* javax.net.ssl.keyStoreType. *The trust manager properties are* javax.net.ssl.trustStore, javax.net.ssl.trustStorePassword, *javax.net.ssl.trustStoreProvider, and* javax.net.ssl.trustStoreType.

If the javax.net.ssl.trustStore *property is not set, the system will look in the JVM's security directory for the file* jssecacerts. *If* jssecacerts *does not exist, the system will use the file* cacerts.

If the javax.net.ssl.keyStoreType *or* javax.net.ssl.trustStoreType *properties are not set, they default to the return value of* KeyStore.getDefaultType().

2. Most Java keystore types allow access to trusted certificate entries without the need to specify a password for loading the keystore file. Why is it important to use a password when loading a keystore with trusted certificate entries?

Providing the password will force an integrity check on the file and help detect any tampering that might have occurred.

3. What class do you use to provide your own KeyManager and TrustManager objects and create your own SSLServerSocketFactory and SSLSocketFactory objects that will be configured using them?

The javax.net.ssl.SSLContext *class.*

4. Usually, an SSL handshake is done when one of the streams involved in an SSL link is written to. This might mean that exceptions thrown during handshaking are hidden beneath other exceptions. What method do you need to use to see explicit handshake exceptions when an SSL connection is initiated?

The SSLSocket.startHandshake() *method.*

Algorithms Provided by the Bouncy Castle Provider

As you can imagine, in an area that is still evolving such as cryptography, any software designed to support use of it can be expected to evolve as well. Consequently, you can expect the list of algorithms and their modes of use presented in this appendix to change.

Updates to this list will appear in the file `specifications.html`, which is distributed in the source code releases of the Bouncy Castle provider. What follows gives you a picture of the algorithms supported by the Bouncy Castle provider as of release 1.28.

Asymmetric Ciphers

The RSA and ElGamal asymmetric ciphers are supported and can be used with the mode NONE, or ECB, and one of the following paddings:

- ❑ NoPadding
- ❑ PKCS1Padding
- ❑ OAEPWith*<digest>*AndMFG1Padding, where *digest* is one of MD5, SHA1, SHA224, SHA384, or SHA512

Certificate Path Validation

The PKIX validation algorithm is supported.

Key Agreement Algorithms

Three key agreement algorithms are supported: DH, ECDH, and ECDHC.

Key Stores

The following keystore types are supported: BKS, UBER, and PKCS12 (BCPKCS12/PKCS12-DEF).

MAC Algorithms

The following symmetric cipher-based MAC algorithms are supported: DES, DESEDE, IDEA, RC2, RC5, and Skipjack.

Two types of HMAC are supported as well:

❑ HMac<*digest*> where <*digest*> is one of MD2, MD4, MD5, RIPEMD128, RIPEMD160, SHA1, SHA224, SHA256, SHA384, or SHA512

❑ PBEWithHMac<*digest*>, where <*digest*> is one of RIPEMD160 or SHA1

Signature Algorithms

The following signature algorithms are available:

❑ DSA, ECDSA, GOST-3410 (GOST-3410-94), ECGOST-3410 (GOST-3410-2001)

❑ <*digest*>WithRSAEncryption, where <*digest*> is one of MD2, MD4, MD5, SHA1, SHA224, SHA256, SHA384, SHA512, RIPEMD128, RIPEMD160, or RIPEMD256

❑ <*digest*>WithRSAAndMGF1, where <*digest*> is one of SHA1, SHA224, SHA256, SHA384, or SHA512

❑ <*digest*>WithRSA/ISO9796-2, where <*digest*> is one of MD5, SHA1, or RIPEMD160

Message Digests

The following digests are supported: GOST3411, MD2, MD4, MD5, RIPEMD128, RIPEMD160, RIPEMD256, RIPEMD320, SHA1, SHA224, SHA256, SHA384, SHA512, Tiger, and Whirlpool.

Symmetric Block Ciphers

The following symmetric ciphers are supported: AES, Blowfish, CAST5, CAST6, DES, DESEDE, GOST-28147, IDEA, RC2, RC5, RC6, Rijndael, Serpent, Skipjack, and Twofish.

Any of the ciphers can be combined with one of the following modes:

❑ **ECB.** Electronic CodeBook mode

❑ **CBC.** Cipher Block Chaining

- ❑ **OFB.** Output Feedback Mode
- ❑ **CFB.** Cipher Feedback Mode
- ❑ **SIC (CTR).** Segmented Integer Counter mode (CounTeR mode)
- ❑ **OpenPGPCFB.** Variation on CFB mode defined in OpenPGP
- ❑ **CTS.** Cipher Text Stealing (should be used with NoPadding)
- ❑ **GOFB.** OFB mode defined for the GOST-28147 encryption algorithm

and one of the following padding mechanisms:

- ❑ **NoPadding.** No Padding
- ❑ **PKCS7Padding (PKCS5Padding).** Padding mechanism defined in PKCS #5 and PKCS #7
- ❑ **ISO10126-2Padding.** Padding mechanism defined in ISO 10126-2
- ❑ **ISO7816-4Padding.** Padding mechanism defined in ISO 7816-4
- ❑ **TBCPadding.** Trailing Bit Complement padding
- ❑ **X9.23Padding.** Padding mechanism defined in X9.23
- ❑ **ZeroBytePadding.** Padding with zero bytes (not recommended)

The following PBE algorithms are also supported:

- ❑ PBEWithMD5AndDES
- ❑ PBEWithSHA1AndDES
- ❑ PBEWithSHA1AndRC2
- ❑ PBEWithMD5AndRC2
- ❑ PBEWithSHA1AndIDEA
- ❑ PBEWithSHA1And3-KeyTripleDES
- ❑ PBEWithSHA1And2-KeyTripleDES
- ❑ PBEWithSHA1And40BitRC2
- ❑ PBEWithSHA1And40BitRC4
- ❑ PBEWithSHA1And128BitRC2
- ❑ PBEWithSHA1And128BitRC4
- ❑ PBEWithSHA1AndTwofish

Symmetric Stream Ciphers

The only stream cipher currently supported is RC4 (ARC4).

Using the Bouncy Castle API for Elliptic Curve

Prior to JDK 1.5, there was no standard API for doing elliptic curve cryptography available in Java. This meant the cryptography service providers needed to provide their own API if they wanted to provide elliptic curve support.

The Bouncy Castle provider has provided support for elliptic curve since release 1.04. This was done primarily to provide support for X9.62 ECDSA, so if you happen to have a copy of the standard available, you'll see that the API follows its ASN.1 structures fairly closely.

The math support for elliptic curve is provided in the package `org.bouncycastle.math.ec`, and you can find the classes and interfaces associated with its use in cryptography in the packages `org.bouncycastle.jce.spec` and `org.bouncycastle.jce.interfaces`. You will need to use these two packages if you are using JDK 1.4 or earlier. With the advent of JDK 1.5, the two packages were adjusted slightly so that JDK 1.5 API and the Bouncy Castle could exist side by side, and for the most part, you won't need to use the Bouncy Castle package anymore. There is one interface and one class that is still relevant in JDK 1.5 and may still be useful. They are the `ECPointEncoder` interface and the `ECNamedCurveSpec` class. You'll look at the interfaces first.

Elliptic Curve Interfaces

The interfaces representing elliptic curve keys are in the package `org.bouncycastle.jce.interfaces`. Although most of them are no longer relevant when you move to JDK 1.5, the `ECPointEncoder` interface is still useful if you need to work with other providers that cannot handle points encoded in compressed format.

The ECKey Interface

The `ECKey` interface has a single method, `getParameters()`, which returns an `ECParameterSpec` representing the domain parameters for the elliptic curve the key is associated with.

The ECPrivateKey Interface

The `ECPrivateKey` interface has a single method, `getD()`, which returns a `BigInteger` representing the private value for the elliptic curve private key.

The ECPublicKey Interface

The `ECPublicKey` interface has a single method, `getQ()`, which returns the `ECPoint` representing the public point for the elliptic curve public key.

The ECPointEncoder Interface

All Bouncy Castle elliptic curve keys implement this interface, even after JDK 1.5.

The `ECPointEncoder` interface has a single method, `setPointFormat()`, which takes a string representing the style of encoding you want to use when the EC key implementing this interface has its `getEncoded()` method called.

By default, Bouncy Castle elliptic curve keys encode using point compression. This can cause problems with other providers that do not support it. If you pass `UNCOMPRESSED` to the `setPointFormat()` method, points will be encoded uncompressed.

Elliptic Curve Classes

A group of classes for representing key and parameter specifications that can be used with elliptic curve cryptography are also provided in the `org.bouncycastle.jce.spec` package.

The ECNamedCurveParameterSpec Class

The `ECNamedCurveParameterSpec` class can be used in any JDK, although it will probably be easier to use its successor the `ECNamedCurveSpec` when you are using JDK 1.5. `ECNamedCurveParameterSpec` provides a mechanism for representing a parameter spec for a named curve. You can use this class for creating keys that will encode their parameters as *named curves*, rather than storing the numbers making up the curve parameter information explicitly. This results in smaller encodings, but it does mean anyone using the certificate will have to know how to re-create the curve parameters from the curve parameter name (usually stored as an OID) that is carried in the certificate with the public key.

The provider supports the following named curves from X9.62:

- ❑ prime192v1
- ❑ prime192v2
- ❑ prime192v3
- ❑ prime239v1
- ❑ prime239v2

❑ prime239v3

❑ prime256v1

It also supports the following named curves for use with ECGOST3410 (GOST-3410-2001):

❑ GostR3410-2001-CryptoPro-A

❑ GostR3410-2001-CryptoPro-B

❑ GostR3410-2001-CryptoPro-C

❑ GostR3410-2001-CryptoPro-XchA

❑ GostR3410-2001-CryptoPro-XchB

The ECNamedCurveSpec Class

The ECNamedCurveSpec class exists only in JDK 1.5 or later. It provides a mechanism for representing a parameter spec for a named curve. Like its predecessor, the ECNamedCurveParameterSpec, this class creates keys that will encode their parameters as named curves, rather than storing the curve information explicitly.

The ECParameterSpec Class

The ECParameterSpec class is a simple value object for holding the domain parameters for an elliptic curve. In JDK 1.5, it has been replaced with a class of the same name in the java.security.spec package.

An ECParameterSpec can be constructed using a curve, base point (G), the order (N), the cofactor (H), and the random seed used to generate the curve if it is available and it has a series of get() methods for retrieving these values.

The ECPrivateKeySpec Class

The ECPrivateKeySpec class is a simple value object that holds the parameters required to create an elliptic curve private key. In JDK 1.5, it is replaced with a class of the same name in the package java.security.spec.

An ECPrivateKeySpec can be constructed with a private value and an ECParameterSpec. There are get() methods on the class for retrieving these values.

The ECPublicKeySpec Class

The ECPublicKeySpec class is a simple value object that holds the parameters required to create an elliptic curve public key. In JDK 1.5, it is replaced with a class of the same name in the package java.security.spec.

An ECPublicKeySpec can be constructed with a public point and an ECParameterSpec. There are get() methods on the class for retrieving these values.

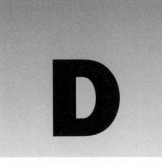

Bibliography and Further Reading

ASN.1 Standards

These are all available on the Web at `www.itu.int/ITU-T/studygroups/com10/languages`:

- ❑ X.680 Information Technology — Abstract Notation One (ASN.1): Specification of Basic Notation

- ❑ X.681 Information Technology — Abstract Notation One (ASN.1): Information Object Specification

- ❑ X.682 Information Technology — Abstract Notation One (ASN.1): Constraint Specification

- ❑ X.683 Information Technology — Abstract Notation One (ASN.1): Parameterization of ASN.1

- ❑ X.690 Information Technology — ASN.1 Encoding Rules: Specification of Basic Encoding Rules (BER), Canonical Encoding Rules (CER), and Distinguished Encoding Rules (DER)

- ❑ X.691 Information Technology — ASN.1 Encoding Rules: Specification of Packed Encoding Rules (PER)

- ❑ X.693 Information Technology — ASN.1 Encoding Rules: XML Encoding Rules (XER)

IETF Working Group Charter Pages

The charter pages are useful places to look if you need to stay up-to-date with the newest RFCs. Here are the home pages for the working groups most relevant to this book:

- ❑ Electronic Data Interchange-Internet Integration (EDIINT) — `www.ietf.org/html .charters/ediint-charter.html`(Working group responsible for AS 2

- ❑ Public-Key Infrastructure (X.509) (PKIX) Charter — `www.ietf.org/html.charters/ pkix-charter.html` — Working group responsible for certificate processing, formats, and validation methods

❑ S/MIME Mail Security (SMIME) Charter — `www.ietf.org/html.charters/smime-charter.html` — Working group responsible for S/MIME and CMS

❑ Transport Layer Security (TLS) Charter — `www.ietf.org/html.charters/tls-charter.html` — Working group responsible for ongoing development of TLS (formerly SSL)

NIST Publications

The FIPS and SP publications are produced by NIST (National Institute of Standards and Technology) in the United States. They are available off the Computer Security Resource Center Web site, which is at `http://csrc.nist.gov`.

The following NIST publications are the ones most relevant to this book:

❑ FIPS PUB 46-3 — "Data Encryption Standard (DES)," `http://csrc.nist.gov/publications/fips/fips46-3/fips46-3.pdf`

❑ FIPS PUB 81 — "DES Modes of Operation," `www.itl.nist.gov/fipspubs/fip81.htm`

❑ FIPS PUB 180-2 — Secure Hash Signature Standard (SHS), `http://csrc.nist.gov/publications/fips/fips180-2/fips180-2withchangenotice.pdf` (linked document includes most recent change notice)

❑ FIPS PUB 186-2 — "Digital Signature Standard (DSS)," `http://csrc.nist.gov/publications/fips/fips186-2/fips186-2-change1.pdf` (linked document includes most recent change notice)

❑ FIPS PUB 197 — "Advanced Encryption Standard (AES)," `http://csrc.nist.gov/publications/fips/fips197/fips-197.pdf`

❑ SP 800-38A — "Recommendation for Block Cipher Modes of Operation(Methods and Techniques," `http://csrc.nist.gov/publications/nistpubs/800-38a/sp800-38a.pdf`

PKCS Standards

The PKCS standards are all available off the RSA Labs Web site, which is under RSA Security's main Web site. RSA Labs are doing on-going standards development in many areas, including elliptic curve cryptography, currently a proposal for PKCS #13, so their Web site makes an interesting read in general.

Here are the PKCS standards referred to in this book:

❑ PKCS #1 — "RSA Cryptography Standard," `www.rsasecurity.com/rsalabs/node.asp?id=2125`

❑ PKCS #3 — "Diffie-Hellman Key Agreement Standard," `www.rsasecurity.com/rsalabs/node.asp?id=2126`

❑ PKCS #5 — "Password-Based Cryptography Standard," `www.rsasecurity.com/rsalabs/node.asp?id=2127`

❑ PKCS #7 — "Cryptographic Message Syntax Standard," `www.rsasecurity.com/rsalabs/node.asp?id=2129`

❑ PKCS #8 — "Private-Key Information Syntax Standard," www.rsasecurity.com/rsalabs/node.asp?id=2130

❑ PKCS #9 — "Selected Attribute Types," www.rsasecurity.com/rsalabs/node.asp?id=2131

❑ PKCS #10 — "Certification Request Syntax Standard," www.rsasecurity.com/rsalabs/node.asp?id=2132

❑ PKCS #11 — "Cryptographic Token Interface Standard," www.rsasecurity.com/rsalabs/node.asp?id=2133

❑ PKCS #12 — "Personal Information Exchange Syntax Standard," www.rsasecurity.com/rsalabs/node.asp?id=2138

RFCs

The following RFCs are referenced in this book:

❑ RFC 1750 — "Randomness Recommendations for Security," www.ietf.org/rfc/rfc1750.txt

❑ RFC 2040 — "The RC5, RC5-CBC, RC5-CBC-Pad, and RC5-CTS Algorithms," www.ietf.org/rfc/rfc2040.txt

❑ RFC 2104 — "HMAC: Keyed-Hashing for Message Authentication," www.ietf.org/rfc/rfc2104.txt

❑ RFC 2246 — "The TLS Protocol Version 1.0," www.ietf.org/rfc/rfc2246.txt

❑ RFC 2253 — "Lightweight Directory Access Protocol (v3): UTF-8 String Representation of Distinguished Names," www.ietf.org/rfc/rfc2253.txt (obsoletes RFC 1179)

❑ RFC 2440 — "OpenPGP Message Format," www.ietf.org/rfc/rfc2440.txt

❑ RFC 2560 — "X.509 Internet Public Key Infrastructure Online Certificate Status Protocol - OCSP," www.ietf.org/rfc/rfc2560.txt

❑ RFC 2712 — "Addition of Kerberos Cipher Suites to Transport Layer Security (TLS)," www.ietf.org/rfc/rfc2712.txt

❑ RFC 2984 — "Use of the CAST-128 Encryption Algorithm in CMS," www.ietf.org/rfc/rfc2984.txt

❑ RFC 2876 — "Use of the KEA and SKIPJACK Algorithms in CMS," www.ietf.org/rfc/rfc2876.txt

❑ RFC 3058 — "Use of the IDEA Encryption Algorithm in CMS," www.ietf.org/rfc/rfc3058.txt

❑ RFC 3161 — "Internet X.509 Public Key Infrastructure Time-Stamp Protocol (TSP)," www.ietf.org/rfc/rfc3161.txt

❑ RFC 3211 — "Password-based Encryption for CMS," www.ietf.org/rfc/rfc3211.txt

❑ RFC 3218 — "Preventing the Million Message Attack on Cryptographic Message Syntax," www.ietf.org/rfc/rfc3218.txt

❑ RFC 3268 — "AES Ciphersuites for TLS," www.ietf.org/rfc/rfc3268.txt

- ❏ RFC 3274 — "Compressed Data Content Type for Cryptographic Message Syntax (CMS)," `www.ietf.org/rfc/rfc3274.txt`

- ❏ RFC 3280 — "Internet X.509 Public Key Infrastructure Certificate and CRL Profile," `www.ietf.org/rfc/rfc3280.txt` (obsoletes RFC 2459)

- ❏ RFC 3281 — "An Internet Attribute Certificate Profile for Authorization," `www.ietf.org/rfc/rfc3281.txt`

- ❏ RFC 3370 — "Cryptographic Message Syntax (CMS) Algorithms," `www.ietf.org/rfc/rfc3370.txt`

- ❏ RFC 3546 — "Transport Layer Security (TLS) Extensions," `www.ietf.org/rfc/rfc3546.txt`

- ❏ RFC 3565 — "Use of the Advanced Encryption Standard (AES) Encryption Algorithm in Cryptographic Message Syntax (CMS)," `www.ietf.org/rfc/rfc3565.txt`

- ❏ RFC 3686 — "Using Advanced Encryption Standard (AES) Counter Mode with IPsec Encapsulating Security Payload (ESP)," `www.ietf.org/rfc/rfc3686.txt`

- ❏ RFC 3749 — "Transport Layer Security Protocol Compression Methods," `www.ietf.org/rfc/rfc3749.txt`

- ❏ RFC 3851 — "Secure/Multipurpose Internet Mail Extensions (S/MIME) Version 3.1 Message Specification," `www.ietf.org/rfc/rfc3851.txt`

- ❏ RFC 3852 — "Cryptographic Message Syntax," `www.ietf.org/rfc/rfc3852.txt`

Other Useful Standards

Some other standards documents, not all referred to directly in this book, but certainly useful nonetheless, are as follows:

- ❏ X9.62 — "Public Key Cryptography for the Financial Services ECDSA," available from `www.x9.org`

- ❏ SEC 1 — "Elliptic Curve Cryptography," `www.secg.org/download/aid-385/sec1_final.pdf`

- ❏ SEC 2v — "Recommended Elliptic Curve Domain Parameters," `www.secg.org/download/aid-385/sec1_final.pdf`

The last two are of particular interest if you are using elliptic curve cryptography and are under ongoing development as well. You can find more information on them off the SECG (Standards for Efficient Cryptography Group) Web site at `www.secg.org`.

Useful References

Bleichenbacher, D. *Chosen Ciphertext Attacks against Protocols Based on RSA Encryption Standard PKCS #1.* In *Advances in Cryptology — CRYPTO '98*, LNCS vol. 1462, pp. 1–12. New York: Springer-Verlag. Available on the Web at `www.bell-labs.com/user/bleichen/bib.html`.

Ferguson, Niels, and Bruce Schneier. *Practical Cryptography.* New York: John Wiley & Sons, 2003. ISBN 0471223573.

Larmouth, John. *ASN.1 Complete.* San Francisco: Elsevier-Morgan Kaufmann, 1999. ISBN 0122334353. Also available on the Web at `www.oss.com/asn1/larmouth.html`.

Menezes, Alfred J., Paul C. Van Oorschot, and Scott A. Vanstone. *Handbook of Applied Cryptography.* Boca Raton, FL: CRC Press, 1996. ISBN 0849385237. Chapters of this book are also available on the Web at `www.cacr.math.uwaterloo.ca/hac/`, with some restrictions.

Schneier, Bruce. *Applied Cryptography: Protocols, Algorithms, and Source Code in C. 2nd ed.* New York: John Wiley & Sons, 1995. ISBN 0471117099.

Useful Web Links

The following Web links are useful both in conjunction with reading this book and doing further research:

- ❑ `www.bouncycastle.org` — Home of the Legion of the Bouncy Castle and the open source Bouncy Castle provider
- ❑ `http://java.sun.com/products/javamail/` — Home of the JavaMail API
- ❑ `www.schneier.com/crypto-gram.html` — Home of the monthly Crypto-Gram newsletter by Bruce Schneier
- ❑ `www.rosettanet.org` — Home of the RosettaNet series of standards efforts

Index